The Collected Clinical Work
Volume 9

Case Histories

Problems of Neurosis

The Case of Mrs. A.

The Case of Miss R.

Alfred Adler

Edited by Henry T. Stein, Ph.D.

Classical Adlerian Translation Project

Published 2005 by The Classical Adlerian Translation Project.

First printing 2005
Second printing 2012 revised
Third printing 2012 revised
Printed in the United States of America

0-9715645-9-0

Table of Contents

Editor's Preface 2005 iii
Part 1: **Problems of Neurosis** 1
    Chapter I: Goals of Superiority 2
        Boy 17: Fear of Decisions 3
        Man 35: Agoraphobia and Heart Symptoms 5
        Man 40: Fear of Heights 6
        Woman 27: Suffering from Obsessions 6
    Chapter II: Not Meeting the Problems of Life 13
        Boy 18: Schizophrenic 13
        Elderly Woman: Depression 15
        Woman 46: Domination with Depression 15
    Chapter III: Deficient Social Feeling, Masculine Protest 20
        Boy with Obsessive Guilt Feelings 25
        Woman 26: Who Wanted to be a Man 28
    Chapter IV: Problems in Love and Marriage 31
        Man 23: Dominating Through Drinking 34
        His Wife Takes Morphine 35
        Mistress with Headaches and Palpitations 38
    Chapter V: Neurotic Style of Life and Psychotherapy 42
        Boy 15: Believed He Was a Prophet 45
        Man 40: Clairvoyant and Speechless 46
        Principles of Psychotherapy 46
        Man 32: Escape Through Drinking 49
        Suicidal Medical Student 53
    Chapter VI: Neurotic Use of Emotion 55
        Man 50: Depressed When All is Well 55
        Man 36: Impotence and Polygamous Desires 56
        Man 50: Beggar as King 58
        Man 53: Agoraphobia – Avoidance of People 60
    Chapter VII: The Family Constellation 63
        Position of the First Child 63
        Effects of Dethronement 64
        First Child May Keep Position 65
        Attitude of Eldest Toward Authority 66
        Position of Second Child 67
        Position of Youngest Child 70
        Difficulties of an Only Child 72
        Case of Homosexual Development 73
        Importance of Evaluation of Men and Women 77

Chapter VIII: Earliest Recollections 79
Chapter IX: Further Useless Goals of Superiority 84
    Sadism and Masochism 85
    Man 32: Erythrophobia 87
    Man 45: Swallowing Air 88
    Man 40: Wanting to Marry His Cousin 89
    Woman 60: Jealousy 90
    Woman: Neurotic Heart and Jealousy 91
    Man 38: Agoraphobia and Fear of Syphilis 92
    Boy 14: Shirking the Masculine Ideal 92
    Woman 20: Masochistic Fantasies 93
Chapter X: Occupational Choices and Sleep Postures 96
    Body Postures and Sleep Postures 100
Chapter XI: Organ Dialect and Dreams...........................102
    Woman 25: Anxiety Neurosis 102
    Critical, Compulsive Housewife 102
    Organ Dialect 103
    A Woman's Revenge Against Her Father 104
    Depression as Safeguard Against Marriage 106
    Sleep and Hypnosis 106
    Antagonism to a Wife Awake and Dreaming 109
Part 2: **The Case of Mrs. A**. 112
General Introductory Comments 113
The Case of Mrs. A. 116
Part 3: **The Case of Miss R.** 141
Preface 142
Chapter I: Early Childhood 150
Chapter II: Adolescent Difficulties 160
Chapter III: The Development of a Neurosis 168
Chapter IV: The Style of Life 178
Chapter V: The Jealousy Mania 193
Chapter VI: Sexual Development 200
Chapter VII: The Problem of Love 213
Chapter VIII: The Shock of Sexual Knowledge 228
Chapter IX: The Masculine Protest 244
Chapter X: A Lupus Phobia 260
Chapter XI: Yes! But-- 282
Chapter XII: The Goal of Superiority 303

Index 321
Appendix: "Basic Principles of
Classical Adlerian Psychology" 339

Editor's Preface – 2005

Volume nine brings together three of Adler's books on case histories: *Problems of Neurosis*, *The Case of Mrs. A.*, and *The Case of Miss R.* Although these books were previously published in English, the text required substantial editing for readability. Adler's diagnostic brilliance now shines through without the distractions of dated terminology and awkward phrasing.

Adler takes us on a fascinating journey of life style analysis through progressive levels of understanding. In *Problems of Neurosis*, he offers us vivid thumbnail sketches of thirty-three cases, spanning the symptoms of depression, obsession, compulsion, alcoholism, schizophrenia, clairvoyance, agoraphobia, impotence, sadism, masochism, and jealousy. He also discusses the general topics of family constellation, earliest recollections, body postures, sleep postures, organ dialect, and hypnosis.

In *The Case of Mrs. A.*, Adler takes us further into a single style of life. Working from the notes presented by another physician, he spontaneously comments on each segment of information offered to him. Using the diagnostic process common in medicine, he gathers data, makes conjectures, then tests them until he establishes a coherent theme. He even ventures to predict the consequences of behavioral patterns. In a presentation of modest length, he achieves his goal of clearly illustrating the unity of a style of life.

The Case of Miss R. takes us into deeper waters. In the mid-1920's, a journalist presented *The Diary of Claire Macht* to Adler. After studying the material, he offered his comments in a series of eight presentations to an Individual Psychology Association. Originally titled *The Technique of Individual Psychology, Volume 1: The Art of Reading a Life-and-Case History*, it was first issued in Germany, then translated into English and published in 1929. In her autobiographical narrative, a young working-class woman recalls her sexual awakening in early twentieth-century Vienna with striking candor No doubt shocking to a reader in the 1920's, the sexually explicit material is commonplace in psychological literature today. However, Adler's artful construction of a unified psychological portrait is compelling to follow. He weaves early family influences and social conditions into a unique, logically and emotionally coherent tapestry.

Volume nine is a "must read" for anyone interested in the art of life style analysis. His remarkable theory springs to life in this series of richly varied case histories.

For readers unfamiliar with Adler's ideas, a brief overview, titled "Basic Principles of Classical Adlerian Psychology," is included in the appendix.

Part 1

Problems of Neurosis[1,2]

A Book of Case Histories

---

[1] First published in 1929 by Routlcldge & Kegan Paul, Ltd., London. Edited by P. Mairet.
[2] Additional editing by Henry T. Stein, Ph.D., 2005.

Chapter I

Goals of Superiority

The problem of every neurosis is, for the patient, the difficult maintenance of a style of acting, thinking and perceiving which distorts and denies the demands of reality. Usually, only when this way of life has become arduous to the verge of breakdown is the case brought to the physician, whose task is to find the right method for its correction. Therefore, the common problem of both patient and physician, and the basis of their cooperation, is to understand the nature of the patient's mistakes. This understanding demands not only an accurate outline of his significant history, but also a perception of the dynamic unity of that history as a continual striving toward an implied conception of superiority.

As the work of Individual Psychologists has abundantly proved, an individual goal of superiority is the determining factor in every neurosis, but the goal itself always originates in, and is strictly conditioned by the actual experiences of inferiority. The physician's first line of approach is to identify the real causes of the feelings of inferiority, which the patient disguises from himself in various degrees and in his individual manner. Since the feeling of inferiority is generally regarded as a sign of weakness and as something shameful, he naturally has a strong tendency to conceal it. Indeed, the effort of concealment may be so great that the person himself ceases to be aware of his inferiority as such, being entirely preoccupied with the consequences of the feeling and with all the objective details that serve its concealment. So efficiently may an individual train his whole mentality for this task that the entire current of his psychic life flowing ceaselessly from below to above--that is, from the feeling of inferiority to that of superiority--occurs automatically and escapes his own notice.

It is not surprising, therefore, that we often receive a negative reply when we ask a person whether he has a feeling of inferiority. It is better not to press the point, but to observe his mental and psychic movements, in which the attitude and individual aim can always be discerned. In this way we soon perceive a greater or lesser degree of the feeling of inferiority in everyone, together with a compensatory striving toward a goal of superiority. Such a universal feeling is not in itself indictable; its meaning and value depend entirely on how it is used. The most important discovery of Individual Psychology is that the inferiority may be used as a stimulus to continue on the useful side of life.

Boy 17: Fear of Decisions

These general observations clearly apply to the case of a seventeen-year-old boy, the second child in the family, who was brought to me because he suffered from anxiety, and became extremely angry when confronted with difficulties. He also had stomach trouble and diarrhea when he went mountaineering, a sport which he sometimes shared with his comrades. His mother was intelligent and liked him, but apparently preferred his elder brother who gave her less trouble. This elder brother was much stronger, taller, and a good sportsman. The father was a capable man and the patient esteemed him highly.

This boy was afraid of making any decisions because his feeling of inferiority was too great for him to trust himself. He was unwilling, however, to admit that this feeling was due to any cause within his control. He insisted that he was born such as he was and his nature was not his responsibility.

The patient's attitude toward life was one of hesitation. When confronted with problems he created difficulties, but though he thus "slowed down," he did not stop altogether. He was a good pupil at school, but in constant fear of losing even this advantage, and he could not decide at all what to do upon leaving high school. He made no friends, did not like girls, and was afraid of sexual experiences. He believed some of his difficulties resulted from masturbation and nocturnal emissions. This behavior shows typical indecision and lack of confidence in regard to the three problems of life: friendship, occupation, and love. The response to all three problems was evaded or postponed. He disguised his sense of general inadequacy by making various causes responsible, thus reassuring and convincing himself of worth. It is notable, however, that the patient went on in spite of difficulties. He studied well, and he climbed mountains, which by the way, is a common activity of people who feel overburdened with life, to give themselves feelings of superiority. To review and emphasize the difficulties of life from the viewpoint of a superior feeling is the next best thing to being able to boast that one has overcome them. It was in order to escape from the consciousness of his inferiority feeling that this patient blamed his weakness on natural difficulties and masturbation, and especially on inherited deficiencies.

The theory of heredity must never be emphasized in education or in the theory and practice of psychology. Except in cases of congenital mental retardation, everyone can do everything necessary. This is not, of course, to deny the differences of inherited physical and mental capacities, but what counts is the use we make of them. Only in this way do we see the enormous significance of education. Correct education develops the individual, with all his inherited abilities and disabilities. With courage and training, disabilities may be so compensated that they even become great abilities. When correctly encountered, a disability becomes the stimulus for higher achievement. We are no longer surprised to find that those who have attained remarkable successes in life have often been handicapped in the beginning with disabilities and great feelings of inferiority. On the other hand, we find that a person who believes himself the victim of inherited deficiencies and disabilities, lessens his efforts with a feeling of hopelessness, thus permanently hindering his development.

Teachers exaggerate the harmfulness of hereditary factors to excuse the inefficiency of their own methods. It is interesting to read in Einhardt's biography of Charlemagne that this great Emperor could learn neither reading nor writing, from sheer lack of talent for such things. Now, with the proper development of educational methods, no normal child finds these tasks beyond him. This and many other examples show that whenever authors, teachers or parents fail to find a method to correct errors by education, they blame the child's inherited deficiencies. This superstition is one of the greatest difficulties and the most commonly encountered in education and in handling "problem children," not to mention the treatment of criminals, neurotics, and psychotics. Yet for the treatment of these conditions, the only reasonable assumption is the one made by Individual Psychology: that everyone is equal to his life-task. This does not mean that the results are or can be equal, for of course, we must consider inequalities of training, method, and above all the degree of courage shown.

To return to the case in question, the ability of this boy's father was an additional reason for his feeling that he could not make good in life. It is well known that the children of great men are often unsuccessful; they feel incapable of ever attaining positions as high as their fathers held, and therefore do not seriously attempt anything at all. In the case of this patient, the high achievements of his elder brother also lengthened his distance from the goal of superiority in the family circle. He felt himself hopelessly surpassed. The neurosis which he developed was a protection from the painful consciousness of this inferiority. It was the adoption of an attitude which signified to him: "If I were not anxious, if I were not ill, I would be able to do as well as the others. If my life were not full of terrible difficulties, I would be the first." With this attitude, a person can still feel superior, for the evaluation of his worth and value is placed beyond proof, in the realm of possibilities. His chief occupation in life is to look for difficulties, to find means of increasing them, or at least of increasing his own sense of their gravity. He carefully collects and exhibits the most ordinary difficulties of life, common to everybody. He does this more to impress himself than others, but naturally other people take his burdens into account and do not expect so much of him. Any success he may have, moreover, is magnified by this heavily-advertised handicap, so that it becomes his most useful possession. He uses it to win his way to a privileged life, judged by a more lenient standard than others. At the same time, he pays the costs of it with his neurosis.

Man 35: Agoraphobia and Heart Symptoms

Another case of anxiety neurosis, in the form of agoraphobia accompanied by heart symptoms, occurred in a man of thirty-five. Anxiety neurosis is always symptomatic of a timid attitude toward the three problems of life, and those who suffer from it are invariably "spoiled" children.

This man dreamed, "I crossed the limit of the border between Austria and Hungary, and they wanted to imprison me." (Such short dreams, by the way, are the best for analysis.) This dream indicated the man's desire to come to a standstill because of the fear that he would be defeated if he went on. Its interpretation clearly confirms our understanding of anxiety neuroses. The man wanted to limit the scope of his activity in life, to "mark time" in order to gain time. He came to see me because he wished to marry, and the imminent prospect of doing so had brought him to a halt. This fact itself, that he came to consult me about his marriage, clearly indicated his attitude toward it. Similarly, the way he would behave in marriage was mirrored in the dream, in which he commanded himself, "Do not pass the limit!" The prison in the dream also reflected the dreamer's view of marriage. We often deceive ourselves by such images in dreams. We use them to train ourselves to tackle the problems of the near future in a manner consistent with our style of life, but not in accordance with the logic of the situation

The style of life is established in the first four or five years of childhood. This period closes with the full development of the ego and consequently a fixed attitude toward life. From this time onward, the answers to the questions presented by life are dictated, not by the truth of relationships in themselves, but by certain automatized attitudes, which we call the style of the individual. Thus, we explain how a certain mistake of adaptation, such as the desire to be the center, to be overburdened, not to be forced, not to be curtailed, etc., may persistently continue throughout a lifetime.

Man 40: Fear of Heights.

A very successful man, forty years old, complained that he could not go up into a high building without having an impulse to jump out a window. He said he had always been afraid of everything. The youngest of six children, he had been very spoiled by his mother. This case reveals at a glance the wish to be thought overburdened and in danger. The patient cannot avoid going upstairs, but he colors this procedure with his desire to be in a dangerous situation, clinching the danger by developing an impulse to jump.

In this case and the two previously cited, the goal of superiority is similar, regarding the motive of being overburdened. But this man goes further. He has a desire to jump from a window, but lo, ! he overcomes it and still lives. He is even stronger than himself.

In support of this diagnosis, I will add a recollection from the patient's childhood. "I went to school when I was six years old. I was not very happy. The very first day a boy attacked me. I was dreadfully afraid and trembled but . . . I sprang at him and threw him down." This fragment of memory records the two typical motives of the man's life-style. He trembles at first, but only to overcome. And that little word, "but," holds the rich meaning of his compensation for feelings of inferiority.

Woman 27: Suffering From Obsessions

A woman of twenty-seven came to consult me after five years of suffering. She said: "I have seen so many doctors that you are my last hope in life." "No, I answered, "not the last hope. Perhaps the last but one. There may be others who can help you, too." Her words were a challenge to me; she was daring me not to cure her, in order to make me feel bound in duty to do so. This is the type of patient who wishes to shift responsibility onto others, a common development of spoiled children. We can assume that in childhood she constantly contrived to keep another person occupied with her, and we may infer that it was probably her mother. We need additional facts to verify this impression, but we can use certain methods to do so even in the first interview.

It is important, by the way, to evade such a challenge as the one I have recorded here. The patient may have worked up a high tension of feeling about the idea that the doctor is his "last hope," but we must accept no such distinction. To do so would prepare the way for grave disappointment, or even suicide.

This woman was a second child, whose elder sister was more beautiful than she, besides being very clever and popular, so that the patient's life had been like a breathless race to overtake her rival. The sister married happily. The patient also developed well, especially intellectually, outdoing her elder sister in school work. However, the sister was much more charming and attractive, and made friends far more readily. The life of the older sister had been smoother and pleasanter, giving her greater self-confidence. The younger, from a sense of insecurity, felt a need to assert herself against others, which inhibited their friendship. Doubtless none of these two girls' acquaintances recognized the true nature and origin of this difference between them, but they all felt it unconsciously, being attracted to the one and repelled by the other.

The patient had been in love at the age of fourteen, when she was ridiculed for it, so ever since she had declined to play the part of a loving woman. When her sister married, she fell in love with a married man. Such an attachment cannot, in itself, be automatically judged. Nobody can be sure if such a love will turn out well or not. But we cannot ignore that every girl in such a situation sees the great difficulties involved as clearly as her parents or anybody else can see them. And a woman going through such an experience tells herself, "This is what love is like." Her selection of such a troublesome love is obviously ground for suspicion that she does not wish to see love and marriage through. In this case we see the patient adopted toward this new life-problem of love, the same hesitant, non-committal attitude she had exhibited in the past. She had reasons. She was less attractive than her sister, and she had been ridiculed in her first love affair. A woman of such a competitive nature, bent toward the goal of superiority, is always in danger of losing courage and self-confidence by marriage. She will usually feel marriage as a menace to her sense of superiority. The happy marriage of this girl's sister fed these fears, so did the unhappy marriage of her parents and her mother's inferiority.

The woman's hesitating attitude toward love and marriage came out during frank discussion with her. She said: "I am sure my husband would leave me two weeks after our marriage." When I hinted at the deep feeling of inferiority which was the cause of her evasion of marriage, she tried to retract this statement; but the mere fact that such an idea could appear at all, even in a joke, showed that her mind had been occupied with that specific problem.

Even when the man with whom she was in love wanted to kiss her, she ran away from his caresses. In such ways, she established her distance from the demands of love and marriage, and sacrificed everything to her neurotic goal of superiority. "If this man were not married, I would marry him," was her answer to this problem of life.

"If" is usually the theme of neurotic drama. "If" is the last resort in every neurotic dilemma, and one sure way of escape. For the will to escape has only one reason, and that is fear of defeat, which is the hardest of all reasons to admit. At this point, therefore, we frequently find some fictitious form of anxiety, which the patient interprets to himself in various ways, but never as the simple fear of being beaten. Agoraphobia, anxiety neurosis, and all the forms of phobia may originate at this point, but whichever form it may take, the fear of defeat fulfills its purpose of blocking the way to further activity. Thus, what was desired is attained. The ordeal is evaded without disclosing, even to its owner, the hated feeling of inferiority. All the other neurotic symptoms, such as compulsion ideas, fits, fatigue, sleeplessness, functional disturbances such as heart palpitations, headaches, and so on, develop out of the severe tension of this very stressful concealment.

The organs most disturbed by this tension are those made susceptible by some inherited weakness. Hence, where a whole family tends toward a particular organic weakness, several members suffer from organic illnesses, and others from neurotic symptoms of that same organ. In such cases, we must not overlook the contributory factor of imitation. Unlike other psychologists, however, we find that the only symptoms imitated are those conforming to the neurotic goal of superiority.

This patient held a position in an office, where she played a leading role and was much appreciated, but like all people with an excessive feeling of inferiority, she had an insatiable appetite for appreciation. At the age of nineteen she changed her position, and lost the admiration she had formerly enjoyed. Reviewing her case, we note:

1. She felt she could not compete with her sister, either in making friends or in making a successful marriage.

2. She feared facing the problems of love and marriage.

3. She had lost a favorable position in her work.

In short, all the defeats she had feared had now befallen her; her intense feeling of inferiority had been justified. She did not reason out the situation in this way, but showed by the appropriate mood, that this was how she felt it.

We may now note in passing a typical concentration on, and exaggeration of one point in the life-problem, the fear of defeat. While occupied with the useful side of life, we have to consider the possibilities of defeat, which we normally minimize by regarding occasional reverses as incidental to every human enterprise. But in such a case as we are now reviewing, the possibility of defeat has become the focus of life. The patient subordinates his whole life to it, just as a person with a cleaning mania makes her life revolve around the idea of dirt, and the normal, useful act of washing becomes exaggerated into a ceaseless search for dirt, either on her own person or on furniture, floors or elsewhere, until it has no meaning or value for life. Such a mistaken focus of attention is typical of neurosis in general, and in the case of this girl her earlier life-purpose on the useless side, to surpass her sister, was developing into the still narrower and more negative aim of escaping from any sort of defeat whatsoever.

Neurotic symptoms develop at precisely such a critical point in a life-history. The style of life with its characteristic hesitation at every possibility of defeat does not change, but the individual now expresses this attitude by demanding impossible securities. If he has no means of proving superiority on the useful side, he becomes a problem child, or a criminal, or he may commit suicide. If he has some activity, but an insufficient amount, and more hope, he deceives himself that he is blocked by a fatal hindrance, such as an illness. He selects certain symptoms and develops them until they impress him as real obstacles. His state of tension readily provides the initial mental or bodily disturbances, which vary according to the style of life and the native organic weaknesses. Behind his barricade of symptoms, the patient feels hidden and secure. To the question, "What use are you making of your talents?" he answers, "This thing stops me; I cannot go ahead," and points to his self-erected barricade. We must never neglect the patient's use of his symptoms. Not only does he use them in this way, but, as happens still more in psychosis, they also modify his perception of every vital life question.

To be already overworked by grappling with his own neurotic difficulties is not only an extenuating circumstance, it also provides a patient's inner relief from his striving for superiority; he really expects less of himself. Such a self-protective style of life may also take the form of being overwhelmed with social difficulties.

The best way to understand a neurotic patient is to set aside all his neurotic symptoms, and study his style of life and individual goal of superiority. Only by a firm grasp of these two things can we come to a full understanding of the neurosis itself, the development of which they entirely control. It is the fear of defeat, real or imaginary, which triggers the outbreak of the so-called neurotic symptoms. Life and custom drag the man along in apparent agreement, but in reality a sense of utter abasement has separated him from life, and he is trying to stop or escape.

My experience proves that psychoses such as schizophrenia, mania, depression, and paranoia, appear when the patient feels absolutely checkmated, with no hope of going on, which means that he gives up all attempts to answer any of the three questions of life. A neurotic person, however, is willing to consider one or two of these questions, but has broken down in face of some new and overwhelming difficulty.

The cases I have been describing exhibit such incomplete hesitation. In the one immediately under consideration, the girl appeared to be quite healthy until she suffered the setback in her occupation. Then, more deeply intimidated by the difficulty of life, she began to shelve its problems more and more, and strove for a new kind of superiority in the form of compulsion-ideas.

One day she had a fear that her handbag had come open and that some coins, covered with verdigris, had dropped into the basket of vegetables which she had been carrying for another woman. She feared she had poisoned this woman's entire family. Another compulsion-idea she had, was that the dust of the street was on her hands and would soil her mother's *Bible* if she touched it, which of course she could not avoid doing from time to time. So after each imaginary soiling of the *Bible*, she surreptitiously bought another and replaced it, until she had bought a dozen of them. She attributed this exaggerated holiness to the books in order that she might profane them, and wasted her money on them so that she could be held irresponsible. Thus also, she became a martyr, misunderstood, and a soul degraded by the fouling of sacred things.

If the woman's sole ambition in life had been to become more conspicuous than her sister, she was well on the way to realizing it. But this neurotic aim was involving her in such practical defeats that it was clearly advisable for her to renounce it for another. The goal of her striving was to escape the dreaded decision: "My sister is superior to me."

Closely examined, this escape from a decision also reveals itself as a goal of superiority. Because she will not mix with people, she cannot be defeated socially. As long as she avoids love and marriage, she is not measured against her sister's happy marriage. Whatever happens, she can say, "But I am fully occupied with my compulsion-ideas." She must be occupied with something. Time, the circumstances, and whatever logic her neurosis has not destroyed, demand some occupation, so she busies herself on the useless side with this compulsion-neurosis. Her activity is actually free from competition, and fictitiously superior. This illusion of superiority is shown by her striving, in compulsion-ideas, to make herself feel responsible for the lives of others, or for their purity. This effort to show a superior conscientiousness is her occupation, for she has not stopped. If she had, she would be in a state of stupor, as in catatonia.

Before referring to this patient's dreams, a few general remarks are advisable. A psychology which could not understand and interpret dreams would exclude a great part of the mental life, and would therefore be a most imperfect psychology. Thus, the Freudian conception of dreams is an important contribution. Unfortunately, its author overlooked the most vital principles of dream formation owing to his mistaken assumption of the dominance of the sexual factor. This mistake prevented him from seeing that the sexual attitude in life is determined by the goal of totality or superiority. We must interpret abnormal sexual tendencies as expressions of the entire style of life, looking for the deeper movements which underlie them.

The understanding of dreams owes its furthest practical progress to a contribution of Individual Psychology: the recognition that every dream creates its mood to cope with a specific situation, in accordance with the goal of superiority. This purpose of the dream explains the mysterious fact that people do not understand their own dreams. Dreaming is a process of turning away, in sleep, from reality and common sense toward the individual's goal of superiority. To relate our present problems to this goal by logical planning and thinking is very difficult, but by using feelings it is easy, and their "short cut" is the dream. As I have shown elsewhere, the dream is a dress rehearsal, a trial performance of a step toward the fictive goal. In an automatic way, it produces an illusory picture of how to succeed regardless of the logic of the situation.

This patient dreamed that she fell down. No one can deny that such a dream connotes unpleasant feelings as of defeat, and we must assume that she was diminishing her impulse to proceed. Presumably, she faced a question which she wanted to answer in a discouraged manner. That question proved to be an invitation to a rendezvous with the married man in the case. She responded by giving herself, through the dream, the hopeless mood she wanted, the impulse to denial and escape.

In case the critical reader is unconvinced, I will cite another dream of the patient's on the same night. She was terrified by noticing some blue and red spots on her skin. Was this good preparation for meeting with a lover? That the spots signified the result of a syphilitic infection was not only obvious to me, but also was suggested independently by the patient herself. In discussing this matter, she expressed the opinion that all men were untrue and polygamous. "I am sure," she exclaimed (and this I have already quoted) "that my husband would leave me a fortnight after the wedding. What is the good of marriage, if I constantly expect to be deceived and also infected by my husband?" This clinches the proof of her motive to escape. She added, "I should become less than my sister, whose husband is faithful." Thus, her goal has changed. She no longer wishes directly to surpass her sister, but barricades that path, and looks for another superiority, on the useless side. She was going to avoid all defeat, and to be nobler than anyone else.

Everyone's goal is one of superiority, but in the case of those who lose their courage and self-confidence, it is diverted from the useful to the useless side of life. This escape into a life of unrealities takes place in an automatic way; the fear of defeat itself arranges the emotions, and through them the actions, until a situation is reached which alleviates it. This escape is always felt as a relief, but is not understood as such. If it were, the patient would enjoy it, which would spoil the whole arrangement by removing the justification for his hesitation and escape. He must pay the costs with suffering in order to be excusable. And the neurotic symptoms, built upon the pattern of an illness, really resemble illness, and efficiently safeguard the patient's sense of superiority by enabling him to think, "I could be the first, if only my suffering did not prevent it." Such a style of life automatically excludes happiness quite independently of any adjustment to circumstances.

Chapter II

Not Meeting Problems of Life

Boy 18: Schizophrenic

Every development in an individual's life is conditioned by his life-aim, connecting all successive phases of his life. When the mother of a son who has suddenly become schizophrenic at the age of eighteen, says that he was perfectly normal until that age, we cannot agree with her. Investigating the boy's past life, we find that he was domineering and did not play with his schoolmates. Such a childhood provides bad preparation for facing the real problems of life. In this case it was a preparation for schizophrenia, which was not a sudden development but the result of a life-attitude, and showed itself only when he had to face a really difficult situation. At the age of eighteen, he was faced with the three questions of friendship, occupation, and love, and felt unable to answer them. A patient's unpreparedness for life does not usually show itself in favorable circumstances, or when he is shielded from the real demands of life which are always of a social nature and demand social feeling. Normally a sheltered period of life, childhood may be passed in a way that does not develop social feeling, as in the case under consideration and also in the case previously described where a girl competed with an elder sister. Because she felt her prestige endangered all the time, she was preoccupied with herself. Such a conception of her situation hinders a child's development of social feeling.

The circumstances of early life, such as those of the nursery, kindergarten, school, and companionship, offer the first training and test in social behavior. When a neurosis is developed, we always find that the individual's difficulties were foreshadowed in these childhood relationships. He did not care to do things with others, or he did so with some noticeable difference from others. A neurotic generally remembers his peculiarities and difficulties of adaptation in early life as a justification for keeping his distance from the present social environment. When he is driven by necessity or by his own demands to approach an accepted standard of behavior, the neurotic may apparently try to adapt himself, but in reality he does nothing of the kind. He answers the new demands with automatic responses and trained attitudes which cover his escape from any real contact. He may mix with others superficially, in conversations and customary kinds of cooperation, but

13

he does so according to his own established mechanisms, and behind this screen his psyche slips back into its own secret stronghold. In this behavior of neurotics, psychotics, and problem-children, we must recognize a certain inevitability, a necessary result of their past. The artificial attitudes they have established are the logical consequence of faulty training, and we can do very little good by trying to correct these consequences. We must make a change in the deeper motive, in the underlying style of life, and then the patient will see all his life-tasks in a new perspective.

Every human being must somehow solve the three problems of life which I have already described, for the individual's relationship with the world is three-fold. No one can escape a definite answer to the question of friendship, occupation, or love. Whoever can make friends, pursue a useful occupation with faith and courage, and express his sexual life in accordance with social feeling, is immune from neurotic infection. But when an individual fails to succeed in one or more of these three inexorable demands of life, beware of feelings of abasement, beware of the consequent neurosis. Schizophrenia is the result of failure in all three directions at once.

The boy whose case we are considering was unprepared to grapple with these inevitable problems. From our point of view, he evidently needed re-education at this late stage of his development, a process which demands a special method. The practitioner should realize at the outset that nothing can be done by force. The patient must be appealed to in a friendly way, coaxed into a receptive frame of mind. Indeed, the task of the physician or psychologist is to give the patient the experience of contact with a fellow-man, and then to enable him to transfer this awakened social feeling to others.

This method of winning the patient's good will, and then transferring it to his environment, is strictly analogous to the maternal function. The social duty of motherhood is to interpret society to the individual, and if the mother fails in this obligation, then the duty is likely to fall much later on the physician who is heavily handicapped for the task. The mother has the enormous advantage of the physical and psychic relationship; she provides the greatest experience of love and fellowship the child will ever have. Her duty is to relate the growing child to herself mentally, as he was related to her physically, nourishing the child's growing consciousness with true and normal conceptions of friendship, work, and love. In this way, she gradually transforms the child's love for her and dependence upon her into a benevolent, confident, and responsible attitude toward society and the whole environment. This is the two-fold function of motherhood: to give the child the completest possible experience of human fellowship, and then widen it into a life-attitude toward others.

Elderly Woman: Depression

What we call psychosis is liable to occur when the individual breaks down before all three questions of life, and defies logic with every step he takes. By "logical," we mean that which is intelligible as an attempt to solve a real problem of life. An example of psychotic development is shown in the life of an elderly woman, excluded from occupation and love. She is offended because society, her children and sons-in-law, do not take enough interest in her. If she has not developed sufficient social feeling to take a keen interest in the lives of others, her case is indeed a difficult one; for the goal of superiority still attracts her as much as anyone, and keeps her striving without any definite objective. But she finds it possible to impress others by exploiting her weakness. She can become a focus of attention again, and once more an actress on the stage of life, by playing the role of an entirely hopeless person. She will forestall the destruction of her personality by identifying herself with a lost person, and rather than allow others to make her miserable by neglect, she will plunge herself into excessive gloom, giving her a little dismal power over other people's feelings. We find that the pride and ambition of neurotic individuals prohibits their confessing that they feel neglected, so they are unable to directly accuse others. Therefore, the anger and rage we would expect to find in this phase of life is generally suppressed and hidden, though it may break out occasionally, and they rationalize their hopeless attitude by turning their accusation against themselves. In cases of depression, many actually kill themselves in an excess of self-condemnation, while sometimes ostentatiously exonerating others.

Woman 46: Domination With Depression

A very intelligent woman, forty-six years of age, had suffered from depression for three years, eight years before she came to me. She had been married at the age of sixteen, and having no children for the first ten years of her married life, she adopted a child, but did not tell the child that she was not its real mother. This situation is one which usually leads to unhappiness for the child later on. Afterward, the woman had two daughters of her own. She worked in her husband's office after marriage, so she knew all about his affairs, and after some years, when he took a partner into his business, she did not want to be in the office because of her diminished importance. She quarreled continually with the partner until her father became ill, when she withdrew from the business to nurse him, and as soon as the father's health was restored, she developed depression. She suspected her husband of concealing his business affairs from her, and cried if he did not immediately tell her everything she wanted to know. Wanting to dominate her husband, she sought to subdue him by crying. Crying is usually an accusation against another person. Her husband's business was financially satisfactory, and it was not necessary for her to know all the details of its working, but she felt herself excluded and inferior if she did not know all about it.

This strong woman had married a weak man in order to rule him; of course, the choice of an equal mate generally indicates a higher degree of courage. Marriage is a constructive task for two individuals determined to live together in order to help and enrich each other's lives; when anyone chooses a weaker partner, lower in the social scale, or with vices such as alcoholism, morphine addiction, or laziness, in the hope of "saving" him, he betrays the hidden desire for superiority.

This woman showed the principal signs of a true depression. She decreased steadily in weight, was unable to sleep, and was routinely more depressed in the morning than in the evening. She feared that the whole family would face poverty and starvation. In treating the case, my first objective was to reconcile her with her husband. I tried to show her that her husband was getting older, that she should not be angry with him, but handle him more diplomatically. I explained that there were better methods of making him subservient than crying; that the weaker person puts up some kind of resistance, as no one can endure constant domination, and that people must treat each other as equals if they are to live together harmoniously.

I use the simplest and most direct method possible in the treatment of neurotics, but it would be of no use to tell the patient in this case, "You are a domineering woman, trying to rule by means of illness," for she would be offended. I must win her first, and take her part as far as possible. Every neurotic is partly in the right. If this woman did not feel deprived of value by her advancing age, a real hardship of women in our present culture, she would not cling to her prestige in such unseemly ways. But I can only very gradually bring her to face the truth about what she is doing.

At the same time, this patient developed a guilt complex which often happens in such a situation. She remembered that she had deceived her husband with another man some twenty-five years before, during which time this event had played no further part in her life, but all at once she told her husband and accused herself. This so-called guilt-complex, which we would entirely misunderstand with the Freudian interpretation, was clearly an attack upon the husband who was no longer obedient. She could hurt him by confession and self-accusation. Who is so simple as to think it is a case of the majesty of the truth vindicating itself after a quarter of a century? The truth is often a terrible weapon of aggression. It is possible to lie, and even to murder, with the truth.

Nietzsche, with a most penetrating vision and from the same standpoint as Individual Psychology, described the feeling of guilt as mere wickedness. In the majority of neurotic cases, a guilt-complex is used as a means to entrench its maker on the useless side of life. We often see this behavior in a child who tells a lie and gets a complex about it, so that he can play a role of distinguished uselessness. Everyone will be struck by his honesty if he worries so much about having told a fib.

To return to the indirect method of treatment, I recommend it especially with depression. After establishing a sympathetic relationship, I give suggestions for a change of conduct in two stages. In the first stage, my suggestion is, "Do only what is agreeable to you." The patient usually answers, "Nothing is agreeable." "Then at least," I respond, "do not exert yourself to do what is disagreeable." The patient, who has usually been exhorted to do various uncongenial things to remedy his condition, finds a rather flattering novelty in my advice, and may improve in behavior. Later I insinuate the second rule of conduct, saying, "It is much more difficult and I do not know if you can follow it." After saying this I am silent, and look doubtfully at the patient. In this way, I excite his curiosity and ensure his attention, and then proceed. "If you could follow this second rule, you would be cured in fourteen days. It is: to consider from time to time how you can give another person pleasure. It would very soon enable you to sleep and would chase away all your sad thoughts. You would feel yourself to be useful and worth while."

I receive various replies to my suggestion, but every patient thinks it is too difficult to act upon. If the answer is, "How can I give pleasure to others when I have none myself?" I relieve the prospect by saying, "Then you will need four weeks." The more transparent response, "Who gives me pleasure?" I counter with what is probably the strongest move in the game, by saying, "Perhaps you had better train yourself a little thus: do not actually do anything to please anyone else, but merely think about how you could do it."

Depressed subjects who reply, "Oh, that is quite easy. It is what I have always done," are to be suspected of dispensing favors in order to exploit others. To them I say, "Do you think the people you favored were really pleased by it?" I sometimes give in, admitting that it is too difficult at present because the patient needs practice and training, so I suggest a milder compromise in these terms: "Remember all the ideas you have in the night, and give me pleasure by telling them to me the next day."

The next day such a patient when asked for his midnight reflections, quite probably replies, "I slept all night," even though he had not previously slept for many days. But let the physician beware lest he triumph too soon. He should continue to collect industriously all the useful facts and reconstruct the patient's style of life.

In treating these cases, I have never had a suicide, the disaster which so commonly occurs, and I believe this is because the indirect treatment reduces acute tension. But all those who are in the patient's environment must be made to understand that they cannot scold, force, or criticize, but must assist the patient into a more favorable situation. With depression, the people in the environment suffer more than the patient, and at times the relatives can no longer endure the strain. My advice is, "When you feel you can no longer control the patient, call for medical help." This is the phase in which the potential for suicide is critical.

Mania, depression, and the severer neuroses are a barricade erected by the patient to block his own approach to the real business of life, and they are sometimes preliminary to the establishment of psychosis in the form of manic-depressive insanity. The first formidable phase of mental disorder, as we have seen, is invariably when some urgent problem presses for solution and the patient has lost courage. In mania, we see an effort to overcome this cowardice of the soul, and the patient pushes himself forward, exaggerates his actions, and talks and laughs with needless excitement. He is high-spirited and irritable, has great projects, is very superior and boastful of his power, and displays strong sexual inclinations. These patients need watching or they may do damage, but this phase of their illness is a sudden blaze which soon consumes its fuel. The natural and usual sequel is a phase of depression in which the patient must on no account be prevented from withdrawing. Individuals show alternations in manic-depressive insanity who showed slight phases of the same pattern in their earlier life. They begin with excitement which rapidly wanes into depression. This tendency is shown even in their handwriting, in which the first letter of a word is written very large, while the others decrease in size and droop below the line. Brilliant beginnings and sudden anti-climaxes are repeated at intervals throughout their life-histories.

Manic-depressive insanity, like a cyclothymia beginning late in life, may appear so similar to general paralysis as to cause confusion in diagnosis. In such a case, the clinical symptoms must be supplemented by an examination of the spinal fluid. This is important, because we find many cases where only a single attack of paralysis occurs; whereas cyclothymia is, of course, recurrent. I once had a patient of this kind whose mania stopped very quickly. I was visiting him at the asylum when he begged me to take him home because the attendants had treated him roughly a few days before. He had begun to recover and his condition was improving every hour, so I took him home. As we sat down at the table, he remarked with satisfaction, "You see, it has always been like this in my life. I have always gotten whatever I wanted." While I was thinking only of the hard knocks he had suffered, he was thinking of nothing but having gotten out of the asylum. That is the difference between the objectivity of common sense and the sort of "private logic" which is the basis of mania.

Chapter III

Deficient Social Feeling, Masculine Protest

Individual Psychology views the conscious and the unconscious, not as separate and conflicting entities, but as complementary and cooperating parts of the same reality. Not of a physiological or biological nature, that reality eludes any chemical or technical tests. For instance, the fact that anxiety affects the sympathetic and parasympathetic nerves does not reveal the cause of an anxiety. The origin of anxiety is in the psychic, not the somatic realm; we attribute it neither to the suppression of sexuality, nor to the conditions of childhood, although we have given all due importance to these factors. What appears most important to us is that a child, for instance, will make use of anxiety in order to achieve his goal of superiority by means of control over the mother. The most exact physiological and neurological description of anger appears to be of almost negligible practical value compared with our actual experience of how anger is used to dominate a person or situation. In this respect, we claim to hold the only position which is correctly and purely a psychological one; that is, we believe the attribution of feelings, emotions and thoughts to bodily conditions and inherited instincts, which is the basis of almost all other psychologies, always leads to exaggerations and mistakes. We are far from disputing that every mental and bodily function is necessarily conditioned by inherited material, but what we see in all psychic activity is the individual's use of this material to attain a certain goal. In all the cases I have hitherto described, the feelings and emotions were developed in the direction and to the degree required for the attainment of a particular goal, which in these instances was of neurotic character. Anxiety, sadness, and every other manifestation took the direction we could have predicted from the style of life. We have seen how dreams also played their part in arranging the feelings into conformity with the general striving, their action giving us a remarkable insight into the workshop of the soul.

If sadness is necessary to the attainment of his goal, an individual is naturally incapable of happiness, for he can be happy only when miserable. But we notice that feelings appear and disappear as required. A person suffering from agoraphobia loses the feeling of anxiety when at home, or when he successfully subordinates another person to himself. The tendency of the neurotic is to exclude from his experience the whole sphere of life except those parts in which he has the sense of being a conqueror. By manufacturing certain moods or emotions in himself, he finds he can repel and shut out the undesirable, unconquerable remainder of his world. He even comes vainly to hide his head in the moods themselves, like an ostrich.

Beneath all fluctuations of mood, however, and ruling them, lies the real, relatively unchangeable character. A coward, for example, even though he shows arrogance against a weaker person or courage in a shielded position, still remains a coward; his freedom from anxiety, when surrounded by watchdogs, guns and policemen, does not deceive us. The excessive protection he demands reveals his character. The proud man may even be very gracious and yielding, but he surrounds himself with inferiors. To estimate the true character of an individual, we must give full significance to the environment he has chosen or permitted for himself.

What we call social feeling in Individual Psychology is the true and inevitable compensation for all our natural weaknesses. Even from the biological standpoint, the human being is clearly a social creature, needing a much longer period of dependence upon others before its maturity than any animal; the human mother is also more dependent before, during, and after giving birth. The high degree of cooperation and social culture which man needs for his very existence demands spontaneous social effort, and the dominant purpose of education is to evoke it. Social feeling is not inborn, but an innate potential which must be consciously developed. We are unable to trust any so-called "social instinct," for its expression depends on the child's conception or vision of the environment. In the growth of this vision of society, the most vital factor is the mother, because in his mother every child makes first contact with a trustworthy fellow-man. In the four or five earliest years of life, the child builds his own prototype by adjusting his inherited abilities to his earliest impressions, and lays the irrevocable foundation of his style of life. This prototype develops later into the more elaborate life-style, conditioning his answers to the three questions of life. In the earliest period, the psychic soundness of the mother is most essential; in the second period, her mentality and breadth of outlook are very important.

The mother influences the first important and specifically human change in the child's behavior. Under her influence, the child first inhibits his desires and organic impulses, introducing delays and circuitous methods into his striving for what he wants. The goal of all striving, to overcome the difficulties of life and gain superiority, is also the stimulus of childhood, which begins with a sense of almost total, practical impotence. To the child, the attentive, benevolent mother is the guardian of his goal, even the goal itself in concrete form. But such a goal is not permanently possible, and the art of motherhood is to give the child freedom and opportunity for success by his own efforts, so that he can establish his style of life and seek his superiority in increasingly useful ways. Then, she must gradually interest the child in other people and in the wider environment of life. To the degree that she performs these two functions: bestowing independence and imparting a true, initial understanding of the situation in the home and in the world, the child will develop social feeling, independence, and courage. To that same degree also will the child find his goal in being a fellow-man and friend, a good worker and a true partner in love. Such an initiation into life unites the ineradicable will to superiority with social feeling, in courageous and optimistic activity on the useful side of life. All the feelings of an individual, throughout his life, are modified by the amount of communal feeling involved in his individual striving for prestige.

Every action on the useless side of life, such as the behavior of problem-children, neurotics, criminals, sexual deviants, prostitutes, and suicides, can be traced to the lack of social feeling, with the consequent loss of confidence. For we must realize that every adaptation we have to make in life, from kindergarten to business management, from school chums to marriage is, directly or indirectly, a social action. From the earliest times, we face new thoughts and events in a manner which is dominantly social or antisocial; it cannot be neutral. Suppose, for instance, that a boy is terrified by illness and death in his environment. He may allay his fears with the determination to be a doctor, and to fight against death. This is obviously a more social idea than that of being a grave-digger, the one who buries the others, a reaction I have also found in a boy in that situation. When social feeling has been instilled from the beginning into the upward striving of the psyche, it acts with automatic certainty, coloring every thought and action, and where this automatized social feeling is deficient, the individual's interest is too self-centered, and he feels he is impotent or a nobody. All his other feelings are connected with this feeling. They do not exist by themselves, nor do they control action, although they are often used to do so—and, of course, they influence our secondary decisions from time to time.

The sense of impotence, or the "feeling of inferiority," is the root-conception of Individual Psychology. Whatever form it may take, it can be correctly estimated only from an adequate study of the individual's actions. Its accurate diagnosis is perhaps more difficult in early life, where we see many efforts to circumvent the instincts and to conceal the feeling itself from its possessor, but most of these early expressions are connected with the strength or weakness of the organs and the friendliness or hostility of the environment. Yet neither the inherited organism nor the environment is entirely responsible for the sense of impotence, nor is it caused by both together. Both these factors, plus the reaction of the child determine the degree to which it is felt. As a conscious connection between its organism and environment, the child's psyche seems to have an indefinite causal power, so that, normal or abnormal, it never reacts with anything like mathematical exactitude. Life, as opposed to dead material, always reacts thus, in a more or less inaccurate, spontaneous manner.

However, for convenience, we may classify common variations of the sense of impotence according to typical causes. Thus, we find three types of neurotic children: those with defective organs, those who are spoiled, and those who are hated. Physical defects, whether congenital or acquired, invariably cause feelings of inferiority, and we can generally trace a special effort to compensate for the specific defect. For example, many who are naturally left-handed and who have been trained to use the right hand exclusively, conceal their sense of manual inadequacy by taking to the arts. Extreme dexterity and finesse of handling such as that of an instrumentalist or a painter becomes an integral factor in their life-goal. Many painters' and poets' choice of vocation was influenced by bad eyesight. Milton and Homer are conspicuous examples of this latter compensation. In the deafness of Beethoven and the stuttering of Demosthenes, we also see the points upon which their strivings were concentrated.

Many people have resented the attention that my colleagues and I have drawn to this compensatory factor in the work of artists of genius or high talent, and they attempt to deny what our experience constantly confirms. But they object because of a misunderstanding of Individual Psychology. We are not so foolish as to suppose that organic imperfection is the actual cause of genius. Many of the Freudians have indeed supposed that the sublimest works of human genius were directly caused by sexual repressions, but we make no such eccentric generalization. In our view, a man of genius is primarily a man of supreme usefulness. If he is an artist, he is useful to culture, giving distinction and value by his work to the recreative life of many thousands. And this value, where it is genuine and not merely empty cleverness, depends on a high degree of courage and communal intuition. The origin of genius lies neither in the inherited organism nor in the environmental influences, but in that third sphere of individual reaction to which I have already referred, which includes the possibility of socially affirmative action. In the choice of its specialized expression, however, the highest talent is conditioned by the organism with which it is endowed, from the greatest defect of which it gains its particular mode of concentration.

A knowledge of this principle, which can only be correctly gained by much observation, is of the greatest service in the treatment of organically defective children, as it enables us to protect them from many dangers of over-compensation.

Receiving too much from others, the spoiled child never proves his own powers to himself. Formed in accordance with his experience, his goal is to be the center of the family, the focus of attention and care. The usual symptoms are: anger, discontent, disorderliness, anxiety, enuresis, a struggle to avoid isolation, and unwillingness to go to school. Treatment readily suggests itself; but we often have to take into account an unusually intense feeling of insecurity.

The hated child is in the worse position of never having been spoiled by anyone. His goal is to escape and get at a safe distance from others. Cruelty, slyness, and cowardliness are some of the symptoms. Such a child often cannot look a person straight in the eyes, cannot speak, and hides his feelings in fear of abasement. In some instances, constant tendency to find fault may be developed in the direction of useful criticism.

No soul develops in complete freedom. Each one is in mental, emotional, and nutritive dependence upon his immediate environment on the earth and in the cosmos, yet independent to the degree that he must deal with these relationships consciously; he must answer them as the questions of life. Everything he does is an answer; no doubt it is the best he can give. We are not blessed with omniscience, and our greatest reasonable hope is not to answer with a great mistake, so that we should test all views, including that of Individual Psychology, and prove them carefully. Our best science must be applied with common sense.

Hated children also take life as they find it, respond to it with the best reactions they can devise, and gradually fix these reactions into a mechanical pattern of life. The three life-problems, in whatever successive forms they present themselves, will thenceforward be encountered by that fixed pattern of behavior, however it may be elaborated by experience. The unusual tension of their life makes these children postulate a higher goal of security and superiority than that of the average child. All the impressions, perceptions, and attitudes are conditioned by the perspective of their prejudiced situation, so that what they learn from life is seldom any new point of view, but merely how to fill in the old one with more detail.

In these three types of children, we encounter the three typical accentuations of the feeling of inferiority. They all weaken the social contact, and tend to isolate the individual in an ever-narrowing sphere of interest. Unsocial types take on very deceptive appearances at times. I once called to see an old lady I knew, who was well known for benevolent actions, and found her crying while an old man, also in tears, stood before her. "What is the matter?" I asked. "Look at this poor old man," she sobbed. "He has five starving children, and is to be turned out of his house if he doesn't pay the ten shillings he owes, and I have only five to give him!" "Don't cry," I replied, "Let me add to your generous gift a little gift of five shillings." She thanked me effusively, saying she had always known me to be a good man. Now I knew that this old lady was not only very rich, but also that she had no real social interest. She consorted only with her own relatives, and even with them in a very dominating spirit. Her charitable action did not contradict her character; her pity and sadness over this poor man gave her the kind of feeling of superiority she lived for. It is of no use to judge an isolated demonstration of feeling apart from the whole style of life. For a psychological understanding, we must perceive the goal toward which all the feelings lead.

Boy With Obsessive Guilt Feelings

I have already called attention to the use of guilty feeling in building up a neurotic and imaginary superiority. One of the clearest examples in my experience was the case of a boy, the second child in the family, whose father and elder brother were both notable for honesty of character. As usual with second children, this boy's striving was largely concentrated on the effort to surpass his elder brother. At the age of seven, he lied to his teacher, pretending that a piece of work on which his brother had helped him was all his own. This gave him a feeling of guilt which he concealed for three years, after which he went to the teacher and confessed that he had lied. The teacher refused to take the matter seriously, but only laughed, so the boy went and unburdened himself to his father with great emotion and sadness. Gratified by what he took to be a profound love of truth, the father consoled and praised his son. But the boy's depression did not vanish with this paternal absolution. He continued to think, with a neurotic compulsion, that he was a liar. The high moral atmosphere of the home, and the feeling that he was worse than his brother, both in school work and in popularity, had combined to

25

set him striving for excellence in the supreme family virtue. He was secretly dedicated to proving, even by the life-long expiation of a trifling transgression, that his integrity was greater than anyone's.

The boy's neurosis developed. He acquired other self-reproaches, for not being entirely honest in work, and for masturbation. These behaviors became most acute just before an examination. By amassing difficulties in this way, he felt excused for not surpassing his brother. He planned a course of technical training after leaving the university, but by that time his compulsion neurosis had increased so much that most of his time was employed in prayer to God to forgive him, of course, putting work out of the question. He was admitted to an asylum, where they supposed him incurable, but his condition improved and he left the asylum, asking to be re-admitted if he had a relapse. At this point, he changed his occupation and began to study the history of art. Before sitting for an examination in this subject, however, he put it beyond the bounds of possibility with a piece of extraordinary behavior. He went to church on a special festival day, when the building was crowded, and prostrated himself publicly, crying out that he was the greatest of sinners.

In this striking achievement of a central position in a large public assembly, we can detect the same pattern of ambition he had in childhood. To be the greatest penitent among all the worshippers in a church is the same kind of distinction as to have the softest conscience for a lie in a family of supreme honesty. It is better than the best. He made another exhibition of himself when he returned to the asylum, by coming to lunch one day entirely naked. He was a well-built man and quite equal to the rest of his family in bodily appearance.

This patient's escape from work and examinations was because of fear that he would not shine in these normal situations. The guilty feeling, especially intensified when required, must be regarded as an intentional exclusion of activities in which he had no confidence of success. He also had a tendency to score a cheap success of notoriety in keeping with his general aim, which prompted him to appear naked at the meal and to engage in other eccentricities of behavior.

The task of the physician is to enable such a patient to realize what he is doing, and to transfer his egocentric interest to social life and useful activity. This is an art, in which the Individual Psychologist must train himself by practice and collaboration, for science and the knowledge of principles alone will never enable him to win the complete confidence which is required. In the case I have just described, for example, I had to recognize correctly, in the first quarter of an hour of the patient's visit, the kind of superiority for which this style of life was designed. If I had failed to do so, I would certainly have provoked prompt resistance. Step by step, I had to induce his correct statement of his difficulties in childhood, to make him reveal, with less and less reluctance, his deep feelings of worthlessness compared with his brother. Then, it was easier for him to admit to himself how he impressed his father with his honesty and how he had maneuvered himself into limelight positions.

The method of Individual Psychology, because it requires the admission and correction of mistakes still dear to the patient, involves the utmost art and craft of the practitioner. We are far from denying that other schools of psychiatry have their successes in dealing with neuroses, but in our experience they do so less by their methods than when they happen to give the patient a good human relationship with the physician, or above all to give him encouragement. A quack sometimes improves a person's attitude toward life to a considerable extent; so also may a visit to Lourdes. But we remain convinced that the cure of all mental disorder lies in the simpler, if more laborious process of making the patient understand his own mistakes.

As we have already seen, the style of life of most of our patients can be traced to three typical positions of inferiority in childhood. Certain mistakes of adaptation prevent the establishment of a normal style of life, and appear even before the child faces his first social problems beyond the home. One of these mistakes of childhood is a refusal to accept the sexual role, in which case a boy grows up like a girl, or vice versa.

Such errors are very common, and indeed nearly everyone shows some slight tendencies toward them. Perhaps every man has something in either body or behavior which we feel to be feminine, and women often have masculine traits of a physical character without a corresponding masculinity of mind. More often, however, the wrong sexuality is in the mind and not the body.

The sex glands, it is true, have an extensive influence on the body. But they have a very limited power to determine the individual's conception of superiority. This individual goal of supremacy is chiefly responsible for a person's confusion about his true sexual function. When we deal with the mental symptoms of inverted sexuality, we must remember this and not blame too much on the glands. It is probably equally true that the mental striving affects the glands themselves in the long run. We must first see how the patient relates his ideas of sexuality to his goal.

Woman 26: Who Wanted to be a Man

The goal of superiority is usually identified with the masculine role because of the privileges, both real and imaginary, with which our present civilization has invested the male. A girl's feeling of inferiority may be markedly increased when she realizes that she is a female, and a boy's also when he doubts his maleness. Both compensate with an exaggeration of what they imagine to be masculine behavior. This form of compensation, which may have the most varied and intricate consequences according to circumstances, is what I have called the masculine protest. Its chief symptom both in mind and in outward conduct is a needlessly domineering attitude toward the opposite sex. It is noticeably connected with a very ambitious style of life, with a goal of super-man or of an excessively pampered woman. The behavior is over-exaggerated, which may be veiled in favorable situations, but is revealed clearly in times of defeat. The masculine protest is indicated to a certain degree in some of the cases I have cited, but I will give a more typical instance.

A neurotic, twenty-six-year old woman who came to consult me, had lost her mother at six, after which she lived with an indulgent father until she was thirteen. Her earliest memory was: "I hated to play with dolls." This was a sign of her unwillingness to develop in a normal manner; she preferred to play with toy railway-trains. She wanted to be wild in conduct, and played only with boys, like a typical tomboy. If she did play with girls, she pulled their hair and annoyed them in other ways. To my question, "What do you think about men and women?" she replied, "Women are always scheming; men are straightforward." This is a still more definite sign of a will toward masculine development.

In parenthesis, I would never forbid a girl to play with trains, climb trees, or play any boys' games, but I am fully convinced that much trouble would be saved in the later life of children if they were brought up from the first with knowledge and preparation for their correct sexual role. This training is impossible, of course, in an atmosphere charged with suggestions of feminine disability and masculine privilege, as we so often find. All those who depreciate women as a sex incur inevitable punishment, because they develop an attitude which contradicts truth and reality.

I asked my patient to tell me about her feelings toward men and women. She said that when she was thirteen, she laughed when she heard that people fell in love. She knew nothing of love until her twentieth year. Combined with her vigorous athleticism, this refusal to acknowledge love confirmed the ostrich-like flight from her sexual role;

she wanted to laugh love out of the question and deny her femininity by excelling in athletics. I expected to find difficulty in menstruation, often experienced by girls who have a grudge against their feminine nature, giving them great pain and tendencies toward anger, but this was not the case with her. We would have expected her to show signs of anger at the age of thirteen when her father married again, but she did not. She scorned to do anything so womanly, but said she was glad her father was married so that she could be free. However, trouble with her father began from that time, and she fought in the home, saying that she wanted to be free to leave home and become a social worker. She wanted to conquer her father by means of financial independence. Her desire to be a social worker was colored by the thought of ruling over her children.

We are familiar, of course, with the desire that patients often express not to take any money from their families. When a patient tells me he does not intend to take any more money from his family, I often say, "Better take it. It will be cheaper for them in the end."

This patient had many men friends, but was never in love. It is usual for boys and girls to fall in love about twelve or thirteen, and not uncommon when they are five or six. An individual who reaches the age of twenty-three without any such experience is not prepared for it. Love is a necessary life-task for which an early preparation is needed, and training for love is an integral part of our education for life. Both normal love and all its deviations such as homosexuality are a matter of training and education.

At the age of twenty-three, this girl had a feeling she thought was love; she liked the man better than she had ever liked anyone before, and the affair led to intercourse. This sexual relationship was part of her striving for independence, expressing her opposition to her father, and her determination to be manlike. The man's feelings changed, and he disappeared for a time. Unable to bear this defeat the girl tried to follow him, with the predictable result in our civilization, where men are taught to think it beneath their dignity to be wooed, and are afraid of surrendering easily. The man cooled off more and more, and she saw him at last with another girl, for which she reproached him. In quarreling with her, the man told her she was a common girl. After this, he disappeared entirely and married the other one.

For some time after this incident, my patient kept up only her sporting and athletic activities with men, and was frightened if they made any other advances; she ran away when a man friend wanted to kiss her. Later on, she became the mistress of a second man, but she was unhappy, fought with him constantly, and would not consent to marry him. The man took a voyage to Africa, thinking it would be better to absent himself for a while, but her unhappiness continued, and was now fraught with memories of her first lover. In her continual quarrels and her return to the image of the married and therefore unattainable lover, we see her excuse for not marrying. A typical symptom was that sexual relations did not satisfy her. She had not been prepared for marriage.

This girl associated being a woman with defeat. Thus, if she behaved like a girl and considered the prospect of marriage, she could not endure it; it was easier to continue playing at being a boy by keeping up her athletic pursuits. On the other hand, she felt that marriage was a natural and logical social demand. In this conflicting situation, she was further discouraged by two great defeats: by her father, when he ceased to spoil her and married again, and second, by the desertion of her first lover. To safeguard herself against another defeat, she put love and marriage at the greatest possible distance. Then, to justify her halt before this problem and to ensure it, she persuaded herself that it was impossible for a girl to keep a man's love. The fundamental difficulty in this case, as in many others, was the idea that the feminine function is of definitely second-rate importance, and therefore not really valuable. One of the chief causes of unhappiness in love and marriage, this mistaken belief is the illusion which forms the basis of the masculine protest.

Chapter IV

Problems in Love and Marriage

At the end of my lectures, I have to reply to questions about love and marriage. My questioners often seem to have been misled by some psychological reading into believing that the sexual impulse is the central motive to which every other activity is related. I have never seen the reason for placing this unnatural emphasis on one single function of life. Of course, I admit its great, although varying importance. But the detection of transposed and sublimated sexual elements in a variety of manifestations is not practically useful, even if it is possible; our experience is that the sexual components cannot even be correctly interpreted except in relation to the individual style of life.

The erotic phases are functions of this individual lifestyle, and we can gain insight into the erotic life, with all its waywardness, hesitation and elusive subtleties, only so far as we grasp the individual's style in the prototype. By the prototype, I mean the original form of an individual's adaptation to life. The psychic prototype is a finished creation by the time the child is four years old. It is the baby in the man or woman, which never grows up any further, but rules the whole life to its end. It is no wonder that certain religions have worshipped an infant, for this prototypical being is the greatest power in human life. The prototype is the constant factor, although we may improve its later manifestations to an indefinite extent when we come to recognize and understand it.

This prototype in each individual is the baby Cupid who rules his behavior as a lover. If the prototype is sociable and interested in others, the personality into whom it develops will solve all love-problems with loyalty to the partner and responsibility to society. If the prototype is struggling to attract notice and to suppress others, its later manifestations will include the use of sexuality toward the same ends; that person will establish sexual relationships in order to rule. A prototype formed by attaining superiority in a limited sphere of activity which excludes the opposite sex will later tend to produce homosexuality or other deviations. The main outlines of the erotic life are thus strictly pre-conditioned.

Therefore, we can interpret the various sexual urges by the goal, especially in its most prototypical form, while the converse is not true.

The study of instincts or urges will never enable us to understand the structure of an individual psyche; and it is interesting to note that psychologists who endeavor to explain the mind's working from such observations instinctively presuppose a style of life without noticing that they have done so.

From the standpoint of Individual Psychology, love and marriage are the normal responses to the sexual question, one of the three vital questions of life, and our task is to understand the special difficulties they present to individuals. An individual who has been well prepared for social life in childhood will not have great difficulties in his sexual life. Courage, an optimistic attitude, common sense, and the feeling of being at home on the earth, will enable him to face advantages and disadvantages with equal firmness. His goal of superiority will be identified with ideas of serving humanity and of overcoming its difficulties with his creative power. Deviations from the norm of sexual expression will be instinctively excluded as unattractive. His useful goal will arrange all his emotions and actions so that he approaches love in a feasible form, while adolescent love-affairs and the experiences of his friends will train him for love and strengthen his position. The literature of unhappy love and disastrous marriage (a common source of mischief) will be unable to mislead him; and even if he has disagreeable experiences with an unsuitable marriage-partner, it will not corrupt his course of life. His ideals of social life, work, and beauty will survive ordinary defeats, and the sense of beauty itself will be transferred to the beauty of adaptation to life.

Those whose social contact is poor, who have lost real interest in the lives of others, face an entirely different fate. They approach love without the right preparation, for every love-problem is a social problem in the sense that it is a question of behavior toward a sexually attractive person, and their unprepared souls feel as if the difficulty is insurmountable when it comes to marriage, the most intimately and intensely social of all situations. Such a person has been educating himself for an isolated life, and does not really want to share life with someone else, so he tends to shut his partner out from all but a few activities in which partnership seems necessary or advantageous. He does not perceive marriage as a complete human relationship. His difficulties are often increased by having learned about love and marriage from parents who were not happily united; and he gathers confirmation from his environment and literature. In popular fiction, the marriage situations are usually portrayed as unhappy; unhappy love stories are probably in a majority because of the use which readers make of them.

One of the chief obstacles to marriage lies in the prevailing opinion that the man is functionally superior, leading men into vain expectations of domination and making girls rebel against their feminine function; they naturally act a role of servitude in a "man-made world." Much suspicion, jealousy, and quarrelling spring directly from this antagonism, for if an individual feels victimized by love or marriage, it disturbs every association of life. For instance, if a girl feels that the feminine a position is worse or lower than the masculine, she will enter into some sort of competition with the man in her striving to show superiority. If either partner is looking for a weaker mate with the expectation of dominating, disappointment is certain. It appears to be an immutable law of love and marriage that it can succeed only where the attitude is one of giving. When an individual's attitude toward love and marriage is hesitant, halting, or expectant, it indicates a general unpreparedness for social life, and we may safely infer a tendency to exclude a large part of the potential of life. In such cases the individual will always justify his actions, but his real purpose appears in the result, which is that love and marriage are indefinitely postponed. In this goal of evasion or exclusion, the means taken are interesting. They include all the neurotic symptoms which are more or less connected with sexual functions. The individual is like a stammerer in the sexual sphere. Ejaculatio praecox, lack of sexual interest and satisfaction, vaginismus and frigidity, are all signs of a determination to exclude actions which the individual claims he is willing to perform.

Normally, of course, the sexual objective is in harmony with the life-goal, is indeed one aspect of it, and as soon as approach to this objective becomes possible, it produces the appropriate thoughts and feelings, excluding all contradictions and conflicting tasks. But in the case of the neurotic, thoughts and feelings are produced which belong to other duties or functions of life; irrelevant considerations are admitted which inhibit, obstruct, or pervert normal conduct along the sexual line. The impotence or other sexual disability thus produced is dictated by a neurotic goal of superiority and a mistaken style of life. Investigation always reveals a fixed intention to receive without giving, with a lack of social feeling, courage and optimistic activity.

We can find other ways of excluding sexual partnership, of course, besides functional disability. Exclusion is often contrived by an exaggerated and unpractical ideal of marriage, and sometimes by a desire to mate with someone obviously ineligible, much older, incurably diseased, or below the age of consent. When the patient has postponed marriage for a long period, perhaps attributing the indecision to polygamous tendencies, investigation will often disclose the under-structure of a perversion, which must not be mistaken for the motive, but recognized as a coordinate of the hesitant attitude.

Man 23: Dominating Through Drinking

The efforts to exclude love and marriage, either before or after the contract, are modeled on the prototypical or infantile pattern of adaptation, as shown in the marriage-history of a young man who was twenty-three when he first came to see me, without occupation and without friends. A year earlier, he had married a girl with whom he had relations for two years. His attitude toward her was one of continual jealousy, advice, and criticism. The girl appeared to be very docile while she was hoping to be married, and the man enjoyed a sense of superiority through her behavior and in the knowledge that the marriage would antagonize his mother. After marriage, however, his wife was not so obedient, and he occasionally showed high temper. He behaved as he had behaved in childhood to his mother and his elder sister when they failed to gratify his wishes. Then he had screamed, run away from lessons, broken toys, torn his clothes, and in every possible way assailed his mother by attacks upon himself or his own toys. Now, after scenes with his wife, he drank heavily and come home intoxicated.

This man was a spoiled child, who lost his father at the age of two years, and was pampered by his mother. He became the tyrant of the family, as children in such a position are likely to do, and from eight years old to thirteen he suffered from fainting-fits.

The connection between fainting and anger may in certain cases have an organic basis. I have found a type of patient who loses consciousness in a rage, and suspect some peculiarities in the blood-circulation of the brain. In such cases it is possible that an epileptic fit occurs in varying degrees, petit mal, for example. If an outlet presents itself, the fits may stop, and as it happened, this patient was not obliged to repress his rages.

In accordance with the view of Individual Psychology, we can predict the repetition of this childhood behavior and expect the patient to take the same direction in any vital conflict with others, to hurt them by damaging himself. As such behavior breeds callousness in the environment, the resentment and injury are correspondingly increased. In this case, when drunkenness ceased to punish the wife sufficiently, the man attempted suicide after a quarrel with her. He hurt himself severely and recovered very slowly. The inheritance of a large fortune from his father had lessened the patient's necessity for self-control. He could never keep a position in his occupation, a failure which he justified by complaining of terrible working conditions.

This case clearly illustrates the inability of a pampered child to seize upon the best means to become a conqueror. It also confirms the insufficiency of treating such conditions as drunkenness without recognition of the psychic prototype, which can assimilate any change of conditions to its individual kind of striving. It is not interest in drink, but in himself and his own superiority that misleads such a patient toward the useless side of life. The object of treatment must be to increase the social interest in whatever way possible.

His Wife Who Takes Morphine

The use of love and marriage as a means of domination is, of course, intolerable to the marriage partner, so this man's wife gradually lost all interest in him. He obtained a divorce and married again twice. He took as his third wife a divorced woman who had attempted suicide during her first marriage, when she was found to have been unfaithful to her first husband because of his neglecting her. Her mother had been very critical and cold to her, failing in both of the two maternal function; she had predictably turned to the kinder father, and he had spoiled her. This woman seemed to be of a gentle disposition, but it did not stand the test of unfavorable situations. At school she had constantly made trouble in the class. She had only one friend, and was not sociable.

Her second husband was a youngest child, left-handed, and with a clumsiness which drew the constant derision of his elder brothers. However, he was ambitious and anxious to outshine the brothers, who in childhood had surpassed him because of his handicap, and this stimulated him to the acquisition of wealth; he became rich and highly esteemed. Fear of defeat and escape from derision made up his prototype, so that he liked and sought isolation. Women who flattered him enticed him into his first two marriages. The second appeared when he had lost a great part of his fortune, which to him stood for superiority over his brothers. This woman tried to console him with morphine, which he continued to take after she died.

The third wife, described above, married him with a determination to save him from the drug habit, and her first efforts revealed her inability to do so. Like the spoiled child she was, she was infuriated at her lack of power over him, and began taking morphine herself in order to punish him. She had the idea that he would reform himself if he saw the terrible consequences of his action; but as nothing of the kind happened, both continued to abuse the drug, and soon each one noticed that the other was looking about for another partner.

This couple tried several morphine cures without success, which is not surprising when we review the complex of motives at work. One was the man's childish goal of superiority, to escape derision or disrespect. Another lay in his attitude toward his business worries, from which he found not only partial relief in morphine, but also a subjectively valid excuse. He could blame his diminished success on the morphine, without which, he could believe, he would have triumphed over everything. He sometimes spoke of the habit in both ways, as a relief and as an excuse, without understanding the connection or the contradiction between them. To recognize the connection would have been to relate these manifestations to his style of life, to understand his exaggerated demand for esteem, in which case he might have chosen better means to attain it. His polygamous tendencies and his exclusion of friends showed a lack of social adjustment; and he could not possibly have been cured by taking away the morphine. The whole personality needed to be changed by the recognition of its prototype. In lighter cases, a patient with varied symptoms may lose them before he or the doctor grasp their coherence. When this happens, it is either because of a favorable change in the patient's situation or because the doctor, by encouragement or by chance, renews the patient's interest in others.

The wife was far from being cured of the drug. Feeling in danger of losing her second husband, she gave up attempts to cure him. Indifferent to the criticism of others, and courting the displeasure of her mother, she increased her own doses of morphine to the most dangerous excesses. This was a repetition of her conduct in her first marriage where she was neglected. This drug habit was a kind of suicide. Because she was a youngest child and the father's favorite, both her desire for conquest and her feeling of inadequacy were intense; she lived according to the neurotic formula: "All or nothing." In these cases, when the hope of gaining all begins to fade, nothing is left; and this must be expressed by bad habits, suicide, or insanity. The feeling that suicide gives mastery over life and death is the supreme expression of the goal of superiority on the useless side of life. But we must note, of course, her father and husband began to watch the patient with apprehension. Everybody became more tender toward her, giving her a sense of augmented power and importance.

Such are the underlying difficulties which obstruct so many attempts to cure drunkenness, drug-habits, and suicidal tendencies. There is a method for everything in life; and to solve any problem we must find the right one. For instance, we have two ways of trying to pass through a doorway only five feet high. One of them is to walk erect, and the other is to bend one's back. If I try the first method, I not only bump my head on the lintel, but I also have to fall back on the second method after all. I call this the law of the low doorway. Nothing compels me to stoop, but if I do not realize the relationship between my height and the aperture, I cannot possibly pass through it. We stand in an equally definite relationship to the critical personal problems of life. If we do not realize the fact and adapt our method accordingly, we collide with reality.

Every child confronts reality, and finds his method of coping, more or less successfully, in his prototype. These individual responses to reality are so wonderfully varied that the ancient poets and fable-writers compared them with species of animals such as the hare, the tortoise, the ant, and the grasshopper. Prototypes are indeed like animal souls, each moving toward its own goal, in its own interest, and in its own characteristic manner.

The tension between the child and his environment, which is never entirely absent, is not exactly calculable, for besides the many possibilities of variation in the family constellation, each child has his individual sensitivity and an original responsiveness. Thus, against a fairly typical position of inferiority, different children will erect most diverse concrete goals of superiority. For example, many children are at a similar disadvantage through weak muscles and poor eyesight, but they may compensate in directions which could lead them to be acrobats or artists or toward a hundred other developments, according to the originality of their reaction, the degree of their courage, and their social feeling. Moreover, the defects for which they have to compensate contain many subtle, individual differences.

For this reason a child who has deviated from a normal line of life cannot be re-educated by normal methods. The method must be specially adapted because the child with an abnormal endowment or development will feel suppressed in perfectly normal situations. A child with stomach trouble, for example, may fail to gain weight, and develop poorly; and if the circumstances are not carefully adapted, the usual consequences will ensue: a pessimistic and hostile attitude, perhaps with pugnacity and irritability. Such a child is liable to acquire an envious disposition by comparing himself with others. He may show an abnormal interest in eating and food, and his tendency to collect and hoard things may develop in later life into a concentration on money-making. We often find troubles in early nutrition in families which produce successful money-makers. As a rule, when a child displays exaggerated consciousness of his stomach and a tendency to anxiety, we should do something about it, for it is a common beginning of neurosis. He feels diminished and loses interest in others, which bode ill for the child's future.

Children with stomach troubles are a familiar source of concern to parents and physicians, but the difficulties are due far more to imperfect methods of child-rearing than to the constitutional deficiency. This is the case with other physical disabilities; the better we understand their connection with the general line of life, the better the methods we can devise. We cannot claim we have found the universally perfect method, but the continued search for correct methods according to the principles of Individual Psychology certainly enables us to avoid many mistakes.

Mistress With Headaches and Palpitations

The following case exemplifies the dominance of the prototypical attitude in love and marriage. As a girl, the patient was the second child of the family, very weak, very pretty, spoiled by her mother and ill-used by a drunken father. She lost the mother's favoritism at the age of three when a baby sister was born, and protested by becoming truculent and high-tempered. She was supposed to inherit bad temper from her father, and some psychologists would uphold this mistaken opinion, but any child might follow this line of development in such an unfavorable turn of circumstances. Indeed, from the attitudes of aggressive, disobedient, or domineering children, we are often able to guess correctly at some salient feature of the home environment, such as displacement by a younger child.

This girl became an actress and had many love affairs, which culminated in her becoming the mistress of an elderly man. Such an obvious exploitation of advantage indicates deep feelings of insecurity and cowardice. This relationship, however, brought her trouble; her mother reproached her, and although the man loved her, he cold not get a divorce. During this time, her younger sister became engaged.

In the face of this competition, she began to suffer from headaches and palpitations, and became very irritable toward the man. Her neurotic impatience was the cause of her coming to consult me. In a certain type, we find that severe tensions of anger regularly produce headaches. The emotion accumulates, so to speak, during a period when the patient shows no symptoms. The emotional tension may actually result in circulatory changes producing attacks of trigeminal neuralgia, migraine and epileptiform seizures. The well known respiratory spasms and sensations of choking induced by violent rage illustrate such circulatory disturbance.

In those cases of trigeminal neuralgia with no organic basis, I have already emphasized (1910) the importance of psychological factors. These may, of course, act through vascular disturbances induced by emotion, and the frequent repetition of such interferences with the blood supply may in the end cause organic damage to the tissues of the nervous system.

The tendency to anger is related to excessive ambition both of which originate in a competitive striving to escape from a sense of being overcome. They occur in antisocial natures, who feel uncertain of attaining their goal by patient striving, and often try to escape to the useless side with an outburst of temper. Children use such explosions to conquer by terrifying, or at least to feel superior; and in a similar way, they use the consequences, their headaches. The scientific world did not know the neurotic origin of headaches when I first spoke of it in 1910, but it must have been well known in antiquity. Horace, in an ode to Maecenas, wrote of those ambitious people who do not want to alter themselves, but merely to change others; and he refers to their headaches and sleeplessness.

To return to the case: the girl's condition was the result of a neurotic, but effective method of striving to hasten her marriage. The married man was greatly worried by her continuous headaches, and tried to get a divorce, but he was not very courageous and made slow progress against the opposition to it. The girl then broke with him and wanted to marry another man; but she soon discovered he was too uncultured, so she returned to her former lover. He (the married man), then came to see me about my patient, saying that he would hurry and divorce and marry her.

Treatment of the immediate illness was easy; in fact, it would have cleared up without me, for the girl was powerful enough to succeed with the help of her headaches. Her goal was to force the man to get a divorce quickly; it was the goal of her childhood not to be surpassed by her younger sister, and as soon as the divorce proceedings began, the headaches disappeared.

I explained to her the connection between her headaches and her competitive attitude toward her sister. She felt incapable of attaining her goal of superiority by normal means, for she was one of those children whose interest has become focused on themselves, and who tremble for fear they will not succeed. She admitted that she cared only for herself and did not like the man she was about to marry.

Her palpitations were because she had twice been pregnant and both times had resorted to abortion, when she justified herself to the doctor by saying that her heart was too weak for her to bear children. It was true that her heart was irritated by tense situations and suppressed anger, but she used this symptom increasingly and exaggerated it to justify her intention never to have children. Self-absorbed women generally show their lack of human and social interest by an unwillingness to have children; but sometimes, of course, they desire children for reasons of ambition or for fear of being considered inferior.

A dream of this patient is worth recording. She dreamed that she was well dressed and held a naked baby in her arms. She said to the baby, which was of a brown and jolly complexion, "I cannot take care of you; I must give you up." The baby answered, "Yes, you are right." Then she began crying in her dream, and a man passed her, but she turned her head to avoid being seen. The man, however, wished to see her and looked at her.

By the nakedness of the baby, she meant that she was too poor to have children. Her sister was to be married to a rich man, whereas she had merely enough money for her own clothes, none to spare for a child. The baby's brown complexion meant that she could have a healthy child, but the dream-child reassured her, by agreeing with her, that everyone could see it was impossible for her to have children. The patient said at this time that she felt perfectly well, but suffered form palpitations of the heart night and morning, which showed she was clinging to the idea that her weak heart excused her from having children. She was too egotistical and much too eager to stay in the center of the stage of life to entertain the prospect of children; moreover, she saw the child as a potential rival because the tragedy of her infantile life was one of rivalry with her baby sister. The man who passed by her in the dream must have been me, and her turning away was a sign that she did not wish to be entirely open with me. She was afraid that I would blame her, and as she knew I wished to develop her social feeling, she thought I would want her to have a child.

The decision whether a woman should or should not have a child should rest entirely with the woman; such at least is my personal belief. I cannot see the use of forcing a child on a woman who is without social interest or love for children, for she is almost certain to bring it up badly. In such cases I prefer to adjust the woman socially, and then, she may wish to have a baby without suggestion or pressure from anyone else.

It is, or used to be, the frequent conclusion of Freudian psychologists that the person who excludes love is repressing his libido, but it is a vast improvement both in diagnosis and treatment when we relate this exclusion to the individual's goal of superiority. If the exclusion of normal possibilities of mating is very persistent and obstinate, it is a sign that the person is neurotic in other relationships also, and does not want to see marriage in the obvious light of social necessity because of a more general exclusion of social behavior. We then see a hesitating or evasive attitude before the love-problem, or an unnatural tendency in the love relationship, both of which proceed from a mistake in understanding the connection between the individual's prototypical needs and the possibilities of his situation. A better understanding would produce better behavior. For individual goals are not unattainable, nor are they attainable in one way only, but every method of attainment has its own sequence of necessary obligations. The neurotic pays the price of taking the most difficult, lonely, and impractical way to the summit of his ambitions, when much easier, better paths are available. In a sense, the prototype never relinquishes its rule over the individual's life, but better ways of fulfilling its law can be found.

We must regard the love task as the most intimate and organically determined form of social behavior, a view which tends to reveal a range of mistakes. This view of Individual Psychology may not bless us with an absolute truth; it may not enable us to foresee the future of a marriage as accurately as we can calculate the path of a falling stone. But the stone lies in a world of truth, whereas we live in the realm of human mistakes. Our method enables us to replace the large mistakes with small ones, justifying our belief that we can often help others approach their own goals with a method which, if perhaps not infallible, is better than theirs in social direction. In the world of the psyche, no principle of individual orientation exists beyond our individual beliefs. The consequences of these beliefs are great. Big mistakes may produce neuroses, but little mistakes make a nearly normal person.

Chapter V

Neurotic Style of Life and Psychotherapy

Because it is natural for an individual to express himself with his whole body, we can often learn more by watching a person's movements--how he walks, sits, smiles or fidgets--than by listening to what he says. We may go further, and apply this principle to the evaluation of symptoms. Vomiting, for example, commonly indicates that the person who vomits does not wish to agree. It represents an attack on someone, or the rejection of an approach. Fainting may also be the effective rejection of a situation in which a person feels entirely powerless.

How could I cure a stutterer if I believed stuttering to be caused by some subtle and unknown organic deficiencies? I have plenty of evidence that the stutterer does not want to join with others, and he can generally talk quite well when he is alone; he may even be able to read or recite excellently. Therefore, I can interpret his stammer only as the expression of his attitude toward others.

However, the belief, common in America, that stuttering is caused by training left-handed children to use the right hand has some merit, although this is merely because wrong educational methods are used, which give the child an antisocial bias in reaction to unsympathetic criticism. A mechanical and competitive method of teaching makes no proper allowance for the fact that the left-handed child has more actual difficulty in adapting itself, and the child retaliates with an impediment which worries or irritates his teachers. We can find no physical reason why children should not be taught to use the right hand. Since we live in a right-handed culture, left-handedness may sometimes be felt as if it were an inferiority in later periods of life. In many technical and commercial positions and even in social life, left-handedness may be a noticeable disability or hindrance. But the training of these people for a right-handed world should be done with the correct method, for they are a large minority whose rights should be protected. In early life the left-handed child certainly has greater difficulties, for often the peculiarity is not recognized, and the child is blamed for clumsiness. Such a child connects his imperfect dexterity with all other difficulties at home and at school, and suffers from depression which focuses his interest too much on himself. Thus left-handed children often acquire the feeling that the world is a dangerous place, and become more vulnerable to neurosis than others.

I believe about thirty-five per cent of all people are left-handed, and most of them do not know it. There are several ways of detecting the left-handed: the best known and simplest is to ask the person in question to clasp his hands together; the left-handed subject will instinctively do this so that the left thumb is over the right thumb. The eyebrow on the left side is frequently higher in a left-handed person, and the whole symmetry of the body more developed on the left side. Even in the cradle, we can see when a baby tends to use the left side of the body more than the right. The adaptation to right-handedness is a rather severe test for these children. Generally, when I see very bad handwriting, I know it is that of a left-handed person whose courage is below par. On the other hand, if I see excellent handwriting I know it is also from a left-handed person, but one who has successfully grappled with his difficulties. The left-handed who develop their right hands tend to some artistic or craftsmanlike talents. We find many left-handed painters who paint equally well with either hand.

Few people realize that left-handed children often have considerable difficulty in learning to read because they spell in reverse from right to left; a mistake they can correct if it is properly explained to them[3].

Imperfections in the sense-organs limit the means which a child has of sharing in the life of others. They impose necessary differences of behavior which may be felt as a burden if we do not use wise measures of encouragement. Children with imperfect sight walk cautiously because they are conscious of danger in movement. They are more interested in seeing because it is difficult for them, and if they compensate well, they will become visual types. Poor hearing and handicaps in movement have corresponding compensations.

Gustow Freytag, for example, was very short-sighted and did not wear glasses. Not being able to see much, his attention was focused on imagining what his environment was like, and his great quality as a writer was the high development of his imagination. Goethe, Schiller, Milton, and many other fine poets were afflicted with poor sight, and also many of the greatest painters. A child with perfectly normal sight is not likely to concentrate his attention on the phenomena of visibility, but takes them for granted. We must never assume, however, that defective

---

[3] These and other facts are collected and discussed by Dr. Alice Friedman in an article published in the *International Journal of Individual Psychology,* 5th year: published by S. Herzl, Leipzig, 1927.

visual powers will be necessarily compensated with talent or brilliance, or indeed in any socially useful way. An individual will compensate well only if he has courage or a favorable situation. Then we may count on a special development, either relative to the same sense function, or to another, such as hearing. If the child lacks courage or his situation is unfavorable, he will compensate negatively, i.e. he will not want to see anything.

Those whose eyes are normal sometimes develop interests which depend on visual powers, but not unless they have at some time been confronted with the necessity of seeing. No advance is ever made without the consciousness of a hindrance. The thing which appears to be a deterrent acts as the incentive whenever we find a courageous struggle for success. I have already referred to the aural difficulties of Beethoven, Smetana, Dvorak, and other musicians.

Our civilization is not only a right-handed but also a masculine one, so the striving for superiority tends to elaborate an over-masculine attitude. Several great philosophers have remarked on this, as Kant did when he said, "No man ever wants to be a woman." I do not entirely agree with this, for I have known cases in which men wished to be women. A bow-legged man, for instance, told me he wished he were a woman with skirts to cover his unshapely legs, and some spoiled boys would like to be women in order to be indulged.

I would never oppose women for taking their place in the world on an equal footing with men, but I have seen that it is better to bring up boys and girls from the earliest age to be reconciled with their respective social roles. When a girl believes that she may change into a boy, it is because the female role has not been presented to her as fundamentally equal to the male. She rebels against what she feels to be a prospect of permanent inferiority. The Freudians have interpreted this fact as the so-called "castration complex," because girls frequently have the fantasy that the male organs have been surgically removed from them; but this is to mistake the effect for the cause. Almost every girl wishes at times to be a boy, even when she says that she prefers being a woman, because the masculine position appears to be safer. She shows that she has weighed the advantages and disadvantages of both. In Herder's collection of songs of brides, we cannot help being struck by the sadness of all the songs, showing the girl's apprehension that she will not be appreciated or esteemed in marriage. In the crisis between girlhood and womanhood, she fears the loss of virginity as if it were the loss of potential or dignity. This feeling accounts for various manifestations in women, such as a suspicious attitude, desire to escape from love and marriage, vaginismus, shyness before pregnancy, and also perversions.

Girls often want to dress as boys, play like boys, and even be called by boys' names. I was once walking with a five-year-old girl, and she led me to a store with boys' clothing displayed in the window. She asked me to buy her a boy's suit. I resorted to artfulness and said, yes, I would buy it for her if she wanted it, but no boy would want to wear a girl's dress. She was silent for a while and then pointed to a boy's overcoat and said, "Please, won't you at least buy me that coat."

In such a child, we may infer that at the age of two or three she had felt some uncertainty about the unchangeable nature of the sexual role, and this uncertainty had influenced the formation of the psychic prototype. If a girl is stimulated to imitate boys by her environment or her education, it will increase her difficulties later when she has to face the problems of life. Girls should be educated, not as if for a lower function, but with a view and a sense of their special social responsibilities and possibilities. Without this preparation, girls are likely to show the need of it later, especially in adolescence, when they first encounter a little freedom and independence; then they often like to exaggerate masculine ways and manners, and especially to imitate the bad ones, such as drinking and sexual liberties. At the present time, the masculine protest is rampant and widely displayed by women of all ages, who smoke, wear short skirts and short hair, doing everything possible to approximate masculine behavior.

Boy 15: Believed He Was a Prophet

A boy of fifteen was brought to me from a sanatorium, after being treated by many physicians for making unaccountable motions with his hands, contorted facial expressions and abnormalities of speech; he often screamed without any apparent reason. His symptoms resembled schizophrenia, but eventually he told me his secret. "I know my behavior is rubbish," he said, "but I believe I am a prophet. No one must know my secret." In a few days I was able to cure him. He did not wish to associate with others, and he was isolating himself by his extraordinary behavior. He had a younger sister, always a difficult position for an older boy. Although his school record was a good one--in fact, he was the best pupil in the school--his determination to play a unique part in life had made him universally disliked. His flight into the world of unreality, where alone he could feel a sufficient degree of superiority, was caused only by cowardice. Finally it had become necessary for him to speak a different language from the others, and to regard all his schoolmates together as one victorious and foreign nation, for they had teased and beaten him. Meanwhile at home, he felt more and more that his sister was advancing, so that for the second time he would lose his superiority, and this upset him altogether. He had no courage to tell his parents that he felt suppressed, and at school he escaped into fantasy. In his dream-world, therefore, he made himself a prophet. The singular contortions and grimaces he had begun to use were modeled on gestures he had originally invented to attract his parents' attention.

He was able to take an optimistic line with me, because he felt able to reveal to me alone the secret of his greatness. On the basis of this mutual confidence, he could discuss and reconsider his relationships with others, and with the help of my explanation and encouragement, he recovered the natural desire to adapt himself to life. I have had similar cases, in which spoiled children have suffered greatly from the cruelty of their comrades.

Man 40: Clairvoyant and Speechless

Another case in which neurosis involved a prophetic role was that of a merchant, forty years old, who came to me for help because he found himself unable to speak to people. In social surroundings he was overcome by a tension like stage-fright; he trembled, was abashed, and felt a sensation of choking. He had married a widow twelve years his senior, who spoiled him very much as his mother had done before. With her and with a few intimate friends, as well as with his customers, he could converse without any difficulty, but his behavior could not stand the test of any wider circle of society.

I could not find the clue to this strange situation until the man mentioned that he had prophetic dreams. Then I suspected at once that his goal of superiority was to be a prophet, in a privileged and unique relationship with God. I cautiously hinted at this idea to him, beginning with a "perhaps," and he at once replied, "All my friends know that I am a clairvoyant, and so does my wife. Many cases have proved it." This, of course, was the cause of his difficulty. If he spoke freely in society, he would be in danger of betraying some error in his knowledge, which might ruin his fame as a clairvoyant. In the tension of facing this possibility of defeat he choked, and his clairvoyance was thus defended by a mysterious speechlessness.

Principles of Psychotherapy

In the first interviews with a patient, we have to make sure whether the case is really one of neurosis. My own practice, after hearing the patient's complaints, is to proceed in one of two ways. If I suspect no real organic difficulty, I may temporarily exclude that aspect of the case from consideration, and proceed to investigate the circumstances and style of life. On the other hand, if organic disturbance is evident, I consider whether the complaint and suffering are greater than the illness itself would justify, i.e., whether organic and psychic illness are combined. I have often found more pain than the illness warrants, for instance, and also unaccountable excitement accompanying an injurious illness, which may increase the course of the fever. In organic illness, the appetite also varies according to the general outlook, and a serious illness may be prolonged or even fatally influenced if the patient turns pessimistic or becomes psychically lethargic.

In these cases the most urgent need is to find out whether the patient faces a problem he feels unable to solve. Hardly ever, of course, can we get at this directly. If possible, I discuss the course of the patient's life with him from earliest childhood, noting especially the incidents or phases which reveal or conceal the most painful sense of weakness and impotence; and at the same time I keep myself alert to the signs of organic inferiority. Wherever we can surely detect a disposition to hesitate, halt, or escape, we also have a clue to the present position. When the illness proves to be both organic and psychic, the treatment must proceed along both lines at the same time. If the disturbance is dominantly or entirely of a psychic nature, I explain to the patient what I have discovered from the first conversation, but in such a way that it cannot be discouraging, and taking the greatest care not to tell the patient anything he is not yet able to understand.

To verify my findings, I check one indication against another, eliciting information of various kinds. I ask, for instance, "What would you do if I cured you immediately?" a question which I expect will draw a reference to some present problem not hitherto discussed. I ask for the patient's earliest remembrance to get a hint of the dominant interest in life. I try to understand what is happening by noting what activities, of a kind normally expected, the patient is excluding. At the same time, I am careful to ask myself if I would have been of the same type as I think I have before me, if I were in the same circumstances and following the same style of life. As soon as I feel I have grasped his circumstances, I inquire whether the patient's thoughts, feelings, actions, and characteristics are all working in the same direction, toward the exclusion or at least the postponement of the present problem. The accumulated experiences of Individual Psychology justify us in looking for this unity in the life-plan, and a wide knowledge of the literature and working tradition of Individual Psychology are of great value in diagnosis, as they help us identify the typical neurotic factors, such as the lack of social interest, failure in courage and self-confidence, and rejection of common sense. We can thus more easily comprehend the style of life; and if we always check and verify each impression with others, we will not be misled into mere generalizations.

The discussion invariably reveals an accented "*if*." "I would marry *if*"; "I would resume my work *if*"; or "I would sit for my examination *if*"; and so on. The neurotic collects some more or less plausible reasons to justify his escape from the challenge of life, but he does not realize what he is doing. The patient must be led very carefully, and the psychologist's duty is to train his patient with simple and direct explanation.

The psychotherapist must lose all thought of himself and all sensitiveness about his position of dominance, and must never demand anything of the patient. His is a belated assumption of the maternal function, and he must work with a corresponding devotion to the patient's needs. What the Freudians call transference (as far as we can discuss it apart from sexual implications) is merely social feeling. The patient's social feeling, always present in some degree, finds its best possible expression in the relationship with the psychologist. The so-called "resistance" is merely lack of courage to return to the useful side of life which causes the patient to put up a defense against treatment, for fear that his relationship with the psychologist might force him into some useful activity in which he will be defeated. For this reason we must never force a patient, but guide him very gently toward his easiest approach to usefulness. If we apply force, he is certain to escape. My own practice, also, is never to advise marriage or casual sexual relationships. I find it invariably leads to bad results. A person who is told that he should marry or seek sexual experience is quite likely to develop impotence. The first rule in treatment is to win the patient; the second is for the psychologist never to worry about his own success; if he does so, he forfeits it.

The elimination of all constraint and the freest possible relationship are the indispensable conditions between patient and physician. A cure depends on their unity in understanding the patient's goal which has been hitherto a heavily-guarded secret. I have already alluded to this necessity for the truth underlying the individual life-style in reference to the treatment of drunkenness, morphine use, and similar habits. Merely to take away the poison and say some encouraging words is useless. The patient must realize why he took to drink. Insufficient also would be his recognition of the general principles of Individual Psychology, that those who turn inebriate have lost social courage and interest, or succumbed to fear of an imminent defeat. It is easy for the physician to say, and even for the patient to believe, that he turned to drink because of a sense of inferiority which originated in childhood, but nothing will come out of the mere phraseology. The physician must grasp the special structure and development of that individual life with such accuracy, and express it with such lucidity, that the patient knows he is plainly understood and recognizes his own mistake. When patients or practitioners come to me and say: "We have explained everything," or "We thoroughly understand, and yet we cannot succeed," I consider their statements ridiculous. If I take on such a case of failure, I find that neither physician nor patient have understood the matter nor explained anything. Sometimes the patient has felt inferior and suppressed by the physician, and resisted all true explanation. Ocassionally the tables have been turned and the patient has been treating the doctor! Often, an inexperienced practitioner teaches the patient the theories of Individual Psychology, in such phrases as, "You lack social courage, you are not interested in others, you feel inferior," and so forth, which may be worse than useless. A real explanation must be so clear that the patient knows and feels his own experience in it instantly.

Man 32: Escape Through Drinking

I treated a case of drunkenness in a man thirty-two years of age, very intelligent, well-educated and perfectly healthy, who had regular bouts of drinking at intervals of four weeks. He had had many treatments and remedies, including injections of the extracts of various glands. He had spent months in the lock-up, but nothing had changed his habits.

The man was very shy, trembled, and smoked cigarettes incessantly. This behavior confirmed the impression I had formed at the first glance, that he felt me as a superior and an enemy; and he clung to his cigarette in order not to be submerged by his feeling of comparative worthlessness. In answer to my questions, he said he had no friends and did not go into society, had no occupation, and was not in love. He preferred to remain alone, and if he was urged to join in any social gathering, he became highly excited. He lived extravagantly at the expense of his parents, paying the highest prices for more or less useless things whenever he chose to do so. We can guess his answer to the sexual problem: It was masturbation, which is the style of sexual life adapted to confirm isolation and avoid love and marriage.

Such a way of living usually originates in the prototypical attitude of a pampered child, who feels obliged to keep out of the firing-line of life because he is not prepared for it. This man made his escape by being a drunkard. When he faced the problems of friendship, work, and love, unsupported by others, he experienced strained situations and tense attitudes, so that uncontrollable bouts of drunkenness were an appropriate solution of his problem on the useless side of life.

The usual tensions of every day were not severe enough to drive him to drink, and he was able to use his sober intervals to display good intentions of giving up the habit altogether. He did not strive to make his environment hopeless, as the fighting type of child often does, but was able to continue in his own line of error by means of these intervals of remorse and repentance, which always induced others to give him another chance and hope that "this time really was the last." The drunkenness would begin sometimes when he was expected to go into society, and sometimes when actually in company with others or at a party. It appeared with a demand of duty, or if he met a girl who regarded him as a possible husband; when he was short of money and his parents did not wire a remittance to him quickly enough, he also resorted immediately to drink. He was partly conscious of the use he made of his indulgence, but he never understood its general purpose as an escape, nor that he was ready to compromise himself and make himself impossible.

His evident aim was to be relieved of every responsibility and be supported for his own sake alone. Self-centered and wholly lacking in social adjustment, he had nevertheless attained a position of superiority by the elimination of defeat. He had no defeat in society for he did not enter it; no defeat in work, for he had no occupation; no defeat in love-- he avoided it. Subjectively, he triumphed over life, lived it upon his own terms entirely; but objectively, of course, the terms he obtained were almost the worst possible.

He proved to have been a spoiled child, who wanted to face every situation by leaning on parental support. He was an only boy among three sisters. He was carefully educated and succeeded at school because the parents persuaded the teachers to pamper him. When he grew out of his sheltered years, life looked impossible to him, so he made his escape. This patient's father used to drink, and he knew from an early age how this habit worried his mother, occupying her thoughts with the father. One day before a school examination, he got drunk for the first time. His mother was very worried, believing this was a hereditary defect in his disposition, and took greater care of him in the hope of curing him. Not to lose this success, the patient continued to drink.

His earliest memory referred to a time when his parents were away, and he was left to the care of his grandmother. He did not feel well during this period. Once, when his grandmother criticized him, he packed up some of his belongings and ran away, and the grandmother had to follow him. He was four years old at the time, and this recollection indicates his prototypical attitude to life. Whenever he did not feel indulged, he escaped into drunkenness. All neurotic persons who have developed from a pampered prototype expect to be appreciated before they do anything of social value instead of after having done it, thus expecting the natural course of things to be reversed in their own favor.

This patient had to be trained to feel at home in the wider environment of the world, and encouraged until he could recognize its real and necessary demands. As I have said before, this involves the assumption by the psychologist of the two maternal functions: first, winning the patient's trust as a fellow-man, and then, directing this new confidence toward other people and toward the advantages and disadvantages of real life. His mother had failed in the second function, so it had transferred to me.

In the beginning of the treatment, he might possibly have hurt himself or others with a more desperate escape into intoxication than ever, so steps had to be taken to watch him. No rule can be given how best to do this, but whatever is done must be arranged with the agreement of the patient. Otherwise, the patient would fight the physician in the same way that he fought the parents, by exploiting his own weakness: the drunkenness. If it is necessary to keep him under supervision against his will--in an asylum, for instance--let someone else place him there. The physician must in no way force him, then he will not be hindered by the patient's antagonism.

In relation to nature as a whole, man is in an inferior position, obliging him to develop on the side of strategy and trickery. In our over-intellectualized civilization especially, practically everyone is wonderfully adept at the use of his own individual tricks. The really important differences of conduct are not those of individual cleverness, but of usefulness or uselessness. By useful, I mean in the interests of mankind generally. The most sensible estimate of the value of any activity is its helpfulness to all mankind, present and future, a criterion that applies not only to what serves the immediate preservation of life, but also to higher activities such as religion, science, and art. While we cannot always decide what is strictly worthwhile from this point of view, we know when we are guided by the impulse to act usefully, and the better a person's social adjustment, the nearer he approaches accurate perception of usefulness. A person on the path of self-isolation and withdrawal may perhaps get to know or acquire valuable potential, but even then society does not benefit by these new possibilities until they are realized through the socially directed activity of himself or others.

Whether a given line of life is really due to a social or an asocial impulse is shown by contact with reality. A life may develop remarkably well or ill, perhaps at a late stage, and people are astonished by it, and try to explain it by chance, by inherited tendencies, or by destiny, when it is really due to the inherent social or anti-social feeling in the goal of the individual. And the asocial tendencies and mistakes which we can trace in the early life of a child can also be seen in the behavior of a whole family or in certain national attitudes. The only way we can hope to avoid these mistakes is by learning to increase our social feeling, which alone can save us from worthless and injurious activities.

It is almost impossible to exaggerate the value of an increase in social feeling. The mind improves, for intelligence is a communal function. The feeling of worth and value is heightened, giving courage and an optimistic view, and we gain a sense of acquiescence in the common advantages and drawbacks of our lot. The individual feels at home in life and feels his existence to be valuable just so far as he is useful to others and overcomes common instead of private feelings of inferiority. Not only our ethical nature, but the right attitude in aesthetics, the best understanding of the beautiful and the ugly will always be founded on the truest social feeling.

While the child is embedded in the family group, it is not easy to be sure whether he is developing social feeling and useful interest. This appears with certainty only when he encounters his first new situation, generally the arrival of a baby brother or sister, or the entrance into kindergarten. In one of these situations, the child either passes or fails in his first examination in fitness for life. A child who refuses to go to school, does not pay attention when he is there, works badly or will not associate with his schoolfellows, shows the inadequacy of his preparation. If allowed to develop such a plan of life, he will probably be unable to take his place in society.

Neurosis invariably gives relief to the subject, not in the light of objectivity and common sense of course, but according to his own private logic; it secures some triumph or at least it allays the fear of defeat. Thus neurosis is the weapon of the coward, and the weapon most used by the weak. We cannot ignore the heavily-veiled aggressive or vindictive element in most neuroses.

Suicidal Medical Student

I had a case of a medical student who wanted to commit suicide, an undersized man, who consequently wanted to be tall. He was greatly spoiled by his mother, who was the wife of a physician, a tyrannical husband with whom she was not happy. One day the cook came into the room screaming and crying out that the father had assaulted her sexually. From this time, the mother became depressed and cried continually. The boy could not understand her behavior, and wanted me to explain it to him. He had already asked his mother how she could be so much depressed by the unfaithfulness of a husband for whom she neither had nor professed any affection; but she interrupted his question by screaming, "You cannot possibly understand this!" The student said, in answer to my inquiry whether the father's behavior was as brutal or rough as before, that on the contrary he was very quiet, calm, and considerate.

"Do you think?" I then asked, "that your mother will give up her only means of taming this tyrant? She pays the price with her depression, but she feels that she is the conqueror. You are doing something very similar. You used to be your mother's favorite, but now you are alone in a foreign city, deprived of the attentions of your mother, who is busy taming your father. You are failing in your work at the university, and are not prepared to be independent, so you wish to impress your mother with your suicidal impulses just as your mother impresses your father with her depression. You have been trained, as pampered children often are, to succeed by a display of weakness."

In the investigation of a neurotic style of life, we must suspect an opponent, and note who suffers most because of the patient's condition. Usually this is a member of the family, and sometimes a person of the other sex, though in some cases the illness is an attack on society as a whole. Neurosis contains this element of concealed accusation, where the patient feels as though he were deprived of his right--i.e., of the center of attention--and wants to fix the responsibility and blame on someone. By such hidden vengeance and accusation, by excluding social activity while fighting against people and rules, the problem-child and the neurotic find some relief from their dissatisfaction. In some cases the revenge-motive is fairly obvious, as it was with a neurotic woman I treated whose marriage was entirely unhappy, and yet she would not divorce her husband, preferring to remain as a continual accusation against him. However, we must remember that neurotics generally, like perverts, drunkards, and morphine-addicts, have not entirely denied their social feeling, which still keeps them from crime and suicide.

Chapter VI

Neurotic Use of Emotion

Man 50: Depressed When All is Well

A curious case of depression I once treated clearly illustrates how sadness may be used to heighten the feeling of superiority. A man of fifty said he felt perfectly healthy except when he was in a notably comfortable situation. When he was at a concert or theater with his family, however, a fit of melancholy would descend upon him; in such depression, he always remembered an intimate friend who had died when he was twenty-five. This friend had been his rival, not only in business but also as a suitor for the hand of his wife—an unsuccessful rival, however, for by the time he contracted his fatal illness, my patient already had the advantage over him both in love and in business.

Success had been his lot, both before and after the friend's death; he was the favorite of his parents, unsurpassed by brothers and sisters, and prosperous in the world. On the other hand, his wife was an ambitious character who strove to solve every domestic problem by a personal triumph or conquest, moral or otherwise; between two such persons, the struggle was naturally continuous and severe. The wife sometimes gained the upper hand very cleverly, not by quarreling or dominating in any way, but by becoming nervous in disadvantageous situations, and conquering him by her painful condition. She never expressed her excessive jealousies, but sought to shackle him as required by her fits of anxiety. Thus, successful as he was in all but one relationship of life, the man felt uncertain of having reached his goal of superiority, and his excessive ambition demanded compensation.

I know that many psychologists would seek a "guilt complex" to explain this depression. They would investigate the patient's childhood to find an early desire to kill someone, probably the father. This patient, however, had been the favorite of his father. He had no reason to have desired his death because he had always been able to manage him in his own interest. Such a mistaken search for a "guilt complex" might also lead a psychologist to think that the patient had secretly wished to murder his friend and rival, and that after having triumphed over him and having had the death wish granted by fate, he remained still unsatisfied. If that were so, the guilt complex might be developed by the striving of the patient to see himself in a stronger light. He would want to express his good feeling and liking for his former rival with the highest sincerity and honesty; at the same time, he would be shaken by the memory of his rival's fatal end and the thoughts which he had been unable to entirely dismiss before it happened. This would amount to the complicated state of self-accusation and repentance at the same time, which we call a guilt complex, a superiority-striving on the useless side of life. As I have already observed, it means: "I have reached the summit of error," or "My virtue is so lofty that this slight stain on it is killing me."

However, in this case I found no indications of the kind, and the man's appraisal of honesty as a virtue was not abnormally developed. His depressions were an attempt to show himself superior to his wife. To be depressed in favorable situations called attention to his good fortune much more than if he had allowed himself to enjoy them. Everyone was surprised at his depression, and he constantly asked himself, "You happy person, why are you depressed when you have everything you want?" The unmanageable wife was the one sorrow in his comfortable life, for which he compensated by remembering his victory in the most difficult phase of his history: when he outstripped his friend and won the woman from him. Loyalty forbade him to rejoice in the memory of his dead friend, but he could nevertheless feed upon this ancient triumph by being depressed in the box of the theater. The more melancholy he was and the brighter the occasion, the more he was able to think of his past conquest and elevate the consciousness of his status. Deeper inquiries confirmed my conclusion. His friend had died from paralysis after syphilis, a disease which they had both contracted at the same time. My patient was cured, however; now, surrounded by his healthy wife and six children, he could not recall, together with the triumph over his friend, his conquest of the disease.

These were his consolations. In his marriage this man did not feel superior; but at least his wife was the woman his friend had desired, and she had chosen him instead. By contemplating his friend's disaster in a discreet gloom, he heightened the sense of victory. Consolation of this nature is on the useless side, however, and tends, as we see, toward illness.

Man 36: Impotence and Polygamous Desires

A man of thirty-six came to me for advice about sexual impotence after having tried various treatments. He was a self-made man, in a good career position, and physically healthy. Not very well-educated himself, he had a love relationship with a well-educated girl. He was a second child between two girls, and had lost both parents at the age of five. He remembered that although his family had been poor, he had been a spoiled child, pretty and quiet, to whom the neighbors liked to give presents, and he exploited their generosity, behaving like a beggar. One of his earliest remembrances was of walking the streets on Christmas Eve and looking into the shop windows at the Christmas trees destined for others. In the orphanage, to which he was transferred at the age of five, he was strictly treated, but his habitual docility and the striving nature he possessed as a second child enabled him to surpass others. His servility stood him in good stead, for he was promoted to be the principal servant of the institution. In this occupation, he sometimes had to wait a long time at an old, deserted railway station in the country; and at these times, when only the humming of the telegraph wires relieved the dead stillness of the night, he felt utterly isolated and alone in a friendless world. He preserved strong memories of this experience.

In later life, he often complained of buzzing in the ears, for which no audiologist could find the cause. It proved, however, to be quite coherent with his style of life. When he felt isolated, which happened frequently, the memory of the humming wires returned with all the liveliness of a hallucination. After this had been explained to him, and he had been a little more socially reconciled and encouraged to marry his sweetheart, the humming ceased.

It is quite usual for children who are brought up in an orphanage to make the strongest efforts to hide the fact, as though it were a disgrace. This man justified his concealment by asserting that many orphans do not succeed in later life. He regarded failure in life as the inexorable fate of orphans, which gave him his tense, striving attitude in business. For the same reason, he halted before the problem of love and marriage, and his neurotic impotence resulted from this profound hesitation.

This man's style of life was to be a beggar. In business, however (as previously in the orphanage), begging had paved the way to domination. In business he enjoyed nothing more than a begging attitude on the part of his subordinates. He was a beggar only until he could be a conqueror; then he played the second role as heartily as the first. I see no need to drag in the idea of "ambivalent" characteristics, as some psychologists would do immediately. Rightly understood, this entire mental process, working from below to above, expressing an inferiority, but compensating with a superiority is not ambivalence but a dynamic unity. Only if we do not understand it as a whole do we see it as two contradictory and warring entities. In his business, we find the male with a "superiority complex"; but if he were to lose his position and have to start again, he would promptly go back to the expression of inferiority and make capital out of it. In his love-problem he was, for the time being, following the submissive line of action, begging for love, but trying to reach domination. His sweetheart liked him and wanted to marry him, so she responded to his hesitancy by taking up more and more of a begging attitude toward him! He was well on the way, in fact, toward getting the upper hand with her and frequently did so in minor matters.

He still had not overcome his hesitant attitude, but after having had his style of life explained to him and having been encouraged, his state of mind improved and his impotence disappeared. He then set up a second resistance which was that every woman attracted him and these polygamous desires were an escape from marriage. At this time he dreamed that he was lying on a couch in my room, became sexually excited, and had an emission.

My consulting room has no couch. My patients sit, stand, or move about as they please; but the couch in this dream was in the room of a doctor who had formerly treated him for a few months. This dream extracted a confession which he had never made before. He believed that both the other doctor and I belonged to a secret society, the object of which was to cure patients such as himself by providing sexual intercourse for them. For this reason he had been trying to find out which of my women patients would be chosen for him. The fact that he missed the couch in my room was like an accusation against me. I was not the right doctor. He had come to me begging, expecting me to settle his difficulties, take over his responsibilities, and assist him in escaping from marriage. My collusion in stopping his marriage was supposed to include being his procurer, a fantasy to which his fright, impotence, and polygamous tendencies all contributed. Failing that, he would solve his sexual problem with emissions, as others might resort to masturbation or perversion.

He married, but it was difficult to prevent him from developing a tyrannical attitude toward his conciliatory wife.

Man 50: Beggar as King

Another case of the begging attitude was brought to me by a man fifty years old, the youngest of a poor family. Indulged by his mother and the neighbors because of an apparent weakness, he had developed a timid manner early in life. He tried to lean on his mother and appeal to the sympathies of the weak, especially in difficult times when he exhibited great depression and cried until help came. We have already seen how both children and adults use crying. This man's earliest memory was that he had fallen down and hurt himself. The choice of this incident to treasure in the memory out of all possible recollections is explained only by his desire to impress himself with the danger of life. His technique of life was to perfect himself in the role of a beggar, to attract support, consolation, and favor by calling attention to his infirmities. He made every incident into a matter for tears.

As a child, the man had been slow in learning to talk, and his mother, as always happens in such cases, had to attend all the more carefully to him to find out what he wanted. In this way, he was able to feel like a little king. As Lessing said, "The real beggar is the only real king." He became a master of the begging art, expressing his inferiority in the power of his plight over others. "How can I make the poor, weak child a king?" was the problem of life as he saw it, and he answered it by elaborating his own individual and essentially mendicant style.

This is one way of living, and so early an apprentice becomes a master of its technique. He will not change it, unless the cost becomes clearly too great, when he may be brought to see that his childish method is inadequate for present problems. Otherwise, change is impossible for him because all his life he has ascribed every success to the begging art and every failure to lack of proficiency in it. A goal like this is not predictable from inheritance or environmental stimuli, for the child's individual conception of the future is the dominant causal factor, and this patient's conception was such that whenever he wanted to attain superiority he had to make a mistake or get himself into a mess of some kind. All his feelings were appropriately directed toward the goal of thus getting something for nothing.

After a few days' treatment, this man was very impressed by what I told him; he sent me a pamphlet he had written some years before. It was entitled "An Association of Beggars."

Habitual criticism, anger, and envy indicate useless striving for superiority; they are motions toward the suppression of others, either in reality or fantasy, to be supreme. Useful criticism of a constructive tendency is always in some comprehensible relationship with social feeling, but where the motive is merely relative self-evaluation by lowering or degrading others, the tendency is neurotic. Neurotics often make use of the truth in order to undervalue others, and it is important, when checking a neurotic criticism, not to overlook the element of truth in the observation.

Anger usually indicates that the person who is angry feels at a disadvantage, at least temporarily. Neurotics use' it freely as a weapon to intimidate those responsible for them. Although occasional anger is an understandable attitude in certain critical situations, when it is habitual it shows anxiety, impatience, or feelings of helplessness or suppression. Patients with the anger habit are often clever in the selection of vulnerable points to attack in others, and are also great strategists in preparing situations so that they put others slightly in the wrong before they begin a fight.

Envy is universally an expression of inferiority, though it may sometimes be a stimulus to useful action. In neurosis, however, envy of another does not go so far as practical emulation. It stops like a tram before the journey's end, leaving the patient irritable and depressed.

In a certain popular music-hall act, the "strong man" comes on and lifts an enormous weight with care and immense difficulty, and then, during the hearty applause of the audience, a child comes in and gives away the fraud by carrying the dummy weight off with one hand. Plenty of neurotics swindle us with such weights, adept in the art of appearing overburdened. They could really dance with the load under which they stagger like Atlas bearing the world on his shoulders. Yet it cannot be denied that neurotics suffer intensely from their burden. They may be continually tired. They may sometimes perspire freely, and their symptoms may suggest the possibility of tuberculosis. Every movement is tiring, and they often suffer from palpitations of the heart. Usually depressed, they continually demand more zealous care from others, and yet find it continually insufficient.

Man 53: Agoraphobia – Avoidance of People

I had a case of agoraphobia in a man of fifty-three, who found that he could not breathe properly when he was with others. He was living with his sister, and had a son with characteristics like his own. When I investigated the cause of this man's unusual concentration of interest on himself, I found he had been orphaned at ten and he had two elder brothers. When they quarreled, he had his first attack. This indicates the tendency to meet a difficult situation with a breakdown. The man was the youngest of a family of eight and educated by his grandfather. A grandparent is usually a spoiling foster-parent. The patient's father and mother had been happily married; the father was superior and the mother rather cold, so the boy was attracted to his father.

A child's first good-fellowship in life is always with the mother if she is present, so that if he inclines more toward the father, we may assume that the mother does not give the child sufficient attention. She is probably unkind, otherwise occupied, or more attentive to a younger child. In such circumstances, the child turns to the father if possible, and in this case the resistance to the mother was considerable.

People are often unable to correctly remember their earliest situations, but experience enables us to reconstruct their circumstances from comparatively slight indications. One man said he could only remember merely three incidents from early childhood which had deeply impressed his memory. The first of these occurred at the age of three, when his brother died. He was with his grandfather on the day of the funeral, when his mother returned from the cemetery, sorrowful and sobbing, and when the grandfather kissed her, whispering some words of kindness and consolation, the boy saw that his mother smiled a little. He was very upset by this, and for long afterward resented his mother's smile on the day that her child was buried. A second memory that he had preserved was of a friendly reproof from his uncle, who had asked him, "Why are you always so rough toward your mother?" A third remembrance from the same period of his life related to a quarrel between his parents, after which he turned to his father, saying, "You were brave, daddy, like a soldier!" He depended greatly on his father, was pampered by him, and admired him more than his mother, although he realized his mother's character was of a better type.

All these memories, which appeared to date from his third or fourth year, showed his fighting attitude toward his mother. The first and third remembrances were clearly ruled by his goal, which was to criticize his mother and justify him in turning toward his father. His reason for turning away from his mother is easy to guess; he had been too spoiled by her to be able to put up with the younger brother's appearance on the scene, that same younger brother who figures in an apparently innocent manner in the first recollection.

This patient had married at the age of twenty-four, and marriage had disappointed him because of his wife's demands. Marriage between two spoiled children is always unhappy because both retain their expectant attitude and neither begins to give. This man went through varied experiences and tried different occupations without success. His wife was not sympathetic, and complained that she would rather be the mistress of a rich man than the wife of a poor one, so the union ended in divorce. Although the man was not really poor, he was stingy toward his wife and she divorced him out of revenge.

After his divorce, he turned misogynistic and developed homosexual tendencies; he had no actual relationships with men, but felt a desire to embrace them. This homosexual trend was as usual a kind of cowardliness. Women had defeated him twice, first his mother and afterward his wife, and now he was trying to divert his sexuality toward men in order to evade women and further possibilities of humiliation. To confirm himself in such a tendency, a man can easily falsify the past by recollecting and magnifying the importance of certain common experiences which he then interprets as proof of inborn homosexual tendencies. Thus, this patient remembered that he had been in love with a schoolmaster, and that in his youth a boy friend had seduced him into mutual masturbation.

The determining factor in this man's behavior was that he was a spoiled child who wanted everything for nothing. His agoraphobia resulted from the fear of meeting women on the one hand, while on the other hand it was also dangerous to meet men because of possible erotic inclination toward them. In this tension of feelings about going outside, he developed stomach and respiratory troubles. Many nervous people begin to swallow air when they get into a state of tension, which causes flatulence, stomach trouble, anxiety, and palpitations, as well as affecting the breathing. When I made him realize that this was his condition, he asked the usual question: "What shall I do not to swallow air?" Sometimes I reply: "I can tell you how to mount a horse, but I can't tell you how not to mount a horse." Or sometimes I advise: "If you want to go out, and feel in conflict about it, swallow some air quickly." Like other patients, this man swallowed air even in sleep, but after my advice he began to control himself and discontinued the habit. Air-swallowing at night and vomiting upon waking occur in these patients who suffer from stomach trouble and anxiety when they face a difficulty which must be confronted the following day. The patient in question began to recuperate when he came to understand that, as a pampered child, he expected to take continually without giving. He now realized that he had first stopped his normal sexual life, looking for something easier, and afterward adopted a fictitious homosexuality in which he also stopped short of danger, the whole process being an elaborate way of coming to a standstill. The last obstacle to be removed was his fear of mixing with strangers who did not care for him, such as the people in the streets. This fear results from the deeper motive of agoraphobia, which is to exclude all situations in which one is not the center of attention.

Chapter VII

The Family Constellation[4]

It is a common misconception that children of the same family experience the same environment. Of course, children in the same home share certain conditions, but the psychic situation of each child differs because of the order of their birth.

My classification based on position in the family has been somewhat misunderstood. The child's number in the order of births does not influence his character, but rather the situation into which he is born and the way he interprets it. Thus, if the eldest child is feeble-minded or suppressed, the second child may acquire a style of life similar to that of an eldest child; and in a large family, if two are born much later than the rest, and grow up together separated from the older children, the elder of these may develop like a first child. This dynamic also sometimes occurs with twins.

Position of the First Child

Having been the only one at the beginning of his life and thus the central focus, the first child is generally spoiled. He resembles the only child in this respect, and spoiling is almost inevitable in both cases. The first child, however, usually suffers an important change of situation, being dethroned when the second baby is born. Typically unprepared for this change, the firstborn feels he has lost his position as the center of love and attention. Far from his goal, he suffers great tension and begins striving to regain favor. He uses all the means by which he has formerly attracted notice, of course, he would like to be beloved for his goodness; but good behavior often goes unnoticed when the newcomer keeps everyone busy. He is then likely to change his tactics and resort to old activities which previously attracted attention, even if it was unfavorable attention.

If intelligent, he acts intelligently, but not necessarily in harmony with the family's demands. Antagonism, disobedience, attacks on the

---

[4] Published in the *Int. J. Indiv. Psychol.,* Vol. 3, pages 211-227, 1937. Also published in *The Collected Clinical Works of Alfred Adler, Volume 7,* as chapter 25.

baby, or even attempts to play the part of a baby, compel the parents to give him renewed attention. A spoiled child must have the spotlight on himself, even at the cost of expressing weakness or imitating a return to babyhood. Thus, under the influence of the past, he attains his goal in the present by unsuitable means: a sudden inability to function alone, needing assistance in eating and excretion, and requiring constant watching by flirting with danger and terrifying the parents. The appearance of such characteristics as jealousy, envy, or egotism has an obvious relation to the new circumstances, but he may also indulge in, or prolong, illnesses such as asthma and whooping cough. The tension in certain types (depending upon the bodily organization) may produce headache, migraine, stomach trouble, petit mal, or hysterical spasms. The child may also impress his parents with the slighter symptoms of a tired appearance and a general change of behavior for the worse. Naturally, the later the rival baby is born, the more intelligible and understandable will the methods appear which the first child uses in his change of behavior. If dethroned very early, the eldest child's efforts are largely "instinctive" in character. The style of his striving will in any case be conditioned by the reaction of others in the environment and his evaluation of it. For instance, if the dethroned child finds that fighting does not pay, he may lose hope, become depressed, and score a success by worrying and frightening the parents. After succeeding with such methods, he will resort to ever more subtle uses of misfortune to gain this end.

An example of the type of adult activity based on the childhood prototype was shown in the case of a man who became afraid to swallow for fear of choking. Why did he select this symptom instead of another? The patient had an immediate social difficulty in the behavior of an intimate friend who attacked him violently. Both the patient and his wife concluded that he must put up with it no longer, but he did not feel strong enough to face the struggle. Inquiring about his childhood, I learned that he had had a similar difficulty with swallowing before. The eldest child, he had been surpassed by his younger brother, but by means of difficulty in eating, he had made his father and mother watch over him. Now faced with a personal defeat in later life and not knowing what to do about it, he fell back upon his old line of defense, as though it might make someone watch over him and help him.

Effects of Dethronement

The dethronement of the first child by another may make him turn away from the mother toward the father, and adopt a critical attitude toward the mother. Afraid of being "pushed back" all through life, a person of this type likes to make one step forward and one backward in all his affairs, so that nothing decisive can happen. He feels justified in fearing that a favorable situation will change. He will face all three life tasks with a hesitating attitude and neurotic tendencies. He will feel that problem behavior and symptoms are a form of help and security. For example, he may approach society with a hostile attitude; he may constantly change his occupation; and in his sexual life he may experience failure in functioning, and show promiscuous tendencies; if he falls in love with one person, he quickly falls in love with another. Skeptical and indecisive, he becomes a great procrastinator. I met a perfect example of this type once, and his earliest remembrance was this: "At three years of age I caught scarlet fever. By mistake my mother gave me carbolic acid for a gargle, and I nearly died." He had a younger sister who was the favorite of his mother. Later in life, this patient developed a curious fantasy of a young girl ruling and bullying an older one. Sometimes he imagined her riding the old woman like a horse.

First Child May Keep Position

By virtue of his native endowment and development, or because of the second child's inferiority, ugliness, organic handicap, or bad behavior, the eldest child may be so firmly fixed in his parent's favor that he cannot be supplanted. Then, the second child becomes the problem, and the eldest may develop very well as in the following case.

Of two brothers four years apart, the elder had been strongly attached to the mother, and when the younger was born the father had been ill for some time. The mother spent all her time and most of her attention caring for the father. Trained in friendship and obedience to her, the elder boy tried to help her, and the younger boy was cared for by a nurse who spoiled him. This situation lasted for some years, leaving the younger child no reasonable chance to compete with the elder for the love of the mother. Soon abandoning the useful side of life, he became wild and disobedient. His behavior became still worse four years later, when a little sister was born, to whom the mother was able to devote herself because of the father's death. Thus, twice excluded from his mother's attention and spoiled by the nurse, this second child turned out to be the worst pupil in his class, while the elder boy was the best. Feeling hopelessly handicapped in competition with his brother, unloved at home, and reproached at the school (from which he was finally expelled), this second son could find no goal in life but to dominate his mother by worrying her. Physically stronger than either his brother or sister, he tyrannized them. Trifling away his time, at puberty he began to waste money and incur debts. His honest and well-meaning mother provided a strict tutor for him who did not, of course, grasp the situation, and dealt with it superficially by punishments. The boy grew into a man who tried to get rich quickly and easily. Easy prey to unscrupulous advisers, he followed them into fruitless enterprises, and not only lost his money but involved his mother in his dishonorable debts.

All the courage this man ever displayed resulted from his unsatisfied desire to conquer. He occasionally played an odd game, especially when things went against him. Now an old woman who earned her living in the family as a head servant, the nurse still worshipped the second boy and interceded for him in his numerous scrapes. The unusual sport in which he indulged was to lock her in a room with him and make her play soldiers, commanding her to march, fall, and jump up again at his orders; and sometimes he quickened her obedience by beating her with a stick. Although she screamed and resisted, she obeyed.

This singular sport revealed what he really wanted, the completest domination in the easiest way. Some writers would describe this as sadistic conduct, but I demur[5] at the use of a word which implies a sexual interest, for I could discover nothing of the kind in it. In sexual matters the man was practically normal, except that he changed his partners too frequently and always chose inferiors. Genuine sadism is a domineering tendency expressed sexually, owing to the discouragement of the individual in other spheres.

This man ended in very bad circumstances, while the elder brother became successful and highly respected.

Attitude of Eldest Toward Authority

The eldest child, partly because he often acts as the representative of parental authority, usually believes strongly in power and the law. The ancient and persistent custom of primogeniture shows an intuitive perception of this fact. It is often observable in literature. Thus Theodore Fontane wrote of his perplexity at his father's pleasure in hearing that ten thousand Poles had defeated twenty thousand Russians. His father was a French emigrant who had sided with the Poles, but to the writer it was inconceivable that the stronger could be beaten; he felt that the status quo should be preserved and that might must, and ought

---

[5] The contemporary use of "sadism" differs from Adler's. Today, it does not necessarily imply sexual interest, but refers primarily to the enjoyment of inflicting pain on others.

to, succeed. This was because Theodore Fontane was a first child. The lives of scientists, politicians, artists, and others show that the eldest is readier than most to recognize power, and likes to support it. Even revolutionaries harbor a conservative tendency, like Robespierre.

Position of Second Child

Never having had the experience of being the only one, the second child is in a very different situation. Though at first, he is never the sole center of attention. From the beginning, life for him is more or less a race; the first child sets the pace, and the second tries to surpass him. What results from competition between two such children depends on their courage and self-confidence. If the elder becomes discouraged, he will be in a serious situation, especially if the younger is really strong and outstrips him.

If the second child loses hope of equality, he will try to shine more rather than be more. That is, if the elder proves too strong for him, the younger will tend to escape to the useless side of life. In many cases of problem children, laziness, lying, or stealing begin to pave the way toward neurosis, crime, and self-destruction.

As a rule, however, the second child is in a better position than the first. His pacemaker stimulates him to greater effort. Also, the first child often hastens his dethronement by fighting it with envy, jealousy, and belligerence, which lower him in parental favor. A brilliant child puts the second child in the worst situation.

Even when dethroned, however, the elder child does not always suffer most. I say this in the case of a girl who had been the center of attention and extremely spoiled until she reached the age of three, when a sister was born. After the birth of her sister, she became jealous and developed into a problem-child. With sweet and charming manners, the younger sister grew up the more beloved of the two. But when this younger sister went to school, she was no longer spoiled and being unprepared to encounter difficulties, was frightened and tried to withdraw. To escape defeat both in fact and in appearance, she adopted a common device among the discouraged, she never finished anything she started, escaping final judgment, and wasting as much time as possible. Time is the great enemy of discouraged people because under the pressure of the requirements of social living, they feel as if time continually persecutes them with the question, "How will you use me?" Hence their strange efforts to "kill time" with silly activities. This girl habitually came late and postponed every action. She did not antagonize anyone, even if reproved, but her charm and sweetness, maintained as before, did not prevent her from being a greater worry and burden than her aggressive sister.

When the elder sister became engaged to be married, the younger sister was desperately unhappy. Though she had won the first stage of the race with her rival by gentleness and obedience, she had given up in the later stages of school and social life. Feeling her sister's marriage as a defeat, her only hope of regaining ground would be to also marry. However, she lacked enough courage to choose a suitable partner and automatically sought a second-best. First, she fell in love with a man suffering seriously from tuberculosis. Can we regard this action as a step forward? Does it contradict her preestablished custom of leaving every task unfinished? Not at all. The poor health of her lover and her parents' natural resistance to the match provided sure causes of delay and frustration. She preferred an element of impossibility in her choice. Another scarcely eligible partner appeared later, in a man thirty years older than she was. He was senile, but did not die as the previous one had, and the marriage took place. However, it was not a great success for her because the attitude of hopelessness in which she had trained herself did not allow her any useful activity. It also inhibited her sexual life, which she considered disgusting, feeling humiliated and soiled by it. She used her usual methods to avoid love and postpone relations at the appropriate times. Not quite successful in these evasive maneuvers, however, she became pregnant, which she regarded as another hopeless state. From that time on, she not only rejected caresses but also complained that she felt soiled, and began to wash and clean all day long. She not only washed herself, but cleaned everything that had been touched by her husband, the maid servant, or the visitors, including furniture, linen, and shoes. Soon she allowed no one to touch any of the objects in her room, and lived under the stress of a neurosis, a washing-compulsion. Thus, she was excused from the solution of her problems, and attained a lofty goal of superiority, she felt more fastidiously clean than anyone else.

The neurosis of a "washing-compulsion" vividly expresses the exaggerated striving for an exalted goal of high distinctiveness. A person who feels that sex is "dirty" uses illness as a means of avoiding sexual relations. Invariably, it gives the fantastic compensation of feeling cleaner than everybody else.

However, because he feels life is a race, the second child usually trains himself more rigorously and, if his courage holds, is well on the way to overcoming the eldest on his own ground. If he has a little less courage, he will choose to surpass the eldest in another field, and if still less, he will become more critical and antagonistic than usual, not in an objective but in a personal manner. In childhood, this attitude appears in relation to trifles: he will want the window shut when the elder opens it, turn on the light when the other wants it extinguished, and be consistently contrary.

The *Bible* story of Esau and Jacob describes this sibling situation clearly when Jacob succeeds in usurping the privileges of the eldest. The second child lives in a condition similar to an engine under a constantly excessive head of steam. A little boy of four expressed it well when he cried out, weeping, "I am so unhappy because I can never be as old as my brother."

Some writers attribute children's repetition of the psychic behavior of older siblings and parents to an imitation "instinct" or "identification" of the self with another; but it is explained better when we see that a child imitates only that behavior which offers him a successful way of asserting an equality denied to him on other grounds. Psychic resemblances to the conduct of ancestors or even of savages do not signify that the pattern of psychic reaction is hereditary, but rather that individuals use the same means of offense and defense in similar situations. When we find so much resemblance between all first children, all second, and all youngest children, we may well ask what part remains for heredity to play in determining those similarities. Thus, as psychologists we lack sufficient evidence to accept that the mental development of the individual ought to repeat the development of the race of mankind in successive stages.

In later life, the second child is rarely able to endure the strict leadership of others or to accept the idea of "eternal laws." He will be much more inclined to believe, rightly or wrongly, that no power in the world is invincible. Beware of his revolutionary subtleties! I have known many cases in which the second child used the strangest means to undermine the power of ruling persons or traditions. Not everybody, certainly not these rebels themselves, would easily agree with my views of their behavior. For though it is possible to endanger a ruling power with slander, more insidious ways exist. For example, excessive praise may idealize and glorify someone until the reality cannot stand up to it, as illustrated in Mark Anthony's oration in *Julius Caesar*. Dostoyevsky also successfully used these methods, perhaps unconsciously, to undermine the pillars of old Russia. Those who remember Father Zosima in *The Brothers Karamazov*, and also recall that he was a second son, will have little difficulty accepting the influence played by position in the family.

Of course, the style of life of a second child, like that of the first, may also appear in a child in a different chronological position, if the situation involves a similar pattern.

Position of Youngest Child

The baby of the family, the youngest child, has never known the tragedy of being dispossessed by a younger, the fate shared by most other children. In this respect, he finds himself in a favored situation and often better educated, as the economic position of the family generally improves in later years. The older children frequently join the parents in spoiling the youngest, who thus becomes too indulged. On the other hand, the youngest may also be too stimulated by his elders. In the former case of over-indulgence, the child will strive throughout life to be supported by others. In the latter case, the child will instead resemble a second child, competitively striving to overtake those setting the pace for him, and in many cases failing to do so. Therefore, he often looks for a field of activity remote from the other members of the family, revealing a sign of hidden cowardice. If the family is business-oriented, for instance, the youngest often inclines to art or poetry; if scientific, he wants to be a salesman. Many of the most successful men of our time were youngest children, and I am convinced this is also the case in other ages. In Biblical history, we find a remarkable number of youngest children among the leading characters, such as David, Saul, and Joseph. A particularly good example, the story of Joseph illustrates many of the views we have presented. Because his younger brother, Benjamin, was seventeen years his junior, he played little part in Joseph's development. Joseph's psychological position, therefore, was that of a youngest child.

Interestingly, Joseph's brothers fully understood his dreams. More precisely, they understood the emotion of the dreamer. The purpose of a dream is not to be understood, but to create a mood and a feeling.

In the fairy tales of all cultures, the youngest child plays the role of a conqueror. I infer that in earlier times, when both circumstances and men's apprehension of them were simpler, it was easier to collect experiences and to understand the coherent pattern of the life of the latest-born. This traditional grasp of character survives in folklore, although the actual experiences have been forgotten.

I found a strange type of spoiled youngest child in the case of a physician with a "begging" style of life. Difficulties with his mouth had made him fearful of cancer. Unable to swallow normally for twenty years, he could take only liquid food. He had recently had a dental plate

70

made for him, which he continually pushed up and down with his tongue, causing pain and soreness of the tongue, so that he feared he was developing cancer.

The youngest of a family of three with two older sisters, he had been sickly and much indulged. At the age of forty, he could eat only alone or with his sisters. Every approach to society had been difficult for him. He had no friends, and merely a few associates whom he met weekly in a restaurant. Because he faced the tasks of life with an attitude of fear and trembling, the presence of other people created tension which made him unable to swallow food. Living in a kind of stage fright, he feared not making a sufficiently good impression.

This man responded to the life task of occupation with tolerable competence, because his parents had been poor and he could not live without earning, but he suffered exceedingly in his profession and nearly fainted during his examinations. His ambition as a general practitioner was to obtain a position with a fixed salary and later, a pension. This great attraction to a safe official position reveals a feeling of insecurity. People with a deep sense of inadequacy often aspire to a "safe job." For years, he surrendered to his symptoms. When he became older and lost some of his teeth, he decided to have a plate made, which led to the development of his latest symptom.

When he came to me, the patient was sixty years old and still living in the care of his two sisters. Both suffered from their advanced years, and this aging man, spoiled by two unmarried and much older women, faced a new situation. He feared his sisters would die. Needing to be continually watched over, what would he do in that case? Unable to find a woman whom he could trust with his fragile happiness, he had never been in love. How could he believe that anyone would spoil him as his mother and older sisters had done? It was easy to guess the form of his sexuality, masturbation, and some petting affairs with girls. But recently an older woman had wanted to marry him, so he wished to appear more pleasant and attractive in behavior. The beginning of a struggle seemed imminent, but his new dental plate came to the rescue. In the nick of time, he became anxious about contracting cancer of the tongue.

As a doctor, he doubted the reality of this cancer. The many surgeons and physicians he consulted all tried to dissuade him from belief in it; but he persisted in his uncertainty, continued to press his tongue against the plate until it hurt, then consulted another doctor.

Such preoccupations, "overvalued ideas" as Eernicke calls them, are carefully cherished in a neurosis. The patient shies away from the right objective by fixing his glances more and more firmly upon a point some distance from a good, productive course. He does this in order to swerve away from a direction beginning to be required by logical necessity. The correct solution of his problem contradicts his style of life, and because the style of life rules (as the only approach to life he has learned), he has to establish emotions and feelings which will support his life-style and will insure his escape.

In spite of this man being sixty years old, the only logical solution was to find a trustworthy substitute for his spoiling sisters before their departure. His distrustful mind could not hope to achieve this possibility; nor could logic dispel his doubts, because throughout his life he had built up appearance, the dental plate should have been a help, but he turned it into an insuperable impediment.

In treating this case, it was useless to attack his belief in the cancer. When he understood the coherence of his behavior, the patient's symptoms were greatly alleviated. The next day he told me of a dream: "I was sitting in the house of a third sister at a birthday celebration of her thirteen-year-old son. I was entirely healthy, felt no pain, and could swallow anything." But this dream was related to an episode in his life which took place fifteen years before. Its meaning is very obvious: "If only I were fifteen years younger." Thus, the life-style is maintained.

Difficulties of an Only Child

The only child also has his typical difficulties. Retaining the center of the stage without effort and generally pampered, he forms a style of life based on being supported by others and at the same time ruling them. Very often, he grows up in a sheltered environment. The parents may be fearful people and afraid to have more children. Sometimes the mother, neurotic before his birth, does not feel equal to rearing more children, and develops such behavior that everyone must feel, "It is a blessing that this woman has no more children." Birth control may absorb much of the family's attention, leading to tension and anxiety for both parents. The care then devoted to the only child never ceases, and often impresses him with a belief that not being watched or guarded is a mortal danger. Such children often grow up cautious, and sooner or later may become successful, gaining the esteem and attention they desire. But if they confront different conditions where life is difficult for them, the may show striking insufficiency.

Only children are often sweet and affectionate, and later in life may develop charming manners in order to appeal to others, because they have trained themselves this way. Usually closer to the more indulgent parent, generally the mother, they sometimes develop a hostile attitude toward the other parent.

While the proper upbringing of an only child is not easy, parents can conceivably understand the problem and solve it correctly. Although we do not regard the only child's situation as dangerous, without the best educational methods, bad results frequently occur which having brothers and sisters would have avoided.

Case of Homosexual Development[6]

I now present a case of the development of an only child, a boy attached entirely to his mother. Although the father contributed materially, he was of no importance in the family, and obviously without interest in the child. The mother was a dressmaker who worked at home, and the little boy spent all his time with her, sitting or playing beside her. He played at sewing, imitating his mother's activity, and ultimately became extremely proficient at it, but he never took part in any boy's games. The mother left the house each day at five p.m. to deliver her work, returning punctually at six. During that time, the boy was left with an older girl cousin and played with sewing materials. Always looking for his mother's return, he became interested in timepieces. He could tell the time when he was merely three years old.

The cousin played games with him in which she was the bridegroom and he was the bride, and he looked significantly more like a girl than she did. He came to school unprepared to associate with boys, but he established himself as a favored exception because others liked his mild, courteous disposition. He began to approach his goal of superiority by being attractive, especially to boys and men. At fourteen, he acted the part of a girl in a school play. The audience had not the slightest doubt that he was a girl; a young fellow began to flirt with him and he was very pleased to have excited such admiration.

He had worn girlish clothes during his first four years, and until the age of ten he did not know whether he was a boy or a girl. When he

[6] Whereas Adler's views on the equality of women were ahead of his time, his criticism of homosexuality here (and elsewhere) reflects the common bias of his time and place. These opinions, coming out of the early 1900's in Vienna, do not represent contemporary Classical Adlerian psychotherapy. While we respect every individual's sexual choice, we apply the same psychological criteria to all relationships, promoting increased cooperation, respect, equality, mutual benefit and empathy, and working to eliminate domination, subordination, depreciation, exploitation, or abuse. Adler's comments have been retained in the text in the interest of scholarship and historical accuracy.

learned his gender, he began to masturbate, and in his fantasy he soon connected sexual desire with what he had felt when boys touched or kissed him. To be admired and wooed became his goal in life; to this end he used all his capacities in such a way that he might be admired especially by boys. The only girl he had known, his older cousin was gentle and sweet, but she had played the man's role in their games and otherwise had ruled him like his mother. His mother's overindulgent, excessive care led to his great feeling of inferiority. Married late at the age of thirty-eight, she did not wish to have more children by the husband she disliked. Her anxiety, undoubtedly of earlier origin, and her late marriage indicate a hesitant attitude toward life. Strict in sexual matters, she wanted her child to be educated in ignorance of sex.

At the age of sixteen this patient looked and walked like a flirtatious girl, and soon fell into the snare of homosexuality. In order to comprehend this development, we must remember that he had had, in a psychological sense, the education of a girl, and that the difference between the sexes had been made clear to him much too late in his development. He had experienced his triumphs in the feminine role, with no certainty of gaining as much by playing a man. Clearly he saw the open road to his goal of superiority in the imitation of girlish behavior.

In my experience, boys with this type of upbringing look like girls. The growth of the organs and probably the glands is partially ruled by the environment and the child's attitude toward it; and they adapt to them. Thus, if early environmental training toward femininity is succeeded by a personal goal of the same tendency, the wish to be a favored girl will influence not only the mind, but also the carriage and even the body.

This process clearly illustrates how a homosexual trains himself mentally for his abnormal attitude toward sex. We do not need to postulate an inborn or hereditary, organic deviation.

When the boy in question came to me, he had a relationship with another boy who was the neglected second child of a domineering mother. This other boy's striving was to overcome men by his personal charm, which he used successfully to rule his weak father. When he reached the age of sexual expression, he was shocked. He had based his notion of women on his domineering mother, who had neglected him. Although he felt the need to control, he entertained no hope of ruling women because, in accordance with his early experience of a strong and aggressive mother, he felt that a woman was too powerful to control. His only chance to be the victor was in a relationship with men, so he became homosexual. Consider then the hopeless situation of my patient!

He wanted to conquer by female means, with the charm of a girl, but his friend wanted to conquer men.

I helped my patient realize that, whatever he thought or felt in this liaison, his friend considered himself a conquering man-charmer. Therefore, my patient could not be sure that his was the real conquest, so his homosexuality was accordingly checked. By this means I was able to break off the relationship, for he saw that it was stupid to enter into such a fruitless competition. This also made it easier for him to understand that his abnormality was due to lack of interest in others, and that his feeling of inadequacy, the result of being pampered, had led him to measure everything in terms of personal triumph. He then left me for some months; when he visited me again he had had sexual relations with a girl, but had tried to play a masochistic role with her. In order to prove to himself that his original view of the world was correct, he obviously wished to experience with her the same inferiority that he had felt with his mother and cousin. This masochistic attitude showed when his goal of superiority required the girl to do to him what he commanded. He then wished to complete the act at this point without achieving sexual intercourse, so that the normal was still excluded.

The great difficulty of changing a homosexual lies not only in his lack of general social adjustment, but also in the invariable absence of correct training in the sexual role, which must begin in early childhood. The attitude toward the other sex is strained in a mistaken direction almost from the beginning of life. In order to realize this fact, we must note the kind of intelligence, behavior, and expectations such a case exhibits. Compare normal persons walking in the street or mixing in society with a homosexual in the same situations. The normal majority are interested primarily in the opposite sex, the homosexuals only in their own. The latter evade normal sexuality also in dreams. The patient I have just described used to dream frequently that he was climbing a mountain by a serpentine road. The dream expresses his discouraged, circuitous approach to life. (He moved rather like a snake, bending his head and shoulders at every step.)

In conclusion, I will summarize some of the most disastrous cases I have known among only children. A woman asked me to help her and her husband in the case of their only boy, who tyrannized them terribly. He was then sixteen, a very good pupil at school, but quarrelsome and insulting. He was especially combative toward his father, who had been stricter with him than his mother. Antagonizing both parents, if he could not get what he wanted he attacked, sometimes wrestling with his father, spitting at him, and using bad language. Such development is possible with a pampered only child who is trained to give nothing but to expect everything, until the indulgence can continue no longer. In such cases, treating the patient in his old environment is difficult, because it revives too many old recollections which disturb the harmony of the family.

In another case, a boy of eighteen had been accused of murdering his father. An only spoiled child, he had stopped his education and was wasting, in bad company, all the money he could extort from his parents. One day when his father refused to give him money, the boy killed him by hitting him on the head with a hammer. No one but the lawyer defending him knew that he had killed another person several months before. Consequently, he felt perfectly sure of escaping discovery this second time.

In yet another case of criminal development, an only boy was brought up by a very well-educated woman who wanted him to be a genius. At her death, another experienced woman continued nurturing him in the same way, until she became aware of his tyrannical tendencies. Believing sexual repression to be the cause of his aggressiveness, she had him analyzed. His tyrannical attitude did not cease, however, so she then wished to be rid of him. But he broke into her house one night intending to rob her, and strangled her.

The characteristics typical of certain positions in the family can, of course, be modified by circumstances. Despite the many possibilities of variation, however, the outlines of these patterns will remain substantially correct. Among the possibilities, we may include the position of a boy growing up among girls. If he is older than they are, he develops the same as an elder brother close to a younger sister. The individual pattern of behavior will reflect differences in age, in the affection of the parents, and in the preparation for life.

Where a female majority and feminine influence dominate the environment, a single boy is likely to have a goal of superiority and a style of life directed toward femininity. This dynamic occurs in various degrees and ways: in a humble devotion to and worship of women, in an attitude imitating women, in a tendency toward homosexuality, or in a tyrannical attitude toward women. People usually avoid educating boys in an overly feminine environment because such children develop toward one of two extremes: either exaggerated vanity or aggressiveness. In the story of Achilles, many points reveal that the latter case was well understood in antiquity.

Importance of Evaluation of Men and Women

We find the same contradictory possibilities in the cases of only girls who grow up among boys or in an entirely masculine environment. In such circumstances a girl may, of course, be spoiled with too much attention and affection, but she may also adopt boys' attitudes and wish to avoid looking like a girl. In any case, the result largely depends on how men and women are valued in the environment. Every environment has a prevailing attitude in regard to this issue. Therefore, the child will wish to assume the role of a man or a woman in accordance with the relative value given to men and women in that attitude.

Other views of life prevailing in the family may also influence the pattern of a child's behavior, or lead to difficulties, as for example the superstition about character being inherited, and the belief in fanatical methods of education. Any exaggerated method of education will probably harm the child, as we can often trace in the children of teachers, psychologists, doctors, and people engaged in the administration of laws: policemen, lawyers, officers, and clergymen. Educational exaggerations surface in the life-histories of many problem children, delinquents, and neurotics. The influence of both the superstition regarding heredity and a fanatical mode of training appear in the following case.

A woman came to me with a daughter of nine, both of them in tears and desperation. The mother told me that the girl had only recently come to live with her, after spending years with foster parents in the country. Because she had completed the third grade of her schooling there, she entered the fourth grade in the city school, but her work became so bad that her teacher had her put back into the third grade. Soon afterwards her work became still worse, so she was demoted again and put in the second grade. Thoroughly upset, the mother was obsessed with the idea that her daughter's deficiency was inherited from the father.

From the beginning, I could see that the mother treated the child with exaggerated educational insistence, which was particularly unfortunate because the girl had been brought up in a congenial environment and expected still greater kindness from the mother. But in her eagerness that her child should not fail the mother was overstrict, keenly disappointing the girl. She developed a great emotional tension, blocking her progress both at school and at home. Exhortation, reproaches, criticism, and spanking only intensified the emotion, with consequent hopelessness on both sides. To confirm my impression, I spoke with the girl alone about her foster parents. She told me how happy her life with them had been. Then, bursting into tears, she also told me how she had enjoyed being with her mother at first.

I had to make the mother understand her mistakes. The girl could not be expected to put up with such harsh training. Putting myself in her place, I could perfectly understand her conduct as an intelligent reaction, that is, as a form of accusation and revenge. In a situation of this type, with less social feeling, a child may easily become delinquent, neurotic, or even suicidal. But in this case, I was sure the girl could improve if the mother were convinced of the truth, and impressed the child with a sufficient change of attitude. Therefore, I explained to the mother that the belief in inheritance was nothing but a nuisance, after which I helped her realize what her daughter had reasonably expected when she came to live with her, and how she must have been disappointed and shaken by such disciplinary treatment, to the point of utter inability to do what was expected of her. I wanted the mother to confess to the child that she had been mistaken and would like to reform her method, so I told her I did not really believe she could bring herself to do it, but that it was what I would do in the circumstances. She answered decidedly, "I will do it." In my presence and with my help, she explained her mistake to the child. They kissed, embraced, and cried together. Two weeks later they both visited me, smiling and well satisfied. The mother brought me a message from the third-grade teacher: "a miracle must have happened. The girl is the best pupil in the class."

Chapter VIII

Early Recollections[7]

The discovery of the significance of early recollections is one of the most important findings of Individual Psychology. It has demonstrated the purposiveness in the choice of what is remembered longest, though the memory itself is quite conscious or the recollection is easily elicited upon inquiry. Correctly understood, these conscious memories give us glimpses of depths just as profound as those more or less suddenly recalled during treatment.

Of course, we do not believe that all early recollections are accurate records of actual facts. Many are even imagined; perhaps most are changed to a time later than that in which the events are supposed to have occurred; but this does not diminish their significance. What is altered or imagined also expresses the patient's goal, and although the effect of fantasy and memory differs, we can relate both to the total style of life of the individual, and recognize their unity with his main line of striving toward a goal of superiority.

In recollections from the first four or five years of life, we find primarily fragments of the prototype of the individual's life-style, or useful hints as to why his life-plan was elaborated into its own particular form. Here we may also gather the surest indications of self-training to overcome the organic difficulties or deficiencies felt in the early environment. In many cases, the early recollections reveal signs of the person's degree of activity, courage, and social feeling. Because of the great number of spoiled children who seek treatment, we find the mother rarely absent from the earliest remembrance; indeed, if the life-style is one of a pampered child, the guess that the patient will recall something about his mother is usually correct. If the mother does not appear in his early recollections, that may also have a certain significance; it may indicate his feeling of having been neglected by her. However, he has never understood the meaning of his early remembrances. In answer to my question, he may simply say, "I was sitting in a room playing with a toy, and my mother was sitting close to me." He regards a recollection as a thing by itself with no significance; he never thinks of its coherence

---

[7] Published in English in the *Int. J. Indiv. Psychol.*, No. 3, pages 283-287, 1937. Also published in *The Collected Clinical Works of Alfred Adler, Volume 7*, as chapter 26.

in the whole structure of his psychic life. Unfortunately, many psychologists do the same.

To estimate its meaning, we have to relate the early pattern of perception to all we can discover of the individual's present attitude, until we find how one clearly mirrors the other. In the example just given, we begin to see this correlation when we learn that the patient suffers from anxiety when alone. The interest in being connected with the mother may appear even in the form of fictitious remembrances, as in the case of the patient who said to me, "You will not believe me, but I can remember being born, and my mother holding me in her arms."

Very often the earliest memory of a spoiled child refers to its dispossession by the birth of a younger brother or sister. These recollections of feeling dispossessed vary from slight and innocent reminiscences, such as, "I recollect when my younger sister was born," to instances highly indicative of the particular attitude of the patient. A woman once told me, "I remember having to watch my younger sister, who was lying on a table. She was restless and threw off the coverlets. I wanted to adjust them and I pulled them away from her, whereupon she fell and was hurt." This woman was forty-five when she came to me; at school, in marriage, and throughout life she had felt disregarded, just as in childhood when she had felt dethroned. A similar attitude, even more expressive of suspicion and mistrust, was expressed by a man who said, "I was going to market with my mother and little brother. Suddenly it began to rain, and my mother took me up in her arms, and then remembering that I was the elder, she put me down and took up my younger brother." Successful as he was in his life, this man distrusted everybody, especially women.

A student thirty years of age came to me in trouble because he could not face his examinations. He was in such a state of strain that he could neither sleep nor concentrate. The symptoms indicated his lack of preparation and courage, and his age showed the distance at which he stood from the solution of the problem of occupation. Because of his lack of social adjustment, he had no friends and had never fallen in love. He expressed his sexuality in masturbation and nocturnal emissions. His earliest memory was of lying in a cot, looking at the wallpaper and curtains. This recollection reflects the isolation of his later life, and also his interest in visual activity. Astigmatic, he was striving to compensate for this organic deficiency. We must remember, however, that any strongly developed function related to a strong degree of social interest may disturb the harmony of life. For instance, to watch is worthwhile, but when the patient barricades himself against all other activities and wants merely to gratify his eyes all day, watching may become a compulsion-neurosis. Some people are interested primarily in seeing. But few positions merely require an interest in seeing. Even those positions cannot be found by a person who is socially maladjusted. As we have seen, this patient had not been a real fellow man to anyone, so he found no practical use for his peculiar interest.

Earliest remembrances frequently reveal an interest in movement, such as: traveling, running, motoring, or jumping. This movement is often characteristic of individuals who encounter difficulties when they are required to work in sedentary occupations. For example, a man of twenty-five, the oldest son of a very religious family, was brought to me because of misbehavior. Disobedient, idle, and deceitful, he had accumulated debts and stolen. His sister, three years younger, was a familiar type: striving, capable, and well-educated, an easy winner in the race with him. His misconduct began in his adolescence, which many psychologists would ascribe to an emotional "flare-up" caused by the growth of the sexual glands, a theory which might seem all the more plausible in this case because of premature and mischievous sexual relations, often found in similar cases. But we ask: Why should the perfectly natural period of puberty cause a crisis and moral disaster in this case but not in another; not in the sister's case, for example? We answer: Because the sister was in a more favorable position. From the experience of many cases, we know the brother's situation to be one of special danger. Furthermore, when we go more deeply into his history, we find that he wanted to be first in every situation; adolescence did not change this young man's style of life. Before that time the boy had gradually been losing hope of being "first" in a life of social usefulness, and the more hopeless that direction appeared, the more he wandered into the easier path of useless compensation.

This young man's earliest remembrance gives a clear hint of his great interest in motor activity and movement in general. It was: "I was running round the whole day in a kiddy car." After treatment, when he improved, he was taken back into his father's office, but he did not like the sedentary routine there. He finally adapted himself to life as a traveling salesman.

Many first remembrances concern dangerous situations, and they are usually told by persons with whom the use of fear is an important factor in the style of life. A married woman once came to ask me why she was terrified whenever she passed a pharmacy. Some years previously she had spent a long time in a sanatorium undergoing treatment for tuberculosis, and a few months before I say her a specialist had pronounced her cured, entirely healthy, and fit to have children. Shortly after this complete absolution by the doctor, she began to suffer from her obsession. The connection is obvious. The pharmacy was a warning reminder of her illness, an employment of the past in order to make the future seem ominous. She was connecting the possibility of having a child with danger to her health. Though she and her husband had agreed that they wanted a child, her behavior clearly showed her secret opposition. Her secret objection was stronger than any reasonable and common sense logic which said that for her bearing children was no longer dangerous. As a medical expert, the doctor could minimize the danger to her health, but he could not remove the symptom of fear. In this as in many similar cases, we know in advance that the real reasons for the symptoms are deeply rooted, and can be found only if we discover the main line of striving in the style of life.

Resistance to having children is seldom based on objective fears of childbirth or illness. In this case, the woman had been a pampered child who wanted to be in the center of the stage. Such women do not wish to bring a little rival onto the scene, so they argue against it with every variety of reason and unreason. This woman had trained herself perfectly to be on the lookout for danger, and to perceive opportunities for taking the center of attention. Asked for her earliest recollections, she said, "I was playing before our little house on the outskirts of the town, and my mother was terrified when she saw me jumping on the boards that covered the well."

A student of philosophy came to consult me about his fear of blushing. From earliest childhood, he had been teased because he blushed so easily, and for the past two months this had increased so much that he was afraid to go to a restaurant, attend lectures, or even leave his room. I found that he was about to take an examination. Faint-hearted, timid, and bashful, whether he was visiting in society, working, or with a girl, in all situations he suffered from feelings of tension. Because his blushing had recently worried him more, he began to use it as a pretext for retreating from life. From childhood, this man had had a strong antipathy toward his mother, who he felt was partial to his younger brother. Living in the greatest competition with his brother, he now no longer believed that he could achieve any success. Here is the earliest remembrance: "When I was five years old, I went out with my three-year-old brother. My parents were very excited when they found we had left the house, because there was a lake nearby, and they were afraid that we had fallen into it. When we returned, I was slapped." I understood this to mean that he did not like his home, where he felt that he was slighted, and my opinion was corroborated when he added, "I was slapped, but not my brother." But the discovery that he had been in a dangerous situation had still impressed him, as reflected in his present behavior, which was dominated by his guiding idea: not to go out, not to venture too far. Such persons often feel as though life were a trap.

We can easily imagine this patient's painful experience in the company of a girl. We can understand how he put his blushing between himself and women, thus preventing a relationship with any of them. In this way, he avoided the risk of losing out to another man. He always feared other men would be preferred to him, as he felt his mother had preferred his brother.

When correctly understood in relation to the rest of an individual's life, early recollections contain the central interests of that person. They give us valuable hints and clues in finding the direction of a person's striving. They help reveal values to be aimed for and dangers to be avoided. They help us see the kind of world a particular person feels he lives in, and the early ways he found of dealing with that world. They illuminate the origins of the style of life. The basic attitudes guiding an individual since childhood and in his present situation are reflected in those fragments he selects to epitomize his feeling about life, and to cherish in his memory as reminders. He has preserved these as his early recollections.

Chapter IX

Further Useless Goals of Superiority

The loftiest goals are found in the most pathological cases, the psychoses. In cases of schizophrenia we often find the desire to be Jesus Christ. In manic-depressive cases also, in the manic phases, the patient frequently wishes to be the savior of mankind, while in the depressive phases he often complains of being the greatest evil on earth. In paranoia the patient not only strives to be the center of attention, but actually believes he is that already. Individual Psychology has shown that the goal of superiority can be fixed at such altitudes only when the individual has, by losing all interest in others, also lost interest in his own reason and understanding. Moreover the height of the goal now confronts the individual with such difficulties that common sense has become useless to him in solving them.

This goal of personal supremacy blocks the approach to reality. The more reality presents him with real, or even alluring possibilities of action, the greater the effort a maladjusted person will make to avoid it because his feeling of supremacy is proportionately increased thereby. The end result and logical culmination of such a life-line is, of course, total isolation in an asylum.

Perhaps the most audacious goals of superiority are found in cases of general paralysis, which generally exhibit the most marked loss of social feeling and mental control. But all cases of Caesarian madness show the same goal of godlikeness with an absence of social feeling; moreover—and this is consistent with all our findings—there is always a high degree of cowardice. Similarly, whenever we find a marked insensibility to the pain of others, or undervaluation of others' lives, as with murderers and other criminals, we can trace the preparation for their development; they do it by deliberately breaking through the limits of social feeling, impelled by cowardice to seek relief on the useless side of life. Every murderer is a coward intoxicated with the idea of being a hero. The true psychology of these tendencies ought to be explained to everyone because such instruction would do much to prevent "crime waves." For criminals derive some incentive from the prevalent superstition that crime is at least courageous; whereas in truth, even the most audacious crime is deeply motivated by fear.

The development of a criminal tendency has something in common with the fascination of useless sports; the desire to break a record is sometimes apparent, and one of the greatest inducements to crime is the sense of overcoming the law and the police. This considerable gratification on the useless side can give the individual a feeling of having beaten the world single-handed. And as according to statistics, about forty per cent of all punishable crimes pass without detection of the perpetrator, nearly every criminal has had the experience of committing a crime without being found out. The chance of "thumbing one's nose" at the police is very alluring to a cowardly soul.

The goal of personal superiority invariably magnifies one of the three questions of life out of all proportion. We find that a person's ideal of success becomes unnaturally limited to social notoriety, business success, or sexual conquest. Thus we see the social careerist fighting and jealous; the business magnate extending his interests at the expense of all others; and the amorous intriguer, the would-be Don Juan, collecting his sexual conquests. Each disturbs the harmony of his life by leaving many necessary demands unsatisfied, and then tries to compensate with still more frantic striving in his narrowed sphere of action.

Sadism and Masochism

In the realm of sexual perversion, we find the goal expressed in a purely fictitious form. This is especially evident in the sadistic type, by which I mean the type whose will to dominate is connected with sexual irritation. We made a notable advance in the understanding of the psychic structure of perversion when we could prove that the symptoms of masochistic cases are also governed by a personal goal of superiority. In the fantasies of masochists as well as in their actions, the egotistic tendency has been clearly diagnosed. The masochistic attitude signifies: "I am not governed by your power of attraction; you must do what I want you to do." Although the tendency implied here is more fully expressed in sadism, the demands of the sadist are obviously harder for him to enforce than the masochist's "demand to be bullied." But we find individuals who exhibit a mixture of masochistic and sadistic behavior.

I have found that the purpose of most masochistic subjects is to escape love and marriage because they do not feel strong enough to risk a defeat. They regard the avoidance of defeat, even through ignominious escape, exactly as if it were a goal of superiority. By means of their masochistic tendencies, they exclude all the really eligible members of the other sex. In the case of a man whom I cured of homosexuality, the patient went so far as to have a masochistic relationship with a prostitute. By means of homosexuality, he excluded all women, and in his periods of masochism he excluded all worthwhile women.

Similarly, among girls who indulge in masochistic fantasies, we often note that the superior goal toward which they strive takes the form of celibacy. They can imagine love and marriage only as torture, and this fantasy of celibacy is itself gratification consistent with their masochistic tendencies. In masturbation, whether physical or mental, a certain consistency is always apparent; it is the sexual attitude appropriate to the isolated individual. Correctly interpreted, it is the wish to exclude sexual partnership. In such cases, the patient tends to regard a partner as the author of his or her humiliation; and this idea, although avoided in reality, will be expressed in fantasy.

One way of attaining a feeling of superiority is by the irritation of others. Parents or teachers, husbands or wives, as the case may be, will be subtly exasperated until they burst into a rage and begin to attack or punish. To many children, this proof of their power over others is a great satisfaction, and they often desist when they have produced the desired reaction. Still more antisocial is the goal of superiority through the injury of another. In its service, every trifle of evidence against another person will be collected with malicious intent, such as difference in nationality, standard of living, advancing age in the case of women, and any unusual features such as red hair or prominent nose or teeth. On all these disadvantages of another, real or imputed, the neurotic feeling of inferiority feeds voraciously, as if it could fill its own emptiness by the contemplation of yet greater vacuity elsewhere. And by such activity, of course, feelings of inferiority may be induced in the person who is attacked.

The height of the goal is freely revealed in waking fantasies, where the desire to be the richest man, an emperor, or a pioneer finds imaginary gratification, always an image of supremacy in the subject's own line of life, whatever it may be.

The degree of social interest also finds expression in these imaginings. For instance, fantasies of saving life, of stopping runaway horses and rescuing the drowning indicate a more social tendency than images of torturing or being tortured. Children have the common fantasy that they do not really belong to their parents. It indicates dissatisfaction with their own parents for some reason or other, and enables them to believe they are the secret offspring of noble parents. This particular tendency of the fantasy is demonstrated in mass-psychology, by the belief in myths and legends where the heroes are invariably the sons and daughters of gods or demi-gods, or at least, while no one knows it, they are of royal parentage and the heirs to great power and estates.

Man 32: Erythrophobia[8]

Daydreams of a true sadistic or masochistic nature occur in which the dreamer participates merely as an observer and not as an actor, enjoying the sight of the conqueror's power, or identifying his own feelings with the weaker person. This dreaming of vicarious satisfaction is, of course, a double remove from reality, indicating a still greater lack of courage. Such was the case of a man of thirty-two who suffered from erythrophobia. Believing that people could not help looking at him wherever he went, he blushed continually. He was short, cross-eyed, and suffered from lameness, one leg being shorter than the other. He had been spoiled by his mother, but his brothers and sisters had disliked and repressed him. Thus, when he went to school, he assumed a wrong attitude toward his schoolmates, but tried to maintain his personal dominance by becoming an excellent gymnast. Even this achievement, however, did not maintain him sufficiently in the center of general attention, so he tried to supplement it by exciting the compassion of others; when this also failed to satisfy him, he drew attention to himself by clowning and playing the fool. Finally, despairing of winning the high esteem he wanted, he gave up and tried to escape from both society and love. Wherever he met people, in the street, in restaurants, or in theaters, he experienced acute mental tension, and being the nervous type, he expressed it by blushing and feeling afraid. At the same time, he acquired a paranoid fear that every policeman was watching him as a suspect. The effect of all these symptoms was to make him isolate himself to a great extent and continue merely the lightest and most occasional occupations.

His daydreams, which are the point of his narrative, were largely sexual fantasies. His sexual life was, naturally, one of masturbation, but in these fantasies his great distance from the solution of the sex-problem was expressed by visualizing boys beating each other, while he himself was merely a "smiling third."

As a last resort he tried a career in business, but again finding that he was not appreciated, he developed another paranoid fantasy, that all his comrades conspired against him. He went from his office into a sanatorium, where he met a woman who showed great sympathy for him. Although up to this point he had retreated from every problem of life, he

---

[8] Editor's note: Erythrophobia is the fear of blushing.

now felt the urge to go forward in the matter of love. But the old feeling of hopelessness and lack of courage persisted. He had long ago fixed his position as an observer of the struggle of life, and now a situation had arisen which challenged this position. And so, one day, he shot himself.

Man 45: Swallowing Air

Red hair is sometimes taken as sufficient basis for a feeling of inferiority, and the part it may play in building up a neurosis is illustrated in the following case. A man of forty-five complained of heart trouble, which had been first diagnosed as organic and later as a neurotic disturbance. As a child he had been greatly pampered by his mother, and because of his efforts to rule over his comrades he had been unpopular with them; they had always teased him about his "copper nob." He was too unsociable to make friends, but very successful in his school work.

Later on, he was treated psychoanalytically for two years and the doctor who treated him advised him to marry another of his patients. Naturally, with such a lack of social interest, he could not make a success of marriage. He tried to rule his wife in an absurd manner, and when she resisted him in any way, he became so tense that his pulse increased to a hundred and fifty a minute.

Such heart troubles may often be observed as the result of swallowing air. This habit is also connected with asthma, stomach trouble, peritonitis, and even pseudo-pregnancy. Usually the patient knows nothing about it, and my experience leads me to believe that it often takes place in sleep. It is suspected in cases of morning sickness and particularly in hysterical vomiting. The air-swallowing habit is caused by a great psychic tension, due to exaggerated feelings of inadequacy. It is probably due to some tendency deeply laid in human nature since it so commonly appears in times of crisis, such as during an examination, and while courting.

Air-swallowing was the trouble in this case, also. After the psychic mechanism of it had been explained to him, the man had a dream. He said: "I saw a red frog, bloated with air." It is interesting to see how easily the attention of a patient is diverted from the real coherence of the case. He treated this dream as if it were a mystery which he could not understand. I interpreted it to him, explaining that while he was asleep, he understood perfectly what he was doing, and that his dream was a way of saying: "I am like that red frog, suffering from my abnormal coloring and trying to blow myself up into a bigger being than I am." In his criticism of my explanation, however, the patient evidently did not wish to understand.

Man 40: Wanting to Marry His Cousin

The masculine protest is often apparent in the loftiest goals of personal supremacy. A man of forty came to me in a state of nervous irritation because he felt impelled, as if in a fit of irresponsibility, to marry a cousin. Marriage with a near relative, either in reality or in fantasy, generally indicates fear of the opposite sex, for incest is opposed to common sense, which demands a courageous mixing of blood. We can trace incestuous inclinations to cowardice and a sense of social inadequacy. This patient had resisted impulses toward love and marriage. He denied himself various gratifications, such as play-going and eating meat—he had lately become a vegetarian—attached the highest importance to chastity, and became greatly disturbed if he had to do business with a lady client in his own office. He was an eldest son who had resented his dethronement by a younger brother, and had also felt that he was slighted and pushed into the background by his mother, for which reason he had leaned more toward his father. His criticism of his mother, and later of all women, was very bitter. His earliest memory was this: "When I was four years old we moved. I met a strange woman near the new apartment whom I tried to push into a ditch." He also remembered that his feeling for his grandmother had been very hostile.

This man had now come to an age at which it was natural for him to marry, and he felt the urge to do so, but not in a normal way, so he sought a near relative as a sort of half measure. At the same time, his irresponsibility and sudden regret disclose something deeper in the whole arrangement. What he really wanted was to give himself a deep warning never again to approach a girl as long as he lived. So he staged this little warning interlude, in which, of course, I was cast for the part of the sage counselor who was to tell him not to marry, and that his desire to do so was only a neurotic manifestation.

Jealousy is often employed in order to establish a relationship of superiority. The jealous partner lays down rules for the behavior of the other, and enforces them with reproaches and in terms of moral reprobation. The person against whom such conduct is directed is thereby degraded from the position of a partner to that of a dishonorable servant, which gives the jealous one a sense of relative superiority. Jealousy is also found in connection with paranoia and alcoholism, where its use is fundamentally similar. In either case an acute lack of self-confidence drives the patient to strive for superiority by the fictitious method of torturing the sexual partner. It is not true, as often stated, that alcoholism causes impotence in these cases. In these manifestations the alcoholism, the impotence, and the jealousy are coordinated in the useless striving to compensate for the absence of social adjustment, courage, and self-confidence; and, as a whole, they indicate a progressively egotistic attitude.

Woman 60: Jealousy

Paranoia of the truest type, originating later in life, sometimes yields a case of jealousy which is really a hallucination, created to compensate for the state of helplessness. A case in point was that of a woman who had once been wealthy and had had every luxury, but afterward became poor. Her two married daughters supported her and her husband, and kept them in the luxury to which they had been accustomed. She felt deserted, however, and unable to adapt herself to her new limitations, for she had been too accustomed to extravagance and power. Occupied with their families, her daughters paid her little attention. All that was left to her was her husband, in whom she tried to find compensation for everything she had lost. Naturally, it was impossible for him to succeed in such a position; nothing short of his entire obedience and servitude would have maintained the sense of personal superiority that she required, and his submission to her fell far short of her demands. This situation intensified her already wounded dignity, and in the effort to enforce her dominance, she accused her husband of unfaithfulness, although he was seventy years of age and she was sixty. A young maid lived in the house, and the wife interpreted her husband's kindness to this girl as a sign of intimacy. Thenceforth, she imagined that every sound she heard in the house by day or night was a confirmation of her belief. The servant finally left and took a position in another city, but the patient was convinced that she was still in the neighborhood, believed that she heard her knock at the door at night, and suspected that she was still communicating with her husband through advertisements in the newspapers.

It is not difficult to understand why she needed her jealousy. Her husband's and her daughters' attitude toward her had changed since the time when she had lived in the focus of their attention. She now despaired of reality, but she still had the same goal of supremacy. This jealousy enabled her, by an attitude of accusation, to still keep the circumstances revolving around the question of her personal privilege.

Woman: Neurotic Heart and Jealousy

In many cases, patients indulge in jealousy without for a moment admitting the fact to themselves. This denial is probably because jealousy is considered an inferior feeling, and so conflicts with their conscious self-evaluation.

A particular patient complained of pains in the heart which recurred from time to time, especially when she felt discontented. She had been married for nearly twenty years and the marriage was supposed to be a happy one. The husband was a kind man, although weak; they had an accomplished daughter as their only child and lived in good circumstances. For a year the patient had been suffering from these pains, which radiated from the breasts into both arms, and angina pectoris had been suspected. But as no organic symptoms could be discovered, and as the pains always occurred after a mental disturbance, the diagnosis of a neurosis (pseudo-angina) was justifiable. Some time before the appearance of these symptoms, she had had a peculiar feeling in the legs, as though they were tied and she was unable to move them. The later symptoms she described as very painful, lasting for several minutes and ending with vomiting. Closer inquiry revealed that the pains reached the throat from the sternal region, and were associated with frequent vomiting, flatulence, and occasional peritonitis. Where we find such complications of symptoms, I recommend that the practitioner look for xerophagia[1], a condition which, in the present case, I could observe while I spoke to the patient.

This patient had come to me from abroad, and after arriving in Vienna her husband left her to spend some time in Berlin. On the night of his departure, she could not sleep, and when I asked her what thoughts passed through her mind while she lay awake, she answered: "I kept figuring out how far my husband was from Berlin." This remark convinced me that the woman was constantly thinking about where her husband was and wondering what he was doing. That her marriage was a fortunate one made it all the more likely that she kept a sharp look-out. Such conditions are fertile ground for jealous fears, especially in the case of a woman as ambitious as this one proved to be.

After the second night, she related the following dream: "Someone showed me a calf which was lame and unable to walk. This person commanded me to slaughter it." The inability to walk was reminiscent of some of her own symptoms, so it was justifiable to suppose that she identified herself with the calf. In this connection, the

---

[1] Editor's note: Xerophagia is a condition of dry eating.

slaughter of the calf represented suicide, probably in this case by cutting the throat, but the lameness held more meaning. She helped me a great deal in this interpretation by telling me that a friend of her husband suffered from ankylosis[2] of the knees as a result of gonorrheal arthritis.

Man 38: Agoraphobia and Fear of Syphilis

How wounded jealousy may be used in the service of the neurotic goal is illustrated in the case of a man of thirty-eight who suffered from agoraphobia. He was fairly intelligent, but this weakness precluded both work and social relations. The neurosis followed a disappointment, when the girl to whom he was engaged became unfaithful to him. He was then advised to take a good position in another part of the country so that he might forget his calamity, and he did so, but after a few days' work he had his first fit of anxiety, was scared to death, and hurried back to his mother, with whom he lived from that time until I saw him. He told me that for some days before the first fit of anxiety, he had been thinking continually of syphilis and of how easily he could become infected with it. This behavior must be understood as a self-preparation, by the appropriate meditation, to keep at a distance from all women and to live only under the care of his mother. His behavior was that of a pampered child, readily fleeing from the world and sure of safety only with his mother. His earliest recollection was an epitome of his life-plan: "When I was four years old, I was in a room with my mother; and I remember looking out the window at people working in the street." This fragment of memory conveys his abnormal need of a sheltered position and his interest in watching (he was near-sighted) "how others work." To be with his mother and observe others working was his sole idea of escape from tension and anxiety. When he was cured, he started in business as an interior decorator.

Boy 14: Shirking the Masculine Ideal

Early memories often furnish significant hints of the way in which the sexual attitude has been built up, as well illustrated in the case of a pampered boy of fourteen with a very expectant attitude toward life. He was a bad sport who made great difficulties in learning to swim and was disinclined to work or learn anything, especially mathematics. Mathematics is often the chief difficulty with this type, probably because

---

[2] Editor's note: Ankylosis is the consolidation of two or more bones or tissues into one.

it demands independent work. He confessed to his mother, his best companion, that for some time he had the tendency to feel sexual excitement at the sight of a man's muscles in the swimming pool or elsewhere. The earliest experience he could recall was of walking with his mother, when people often said, looking at his fair and curly hair, "What a pretty girl!" When asked if he would like to be a girl, however, he denied it emphatically. In his conscious opinion, it was better to be a man than a woman, but since he really wanted to have everything more easily, he instinctively shirked the necessary preparation for a masculine role, and his goal was to be wooed and receive attention as though he were a girl. This appeared possible because he was pretty to look at, but in all other ways success looked difficult and doubtful, so he took refuge in laziness or incapacity. Such a style of life, it must be clearly understood, actually gives the patient a sense of relative power or control. It goes with a great aversion to all situations which one is unable to dominate, so that we need not be surprised at this boy's exaggerated fear of thunderstorms. A thunderstorm is a supreme example of a thing which we cannot manage or control. With the lofty ambition of a second and youngest child, this boy's obvious defeats had made him incapable of conceiving of adequate success as a man, hence the attempt to form a homosexual goal, to govern passively by being loved and worshipped.

Woman 20: Masochistic Fantasies

In many cases a fragment of the prototype is revealed when in a dream, fantasy, or early recollection, the patient discloses some notion of a high superiority. Thus, a girl of twenty once said to me: "I had an old and, of course, imaginary memory of having once been high up in a cloud." She had been a pretty child, spoiled by her father who had committed suicide when she was fourteen. As we know, to lean upon the father is a second-best alternative and indicates discontent with the mother, so that as I expected the patient had a younger sister. She changed in appearance at the father's death, losing her good looks. The younger sister was now more attractive than she, and the mother was focusing all her care on an elder brother who had been ill for some time. Left with no one to spoil her, this pampered girl began to fight for attention, especially because her brother was hostile to her. About this time she experienced a nasty shock; returning from school one day, she passed a man who exhibited himself, and she ran home screaming with fear.

Such experiences with exhibitionists occur much more often than is generally known. Many men are too cowardly to strive for a real solution to the life problem of sex. Looking for a relief or substitute, they stop short at some partial manifestation of sexuality. If they are visual types, and their vision is not transferred to other objects, they become voyeurs or exhibitionists. They confirm their cowardice by usually approaching children.

My patient's shock from the exhibitionist marked the beginning of agoraphobia. We must recognize, however, that she was training herself to attain the foremost position along a non-sexual line of life as in the earlier relation with her father. The height of her ambition is indicated by the early recollection, and it had become still more neurotically exalted because the sister had surpassed her, the brother had repressed her, and the mother had neglected her. Such a goal of personal superiority was in danger from love and marriage, so she was naturally trying to exclude these possibilities. She made the most of this first experience of actual sexuality in order to justify herself in an overt rejection of sexual life altogether. I found that she was training herself in this attitude by means of certain daydreams, calculated to intoxicate her with the same idea. In one of these which recurred often, especially when she had a sexual feeling, she imagined that a man resembling her brother threw her down and spat upon her, which she found gratifying.

In my experience, girls commonly indulge in such masochistic fantasies, assumed to indicate an inclination to be subdued, which is supposed to be a female characteristic. On the contrary, however, such a fantasy is a complex fulfillment of a desire which is fundamentally quite simple, but the reverse of submissive, namely, the desire to exclude a realistic sexual objective with its possibilities of defeat and humiliation. We see the fantasy building up the daydreamer's resistance to love at the same time as it gratifies the sensational need; first, because to be satisfied in a fantasy is to teach oneself, "It is not necessary to have a real relationship," and second, because satisfaction mixed with the imagination of a defeat (in this case degradation by a brother who disliked her) teaches one to feel that a real experience would be highly objectionable. Thus, the fantasy is an appropriate meditation like a sort of prayer, in which the individual trains herself to lose interest in others, and to ardently desire escape from marriage. Where masochism is actually expressed in attempts to form masochistic relationships, the aim is fundamentally the same: to establish a great distance from normal behavior and natural conditions.

Nothing, then, could be further from the truth than the idea that masochistic fancies indicate a desire for submission. This patient of mine had been looking for someone whom she could rule, had fastened on her younger sister to be her obedient slave, and had finally prevailed on her to accompany her in everything. Her breakdown revealed her intolerance of the slightest real control over her; she was given a job, and when her employer told her to write something at his dictation, she could not do it.

Chapter X

Occupational Choices and Sleep Postures

Earliest recollections often involve ideas of danger, illness, and death. We can easily understand how the first experiences of these early events, especially if connected with danger and fear, may oppress a child with inferior feelings. Probably, only we humans are aware that death is part of life, and this awareness alone is enough to give us a sense of being terribly overpowered by nature. If a child experiences a brusque contact with death at an early age, his whole style of life may be largely molded by that single impression. In such a case the importance of death is invariably exaggerated, and we can often perceive how the child directs his actions and reactions in order to find relief from the oppressive idea, or compensation for it. Children adopt various tricks in their struggle against death. Some take an ostrich's refuge, avoiding every possible reminder of the subject, some develop other anxieties which keep the real terror out of consciousness, and others, more actively disposed, strive to protect and arm themselves, and to overcome death. In all these types, the so-called instinct of self-preservation is unusually evident.

We have two methods of fighting death with some certainty of victory. The first is to preserve the race by producing and raising children. In so struggling to conquer the destiny of the individual, the strongest instincts may be allies, and our interest may be intensified toward society and the future of mankind. This commonsense compensation for the fear of death naturally involves the healthiest conceptions of love and the exclusion of all perversions. The second method, suited to more individual ambitions, is to live in a way that will influence the future. This has been the ruling motive of many great men who have done enduring work in art and science; this purpose is also clearly visible in the lives of poets. Both in the procreation of the race and in the progress of its culture, this psychic striving to conquer death plays a leading part.

The fact that the work of many poets and philosophers has been largely motivated by the desire to overcome death is shown by the power of death in their reflections. We see it in Horace's "Exegi monumentum aere pernnius," and in Heine's "Nicht in Dilsseldorf am Rheim will ich stelin auf taubem Steim." And Tolstoy writes: "If I do not know how to act in any situation, I imagine—what would I do if I were going to die tomorrow?"

However, the early fear of death may also provoke a striving worse than useless, even though efficient. I have already made passing reference to the case of a boy of fifteen who had been deeply impressed by the death of an older sister, and often talked about death. When I asked him what he wanted to be, I thought he would say, "A doctor." But he answered: "A grave-digger, because I don't want to be the one who is buried. I want to bury others." And he did so, in his own way, for he became a merchant, a hard man of business who "buried" his competitors.

Children who have had some painful experience with death often choose another way of life. They form an early desire to become physicians and master all medical knowledge in order to survive. In a discussion I once opened in a medical society, nearly everyone present recounted memories of the death, mortal danger, or illness of some member of the family. A professional psychoanalyst who was present objected to my interpretation of this similarity of their experiences, which I could relate to many other cases of the earliest memories of physicians; he insisted that his own first recollection was of quite a different character. He remembered saying to his sick mother, when he was four years old, "Wait a little, and when I am grown up I will buy you all the best and most expensive medicines."

For the individual who fails to find relief in any of these compensations, the fear of death may be relieved by means of religious faith in the immortality of the soul. This faith may appear in complicated forms such as reincarnation, or more directly, as in spiritualism. The latter is founded on the possibility that the spirits of the dead can still move, act, and speak, a possibility which some acknowledge in the absence of more realistic hopes of conquering mortality.

Not only in physicians, but in all workers, the choice of occupation is foreshadowed by some dominant interest of the psychic prototype. The development of this interest into the concrete realization of work is often a lengthy process of self-training in which we can see the same idea adapting itself successively to various material possibilities. Thus, a great interest in playing with toy soldiers, a possible preparation for military life, may also be the prelude to success as the director of a department store. To play at sewing with needle and thread need not reveal a future tailor; it may just as well be the first step toward the career of a surgeon. Playing with dolls indicates an interest which may well develop into marriage and family life, but it may also be the sign of a future nurse or teacher.

Both marriage and occupation demand power of independent action, and readiness to accept the division of labor. These qualities cannot exist without some degree of social feeling and adaptation, and it is often at the time when the choice of an occupation becomes necessary that the lack of social adjustment appears. I believe the attention of children should be drawn fairly early in their schooldays toward the question: "What do I want to do later in life, and why do I want it?" The ideas thus elicited, combined with our knowledge of students' organic deficiencies or peculiarities, can help us greatly in guiding them vocationally. We should look not only for the most highly trained interest, but also seek to understand its root in the psychic prototype. Wherever we find an ability, it is the result of an interest in which the child has trained himself, stimulated by the totality of his circumstances. So clearly does this self-training appear, that we are justified in believing that anyone could accomplish anything, given the right training and the correct method.

By the way the child thinks and behaves and by his characteristic perceptions, his interest is specialized for his future occupation. The interest as a whole, however, is increased or decreased by his sense of the attainability of his goal of superiority. In the course of his development, the child will concretize his goal in various unattainable forms, which he must be able to abandon without any fundamental discouragement. Therefore, our task is to support the child in spirit, but correct his mistaken ideas. The more we educate the child in the direction of social interest, the more common-sense conceptions of superiority he will develop.

A child's idea of superiority is, of course, often influenced by a desire to surpass the father in his occupation. Thus, if his father is a public-school teacher, a boy may want to be a university professor. Usually, we find that the more the choice of profession changes, the more the child understands reality; but in each choice we can detect the impulse toward domination, the determination to attain a goal of importance or of security, or at least to escape difficulty or defeat. The child paints a new picture of his future action from time to time, but always conditioned by the same prototypical motive. When the actual choice of professions has to be made, the child confronts the reality he has long been approaching, and that reality may come in circumstances either hostile or friendly to his own striving. The goal of his working life now has to be established, however, and the youth strikes his bargain with reality by taking up work in an individual manner. Whatever latitude of choice may present itself, he decides how he will confront this necessity for action in accordance with all the facts as he understands them. We cannot expect his conclusions to be perfectly correct. Some degree of individual mistake is invariably involved in his choice. The conception of his function, in its ideal final form, is distorted by irrelevant factors. Money is one of these factors, which in our present civilization has an altogether exaggerated importance. This final form may also be obscured by an interest in long life and health, security, or social ambition, or be warped by dominating and critical tendencies.

Discouraged children generally have a doubtful or despairing attitude, and every struggle reveals movement toward escape from the necessity of a decision. This negative attitude is often shown in the selection of various and inconsistent professions, preference for no profession at all, empty ideals, lack of adventure, or delinquent tendencies.

If we compare all the professions a child chooses in the course of his development, taken as a whole, they disclose the line of action, and the degree of social interest and courage. We should not ignore the oddest and most unrealistic choices because they connect in a metaphorical way to the attitude a child is preparing to assume toward the demands of reality. One boy, for instance, when I asked what he wanted to be later in life, replied, "A horse." He constantly tried to imitate both the movements and the speed of a horse. In his babyhood, he had suffered from endocarditis[1] and had to lie very still in bed for a long time. Later on, he expressed his choice of a profession more realistically by becoming an automobile engineer. Another boy seven years old also symbolized his ambition by wanting to be a horse. When asked for the reason, he said, "My father is ill, and because I am the eldest I will have to support the family."

In either of these cases, it would be ridiculous to look for the cause of the fantasy in hereditary influences of sexual motives. The first boy was interested in movement because the confinement of his illness had given him a specific feeling of inferiority. The second boy's use of the idea of the horse was entirely different. Considering how best to replace and surpass his father, he believed the horse was the symbol of his future as the bearer of a heavy burden. I found another of these animal-fantasies in a boy of ten, who waned to be a buffalo, and used to charge home from school in a posture imitative of an advancing bull. He developed into a bully and his ideal character in history was Achilles.

---

[1] Editor's note: Endocarditis is inflammation of the endocardium membrane lining the heart.

Body Postures and Sleep Positions

Body postures and attitudes indicate the manner in which an individual approaches his goal. A person who faces life directly shows courage, whereas an adult who is anxious and hesitant has a style of life that prohibits direct action, and something of a detour appears in every action. The way an individual gives his hand in a handshake reveals whether he has social feeling and likes to be connected with others. A perfectly normal handshake is rather rare; it is usually overdone, underdone, or betrays a pushing-off or pulling-to tendency. In a streetcar, some people lean sideways; they wish to be supported and are quite oblivious of others' inconvenience. The same social insensitivity is seen in those who cough in front of others, quite thoughtless of infecting them. When entering a room, some seem to keep instinctively at the greatest possible distance from everyone else. All these things reveal, more directly than their conversation, the attitudes that individuals hold toward life.

The attitudes adopted in sleep are as significant as the postures and movements of daily life. Very little children sleep on their backs, with the arms raised; when we see a child sleeping in this position, we may assume he is healthy. If the child changes this position and sleeps with the arms down, for example, we can suspect some illness. Similarly, if an adult is accustomed to sleeping in a certain position and suddenly changes it, we may assume that something is altered in his mental attitude. Organic defects play their part, of course, in conditioning the sleeping posture. A person suffering from pneumonia or pleurisy will always sleep on the defective side, sometimes without knowing why he does so. He does it unconsciously because it eases his breathing. Some people who have heart trouble, or think they have, believe 'they cannot sleep on the left side. There is no organic reason for this, but they feel they must be careful on the weaker side.

When we see a person sleeping on his back stretched out like a soldier at attention, it indicates that he wishes to appear as great as possible. One who lies curled up like a hedgehog with the sheet drawn over his head is not likely to be a striving or courageous character, but is probably cowardly. We should be careful not to assign him a difficult task until we have found out how to give him courage. A person who sleeps on his stomach betrays stubbornness and negativity. By comparing the sleeping postures of patients in various hospitals with the reports of their daily life, I have concluded that the mental attitude is consistently expressed in both modes of life, sleeping and waking.

Some people turn a gradual somersault in sleep, awaking with their heads at the bottom of the bed and their feet on the pillow. Such people psychically express an unusually strong opposition to the world, with the neurotic attitude of often answering, "No," before having understood the question. Also, some patients make a half-turn and sleep with their heads hanging down over the edge of the mattress. They develop headaches from this practice, which are generally used to escape the demands of the following day.

I was considerably puzzled by the discovery that some children sleep in a crouching position, resting their knees and elbows like animals; but I finally found out this is the best position for hearing what is happening in the next room. Children who adopt this position have more than the normal desire to keep in contact with others, even in sleep, and they generally want to go to bed with the door open.

Thus, all postures have a purposive nature. I once treated a man who had become blind, and since then had always wanted to hold his wife's hand while he slept, which prevented her from moving. This desire was a pathetic disguise for a tyrannical tendency. When she resisted it, he developed hallucinations at night, imagining that burglars had caught her and carried her off. This hallucination was a development of the same line of action, to keep her in his power.

Restless sleepers, who keep moving all night, show they are dissatisfied and want to be doing something more. It may also be a sign that they want to be watched by another person, usually by the mother. When children cry in sleep, it is for the same reason; they do not want to be alone but would like to insure notice and protection. The quietest sleepers are those who are most settled in their attitude toward the problems of life. Because their lives are well organized and productive by day, they can use the night for its proper purpose of rest and recreation, and their sleep is generally free from dreaming.

Chapter XI

Organ Dialect and Dreams

Woman 25: Anxiety Neurosis

In cases where the patient begins with a feeling that treatment will of itself endanger the goal of superiority, it is often difficult to make a start. I had such a case in a married woman of twenty-five who suffered from an anxiety-neurosis. At the first interview, when I asked her to take a chair beside me, she went and sat down on the other side of the room.

Her violent attacks of anxiety occurred when her husband was delayed in coming home. She had felt deprived in her life with her family, and her husband was the first person who overindulged her, but now his business obligations made it impossible for him to devote himself so much to her. Wanting to be connected only with her husband and to exclude everyone else, she was hindering her husband's business by the development of an anxiety-neurosis. No one else could demand anything from her, and her husband had to obey. But she paid for this success with painful anxieties, and her husband persuaded her to see me.

Naturally, the situation was an impasse. She felt before coming that I was a danger to her, and symbolized her attitude in her behavior over the chair. If I freed her from her neurosis, she would have no weapon to use against her husband.

Critical, Compulsive Housewife

A similar case was that of a married woman who had been the youngest of a very competitive family. Reproached and teased as the inferior member of the family, as a girl she had found no way of compensating for this unfortunate position, except to prove that other people were wrong. This habit won her the nickname of "the judge."

She married merely to get even with her married sisters. She was not in love with her husband, but was afraid of being despised if she did not prove herself capable of a happy marriage. But although she had three children, she could never feel equal to others, so she defended herself against society with aggression, arrogance, and criticism. Such behavior is often nothing but a neurotic safeguard against disappointment, not the result of inherited psychopathic conditions.

She felt sure that she could not equal her eldest sister in the art of housekeeping, and her husband made a mistake when they were first married by asking her if she would be as orderly as her sister. This question touched her on the sensitive spot, and from that time on she wanted to avoid housekeeping, or at least to fail under extenuating circumstances. A type of compulsion-neurosis followed, which took the form of devoting herself to the linen and laundry work until her care and accuracy were a nuisance and a waste of time. As this left her no time for anything else, she had an excuse if the marriage developed unhappily.

She had another device by which to defend herself which is commonly used by neurotics; she used to judge other people by their likeness or unlikeness to Jesus Christ. Thus, after setting anyone on a pedestal for admiration, she easily discovered faults in him, to prove that he was not a Christ-like character, and then cast him off. She used this defense against the many doctors to whom she went for treatment, and frustrated their efforts because of her prototypical feeling that if she were understood, she would be "put back" to her inferior position of the youngest. Therefore, she had to prove the doctors wrong, tried to forestall their opinions, and constantly worried and reproached, so that they were unable to speak, and the time of the consultations passed ineffectually.

Organ Dialect

As we have seen in a variety of cases, the style of life dominates the organic functions. This relationship is especially noticeable with the lungs, the heart, the stomach, the organs of excretion, and the sexual organs. The disturbance of these functions expresses the direction an individual takes to attain his goal. I have called these disturbances the "organ dialect," or "organ jargon," since the organs reveal in their own most expressive language the intention of the individual totality.

The dialect of the sexual organs is especially expressive, often leading the patient to the doctor. Each case has its peculiarities, but in practically every one the patient expresses by a disorder of the sexual functioning, a stoppage, hesitation, or escape in the face of the three life problems. Whatever partial sexual satisfactions the patient may provide for himself are an escape from the real problem, and the remainder which is left over for a normal expression has to be excluded. In this way the various forms of impotence are traceable to a common root in a disinclination and lack of training for relationships with other people. We can see this common root when we leave the sexual symptoms temporarily out of the picture, and study the nature of the patient's social contacts. Most of the cases I have known, of this specific functional failure, concerned patients faced with the problem of marriage. Ejaculatio praecox varies greatly in its individual meaning, but I have found it a sign of an egotistical character and a feeling of impotence, invariably combined with very poor social adjustment. Failure to ejaculate occurs in egotistical men who are afraid of having children, generally because of their possible rivalry.

Nobody who has understood anything about Individual Psychology would attempt to cure such cases as these by upbraiding the patients with the words I have used, as if we could do good by taking a moralistic attitude. A patient has to be gradually led into wanting to listen and understand. Only then can he be influenced to live what he has understood.

In women the same dialect appears as vaginismus. This condition represents an avoidance of man, accompanied by other mental symptoms signifying the woman's aversion either to a certain man or to men in general. Besides this active avoidance, we may find the passive forms of sexual rejection: frigidity and a display of passivity. This lack of function mirrors an idea in the woman's mind of not being present in intercourse, as though the event were merely the man's affair. In all cases of frigidity, I have found that the woman felt the female role as one of humiliation and degradation. It is important to verify this precisely, apart from the sexual life.

A Woman's Revenge Against Her Father

Ambitious girls who have been too spoiled may easily lose confidence in regard to sexual relations. This was the case with a beautiful girl whom I treated, the youngest of the family and spoiled by everyone, especially by the father until he married a second time. His remarriage undermined her self-confidence. It is very difficult for a stepmother to take her place in relation to her husband's children without provoking their antagonism. I do not know if others have the same experience, but I have found that girls make the most trouble in these cases and if an opportunity arises, they begin casual sexual relations as if in revenge. When they are intelligent and sensitive enough to feel the full difficulty of the situation, they are conscious of a lack of love from both sides, often becoming frigid and eluding` marriage, which was the case with my patient. We might well ask why this girl continued to enter into sexual relations at all, if we consider how much she had against it. She had the memory of being deserted by her father, the experience of a lover who did not pamper her as her father did, and in addition, she had the gruesome experiences of undesired pregnancy and artificial abortion without physical gratification in love. To balance against all these disadvantages, she had nothing but a secret sense of having revenge against her father.

An individual can never settle down into such an unsatisfactory style of life, which excludes marriage but is adapted to social relationships or to work. A state of continual tension results, which becomes acute in the face of every real problem that may present itself, often appearing as headaches and fatigue.

My patient dreamed: "Jesus Christ appeared to me and invited me to go to Heaven with Him, where my task would be to amuse all the other people. If I did not choose to do this, I would go to Hell. Then I found myself in Heaven and saw many angels who looked like the penguins in Anatole France's satire, and I also saw God, shaving His beard and looking and moving like the man in the advertisements in the chemist's shop-windows. I felt a great despair and wanted to go away." This dream is difficult to interpret unless we relate it to the general line of the girl's development; indeed, we would not make any sense of it if we could not estimate, from her history and its related line of action, what emotional idea she was continually trying to intoxicate herself with. This idea of rejecting virtue and embracing vice was motivated by revenge against her father, who wanted virtue of her. Having grasped this fundamental agreement of the dream with everything else the patient does, we can proceed to interpret: "To amuse the other people" corresponds to her notion of the humiliation of the female role, which she conceives as merely an amusement for men. Jesus Christ is her supreme symbol of a man of earnest and unselfish character who proposed to marry her; He had said to her, "I want to sacrifice myself to make you happy." Heaven, therefore, is the heaven He promised her in marriage. But as we have seen, she fears defeat in marriage, so that married life cannot be allowed to seem attractive, on the same principle that the grapes which are too high to reach must be suspected of being sour. So in her dream, this man in his little village appeared to her in the contemplative mood of the Viennese satirist, Nestroy, when he wrote: "What is a man? Getting up, shaving, and going to sleep again!"

Depression as a Safeguard Against Marriage

An extremely spoiled girl, the youngest of eleven sisters and brothers, and correspondingly ambitious, had another way of making the grapes of marriage sour. She had a few sexual intimacies, but only with married men. I am always suspicious if a girl begins with married men, because the difficulties are obviously so much greater, and an impractical choice cannot be simply explained away by insisting upon the uncontrollable power of love. It was easy in this case to find out that the patient had been intimidated by her pampered upbringing, and was especially nervous about marriage because two older sisters had been happily married and feared she would fail to surpass them. Although conscious of this fear, she was not so well aware of what she was doing in her successive liaisons. If one of her lovers waned to get a divorce and marry her, she left him, depressed and crying a little, of course, but firm because of the poor wife, usually a personal friend of hers. The depression soon ceased with the beginning of another affair, but finally, after breaking off an intimacy in these circumstances, she went into a depression that lasted for months.

At that time, she came to me. She was thirty-six years old and living with a brother who was a widower and pampered her. But in their first months together, he had spoken of marrying again and suggested that she should marry, too. Faced with this undesirable prospect and in the act of breaking off a relationship, she used her illness as a device to "kill two birds with one stone!" It gave the brother a warning to take care of her, and herself a lesson not to begin again with another man because of new and more dangerous consequences.

Sleep and Hypnosis

Sleeping is another kind of waking. Of course, we could be equally justified in saying that waking is a variant of sleeping, the truth being that in order to understand them, whether psychologically or biologically, we must give up the idea that they are contradictory states. Biologically considered, sleep is merely a partial termination of the organism's contact with its environment, a decrease of its functional activity. In sleep our attention retains some contact with reality through feeling, hearing, and thinking, but we exclude the greater part of the connections among them. We observe the limits of our movements in bed and do not fall out. We select some noises as important enough to awaken us and neglect others; we can even wake ourselves up at stated hours. All these activities which sleep does not exclude are also carried on in the waking state, often hardly any more consciously.

Hypnotism is also a variety of waking, but it differs from sleep by excluding a different class of activities. The hypnotized subject excludes whatever the hypnotist wishes him to exclude, having first agreed (whether he admits it or not) to accept only the hypnotist's commands. Thus, hypnotism may be called sleeping to order. Apart from hypnotism, this sleeping to order is not uncommon, especially among children. Thus, hypnotism is proof of great obedience. It is often regarded as a justifiable method of medical or psychic treatment, but Individual Psychologists naturally avoid it, knowing that the essence of successful treatment is increased courage and self-control. A patient must prove these qualities by using them himself, not by relinquishing control to someone else. The frequent failures which follow hypnotic methods of treatment are the patient's revenge for having been unexpectedly attacked by suggestion during the hypnosis.

We should not be surprised that hypnosis can remove or mitigate symptoms, though without permanent benefit. The same is true of many suggestive methods, which the patient regards in a magical or semi-religious light, but these things do not of themselves teach a better adaptation to life. Thus, they give temporary relief and seem to be most effective in reducing the neurotic symptoms accompanying particular organic diseases, such as apoplexy, aftereffects of syphilis, and multiple sclerosis. As Ludwig Stein has shown, nearly all organic illnesses produce more symptoms than necessary. These nervous complications are best treated by the method of Individual Psychology, which, though it cannot cure pneumonia or heart disease, may significantly relieve these conditions by encouraging the patient.

Our distinctive method of dream interpretation is based on this recognition of the unity of the waking and sleeping life. This premise improves on the valuable discoveries of Lichtenberg and Freud, that dreams contain signs of vital problems which the dreamer never recognizes in his waking life, discoveries which our work amply confirms. But the dream is not merely the substitute satisfaction of wishes unfulfilled in waking, especially not of Freud's "infantile sexual desires;" rather it is a function of the entire style of life, more dynamically related to the future than to the past, a fact intuitively known in antiquity when dreams were regarded as prophetic, not historical. The dreamer is engaged in molding his attitude and disposition to the coming events of his life, storing up a reserve of feeling and emotion which could not be acquired in the daytime by contact with reality or logical thinking. He thus accumulates an irrational force to sustain him in the pursuit of his goal of superiority in the problems he anticipates, to solve them in his own way or against the demands of common sense.

In dreams, therefore, we never find any other tendencies or movements than those manifested in the style of the waking life when the latter is coherently grasped. We cannot oppose "consciousness" to "unconsciousness" as if they were two antagonistic halves of an individual's existence. The conscious life becomes unconscious as soon as we fail to understand it; and as soon as we understand an unconscious tendency, it has already become conscious.

The dream strives to pave the way toward solving a problem with a metaphorical expression of it, and in itself is a sign that the dreamer feels inadequate to solve it with common sense. A metaphorical conception of one's situation is a way of escaping from common sense, as metaphors may be used to support almost any kind of concrete action. The dreams creating the feelings and emotions of success best illustrate this dynamic, as they produce a kind of intoxication which perfectly resists the logic of communal life. Naturally, the dreamer does not recognize his own metaphor for what it is. If he understood it, it would be ineffective for its purpose. It is essentially a self-deception in the interest of his individual goal. We should expect, therefore, that the more the individual goal agrees with reality, the less a person dreams, and we find this is true. Courageous people rarely dream, for they deal adequately with their situation in the daytime.

There are problematic cases, of course. The claimed absence of dreams may prove to be merely a lack of awareness of their contents, which are entirely forgotten so that only the emotion remains. That is but a further step in the self-deceptive process which dreaming serves, and its purpose is to prevent the individual from getting insight into his dreams. Or the absence of dreams may be a sign that the patient has come to a point of rest in his neurosis and established a neurotic situation which he does not wish to change. Short dreams indicate that the present problems are such that the dreamer desires to find a "shortcut" between them and the individual style of life. Long or very complicated dreams are dreamed by patients seeking excessive security in their lives; they generally indicate hesitation and the patient's desire to postpone even his own self-deception in case it does not work out correctly. The style of life is best shown by frequently recurring dreams which have remained in the memory for many years.

The methods of self-deception we use in dreams can be seen not only in the abuse of comparisons, metaphors, and symbols, but also in a tendency to narrow or distort a present problem until merely a part of it is visible, a part which cannot be judged by the same standards as the whole.   The urgent and necessary solution of a vital problem, for example, may be dreamed of in the form of an unimportant school examination.

Antagonism to a Wife Awake and Dreaming

Dreams played an important part in the case of a man who had been married eight years and had two children, but was disappointed in his wife.   His great complaint against her was that she did not take sufficient care of the children.   Emphasis on the duty to the children in marriage indicates a deeper-lying disagreement with the partner. Whether this man was right or wrong about his wife's neglect of the children, he used his criticism of her to express a deeper reproach and held it as a weapon against her.   This was evident from other details of his behavior, which showed that he worried about her management of matters other than the children, such as her housekeeping.   The real source of his antagonism was his belief that she had not married him for love and he found confirmation in his wife's frigidity.   I have always found that persistent frigidity offends the husband in the highest degree, irritating both partners.   In order to have a powerful proof of his wife's guilt, instead of the real and humiliating reason for his condemnation of her, he developed this exaggerated fear for the children and subsequently came to me because of headaches and a distaste for work.   He was not courageous enough to get a divorce or to seek another woman, having grown up with the feeling that in childhood he had been dominated by his mother.

This man became very jealous, losing all faith in women.   One night he dreamed, "I was in a battle in the streets of a city, and in the midst of the shooting and burning many women were thrown into the air as if by an explosion."   Afterward, he felt great pity in remembering this picture, until my treatment enabled him to understand it.   It reinforced his attitude toward his marriage problem, for in this dream he gratified his rage by picturing a general extermination of women, which he was compelled to repudiate because he was not without social feeling and compassion.   We can see how this pitying afterthought enabled him to maintain the daily attitude he assumed toward his wife; he was not at all angry with her, but merely solicitous for the children.   I analyze the structure of this dream as follows: He selected some terrible pictures from his memories of the war (we call this: the selection of an adapted thought) and then compared the relationships' between the sexes to such warfare.   In this way, he reduced the whole problem of the sexes to a small part of it, a battle leaving out all the more important factors. When he recovered from his fright, and when, after my explanation he understood his self-deception and self-intoxication, he became quieter and the headaches stopped, but he did not wish to be reconciled with his wife. He then had another dream: "The youngest of my three children got lost and could not be found." As we know he had only two children, but he was very frightened both in the dream and after awakening from it.

The line of reproach this patient had always taken against his wife was the accusation of neglecting the children. So if he imagined a third child lost, it was a warning not to have more children and thus increase the danger. With this detour, he could avoid resuming relations with his wife. Again, we see how the selection of an adapted thought enables him to work up a comparison which reduces the whole problem of educating and protecting children to one detail of it. Nevertheless, an astute psychologist may detect, in the selection of the fiction of a third child, the beginning of a movement toward reconciliation. For it is as though the patient glimpsed the possibility of another child, but withdrew, saying, "She may be careful enough for two, but surely not for three."

The self-deception practiced in dreams is often traceable in the waking state, for which I once had interesting proof. I was about to leave Vienna, when a former patient telephoned, asking me to see his sick wife. He had consulted two physicians and neither could decide what was the cause of her fever. Because I was in a hurry, I tried to excuse myself, saying that I was not a specialist in organic illnesses, but I finally yielded to his insistence. I found the patient suffering from typhus, and recommended a consultant skillful in such cases. He still resisted, saying that no physician could tell him more than I could, and I had difficulty in getting away with a promise that I would visit him as a friend as soon as I returned to Vienna. He kept on saying, "But he could not tell me more than you have told me." At last, I persuaded him to call in the expert and left. When I returned to visit him a few weeks later, his wife was recovering and he told me he was well satisfied with the doctor I had recommended. Then, in a positive tone, he observed, "Of course, you told me when you came that Dr. W. had died that morning."

I had told him nothing of the kind, so I denied it. I had only read the news myself on my vacation the day after leaving Vienna. He would not believe this, however, and stoutly maintained that I had spoken of Dr. W.'s death. When I asked him what made him think that I had told him, he answered, "Why, you must have done so. For when the consultant came to see my wife the next day, he had no sooner greeted everyone present than he turned to the doctors and said, 'Do you know my friend, Dr. W., is dead?' 'Yes,' I interposed, 'Dr. Adler told me so yesterday.' The specialist looked surprised and said, 'I know Dr. Adler very well, but I did not know he was blessed with the gift of prophecy.' There must be some mistake, and I wonder if you can explain it."

It was not so difficult to explain. This man had almost unlimited faith in me and when I saw him before my departure, he had repeatedly said, "The specialist cannot tell me anything that you haven't said." He had intoxicated himself with this idea, so that he received the new doctor with an emotional determination that whatever he said would be something I had already told him. Thus, he spontaneously took the first piece of information the specialist uttered and firmly, with perfect self-deception, ascribed it to me.

Part 2

The Case of Mrs. A.[1][2]

Anxiety Disorder
Psychosis? paranoia, delusions

---

[1] First published in the *Indiv. Psych. Pamphl.,* No. 1, 15-46. F.G. Crookshank
was the editor of a series of papers.
[2] Additional editing by Henry T. Stein, Ph.D., 2005.

The Case of Mrs. A.

Alfred Adler

[1931]

From the Foreword by F. G. Crookshank[1]

In January 1931, Dr. Adler visited London and gave a series of lectures. At a special meeting of the Medical Society of Individual Psychology, it was felt that a demonstration by Dr. Adler of his own methods of reading a "life style" would be of greatest interest. Therefore, Dr. Adler requested that at the last moment, case notes by a practicing physician be presented to him for his extemporaneous consideration and impromptu interpretation.

To this end, Dr. Hilda Weber was good enough to transcribe and bring to the meeting, notes taken by her some time previously on the case of one "Mrs. A." who had been under her care. The nature of the case was known to no one other than Dr. Weber until the moment when the notes were handed to Dr. Adler on the platform, in the fashion of what undergraduate examinees call an "unseen." When she first took these notes, Dr. Weber was not personally interested in Individual Psychology, and she made no alteration in them for the purposes of the meeting.

GENERAL INTRODUCTORY STATEMENTS

First, I thank you all for your interest in the process of Individual Psychology. Because you are partly trained as doctors, I asked to receive an analysis of a sick, neurotic, or psychotic person, knowing nothing about the case. So you see that in Individual Psychology, we proceed in the same way as in the general field of medicine. We know that in

---

[1] Although in his original Foreword F.G. Crookshank suggests publishing a verbatim transcript of Adler's exact words, this editor believes that the contemporary reader will gain a better, deeper understanding of Adler's ideas and methods from judicious editing for readability.

general medicine we have to use all of our diagnostic tools because otherwise we would not feel justified in going on to treatment.

In this case we have to deal with psychological conditions and we must have an idea, a diagnostic conception. If a human life can be understood, we will find a psychological development toward an ideal final goal.

Accepting the premise of a final goal means we have to consider at least two points. One is the point from which the symptom expression arises. Wherever we discover a complaint, we will find a feeling of deficiency. The second point is a striving toward an ideal form in order to overcome this felt deficiency. We say that wherever there is life, there is a striving for an ideal final form.

Today, I cannot explain all the details and characteristics of this striving to overcome. It is enough for me to emphasize that in Individual Psychology we look for the problem or difficulty which a person does not feel able to overcome. Therefore, we have to look for the wrong direction in which this person is striving, one that is incompatible with a solution of the problem.

In this direction we find a million variations, which can be evaluated if we have an idea of what cooperation and social interest. We are usually able to determine how far away from a sufficient degree of cooperation we find a patient striving. Thus, it is necessary--and every astute analysis has to bring this out--to discover at what point a person is not adequately prepared for the solution of social problems, not properly prepared because he cannot mobilize what is expected of him: sufficient degrees of courage, self-confidence, social adjustment, and the right type of cooperation. These qualities must be understood because we see how the patient cannot function, how he declares himself unable to solve his problem, and how he shows what I call the hesitating attitude, or the stopping attitude. He begins to evade and wants to insulate himself from a solution of the necessary problem.

On this point we find him in the state of mind that I have described as the inferiority complex. Because of that complex, he constantly strives to advance, feel superior, and overcome his difficulties in the present situation. We must look for the point where the patient feels satisfied with simply feeling superior. He cannot feel superior in regard to a socially useful solution of his present problem, so his superiority is directed in a socially useless direction. In his own imagination, he has reached his goal of superiority and perhaps satisfied himself, but it cannot be validated as a useful goal to anyone else.

This is the initial general diagnosis in each analysis of a psychological case. Again, along the line of general diagnosis, we have to find some explanation of why this person has not been prepared. This is difficult to understand and recognize. We have to delve back into the past of this person, find out in what circumstances he has grown up, how he has behaved toward his family, and ask questions resembling those we ask in general medicine, such as: "What were your parents like?" The patient does not know that in his answers he expresses his general attitude--if he felt pampered and the center of attention, or if he resented one of his parents--but we see it. Always give "open" questions; be sure that you do not insinuate or give a hint to the patient so that he gives you an answer you are seeking.

At this point in the interview, we see the origin of the lack of preparation for the present problem, which is like a test examination. Why the patient has not been prepared for it must be seen and explained in the case history.

After determining a general diagnosis, we must not believe this is sufficient for understanding the patient. The special diagnosis now begins where we must learn by testing our series of guesses. We do the same kind of testing in internal medicine. We must note what the patient says but, as in general medicine, we must not trust our early guesses or conclusions. We must prove them, and not believe--if we find, for example, a certain frequency of palpitations of the heart--that it necessarily means a particular cause. In medicine and surgery, as in Individual Psychology, we have to guess, but have to support our assumptions with other verifying evidence. If the other information does not agree with our guess, we have to be tough and critical enough with ourselves to look for another explanation.

Today, I want to do an analysis the way we might do it in a clinic. The doctor does an analysis of a patient he has not seen before and tries to explain the symptoms. We can also work in this way, for then the whole audience is stimulated, willingly or unwillingly, to think it over.

Individual Psychology expects us to prove every conclusion we make about a case. We must scrutinize each of our assumptions and try to understand the coherence of a case. Our general views may be reflected, but we must be careful not to bias our conclusions by trying to prove a theory. As in other sciences, we must stay open to a wide range of potential influences. This perspective is very valuable, because it keeps us open to intuitive, free guessing and discovery. This freedom will be tempered by the progressive refinement and correction of our thinking about cases, a skill that improves with experience. In this respect, Individual Psychology fully agrees with the fundamental diagnostic procedures of medicine.

THE CASE OF MRS. A.

Here is the case of Mrs. A. We can see that she is a married woman--perhaps a widow--we do not know more. We must focus on each word and turn it over in our mind, so that we get everything possible out of it.

The patient A., who forms the subject of this paper, was thirty-one years old at the time she came for treatment.

Thirty-one years old and a married woman. We know the circumstances in which a woman, thirty-one years old and married, might find herself. There could be a problem with marriage or with children, perhaps also a problem with income. We are very careful. We would not presuppose anything, but we feel sure that--unless we are surprised later--there is something wrong in one of these areas. Now we go ahead.

She had been married eight years . . .

That carries us further: she had married at twenty-three years of age.

. . . and had two children, both boys, now age eight and four respectively.

She had a child very soon. Eight years married and the child eight years old! What you think about that is your own affair. You see the sharp eye of Individual Psychology!

Her husband was an elevator operator in a store.

Then they are probably in poor circumstances.

An ambitious man, he suffered considerable humiliation from the fact that, unlike his brother, he was prevented, he felt, from obtaining a better type of employment because during the war his right arm had been disabled.

If we can trust this description that he is an ambitious man and does not feel happy in his employment, this discontent must reflect in his married life. He cannot satisfy his ambition outside the family. Perhaps he tries to satisfy it inside, tries to rule his wife and children and to "boss" them. We are not sure and we must be careful not to believe it and be convinced, but we have a hypothesis. Perhaps we will find something to confirm it. An ambitious husband.

His wife, however, had little sympathy with his trouble . . .

If we are right that this man wants to prove himself superior in his family life and his wife does not agree and give in, if she has little sympathy with his style of life, there will probably be some dissension in the family. This man wants to rule; his wife does not agree and does not give him a chance. Therefore, there must be trouble in the family.

. . . being far too occupied with the compulsive thoughts and fears of death from which she suffered.

Compulsive thoughts and fears of death! It does not look like a compulsion neurosis; it looks more like an anxiety neurosis. On this point I would like to give you a rule from our experience which can be used. I like to ask: What happens in these cases? What are the results if a married woman suffers from fears of death and perhaps from other fears? What would it mean? She is preoccupied with it, as we can see, and so many of her necessary tasks would not be fulfilled. We see that she is much more occupied with her own person. She is not interested, as we have heard, in the troubles of the man.

Therefore, we are in agreement on these points, but we are not far ahead. We can understand that such a person cannot cooperate properly if she is interested in the fear of death and other fears, and we understand there must be many quarrels in this family.

These fears, indeed, occupied her mind to such an extent that at the time she came for treatment, she had difficulty thinking of anything else.

At this point we are justified in answering our question as to what happens: She cannot think of anything else. This is what we will always find and, if in some cases it appears not to be so for a time, we will find confirmation later in the description. This shows that our guesses are worthwhile, and encourages us because we know that even if our guesses are not reflected in the present circumstances, they predict what will probably happen later.

We read that she is thinking only of her fears.

A careful housewife, she had previously been governed by an almost obsessional hatred of dirt and love of tidiness . . .

This gives another picture, a compulsion neurosis in regard to cleanliness, probably a wash-compulsion neurosis. Because she was afraid of dirt, she must always keep everything clean. She must wash and clean everything and herself. In the same way, she suffers from a fear of death. There must be a mixed neurosis, which is really very rare. In our general experience, the wash-compulsion neurotics do not suffer from a fear of death. They may combine the two ideas and say: "If I do not wash this desk, or these shoes and so on, my husband will die," or whatever it may be. But that is not the fear of death as we find it in many anxiety neuroses. As I explained in a lecture in this room on "Obsessions and Compulsion in the Compulsion Neuroses," there is always an underlying idea. Here the idea is that of cleaning away the dirt.

Now we understand more on this point. This woman is occupied in another way than she is expected to be. She does not cooperate; she is interested only in her own suffering, making everything clean, and perhaps the wash-compulsion. Therefore, we conclude: This is a type that cannot solve the social problems of life; she is not prepared for cooperation, but much more prepared for thinking of herself. We know from our general experience that we find such a style of life mostly in children suffering from imperfect organs, and in the great majority of pampered, dependent children. More rarely we find it in neglected children, because probably a child entirely neglected would die. The great majority of these neurotic children have been pampered, made dependent, and given such an idea of themselves that they are more interested in themselves than in others.

This woman is striving for a high ideal: to be cleaner than all the others. We can understand that she does not agree with normal life; she wants it to be much cleaner. Cleanliness is a pleasant characteristic and we like it very much. But if a person focuses life on cleanliness, she is not able to live a normal life, because if we have really inquired into cases of wash-compulsion neurosis, we will be convinced that it is not possible to achieve the ideal of cleanliness these people strive for. We will always find some dirt and dust. We cannot carry on life by pointing merely to one part--cleanliness, for instance--because it disturbs the harmony of life.

As far as I can see, only one part of life can never be overemphasized and that is social interest. We cannot overemphasize it to the degree that it disturbs the harmony of life. If we point to health and think only of it, we ruin our life; if we think only of money, we ruin our life, in spite of the fact that, as we know, it is unfortunately necessary to think of it. If we turn to family life and exclude all other relationships, we ruin our life. It seems an unwritten law that we can turn only to social interest without risking any damage.

Now we will see more.

. . . hatred of dirt and love of tidiness, both with regard to her home and to her own person. She now began to neglect both of these.

This woman's initial focus was on cleanliness and avoidance of dirt, but now, she was broken down, so she gives up. We do not know why she appears now in this state of mind, but she probably did not succeed in her imagination with this compulsion neurosis and, therefore, she has made one step forward, coming--if I have read and understood correctly--to a state in which she begins to neglect herself and be dirty.

Here is an interesting point. I have never seen individuals as dirty as those suffering from a wash-compulsion neurosis. If we enter the home of such a person, there is a terrible smell. We find papers lying about, and dirt everywhere. The hands and the whole body are dirty, all the clothes are dirty, and the person does not touch anything. I do not know if it is so here, but this is the usual condition among people with a wash-compulsion neurosis, and it is odd that all these people experience some adventures that others never experience. Where there is dirt, they are mixed in it. Probably it is because they look for dirt and are not as clever as others in avoiding it. I have had a strange experience with people who are always soiled when others can avoid it. It is like a fate hanging over them; they continually find their way to dirt.

We do not know what the breakdown means in this case, perhaps a step nearer to psychosis. That happens sometimes with people suffering from compulsion neurosis.

Her fear of death referred to above was related to a definite knife phobia . . .

We can also call a knife phobia a compulsion idea, a frequent one people suffer from if they see a knife. They feel they could kill someone. But they never do. They stop at the idea. The meaning behind such an idea is hidden; we must find out its whole coherence and meaning. It is similar to a person who is cursing and says "I could kill you."

We spoke before of disagreements. The husband is ambitious. As we know from our general diagnosis of neurotic individuals, she is also ambitious. She wants to rule, to be the head. She wants to be the cleanest person, so we can understand how she avoids her husband, his personal approach, his sexual approach, because of his lack of cleanliness. She calls everything dirty. She can call a kiss dirty. We must find how far she is going to look for this dirt. She has two children, but we believe this had not been her wish. Here we see the lack of cooperation. If we look a little closer, we will surely find this woman is frigid. Do you see why? She thinks merely of herself, and the sexual functions between men and women can be correct only if they are fulfilled as a task for two people. If a person is interested only in herself, the sexual feelings are not right. Thus, we have frigidity. More rarely, we may have vaginismus, but it is usually frigidity, and we can be sure that this woman does not cooperate. We can see her lack of cooperation in the form of her sexuality. Therefore, we can be sure and can predict--though we must not allow ourselves to do so, but should wait and be patient--that she resents sexual intercourse.

We next read that this knife phobia was

. . . connected with both suicidal and homicidal tendencies.

Suicide is always a sign of someone not trained in cooperation. Because this type of individual thinks merely of herself, when she faces a social problem for which she is not prepared, she has such a feeling of her own worth and value that she feels sure that, in killing herself, she hurts another person. If you have seen similar cases, then you understand them. Therefore, we can say that suicide represents an accusation and a revenge, an attacking attitude. We must look for the person against whom this phobia is directed. Undoubtedly, it is her husband, with whom, as we have seen, she must be in conflict. He wants to rule and she is interested only in herself, so her revenge, attack, or aggression against somebody must be against the husband. We can guess it, but let us wait to see if we can prove it.

Her aggressive thoughts and feelings toward other people were *shown in other ways.*

We do not know who these "other people" are, but in a way this contradicts our view that she aims her aggression at the husband.

At times, she experienced an impulsive wish to hit her husband.

That is what I said before. As in general medicine, if we have guessed something, we may find proof to confirm it. If we have rapidly diagnosed pneumonia, for instance, we may find signs later that will prove it and which we can predict; when we find such proof, we feel we are on terra firma.

. . . her husband or . . .

We know what must follow: her husband or the children. There is no one else she could accuse. She would not like children. If you asked her: "Do you like children?" she would say, "Yes; my children are my life!" In Individual Psychology, we learn from experience that if we want to understand someone, we have to close our ears. We need merely to look. In this way, we can see as in a pantomime. Perhaps there are other people. Perhaps there is a mother-in-law. It is possible. We would not be astonished. But, as far as we know the situation, we expect the children to follow.

. . . her husband or anybody else who happened to have annoyed her.

Who else can annoy her? We can see this woman is hyper-sensitive, and in general diagnosis, hyper-sensitivity means a feeling of being in a hostile country and attacked from all sides. That is the style of life of the person who does not cooperate and feel at home, who constantly experiences and senses enmity in the environment; therefore, we can understand that she reacts with such strong emotion.

If I felt I were in a hostile country and expected attacks, to be annoyed and humiliated, I would behave in the same way. I would be sensitive too. This is an interesting point. We cannot explain these individuals merely by looking at their emotion; we must look at their mistaken meaning of life and their early childhood. She really believes she lives in a hostile country and expects to be attacked and humiliated. She thinks only of herself and her own salvation, her own superiority in overcoming the difficulties of life. These emotional people must be understood from this point of view. If I believe an abyss is in front of me, whether there is an abyss or not, it is all the same; I suffer from my interpretation, not from reality. If I believe there is a lion in the next room, it is all the same to me whether there is one or not. I shall behave in the same way. Therefore, we must look for the individual's interpretation. It is "I must be safe": a selfish meaning of life.

Now we read:

These characteristics had recently extended in two directions. On one hand, at times she experienced a strong desire to hit any casual stranger she happened to pass in the street.

Is it not as I have described? She lives in a hostile country where everybody is an enemy. To want to hit any stranger she meets in the street means to be impossible, to compromise herself. It means: "I must be watched; someone must take care of me." She forces other people, or one other person, to take care of her. Whether she says it in words or not, she speaks with her attitude in life and forces other people to take care of her when she behaves in this way. But we must also look for the husband's impression. His wife wants to hit every stranger in the street and he lives with her in a social relationship. Therefore, whatever she does affects him. He must do something. What can he do in such a case? We suppose this husband is not a fool or feeble-minded, and we can predict what he has to do. He has to take care of her as far as possible, watch her, accompany her, and so on. She gives him the rules for his behavior in doing so. This ambitious woman, with an ambitious husband, has conquered. He must do what she wants and commands. She behaves in such a way that other people must feel responsible. She exploits him and is the commander; on this point, she rules.

Now let us see more:

On the other hand, she entertained homicidal feelings toward her younger son, a child of four . . .

This we have not seen before, but we have guessed it: that the attacks would be against the children. Here we have the second child specially pointed out, giving us a chance to guess that she wanted to avoid this child, that he was an unwanted child; it finds expression in her fear that she will kill him, that she does not treat him properly. These feelings are sometimes so intense that the husband must watch her. The husband now becomes a slave, and probably this woman imagined long ago that she could make him a prisoner and slave. She would have been satisfied if her husband had submitted in a general way, as husbands sometimes do. But this husband was ambitious; he wanted her to submit, wanted to subjugate her. He has lost and she has conquered. She could not conquer in a usual way, convincing him, or perhaps taking part in all his interests; therefore, she came to a point we can understand. She is right; she acts intelligently. If her goal is to be conqueror, to subjugate her husband, she has acted absolutely correctly. She has accomplished a creative work, a masterpiece of art; we have to admire this woman.

I want to tell you how I handle such cases. I explain in short words. I say: "I admire you; you have created a masterpiece of art. You have conquered." I put it pleasantly.

Now we want to establish a coherence. This woman looks for a fear that she will kill somebody. We have to look for the internal unity. She leans on one point and does not look for others. Other psychologists will say she is surprised, but she is not surprised. I see it clearly. She does not want to see it, because if she did, her remainder of social interest would rise up and contradict it. No person who is not feeble-minded or crazy would agree that she wanted to rule other people in such a way; therefore, she is not permitted to look. But we must make her look, so I prefer to have a pleasant talk and praise her for her cleverness: "You have done correctly."

Then there is the question whether, even before marriage, her goal was to rule everybody. On this point we have to find out whether in childhood she was also "bossy" and wanted to command everybody. If we can prove it as the next step in our understanding, what shall we say of all the skepticism, all the criticism that we do not know anything about this woman and how she was as a child? If we can show that as a child she was "bossy," in what other science can we be so sure that we can postulate something which happened twenty-five or twenty-eight years before? If we ask her for her earliest recollections, I am sure she will tell us something in which we will find a "bossy" attitude, because we will soon grasp the whole style of life of this woman. She is a "bossy" woman who had the handicap of poverty, an ambitious husband, two children very early, and no training in cooperation. She would be defeated in any normal situation, and she is looking for a conquest in a way we could not call socially useful.

Sometimes the idea of killing the boy was so intense that she feared she might carry the intention into execution.

123

The more she was afraid she would execute it, the more her husband must watch her.

She stated that these symptoms had been in existence for one-and-a-half years.

If this is correct, we would be interested to find out what happened one-and-a-half years ago, when this child was two-and-a-half years old. I would understand it better if it had happened before the second child came, but if the symptoms originated one-and-a-half years ago, then we must know what situation the woman was in at that time and what affected her. We will find that she had to offer cooperation and could not; because she was afraid she would be subjugated, she resisted and wanted to conquer. But we must know.

More careful examination, however, seemed to show that definite neurotic traits had been in existence many years, and had been accentuated since marriage. Indeed, she volunteered the information that she "had not been the girl she was since she had been married."

"Since marriage." This is very interesting, because from our general experience we know three situations are like test examinations to show whether a person is socially interested or not: friendship--how to behave with others; occupation--how to be useful in work; and marriage--how to cooperate with a person of the other sex. These are the test examinations for how far a person is prepared for social relationships. If her symptoms have been worse since marriage, this indicates that she was not prepared for marriage because she was too interested in herself.

What of the family history? Many family histories do not say much. We Individual Psychologists are used to hearing of some situations and facts involving the child in a way we can understand, but we reject all descriptions referring only to heredity, such as that an aunt was crazy or a grandmother a drunkard. These do not say anything. They do not contribute to our understanding. We are especially interested in imperfect organs, if we are to grasp a case, because we often find children in a family tree where relatives have suffered in some organs, and we may suspect that the children suffer from lack of strength in those organs; but mostly we do not get much information from these descriptions.

The family history showed signs of neurosis on both sides.

This is valuable because we can see that the family history of the child had been a bad one. Neurotic means that the parents were fighting for things, to boss, to rule, to subjugate others, to utilize and exploit others, so that the children in such an atmosphere are really endangered. On this point, however, I have to say that although they are endangered, we are not sure they really suffer. They can overcome these dangers, find success, and gain some advantage from them. But probability gives us the right to expect that the danger is that the whole make-up and style of life will in some way be selfish.

At the same time, we must remember that the informant on this matter was the patient, whose attitude toward her parents, at least, was not without personal bias.

We want to see what her attitude was. This probably means it was a hostile attitude toward the parents; she has struggled against them.

For example, she felt wronged that both her father and mother were only children. As she pointed out, this meant she had no uncles or aunts and could not receive presents as other children did.

This is a woman who constantly expects presents, thus betraying a good deal of her style of life. She wants to receive, not to give. We understand that this type has many difficulties in life, especially if she meets an ambitious man.

The father was a laborer. The mother was a hard-working woman who did everything to keep the home together. She avoided responsibility, however, in one important particular. If her children needed correction, she preferred to leave that matter to her husband.

This means she did not feel strong enough, and utilized her husband for punishments, as often happens in families. It is bad for the children because they begin to disrespect and ridicule the mother, making a joke out of her because they see her express herself as a weak person who cannot do the right thing.

This fact was unfortunate, since the latter was very sadistic.

I do not think "sadistic" means that he felt sexual satisfaction when he slapped the children, but rather that he was rough and dominating, and subjugated the children. Now we can understand how

125

she has chosen the goal of subjugating others. I have known many cases where the child gets the idea: "When I am grown up, I will do the same with others: rule them and boss them." In his roughness, the father has given this child a goal. What does superiority mean? What does it mean to be the most powerful person in the world? This poor girl, who was always suppressed and mistreated as a child, could have no idea that it is much better to be above and not down, to mistreat others and not be mistreated. Now we see her from this point of view and on this level.

When we learned from his wife that his children had misbehaved in any way, especially with reference to anything that related to money, for instance, if they wore out the soles of their boots quickly, he would beat them almost unmercifully.

On this point, we can learn something in regard to corporal punishment.

The consequence was that the children lived in dread of their father, at the same time that for obvious reasons they did not confide in their mother.

Where should they learn cooperation, if neither from the father nor the mother? Some small degree of cooperation must have been in this girl's mind because she was able to get married. She may have learned it from other children, friends perhaps, but not from her father or mother.

Nevertheless, she maintained that he was a good father, except on Saturday nights, when he frequently came home drunk.

This means that she preferred the father. When I read this, I am impressed with the idea that she was the oldest child. Usually the oldest child, whether boy or girl, turns toward the father. When another child comes, relations with the mother are interrupted and the throne is vacant, which gives the father his chance. But this is only a guess and we have to prove it.

He would then strike his wife as well as his children and openly threaten to cut their throats.

She imitates the father in her compulsion idea: to kill somebody with the knife--child, or husband. Did I not say that the father gave her the chance to form her goal of superiority in this way?

Notice that the father merely cursed; he did not cut the throats of his children. Therefore, I believe I am right in thinking that when she says she could kill somebody, it is just a curse, an idea: "I could kill you!"

This latter point is possibly of interest in view of a similar symptom exhibited by A. Indeed, in many respects her neurotic symptoms tended to imitate her father's characteristics.

The writer, a doctor, goes on to say:

Similar to the father, she was apt to hit her own children without adequate provocation.

We do not agree with this point. She has a provocation. She wants to be superior, as the father wanted to be superior. That is a provocation. "If I want to dominate, I will use my children because they are the weaker ones and cannot hit back."

Though it is true she later regretted her cruelty . . .

Although we often hear about regret and the feeling of guilt, we Individual Psychologists are skeptical in this matter. We do not judge this regret and feeling of guilt very highly. We say it is absolutely empty and useless. After a child is beaten hard, the regret does not matter. It is too much. Either one of these two things would be enough: the regret or the hit, but not both. I would resent it very much if somebody hit me and then regretted it. I have seen the feeling of guilt used as a trick to mask a cruel attitude in bossing others. It means: "I am a noble woman and I regret it." I believe modern society should be warned not to take regret seriously. We often find it among problem children. They commit some act, cry, and ask forgiveness, then do it again. Why? Because if they did not express regret, but only continued doing it, they would be rejected. Nobody could bear it. By making a sort of safety zone where people will not confront them, they feel that they outsmart others. So this woman is cruel and regrets it, but what does that matter? The facts are all the same.

. . . this feeling had little or no power to prevent similar outbursts on a subsequent occasion.

We expected that because the feeling of guilt is often used as a trick in cases of depression. We are not deceived. We guessed correctly.

A. was the second child and girl of a family of eight: four girls followed by four boys.

We know second children generally try much harder, though there are no rules, and we speak only of majorities. They see life like a race, and they want to overcome the first child. The reason I believed she was a first child was that she turned to the father, but in some circumstances the second child may do so, especially if she has been pampered, a third child comes, and she is in a situation which draws her toward him.

We find second children striving to be first, as in the *Bible* story of Jacob and Esau. It is also interesting to see from statistics that among juvenile delinquents in America, second children are in the majority. Individual Psychologists have begun a study of children of one and two years and younger, which can be used for some understanding of their whole style of life. There will be something good or something wrong about second children. It is like a race; they try to overcome the first. Perhaps it was so in this case, but we do not want to say more yet.

As a child, she said, she had been on the whole happy-go-lucky, cheerful, and healthy . . .

If so, she was in the center of the stage and favored. She was perhaps the favorite.

. . . very different from her oldest sister, whom she described as being silent and withdrawn, characteristics which A. interpreted as selfishness.

Surely, it is selfish to be withdrawn because it means to think of oneself. We can see that she was lucky in her striving because the older girl had the aspect of a defeated child who had been overcome. We find this focus on overcoming in A.'s whole make-up. She is easily able to succeed in her goal of being mother and father and of being the boss, because the older sister has given up and been conquered.

The parents seemed to have held a somewhat similar opinion, and treated their oldest child with special severity.

The parents help her in her race by suppressing the oldest child.

She was frequently in trouble, and the severe beatings which she received from her father filled A. with terror.

She was scared because the oldest child had been beaten so severely.

The rest of the family A. regarded with considerable affection, with the exception, significantly enough, of her oldest brother.

That is, the first boy, who when he came was probably worshipped and appreciated in a way she did not like; therefore, we can conclude (though we must really prove it) that her position in the family was endangered by this boy.

As with her sister, so with him, she considered that he was selfish and inconsiderate, "so different from the rest of us, except of course, T." (the oldest sister).

That she agreed with the other children means that she could rule them; they did not make difficulties. This boy and the oldest sister made difficulties, so she did not agree with them.

Medical History: As already mentioned, A. had been a healthy child and prided herself on her robust health. From the age of fourteen to seventeen inclusive, however, she had some degree of goiter from which she subsequently recovered.

We see here a particular imperfection, as we often find among neurotic patients. How far this influenced her we could learn only from the first child, about whom we have little information.

Though she had no return of the trouble, form time to time in the course of treatment she had considerable difficulty in times of stress in getting her breath, a symptom which caused her considerable anxiety.

This symptom was probably not due to pressure of the thyroid, or it would have been recognized and treated. It was most likely a psychological problem; perhaps she could not breathe when she became emotional during the treatment, or when she wished to pretend, or felt she was unjustly treated. All this may have affected her breathing, but it could have been seen clearly if the thyroid was causing pressure.

Her school achievements were quite good and at that time she had no difficulty in making friends.

Do not forget that such people, selfish from the beginning and striving to be in a favorable situation, do not lack all degrees of cooperation. Therefore, we are not surprised that she probably succeeded in the beginning, wanted to be ahead and lead the school, and found it easier to make friends. They may have been friends who were willing to submit to her, but that is a point we could verify in an interview.

She left school at the age of fourteen, but continued to live at home for some months, going from there to daily work which she enjoyed.

In that case she probably had a good job, where she could express her opinion and perhaps also rule others.

But as soon as she entered domestic service away from home, new troubles began.

Domestic service means to submit, and this woman cannot submit. She cannot submit in any way that can be accepted as cooperation. She must rule and here we have new proof. She is not prepared for a situation in which others are ruling. We find many girls who have to do domestic work and cannot submit. For instance, I remember a governess who, when her female employer asked her to clean the parrot's cage, said: "You should ask what I want to do this afternoon, and I will say that I would like to clean the cage of the parrot." Thus, it appeared to be her own idea; she was commanding. You meet the same thing in army training, where the soldier, after he is commanded, must repeat the command in such a way as if it were his own. We can see the wisdom of that procedure.

Within a week of her arrival, she was attacked by such bad carbuncles on her back that the doctor ordered her home again.

I do not go so far as to say that those carbuncles were the result of her dislike, but it is a fact that if a person does not feel well in a particular place, something may happen. My daughter, who is a psychiatrist and has made researches into accidents, found that half of them occur among people who do not like their job. When people hurt themselves at work, it is as though they say: "It is because my father forced me to take this job, and I wanted another job." Half of all the accidents! Therefore, I am quite sure that things like carbuncles can occur if a person does not like a certain situation.

She returned home with considerable trepidation because she knew that her eldest sister, who had once similarly returned because of illness, had had a very bad reception.

She had learned how not to behave.

For a time, however, everything went well. But soon her father became openly dissatisfied at having to keep his daughter "eating her head off" as he put it. Matters came to a climax when, one morning as A. entered the kitchen to have breakfast, her father, without a word of warning, rushed at her with a shovel, obviously intending to hit her over the head.

It was in the morning, so he was not drunk.

She rushed from the house in terror and hid from the family for the rest of the day. It is possibly of significance, in view of her later fear of coffins, undertakers, and all matters relating to the subject of death, that she spent most of this time in the churchyard.

Now a new idea appears. In a way, we can see that this woman's illness and neurotic symptoms are an accusation against the father whether she knows it or not. We are studying the natural history, the biology, of behavior. If we find one bone, such as this neurotic symptom represents, we can relate it to the father. The father is guilty and her symptom is an accusation against him. She might put it in these words: "My father has tortured me so much that it is because of his treatment that I am as I am." The father had been wrong, but does it follow that the daughter must also be wrong? Is it really like cause and effect? Is she forced to be sick and make mistakes because the father made a mistake? This is a very important question because that is what this woman, if we read her correctly, is really saying: that because the father made a mistake, she must also do so. But there is no real causality here, only the causality she has created. She has made something into a reason which is not a reason. I have seen other children who have been tortured by their parents go through this compulsion neurosis. It is not like the causality we find in non-living things; even among non-living things, causality is now beginning to be doubted.

In the evening, she was found by her mother who persuaded her to return home. Her father treated the incident as a joke, laughing at her for "being such a silly." His daughter, however, did not treat the matter so lightly and vowed she would never again return home to live, a resolution she kept for a long time.

Another resolution she had made, as I said before: "I must never be in a situation where another person can rule me." In the childish fashion we always find in neurotic patients, she knows only contradiction and antithesis: to rule or be ruled. Among all the failures in life, and not merely among neurotic individuals, we find that they know only contradiction. They sometimes call it "ambivalence" or "polarity," but they constantly form judgments of contradiction: down, above; good, bad; normal, not normal; and so on. In children and neurotics, and in the old Greek philosophy, we find this looking for contradiction.

In this way, she has vowed never to be ruled.

After this affair, she went once more into domestic service and appears to have worked hard and diligently. However, she showed a preference for rough work. Her dislike for doing "fiddle work," such as dusting, she distinctly stated to be due to her dread of breaking ornaments and so on.

She is a girl of robust health, who values strength and does not like housekeeping. We remember her resentment of the oldest boy because he had been preferred; she probably did not want to be a woman at all. She disliked being occupied with dusting and such little matters. This would explain why she was not prepared to be a married woman. This would be what I have called "the masculine protest." In such a case, if we force a person to do things she does not like, she tries to exaggerate. We see anger, rage, and exaggeration.

This fact is of interest as the possible forerunner of her later openly destructive wishes and feelings. At the age of eighteen she was engaged to a young man whom she appears to have dominated.

We find the writer of this case history has been on the same track as we have, she describes this domineering symptom when she points out that the patient dominated this man.

In time, however, she came to dislike him for what she considered his "stingy ways" and, after two or three years, dramatically broke off the engagement by throwing the ring in his face.

That is not what we expect from a girl; we expect more polite behavior.

She related with pride, however, that he still maintained a somewhat doglike devotion to her, and even at the time she came for treatment still continued to ask after her. In spite of his manifestation of devotion, she never showed any regret about her behavior in the whole matter.

She does not regret because she has no reason to do so.

During the war, she worked in a munitions factory in a provincial town, and there she met the man who is now her husband.

We now remember this man. He is a cripple, and sometimes men and women who want to dominate are fond of cripples and people who are weak in some way, alcoholics whom they want to save, and people of a lower social status than their own. I would warn girls especially, but also men, against choosing in this way because in love or marriage no person can safely be looked down on. They will revolt, as this man revolted.

He was hospitalized at the time, disabled from the war. He fulfilled her ideal of a possible husband in two most important respects: he was tall and he was not an alcoholic.

The father had been strong with his drunkenness, and the reason many people, especially girls, fear alcoholics is that they cannot rule them. They fear alcoholics and creeping things, like mice and insects, because they cannot rule them and can be surprised by them. We understand why she would resent an alcoholic, but why she preferred a tall man we do not know. It may have been the remains of her admiration of her father, or she may have been tall, or have thought it was more worthwhile to rule a tall man than a short one. We could find this out only by asking her.

It is also possible that his injuries appealed to ~~her love of power~~; her wish to ~~assume the dominant role~~ was a notable trait in her character.

The writer has taken the point of view which I explained. We would underline this and say her style of life was characterized by a very domineering, bossy attitude.

For a time all went well. But when her Lance went to London, he then, for reasons best known to himself, wrote letters well calculated to ~~provoke her jealousy~~.

If we understand that she wanted to rule him, to be alone with him and the center of his attention, we know that jealousy is near at hand. She has to avoid being dethroned as she was when the other children came in the family, and when the boy came.

Unhappy and suspicious, A. followed him to London, obtained work as a waitress in a restaurant, and did all in her power to hold onto her Lance.

We see how ~~she strives to keep him~~.

At this point, the attitude of the two lovers toward each other seems to have undergone a change. Not only did the woman assume the more active part in their relationship . . .

Taking the more active part is further proof of her desire to dominate.

. . . but the man, formerly attentive and kindly, now became careless and inconsiderate.

We saw in the beginning that she had forced him to be careful. At this point, we read that he had become careless.

They made appointments for which he either came late, or not at all. A. became suspicious, tearful, and "quite different from her former bright self."

She was afraid of losing her former ruling position.

Matters came to a head when he failed for a second time to keep an appointment with her, after she had waited for him for hours in the cold and fog of a November night.

This is a difficult situation, and undoubtedly the man was also not adapted for such a marriage. Any girl would be right to look on such negligence as an injury. This girl could end no other way than with the creation of a compulsion idea which she could use to conquer him again.

When she learned from him the next day that he had not kept his appointment because he had gone out with some friends, she angrily told him she did not wish to see him again.

She felt defeated. Perhaps we would be glad to get rid of such a partner, but she does not want to be defeated. She wants to keep him.

She did not follow through on breaking off the engagement, however, a fact for which she felt thankful when, three weeks later, she discovered that she was pregnant.

Here is a good chance to speak of sexual relations before marriage. Although it may seem in some cases to be an advantage, I have found that it is primarily a disadvantage and as doctors, we should advise people to wait. It always causes trouble.

She felt desperate about the pregnancy and for the first time had definite suicidal feelings. Her Lance endeavored to comfort her, promising to marry her as soon as possible--which he did three or four weeks later. The question of her residence for the next few months now arose. She dreaded returning home because her father had said he would have nothing to with any of his daughters if they got into trouble. Though his threat proved to be unfounded, and she was allowed by her parents to return home, she felt very unhappy during this time.

Actually, she felt defeated.

depression?

Her misery was accentuated by the birth of a son; both she and her husband had hoped for a daughter.

This is something we would not expect. We would expect them to hope for a son. Why they wanted a daughter could be explained only by these two people. But perhaps if they had had a daughter, the new mother would still have been disappointed.

It may be pointed out in passing that A.'s desire for a daughter and subsequent disappointment were connected with her later hostility toward her sons.

As we cannot verify her statements without asking her, we must assume she disliked the men in her environment: her father, then her brother. Probably, by wanting a daughter and disliking men, she wanted to prove the dramatic contrast between male and female because these neurotic people look on men and women as opposite sexes. You know the widespread notion: the opposite sex. If you exaggerate it, you get antagonism toward the opposite sex, which is often found both in men and women, especially among neurotic individuals.

After the birth, she returned to London to live in two rooms with her husband. However, the situation soon got worse. Initially, she got on well with her neighbors, but soon feelings of inferiority began to assert themselves. These feelings seem to have been connected with jealousy of her husband, who was popular and well-liked generally. She interpreted passing words and looks of those around her as criticisms directed against herself.

She probably looked on the neighbors as subjects she could rule; therefore, good relations never existed.

As a conscious reaction against the sensation that she was despised, she not only avoided making friendships, "keeping herself to herself" as she described it, but she also used to sing hymns in a loud voice to show her neighbors first, that she was not afraid, and second, that she at least had been well brought up. Unfortunately, her criticisms of her neighbors were not without justification, as quarrels and drunken brawls were frequent. In addition, she and her husband found constant cause for disagreement. The methods she employed to gain his sympathy were characteristic. Thus, after a quarrel, she would retire to bed and threaten to kill herself and the child unless the situation improved.

We see how she ~~wanted to use force~~.

So matters continued, going from bad to worse until A.'s neurotic symptoms became so manifest that her husband took her to see a doctor. He diagnosed her condition as nervous indigestion, and recommended that all her teeth should be extracted.

I presume this was meant as a punishment, not as medical treatment!

After some hesitation she decided to take this advice, and with this end in view went to the hospital accompanied by a friend. The latter was then considerably annoyed when A., after an hysterical outburst in front of the doctor and nurses, refused to have her mouth touched.

This suggests that she really understood the situation better than anyone expected.

Naturally, this same friend refused to accompany her a second time to the hospital. Therefore, on the second occasion A. went alone, when it is noteworthy that, though nervous, she was able to have three or four teeth extracted without trouble. On the next occasion, however, matters did not go so smoothly. She had an hysterical outburst following the extraction of twelve teeth, due, she maintained, to the fact that she saw and felt the whole operation although under an anesthetic. The fantastic nature of these "memories" was obvious. In accordance also with her sadistic tendencies, it is hardly surprising that these "remembrances," to which she frequently referred, made a deep impression on her.

Now, imagine this woman: thirty years of age! They extracted, as far as I can count, sixteen teeth! I think a woman who had no "sadistic tendencies" would not look on this fact in a humorous spirit! It makes a deep impression. If you know what it means to a woman or a man to lose the first teeth, you will appreciate that this woman has lost sixteen. And she is jealous of her husband! She explained how she had suffered. I hope I am explaining it correctly, but her "memories" about the operation may have another explanation. This woman ~~likes to explain how much she has suffered~~. She probably had some dreams, as happens in narcosis, so she tells these "memories" to impress others with how she has suffered.

I do not think we should speak of sadistic tendencies in the way that has become common in our time, because they refer to sexual gratification. All forms of attack are not "sadism."

Shortly after this, her second child was born.

We see that it was a time of distress, when she fought hard for her superior position.

The fact that he was a boy caused her great disappointment; she had been quite certain that the infant would be a girl. The impotence of her wishes in the face of reality severely wounded her vanity. From now on, her neurotic tendency became more and more evident. The resentment she felt toward her infant was the obvious prelude to her later consciously felt wish to kill the child.

You will remember that in speaking of the first symptoms and when they occurred, I said I could have understood it if it had been when the second child came, because her importance would weaken and become less since she now has to share with two children, and she wants herself to be the center, not the children. She will feel resentment more strongly, and a desire to kill.

At the same time, a drunken neighbor with a knife in his hand threatened to take her life, giving her a reason for an exacerbation of her symptoms. It also gave her a reasonable excuse for refusing to stay in the house where they were living, although it was impossible to obtain any other room in the neighborhood at the moment.

This house really was not well-suited for a bossy woman. Even the neighbors did not like her. In this case we also find that a paranoid symptom appears; in a way the manner in which this woman behaves is similar to paranoia--as if others would pursue her, be interested in her, and look at her. But even a compulsion neurosis reaches further and touches some symptoms generally described under another title. There are mixtures in this way.

In addition, by this means she was able to leave her husband for a time, she and her children finding a temporary home with her mother-in-law, her husband remaining in London. The arrangement, however, did not prove happy.

The mother-in-law probably did not submit.

This unhappiness was partly because of the critical attitude of the mother-in-law toward her daughter-in-law, and partly because A. felt hostile toward her mother-in-law from the start, owing to the unfavorable comparisons her husband frequently drew between her and his mother.

The usual situation.

By mutual consent, therefore, the arrangement was terminated and A. and her children went to stay with her parents. From there she was recalled to London because her husband had had a "nervous breakdown" in her absence and wanted her to nurse him.

We do not know the husband. Perhaps he also wanted to dominate somebody.

It seems improbable that it was merely a coincidence that at the same time he had been able to find rooms for the family.

He probably used nervous symptoms, wanting to impress her in this way with a "nervous breakdown."

Shortly after her return to London, she was overcome by obsessive thoughts and feelings which gradually came to occupy her attention more and more, to the exclusion of almost everything else. She dated this phase of her illness back to a terrifying dream of angels surrounding a coffin.

This is the thought of death, but we see what it means. It affects the husband. She has a dream of angels surrounding a coffin, so he has to take care of her.

Significantly, she constantly associates this dream with a picture of her old home, at which she frequently gazed when pregnant with her first child.

We understand that at this time she played with the idea of suicide. While looking at the picture, she imagined family members being impressed and fearful at the possibility of her suicide. With this threat, she felt she was "the master of the game."

The rest of the case notes deal with treatment, which is not part of my lecture. I simply wanted to show you the coherence of a life style.

Part 3

The Case of Miss R.[1][2]

The Interpretation of a
Life Story

By Alfred Adler

Translated by
Eleanor and Friedrich Jensen, M.D.

[1929]

---

[1] *Originally titled* Die Technik der Individualpsychologie, Volume 1, Die Kunst, eine Lebens und Krankengeschichte zu lessen. *Published by Bergman, Munich, 1928. Translated into English by Eleanor and Friedrich Jensen and published by Greenberg, Publisher, Inc., New York, 1929.*
[2] Additional editing by Henry T. Stein, Ph.D., 2005.

Translator's Preface

I

Every human problem is a social problem. Every human problem concerns not only one individual, but also the society in which that individual lives. Every person is tied by intangible threads to his community. There exists, or rather, should exist, a mutual give and take between him and the community which lives through him and through which he lives. The community makes possible his early upbringing, his education, and the development of his abilities. The community enables him to live. As a result, he inevitably faces a set of social problems the solution of which is vitally important for establishing his physical and mental balance which, in turn, the community values highly. Out of the infinite number of social problems we can form three main groups: (1) social relationships (attitude toward fellow men, friends); (2) work (occupation or profession in the case of an adult, school in the case of child); (3) sex (love and marriage).

Probably no one has ever solved these great, general problems completely. Such a solution would require perfect objectivity and unbreakable courage, two of the rarest and most precious of human qualities. But a complete solution of these problems is not important. What is important is the honest effort an individual makes to meet and solve his problems, the sincerity with which he tackles them, and the courage with which he faces them. Those who draw back afraid, who make exclusively individual problems out of general social ones to satisfy their secret lust for power, act absolutely against the community, against what Adler terms "social feeling." When that happens, we speak of a neurosis.

This book tells the story of the development of a neurosis. A young girl relates the fascinating story of her unhappy life; the psychologist comments on her remarks, leading the reader to an understanding of the mistakes which have made her life so full of suffering. Dr. Adler originally presented the Individual Psychological interpretation of this autobiography to a group of psychiatrists and educators in Vienna.

Publication of this study in book form makes it available to a larger circle of readers. The interest in Individual Psychology, expressed not only by our professional contemporaries, but by the general public as well, is steadily growing and the radius of its influence is increasing from day to day. Yet many who have heard of this great intellectual movement are not familiar with it; and not all those who will want to read this book will be sufficiently familiar with the system of Individual Psychology to be able to follow its contents with full understanding. With the intention of submitting this extraordinary life story to as extensive a circle of readers as possible, I give a concise survey of the theory and practice of Individual Psychology for those who have little or no acquaintance with it.

The theoretical system of Individual Psychology was founded by the Viennese psychiatrist, Dr. Alfred Adler. Adler's conception of the structure and function of the mind in relation to the body, of the striving of all psychic expressions and activities toward a goal, and of the mutual relationship between the individual psyche and the community is so illuminating and clarifying that it has quickly brought his ideas to the forefront of modern psychology.

Adler proceeds from the fact that bodily defects should not only be considered as signs of physical weakness, but also frequently lead to attempts at compensation and overcompensation. As soon as there is a physical disturbance, the body attempts to compensate for it. Since every bodily disturbance makes an impression on the mind, a mental striving occurs concurrently with the compensatory efforts of the body, with the aim of overcoming or, at least, making up for this defect in some way. For instance, the body may not be able to make a physical compensation for defective vision, but there may be a mental compensation in the form of greater clarity in thought or improved inner visualization (that is, recapturing with greater accuracy the details of things seen). The bodily defect, recording itself on the psyche as well, may direct the mind to an interest in the visible side of life, as it were; just as a defective ear may increase interest in and perfect the comprehension of sound. This would be a mental or psychic compensation. If there is no possibility of compensating for the physical defects by physical means, there still remains a purely psychical compensation in the form of greater clarity of thought, or an ability to recapture the outer world in correct detail before one's inner eye. This can frequently be observed among those whose vision has become weak. In most cases, however, a bodily as well as mental compensation takes place.

The biological law of compensation, as a phenomenon of all living matter, plays just as important a role on purely psychical as on physical ground. It is the power behind psychic preservation and development; the propelling force of the power is life itself.

Adler has termed such defects "organ inferiorities." According to him, every inferiority produces an urge for improvement, for an adjustment to the demands of the environment which will compensate for the inferiority. However, some inferiorities found in a healthy body and normal mind arise solely because of a particular body and mind are comparatively less developed than the majority of human beings. Every child faces this situation in early life.

Because of his limited abilities, every healthy child feels inferior, consciously or unconsciously, in a world of gigantic and apparently self-sufficient adults. This relative feeling of inferiority is compensated under favorable conditions by a striving for recognition on the "useful side of life." The feeling of inferiority or insecurity, like every unpleasant feeling, requires a quick, compensatory balancing. A feeling of superiority or security obviously compensates for a feeling of inferiority. The child learns this process by experience, gradually establishing a fixed, but fictive goal of superiority or security which, according to his own unconscious interpretation or evaluation of his position and faculties, lies more or less close to reality.

We must not assume that the child thinks of such a goal in conscious, logical terms as we do when we race to win a prize or struggle to attain distinction. In only a fraction of cases is the goal ever verbalized in a childish way by expressing the wish to become like the father, or a king or a policeman, which in the child's world, are always dominating positions. We can merely draw the conclusion from the child's actions that he is striving for a perfection which will compensate for his inferiorities. He may never have spoken of these inferiorities and may not even be conscious of them, but he feels them as surely as we can observe them through the mechanism he sets up to compensate for them. Conscious inferiority thoughts are on an entirely different level from the unconscious feeling of inferiority, and serve an entirely different purpose.

When this feeling of inferiority is aroused, he begins to train for the attainment of his fictive goal by employing his psychic qualities, such as sensitivity, volition, perception, memory, and so on, as useful instruments, and develops them in conformity with his interpretation of his situation. The sum total of all forms of an individual's expression is called his character; his method of approaching his personal goal of superiority when confronted with life's tasks is termed his style of life. When we discover the goal of an individual, we are then able to understand his character and style of life, and modify them.

The most satisfactory compensation for the feeling of inferiority is the development of courage, common sense, and social feeling. An individual compensating satisfactorily approaches life in a sincere and fearless manner, tries to solve his problems and accomplish his tasks as they come along, and adapts himself to the community in which he lives.

He trains in an upward direction, toward a superiority concerned with progress, improvement, adjustment to the world, in short, with useful things. Adler calls this "the striving on the useful side of life." What is useful? The shortest definition I can frame is: Everything is useful that promotes life; everything is useless that inhibits life. However, life is not only the living of a single individual; life means the living of all with whom an individual comes in contact, physically and mentally. Striving for useful superiority, that is, for the promotion of life, therefore, means the promotion of all living things or, in other words, the development of social feeling. Just as courage grows out of the successful accomplishment of tasks, social feeling grows out of devotion to others, assisting others, out of firm belief in and appreciation of others. An attitude so oriented cannot be egocentric; it simply has to be other-centered and task-centered. In approaching the great problems of life: work, social relationships, and love, we develop common sense, courage, and social feeling..

However, if the child has a heavier burden to bear as a result of physical defects ("organ inferiorities") or unfavorable social and environmental circumstances, the normal, relative inferiority feeling increases to an absolute one. Again compensation sets in, this time, however, the longer and more deeply the child senses the feeling of inferiority, the greater the drive toward compensation. The visible result of this compensation is an increasingly intense striving for that feeling believed by the individual to be the only sure remedy for the inferiority sting. Such a person will either accomplish something extraordinary, provided he has sufficient courage to direct his intense drive into useful channels (great artists, scientists, and explorers); or he will accomplish little or nothing, by avoiding in a cowardly fashion the difficult road of a useful striving for recognition, and choosing the seemingly easier path to power at any price. These individuals strive with all their might for the illusion of superiority, for triumphs over and the suppression of their fellow human beings because of purely egocentric reasons, in order to elevate their own shattered self-esteem, regardless of how much pain and trouble their antisocial behavior costs them. If all the energy and skill spent in attaining that sort of goal were employed in useful ways, neurotic individuals would achieve far beyond the average of their more courageous and more social contemporaries.

In an organized civilization, an attempt to overcome all assumed competitors by a fictitious superiority has to fail, except perhaps in the small, restricted circle of a family. Thus, its results are uselessness in a generally social sense, and instead of the development of courage, common sense, and social feeling, a constantly increasing discouragement, egocentricity, and asocial or antisocial feelings (criminals) accompanied by feelings of inadequacy, insufficiency, dissatisfaction, and disgust. The futility of all neurotic efforts to master the world in which we live, without appropriate justification, induces such individuals to retreat farther and farther until they reach the vast region where responsibility for their activities is no longer required: the region of disease.

The sick are exempted from duties; they are irresponsible, especially when they are considered mentally ill. To use the cloak of disease as a means to attain one's goal is a dangerous deception, for the patient himself, who does it unconsciously, as well as for everyone who is deceived by it.

This evasion and deception characterizes all neuroses (including nervous breakdowns, neurasthenia, hysteria, delinquency, perversions, addiction to drugs, etc.) and psychoses. Individual Psychology offers understanding, prevention, and treatment of all these neurotic and psychotic conditions. No one is compelled to follow one road or the other. According to Adler, it is unnecessary to believe in inherited character traits. Everyone can achieve everything necessary in life, including his own misfortune. For the neurotic, disease is nothing but the price which the cowardly, asocial egotist has to pay for offending the "logic of life."

II

To make more easily comprehensible the neurotic life scheme and the particular form of nervous disorder discussed in this book, Adler's conceptions of the construction of neuroses in general will be delineated in somewhat more detail in the following paragraphs. What happens in a nervous disorder?

The feeling of inferiority, when compensation takes a neurotic direction, drives the patient to achieve as absolute a domination as possible over his surroundings. The disorder with all its arrangements serves different purposes: (1) to be used as an alibi for evading the problems of life and as an excuse for refusing to assume responsibility; (2) to serve as a cloak when life withholds the desired triumphs; (3) to be able to postpone decisions; and (4) to emphasize achieved ambition because it has been attained despite the disorder.

The neurotic thus has the fictive goal to strive for in order to safeguard his ostensible superiority. His actions are directed from this point and maintain a typical pattern. The compulsion to achieve superiority is so powerful that every psychic phenomenon constitutes,

146

aside from its outward appearance, an attempt to get rid of the feeling of weakness or inadequacy, to rise from below to above. In order to create the desired arrangement and safety from defeat in overcautiously preparing to experience and comprehend the world's events, the neurotic uses a number of rules and formulas in life which, in accordance with his infantile attitude, form a primitive, antithetical "private logic." He perceives only those qualities which correspond to the "below" and "above" in his scheme, and usually tries to relate these qualities to the more easily comprehensible contrast of masculine-feminine. He endeavors to force violently onto a masculine track traits in his character condemned as feminine, such as obedience, cowardice, tenderheartedness, passive behavior, and all sorts of incapacities. He develops hate, cruelty, stubbornness, egotism and other tendencies which are supposed to secure him triumphs ("masculine protest"). This is an aggressive protest, but the aggression may also be expressed by passive means when the neurotic attempts to conquer by his weakness, forcing his environment to be subservient to him. Moreover, this strategy enables him to escape dreaded decisions with ostensibly sufficient reasons.

When an individual feels that the development of "masculine" qualities in life is necessary but impossible for him, he will avoid the struggles and problems of life, fearing he may be accused of appearing "feminine." "In such a case, we find a striving that deviates from the direct road and, because of constant fear of mistakes and defeat, tries to make safe detours." (Adler)

Neurotic purposiveness is based on two unconscious premises: (1) all human relationships are struggles for supremacy; (2) the female sex is subordinate and inferior, its weakness serving as a measure of masculine strength. These two premises can be found in men as well as in women and distort all human relationships. Useful communication is replaced by constant dissatisfaction. The neurotic symptom represents the excessive greed for superiority; it produces a semblance of victory over the environment. According to Adler, to understand the language of symptoms is one of the chief tasks of psychotherapy.

The neurotic's style of life and the arrangement of his particular neurosis are closely connected. The feeling of inferiority, arising from actual facts, then inflated and later maintained, drives the patient to set his goal in early childhood far beyond all human proportions. In order to establish this goal, he surrounds himself with a wide net of precautions in order to maintain his superiority. In a case of washing compulsion, the goal in view is to be the cleanest human being on earth, an entirely useless enterprise, of course. What really happens is that this extraordinarily clean person neglects the simplest duties of life (including cleanliness), avoids responsibilities, exerts pressure on others, retreats from reality with many excuses, but still retains an illusion of superiority ("No one is as immaculately clean as I am ...")--at least in the small circle of the family.

The neurotic scheme of life is rigid and compulsive, and can be traced only when we succeed in comprehending the general goals of the patient. For example, somebody will use a fear of leaving his house (agoraphobia) in order to raise his own prestige in his family and so force his environment to obey him, by unconsciously connecting the thought of being left alone or going out alone, with fear-producing images of personal misfortunes or accidents to others. Every possible defeat is anticipated and exaggerated by connecting it with thoughts of death, illness, or all sorts of mischief. Thus, the neurotic manages to escape a useful life by establishing pessimistic trains of thought.

On the other hand, the neurotic frequently displays extreme expectations. Followed by just as extreme disappointments, these expectations are designed to justify the patient in producing all kinds of demonstrative emotions, such as hate, grief, sullenness, etc. Disappointed expectations are most frequently seen in cases where the patient wants to avoid his sexual problems. Some men, to use a frequent example, divide all women into two classes: madonnas and prostitutes (private logic). The madonnas are unattainably high, the prostitutes despicably low. If such a man becomes acquainted with one of the unattainably high madonnas, his illusions are soon demolished since women are human beings and not madonnas. The disappointment, following such an unwarranted assumption, proves him ostensibly right and permits him merely to keep on wishing. "As long as someone merely wishes, nothing is going to happen," says Adler.

Someone may take the greatest pains imaginable to attain the alleged goal of his wishes. That is his justification. But since he is a victim of his subconscious, fictive goal of superiority, the arrangements he makes to approach the rational goal of normal sexual relations will prove impossible for that purpose, for these arrangements really tend to preserve the fictitious goal of superiority. Normal love relationships, however, are impossible as long as one person believes he must be or is superior or inferior to another. Thus, he is excused and his unconscious goal of superiority is not endangered. Adler has illustrated the neurotic contradiction in the following way: The pretense of desiring a normal goal is expressed by a patient's saying "Yes," the actual goal expressed by an excusing "But." The sequence of "yes-but" typifies the pattern of the neurotic. Example: A man wants to marry, but he does not find a girl. He tries to meet the "right" girl, but does not succeed. That is possible, for a while at least. However, for twenty years he does not succeed in finding a woman to marry, and is "safe." Adler calls the "yes-but" attitude the shortest and most cogent definition of a neurosis.

A third means of escaping defeat and inferiority feelings consists of anticipatory sensations, emotions, and perceptions, ominous "identifications which, in relation to dangerous situations, have a preparing, warning or stimulating effect and which occur in dreams and all forms of neurotic delusions" (Adler). The girl in this book anticipates in graphic fashion a whole string of misfortunes in order to escape the dreaded problems of life and to maintain her dominating position in an imprudent pampering family, no matter how high the price of suffering was for all concerned.

Psychic treatment, therefore, has three essential tasks: (1) the disclosure of the neurotic system or style of life; (2) gradual encouragement in facing reality; and (3) redirecting toward useful goals in social life as described above. The success of the treatment depends as well on the cooperation and sincere efforts of the patient. The tendency to assume the role of the superior induces him to try to defeat his physician at every opportunity. In order not to have to change his goal, the neurotic will do everything possible to forestall a cure by arranging disturbing emotions, falling in love with the physician, or exhibiting a hostile attitude toward him. The physician has to continually investigate and explain the arrangements and constructions of the neurotic style of life until the patient, his position made untenable, gives them up. Frequently, to be sure, he substitutes new mechanisms, still better concealed. Step by step, the patient's unattainably high goal and its purposive, constraining consequences have to be unveiled. The sincere, sensible, and courageous attempt to approach the three main problems (social relationships, work, and love) leads to a useful, harmonious life.

Chapter I

Early Childhood

We usually learn from books, whether we want to or not. At least we hope to discover in them some answer to our own questions and some solution to our own difficulties. This is especially true when we pick up a book about the problems of our psychic life. What other purpose can the study of psychology have if it does not give us some practical help with our difficulties, or at least make it possible to help ourselves?

In this book I attempt to give the reader an insight into the principles and techniques of Individual Psychology. This art of treating the human mind is demonstrable and open to everyone who believes in the connective unity of human life. We must know the handwriting symbols of our speech in order to read the language we speak. Just as with this knowledge we can read an otherwise strange language, so must we know the symbols of the soul in order to read a life.

We often read biographies; many are filled with dramatic and exciting life stories. Most of them concern individuals whose life or achievement was in some way unusual or dramatic. The activity of the individual or the literary form usually makes the biography interesting. Here I take a life story, vivid and colorful, nevertheless the story of a girl of ordinary station and no particular accomplishment. I believe this story will illustrate that the psychological side of biography may well be the most fascinating.

The art of Individual Psychology is based on knowledge and common sense. Only to those laboring under psychological prejudices will it appear odd or tricky. In this book I proceed as I do in my office when I listen to a patient's story for the first time. The comments on the story are based on no more knowledge of the facts than are available to the reader. With intention, I proceed extemporaneously and tell the story as it was given to me, reading it for the first time as I give my interpretation. With every sentence, with every word of the patient, I consider: What is the real meaning of what she is saying? What is her attitude toward life? What do her words mean in light of her deeds? How does she meet the demands life makes of her? How does she behave toward her fellow human beings? How does she perform her duties (or fail to perform them)? Does she move toward reality or illusion?

Provided with the limited information of this story, the gaps in which we gradually fill from our own experiences, we observe this girl endeavoring to achieve a complete expression of her personality and to master the problems of living. We go back to early childhood because I believe the development of a human being is largely determined in the first four or five years.

I now begin the story of Miss R. It is as unknown to me as it is to you, and I comment as I read.

I remember that father frequently asked me . . .

It is worthwhile inquiring: Why not the mother? "Father" has a special significance. This child, a girl, was much more strongly attached to her father than to her mother. What does that mean? Because the child prefers her father, we can conclude that he must be a tender-hearted man. A child is first attached to her mother. That is natural and easily understood. The mother represents to the child her first connection with the world. The mother helps her and usually pampers her. The second phase begins later when the child has become somewhat more independent. She seeks to attach herself to those who treat her best; that is to say, she either remains attached to her mother or turns to others. Here the mother had started to pamper the child, but apparently could not compete with the father in the child's attention.

Do you feel well? Does anything hurt you?

The girl begins her story with a childhood remembrance. Psychological experience has shown us that childhood remembrances are not as meaningless as we had formerly supposed. From the endless store of childhood memories each of us has, only a few are carried over to maturity, emphasizing the importance of these remembered impressions. So when an adult tells us of an early remembrance which is particularly clear to him (it matters little whether it is the first), we are able to interpret from it the speaker's personal attitude toward life. This is, in essence, the attitude he has retained up to the moment of telling, even if that is twenty, thirty, or forty years later. If his attitude toward life changes with time, the childhood memories which occur to him before and after such a change will differ.

A concrete example may clarify this point. Suppose you are in a strange city for the first time and are being taken over a long road from the train station to the house of your host. Of course, you will see a great many things on the way. On arriving home, you are asked what you remember and you may answer: a monument in the park, some flowers in a window, a delicatessen store, a horse being whipped, the shrill whistle of a factory, the severe jolting of the taxi and so on. But because you were being led and at the same time had confidence in your leader, you would pay little attention to the route. On the other hand, were you alone in the city and forced to find your own way on foot, you would notice landmarks, guides, and direction and be able to describe in exact detail the way you had come.

A child is alone in a strange city depending for guidance on his mother, father, or whoever the preferred person is. He will remember only those things which make a sharp impression because they fit into an already established scheme of perception or attitude toward life.

Therefore, we endeavor to draw some conclusions from the early remembrances of this girl. These conclusions are further corroborated in that the girl thought the facts of sufficient importance to put them at the beginning of her story.

Her father must have been an extraordinarily soft, weak man, and the girl must have been a very spoiled child. We infer that this girl will always see to it that she is pampered. She will want to be the center of attention, constantly trying to draw everyone's focus to herself. Difficulties arise as soon as such a child comes in contact with other people who do not give her the same attention she receives from the person who pampers her. In such a case we find a strong tendency to reject, an aversion to strangers, a critical attitude toward and lack of interest in others, and a reluctance to adjust to new situations. This pampering may be based on her father's nature, or she may be in an exceptional position. She is either an only child, growing up under especially unfavorable circumstances, or she may be the only girl among boys, or the youngest child. One of her organs may be deficient in functioning.

I never felt quite well.

We cannot accept literally the statements of our patients. Such statements must not influence us as they influence the patients themselves. What this girl means to say is: I was a sickly child.

I always had some temperature . . .

That is hard to believe.

. . . and my hands were so hot and dry that I had to moisten them with my tongue.

We know there are better ways of moistening the hands; moreover, in a case of fever the tongue is also dry. She may have used her tongue to moisten her hands for quite another purpose than the one she mentions. We can frequently observe children using their tongues for purposes which those around them disapprove of. Her father probably did not like it and the girl has thus drawn her father's attention to herself. We are therefore able to note another trait: The girl has a strong inclination to secure and strengthen her central position by misbehaving.

My father told me later that my life had hung by a thread.

Many healthy people have been told this. At one time, I was also told that my life "hung by a thread." Later, I saw this was not true. In most cases such a remark is an exaggeration which serves to make the speaker or writer more important. He who feels it necessary to exaggerate must feel inferior. The girl does not tell what ailed her. We learn merely that she was a fragile child who did not eat very well, but apparently only because she had been spoiled. We know the practice among children of refusing to eat; it serves the purpose of drawing attention to themselves.

I never had any appetite, never liked to eat anything. I could not stand the taste of food and I chewed the morsels as if they were paper or grass. I remember vaguely that my parents complained about me to our physician. The only thing that had any taste was mother's milk; I am said to have fought desperately every attempt to wean me.

She writes extremely well.

Thus I remained a nursing infant for an extraordinarily long time, in fact, for five years.

That is quite improbable. But even if it were for only two years, we can assume this girl was deeply attached to her mother. This confirms our previous statement; namely, that the attachment to her father represents the second phase. Perhaps incorrect treatment in the child's infancy was one of the reasons for withdrawing from her mother. It is a tragedy for a child as old as two to need weaning.

I can still see my mother's beautiful white breast in front of me.

It is not so certain that the child has remembered this; someone can form such images subsequently. Again we have to bear in mind that such an image serves certain purposes which seem to have nothing to do with the image. We have found up to the present that this girl has been spoiled and, as a consequence, makes other people serve her. Her interest is directed toward the devotion of others to herself. It is painful to her to have to relinquish her mother's breast since much tenderness and attention accompany such an easy method of nourishment. This girl still thinks there was nothing wrong with her upbringing.

I felt ashamed. When we had visitors, I used to whisper in mother's ear, "Come, let me drink." Then she had to seat herself where no one could see us.

The child therefore knew that it was a disgrace.

When mother went to visit the relatives of her dead first husband, she did not know what to do with me. My older sister was willing to take me on her breast, but I said: "It is not the same as when mother takes me. You are blond and mother is dark. I don't like blond hair."

We can observe from this remark what trifles and superficialities play a part in preference for or rejection of a person. Someone is agreeable to us because he has eyes like one of our friends; another we spurn because he speaks like a teacher whom we hated. We like a girl because her hair is the same color, her complexion or her figure the same as our mother's. Often we do not know by what delicate, undetectable mechanisms our sympathies are aroused. Even those persons whom we select to love and marry have, in many cases, appealed to us so strongly merely because they seem to bear a superficial, usually physical resemblance to the former recipient of our affection. In such cases, the connection can remain completely obscured, and usually does.

As we now know, this girl was very much attached to her mother in early childhood and stresses distinguishing characteristics which are of no importance to us.

I myself had dark hair.

She speaks about hair for the second time. She places an odd emphasis on hair.

My father had my hair cut low on my forehead. At that time I wore a blue cape with red lining and I wanted to have a hat. Every time we passed a store, I cried, "Hat! Cape!"

Vanity and a great penchant for externals developed early. There was a strong emphasis on beauty.

They could not get me away from the stores. Finally, my mother had to make a detour around those shop windows.

The child has an influence over her mother strong enough to compel her to use tricks.

Before mother took me out, she would ask my father what dress she should put on me.

The mother is likewise interested in the child's appearance; we can easily understand how vanity is instilled in the girl.

I was very happy about my first shoes; they were hardly put on my feet when I opened the door and tried to run away with them.

That is an attempt to ensure their possession. Her father is a tailor; the whole family is prone to appreciate the external. This is therefore not an inherited trait, but part of the atmosphere of the house.

There were many buttons in the house; I played games with them which I invented myself. They were my money.

The child is prematurely interested in work and money.

Furthermore, I liked to play with silk pads. I used to cut holes in them through which I put the arms of my doll.

Preparation for the occupation of dressmaking.

I liked still more to play with a beer bottle.

We know that children would rather employ their own fantasy than play with mechanical toys. The child learns by imitation. However, she can do that only when she identifies herself with others, when she plays a role which she has assumed from her father and mother. She imitates her father when she patterns a dress.

I rummaged in the drawers, busying with locks.

The child has had great freedom in playing with what she wanted.

My favorite occupation was talking to myself. I could imitate somebody for hours.

She imitates tailoring and talking. For a child who trains at an early age to identify with others or with a role, a logical profession is that of an actress. Many people are unconsciously prepared for certain professions which they never choose because they do not know anything about their early preparation.

I also imitated the baker. My bakery shop was a drawer with remains of bread which I took to bed with me at night.

Intense desire to imitate; the child wants to be a baker even at night when she should be asleep.

Later on I played teacher, using eyeglasses just as my teacher did in school. I cut glasses for myself from red paper. Father's catalogues and notebooks represented schoolbooks and the backrest of the sofa was the blackboard.

We see the stage of Shakespeare.

I threatened the disobedient children and shouted so loudly that my father told me not to get so excited.

Another method of securing her father's attention.

I played merchant with the coffee grinder.

Imagination and imitation strongly developed.

156

There were two people in our house who sold coal. I piled up wood in their store and sometimes ate dinner with them. The food I ate there I would not have touched at home; for instance, sauerkraut, and meatballs. But at their house, I liked to eat everything.

Refusing to eat is an attempt to draw attention to oneself by protesting against an ostensibly important function. When one is hungry, one eats again. As soon as a child notices that she can secure no attention through such useless maneuvers and that she harms only herself in not receiving any attention, she will abandon this trick.

The coal dealer asked me whom I wanted to marry. I always answered, "My father."

This might be thought an incestuous wish. When we consider, however, that this child does not know anything about sexual relations, it is highly probable that the girl's desire to marry her father is possible only because her relationship with him is completely asexual.

I loved my father very much. I was even jealous of him.

If jealousy were always an expression of sexual love, then we would be wrong. But a type of jealousy exists that originates in a striving for power. It is quite possible that all jealousy really springs from a striving for superiority. Someone can be jealous only if he feels inferior to the one of whom he is jealous -- weaker, less intelligent, insufficient. He believes that his abilities and mentality are not adequate to compete honestly with a rival, so he attempts to exert pressure through jealousy; that is to say, to demonstrate his power. The fact that we find jealousy so frequently in love relationships does not justify its being viewed exclusively as an expression of sexual love. Jealousy is often a matter of prestige.

When my mother caressed my father, I frequently interfered, stroked his hair, rolled up his shirt sleeves, and kissed his arms.

I do not believe that this is an expression of sexual love. Any explanation based on sexuality is false.

When I was naughty, my mother would threaten to order a brother or sister from the stork, and I would cry, "I'll throw him out."

Here the jealousy caused by a ~~striving for superiority~~ is plainly evident.

I held the storks in great respect, although I could not understand how they brought the babies. I heard later on in school that babies came out of the belly. How they started, I did not know. I thought we simply ordered them when we married.

The girl has not the slightest idea about the origin of human beings.

When father traveled, he always brought me a present, a toy or a book. Then he took me on his lap and read to me. After twenty-one years, I can remember how my father read to me. I impressed the words on my memory. When I noticed that people read in the café, I took my book with me and memorized the paragraphs aloud. Two women wondered how such a little child could read. Father sent postcards; I always received two and they were always prettier than the others. However, I could not rest until everyone had given me his or her card.

She ~~wants to have everything~~, a phenomenon of the increased inferiority feeling.

Because of my sickly constitution, ~~everybody was submissive to~~ me.

This girl will put her sickliness into the service of her striving for superiority by the way she behaves.

I was sick very often, suffering frequently from tonsillitis.

She will "make a mountain out of a molehill."

I remember being brought to the children's hospital. I disliked having someone look into my throat and I was afraid of the tongue depressor.

There is a tendency to reject the doctor. The pampered child is anxious to be an object of pity.

I was afraid I would suffocate.

We can imagine how this girl will behave in later life.

Chapter II

Adolescent Difficulties

For one year I had whooping cough. For the first six months it grew steadily worse and it was a year before I was over it.

Whooping cough does not last twelve months. When no lung complications or other illnesses set in afterward, whooping cough is over in three to four months at the most. Since no mention is made of such complications, the only conclusion to be drawn is that the child voluntarily retained the symptoms of whooping cough for her own purposes. What could be the reason? Sick people demand and usually receive much more attention, care and tenderness than those who are healthy. Sick people are helpless, in need of protection, and nursing. It does not matter what their age is; they often act like children again.

As we know, the small child lives an egotistically happy existence, without responsibility, and at the cost of his fellow human beings. We might believe this condition desirable for everybody. That is not the case, or we would probably all be sick, or pretend to be. The normal human being is much too attracted by diverse interests and pleasures to like being taken care of and ordered about longer than necessary. On the other hand, some individuals anticipate great difficulties in life and consequently do not develop themselves from healthy human beings to useful ones. Such people frequently regard illness as a suitable means to achieve without effort the semblance of superiority. This use of illness represents ruling through weakness. These people obviously feel inadequate or too weak to compete with their healthy fellow creatures. (Individuals with inferiority feelings tend to look at life as a fight in which they must always be ahead of the others.) Driven by this feeling of inferiority or insufficiency in comparison to others, they seek a way out which will procure for them the triumph of being first, at least in the small circle of their intimates. They seize upon sickness as a welcome means to attain such tinsel triumphs. While they are training their symptoms, they are also training for an ostensible superiority. That goes on until they find the cost of their cowardly attitude becoming too high, and they simply discard their symptoms. Frequently the termination of one symptom is merely the signal for the acquisition of a new one. Or they have arrived at the point where, hopelessly lost in the mazes of their various strivings and completely discouraged, they appear before the doctor.

Even if we knew nothing else about this girl, we might infer from the assertion that the whooping cough lasted twelve months that she felt sufficiently inferior to drag out a sickness as long as she could. We understand this girl's inferiority feeling very well since we learned from some former remarks that she had been badly spoiled. Pampered children always suffer from a strong feeling of inferiority because they grow up like hot-house plants, therefore dreading the raw reality of life as soon as they encounter it. But not only that. In order to retain their favorable position of security, they will purposely exaggerate the harshness and difficulties of life and thereby lessen their courage. Their feeling of inferiority, the result of a wrong interpretation, becomes absolute and the urge to rule, as compensation for the inferiority sting, intensifies in direct ratio to the deepening feeling of inferiority. Thus the deplorable retreat of the neurotic develops out of cowardice and excessive lust for power.

One night I had such a choking fit that I wanted to climb out of the window in my stupor.

Exaggeration.

I was so weak that I could hardly walk; I was brought into the open air in a wheelchair. The people avoided me.

A pampered child does not care about that.

The children were hurried away from me.

Children are typically removed from such a sight.

Since the doctor had recommended humid air, we made excursions to the old Danube. I often vomited when coughing. After each fit, I fell back in my chair, as if dead.

The pampered child seizes every opportunity to make a strong impression with her coughing spells. The more the child is pampered, the more severe the disease seems to be. The child does not want to give up her whooping cough.

At times I heard my father say that he would commit suicide if anything were to happen to me.

Her father is a dreamer. This girl knows that her father has a great affection for her. She is conscious of her power over him.

His eyes were always resting on me with an expression of sorrow. At night my father also washed me.

The spoiled child does not do anything herself. Everyone around her is employed.

I was afraid of water and always struggled against being washed.

That is not innate. This child makes herself important with everything. Washing becomes a rite. She shows her father that he has to make an effort with her.

The worst was cutting my toe nails.

The same tendency as refusing to eat. Children who make trouble are spoiled children.

Then I started to whine as if my toes were being cut off. I also hated having my hair washed.

All children act alike when something does not suit them or when they face situations that are strange or disagreeable to them. They brush them aside; they revolt. Either they ridicule the new situation or struggle against it. Many even have temper tantrums. The supposition that such bad behavior lies hidden in the collective unconscious of mankind (Jung) is quite unnecessary. Just as superfluous is Freud's assumption that conduct deviations prove that the development of mankind is repeated in every single human being.

When Lina (my sister) washed her feet, I crept to her on all fours and lifted her skirts to see what was beneath them.

Early sexual curiosity.

*From the time I outgrew the baby carriage, I slept in my parents'
bed. I went to bed every night in the following way:*

A spoiled child makes trouble when going to sleep, especially
when she is no longer attached to the mother. Going to bed is
painstakingly described.

*First my father had to take me in his arms, dance around with me
and sing a song which ran: "None of the fairies is as pretty and fine as
you, dear little darling of mine."*

Her father appreciates her prettiness.

*He had to shake the pillows, arrange them correctly, and cover
me.*

Pampered child.

*I lay beside my mother; when she was away, I lay beside Father.
He gave me a little bell like one used on Christmas Eve so that I could
ring it when I wanted my mother. I rang the little bell, Father turned on
the light, Lina rushed to my bed. Then I fell asleep again.*

The anxiety that children have during the night is called pavor
nocturnus. This anxiety is a purposeful symptom, like the ringing of the
little bell her father gave her. What happens when the bell tinkles?
Her devotees are awakened and must hurry to her side. She
assures herself of the attention and obedience of her servants. Feeling
her power and satisfied, she falls asleep again. A child neglects certain
functions (such as that which leads to bed-wetting) to attract attention.
Attention-getting behavior like selective neglect or ringing the little bell
is continued as long as its real purpose has not been detected.
Psychoanalysts regard pavor nocturnus as the result of a child's
having witnessed sexual intercourse between his parents. That is
ridiculous.
The anxiety state appears in many forms of varying severity.
Often it is merely a slight disturbance in sleep, sometimes a paroxysm of
fear, according to the strength of the child's striving for superiority. The
intensity of the symptom's manifestation is irrelevant. What matters is
that the symptom always follows the same rigid scheme: to attract notice
by disturbing others.

We had two boarders. One of them was a Hungarian barber by the name of Nagy. He limped. I was afraid of him. He wanted to hug me, but I ran away and hid myself.

She shows an ~~early instilled fear of physical defects~~. That is understandable considering that she has attached herself to one person. Such a fear is sometimes nourished by the environment. Parents frequently pull their children away from the sight of a beggar. Thus, they create fear and aversion instead of sympathy. Our civilization is cruel.

One day I was sitting on the couch with my doll. The barber came into the room and stroked me. I became frightened, fell down and remained as stiff as if I were having a titanic fit. Father and Lina were in agony.

She seems to have fainted which becomes understandable when we remember that the girl resents every person except her father, especially if the other person looks strange. I knew a child, a year and a half old, who cried bitterly when he saw a homely or poorly dressed person. In this case not only is the overestimation of beauty a factor, but also the unaccustomed sight of a disability. Spoiled children are more prone to be upset by abnormalities.

Once in a while, a man with a clubfoot came to the café where we sat. I trembled, tried to hide myself, and buried my face in my father's lap. Sometimes he had to take me home.

Always making trouble. While the parents sit quietly in a café, this girl gives them something to do. She forces them to go away with her.

Every now and then we visited a restaurant where a military band played. As soon as the conductor raised his baton and the music suddenly began, I got a shock. My father had to leave the restaurant with me.

She keeps her father busy with her. It is the same pattern. We can gather something else from these examples. Her memories are primarily visual impressions. She mentions once or twice remembering audible impressions when she tells how her father had to sing to her, and again in her last remark about the military band. She probably belongs to the visual as well as the auditory type. What do these classifications mean?

We know that many people are especially and preferably interested in visible things. They remember what they have seen far better than what they have heard, and they are better able to retain visually striking impressions. We call this the visual type.

On the other hand, another type uses its sense of hearing for the perception of the outside world and remembers primarily things heard. That is the auditory type.

Most people belong to both types with a slightly greater emphasis placed on one or the other. A third type is what we call the motor type. People of this type seem to have a noticeably strong preference for bodily movement.

We have learned from long observation and considerable study that the type to which an individual belongs is not mere chance. In many cases, we can prove that the type to which a person has elected to train himself represents a compensation for a defect in the functioning of one of the five senses, or a deficiency in the organs of motion (limbs). A congenital or acquired inferiority of the eyes, for example, leads to a compensatory endeavor to overcome the inferiority, thereby starting permanent training in the direction of the visual. Even if the original organic inferiority vanishes completely in later years, the individual still pursues the same training pattern. The difficulties in surmounting the inferiority must have made an ineradicable impression to be able to determine the kind of memories carried over to adulthood.

What I have just said regarding the visual type holds just as well for the auditory and motor types, where disturbances of the respective organs form the foundation for the different training patterns.

I was also terribly frightened when I found a feather in my bed. Then I yelled as if it were a monster.

Anxiety is well known in the history of the pampered child. We notice how she arranges for this mood in advance by being interested in everything which can arouse anxiety. Other psychological schools explain the phenomenon of anxiety differently. For instance, the psychoanalysts claim that anxiety is induced by repressed sexual desire. Fear may result from such repression, but perhaps it is just the other way around and the anxiety is the repressed emotion. The advanced psychoanalysts attempted to take this into account by asserting that every anxiety springs from the original anxiety accompanying the act of birth.

However, we believe that a function as intelligent as anxiety cannot take place at birth. Our method of tracing the purpose and effect of an emotional expression has led us to notice that anxiety is a first-rate method of ruling others. This girl summons her father to help her overcome her anxiety. In this life story we hear continually about anxious moments. She uses everyone and everything in her constant mania to dominate.

When I was five years old, the following happened. While I was playing with my doll, I felt myself forced mentally to call my parents and God bad names, such as dirty slut, lousy dog, and so on.

How does this reaction of hate arise in a child? The psychoanalysts would say that it is an outburst of innate sadism.

When we consider this more carefully, we conclude that the girl is a spoiled child who fights desperately against the demolition of her system. This destruction begins when, as she believes (whether or not it is correct is immaterial), she was weaned at the age of five. She feels as if she had been thrown out of the Garden of Eden. Is it not understandable that she rebels with all her might? She suddenly feels herself forced to call God and her parents bad names. (The fact that she does not know why she does it protects her and permits her to continue doing it.) Her behavior is a distinct act of revenge. Given a similar set of circumstances, we can produce the same reaction in every child. She behaves intelligently throughout. The guilt lies with those who arranged for her a paradise of pampering and permitted her to remain in it too long.

I was furious with those whom I liked best.

As we now know, they are the ones to blame.

It was as if the devil had whispered it into my ear. The harder I tried to restrain myself, the more violently I swore.

This is a pattern every patient produces. Our answer is: Then don't try to restrain yourself. Let us see what happens psychically. Exactly this: My thoughts are so strong and I am innocent. Here lies the complete justification of the neurotic who complains that she feels forced to perform certain acts (compulsion neurosis). Why does she have to do this? Because she has no other means. She would rather force her mother to continue to nurse her, but her mother refuses. She could easily force her father, if he could assume the role of wet-nurse. "But I wanted to become healthy," says the patient. The wish is the proof that she is sick; we therefore advise renouncing the wish. Individual Psychologists are skeptical about wishes, in contrast to other psychologists. As long as somebody wishes, she is sure that nothing will happen. The assumption that volition precedes a deed is contradictory to psychology in general. When we hear of wanting, we know that nothing will happen. On the other hand, when something happens, we hear nothing of a wish.

My face often became deeply flushed from the effort I made to repress my thoughts, but the thoughts did not vanish. In order to apologize to myself, I said "The boarder is a dog, not father."

She cultivates useless, compulsive thoughts.

Chapter III

The Development of a Neurosis

Neurotic cases resemble one another to some extent. The burden of a neurosis is always the same: anxiety in anticipation of a defeat in communal life. As a result of such anxiety, the neurosis appears in the exonerating form of an illness, detaching all responsibility from the sufferer and justifying flight from the expected danger. To give a picture corresponding to the viewpoint of a neurotic: The neurotic views life as a battle in which he is constantly in danger (the lives of others being unimportant to him). The closer he comes to the battlefront of life, the greater his nervousness and apprehension concerning his own safety. When his anxiety finally overcomes him, he flees, or attempts to gain some guarantee of safety by burying himself in trenches as far from life's battlefront as possible.

The form a person chooses for his neurosis depends on his behavior pattern and fictive goal. However, the various forms of neuroses do not differ much from each other, and individuals completely unlike in type, but having the same sort of neurosis, frequently choose the same form for the neurotic manifestation. This similarity is especially true of compulsion neuroses. Neurotics are not very original in the expression of their symptoms.

Nevertheless, I suffered from ~~deep remorse~~. *I looked at my parents and thought, "If you knew what abusive remarks I make about you!"*

Anyone not knowing the principles of Individual Psychology might conclude from such a remark that the girl pities her parents. Her conscience pricks her because of her wretched behavior. Speaking of remorse reminds us of an error in the Freudian school of psychoanalysis. The Freudians emphasize the feeling of guilt, but they misunderstand it. The feeling of guilt is an inferiority feeling in disguise. It makes itself apparent when someone breaks the laws of social life, indicating at the same time that the lawbreaker recognizes these social laws as intrinsically correct. Nevertheless, the feeling of guilt shows neither the intention nor any other indication that the delinquent will thereafter obey the laws, making his life conform to or harmonize with social life. Indeed, we believe that what Nietzche says is true: Remorse is indecent.

If remorse really meant what naïve philosophers assume, the feeling would be followed by a change in behavior. Such a feeling, however, is usually the continuation of a useless activity (always remembering that remorse as here used is in connection with a neurosis).

Therefore, we do not interpret the girl's statement as showing pity. We have seen that she wanted to be the center of attention. We do not believe she has given up her constant desire to be first. She now feels superior, for when she says, "If you knew what things I say about you," it means, "I am more than you. You are blind. You understand nothing." Saying, "Father is a dog," means, "I am better than Father." Thus we can see more clearly how the girl attempts to elevate herself above others. Her feeling of remorse does not alter her striving for superiority; on the contrary, the remorse proves that she has endeavored to continue the tendency to degrade her parents. (We find the tendency to degrade others only in those people who feel inferior.) An individual can compensate for his feeling of inferiority by elevating himself over others, or by degrading them. In either case, he has gained a certain height over them. In other words, he can create this distance by elevation of oneself or lowering the others. The degradation of others and elevation of oneself are not in the least diminished by an unquiet conscience. Quite the reverse, for such a person is then given an additional excuse to pity himself, or to elevate himself still more.

Some neurotics feel compelled to demonstrate their superiority to their fellow men. Others are satisfied if their neurotic striving creates a mood which permits them merely to feel superior.

I wanted to escape these thoughts, but they seized me over and over again. They even disturbed me when I prayed at night; then I had to repeat my prayer. It was horrible.

This hammering, this underlining, this absolutely useless emphasis in description are part of the nature of a neurosis; that is, to make something out of nothing. It brings the neurotic closer to his goal of godlikeness.

It stopped only when I went to school.

We observe quite often that school life is able to change conditions. The situation has probably become more favorable. She is no longer confronted as seriously with the problem: Am I more than Father or not? Perhaps her father has begun to spoil her a little more again.

I suffered from sleeplessness very early in life, at the age of six or seven.

Sleeplessness will obviously be noticed; it relates to the environment. If the child cannot sleep, the father and mother are directly involved and participate in a poor night. Nighttime disturbances are the customary methods of children who want special attention. It makes no difference whether they make trouble going to bed or falling asleep, whether they sleep poorly, suffer from pavor nocturnus (fear of the night) or bedwetting, whether they talk in their sleep or walk in their sleep. It always means: Someone has to take care of me. The night is used to keep the people around her busy.

It was very hard for me to fall asleep, and in the morning I was the first to awaken.

The night and sleep are the greatest enemies of all spoiled children. Nervous adults are also furious when others sleep. This disturbance is in the forefront of many neuroses.

At this point, I will make a few observations on nervous insomnia in general. Sleeping, as well as eating, seems of far greater importance than it really is. Certainly we need sleep in order to renew ourselves. But sleeping is like breathing; nature usually compels us to take the amount we need.

Nervous sleeplessness, like all nervous symptoms, serves different purposes. It may be a vital connecting link in the chain of a nervous life style. We have frequently seen that a nervous person thinks constantly of how he can make himself superior. Because sleep is generally considered so important, the inability to sleep can be used as an effective protest against the environment. It usually provides a way to penalize or complain about certain members of one's household. If a patient complains of sleeplessness during psychotherapeutic treatment, he holds the doctor responsible for it as if he were indicating to him the uselessness of his therapeutic efforts. Or the sleeplessness will be used to prove illness as soon as that seems to be the most effective way to the establishment of superiority, and of one's own will. This will is usually directed toward finding a good alibi, in order to plead inability to work or face a problem, and to make rules for others: I am nervous and can't sleep, so everyone in the house must be quiet; doors must be closed gently; voices must be lowered; everyone must be home early, and so on.

The sufferer from sleeplessness emphasizes his symptoms so strongly that we can infer he demands recognition of his difficult situation. This recognition frees him from all responsibility for whatever blunders he may make in life, and as a further consequence, will place twice as much value on whatever success he may have, since he has been successful in spite of his handicap. The neurotic realizes the expediency of this method from his own experience or from having seen the effect of someone else's illness on the environment and on himself. So long as the psychic significance of the situation has not been understood, we are not surprised when the doctor, or whatever remedies may have been tried, obtains for the patient merely a confirmation of his alleged illness.

Thus, nervous sleeplessness serves as shield and weapon to protect the threatened self-esteem. Nervous people who choose the symptom of sleeplessness generally have other characteristic indications of the nervous character. Excessively ambitious, most lack confidence in their ability to attain their end. They place too great a value on success and exaggerate the difficulties of life; cowardly and afraid to make decisions, they love to rule. The thoughts of such a patient during the time when he should be dozing off are either a means of keeping him awake, or they contain the kernel of the psychic difficulty provoking the sleeplessness.

The patient wants to construct a broad chasm between himself and his pernicious, neurotically unattainable goal, which will absolve him of failure and give him a good excuse to cease struggling. The symptom disappears as soon as the patient realizes that his inability to sleep is a way of avoiding responsibility for the solution of life's problems. When he ceases to consider his sleeplessness an inexplicable fate, he abandons this symptom.

My father was so concerned about my poor sleep that he himself could not sleep any more.

The confirmation follows on the heels of our interpretation.

Then I pretended to be asleep, and when Father quietly tiptoed into the room, I breathed slowly and deeply as if I were sleeping.

This sounds loving and considerate. The child, of course, has some feeling of tenderness for her father; she sometimes gives in when she thinks she has gone too far. However, this girl has every reason to feel she needs to be quiet as she notices her father's apprehensiveness. After seeing her father prowling in the dark and then not sleeping for the rest of the night, she may have made the compromise: Since I have gone so far as to force Father out of bed, I am satisfied.

On our floor lived another tailor who had many children, four girls and two boys. One of the boys, Poldi, was my age; I played with him. He was a little roughneck, dirty and barefooted. I imitated him.

Imitating a boy looks innocent and harmless. However, if we could uncover more of what went on in her mind, we would find a wish to change into a boy. It is the small remainder of a common trait, the protest against being a woman in a world where men are generally considered superior; where they have the more advantageous positions, more freedom, and apparently greater physical strength. I have termed this manifestation "the masculine protest."

Our studies have shown that the masculine protest assumes a central position in every neurosis. It originates with the child's natural feeling of weakness in comparison to adults. When this sense of weakness is exaggerated, it grows into a feeling of dependence and a longing for tenderness, a psychological and physiological dependency and subordination. It becomes a branch of the general struggle for supremacy stemming from the exaggerated feeling of inferiority. The name, masculine protest, contains a special connotation.

Because of his intense longing for security, the nervous person tends to divide the world into contrasting parts, live according to extremes, and treat his problems in the same way: all or nothing, victory or defeat, above or below, and so on. The many steps in between might prove perplexing, so they are eliminated.

Two such extremes are found in the term, masculine-feminine. From careless or tactless remarks made by adults, and from his own prejudiced observation of the world in which he grows up, a child quickly learns that in our civilization men are considered superior to women. The man's role seems generally to be more advantageous and better suited to help relieve the feeling of inferiority. The wish consequently develops, "I want to be a man." A boy can fulfill this wish in his behavior, because he can act according to his idea of how a man should conduct himself. A girl cannot do this.

For a boy, however, the wish, "I want to be a man," has a somewhat different meaning than for a girl. He feels obliged to fulfill the ideal of man which our culture has set; whereas, the masculine protest in a girl does not express anything but the wish to enjoy the advantages and privileges of men.

When children are already disposed to nervousness because of an aggravated feeling of inferiority, both boys and girls will interpret this man-woman conception as antagonistic extremes and purposively exaggerate this interpretation. Children will attach to the word "man" all that means superiority (in their own belief), and will associate with the word "woman" everything that points to inferiority. They sense their own feeling of inferiority as strongly feminine and make a desperate attempt to compensate for the imagined deficiency by assuming masculine characteristics. That is the verbal diagram of the masculine protest.

In the strict apperceptive scheme of the neurotic, all qualities considered passive are stamped as feminine, such as docility, mildness, kindness, subordination, cowardice, patience, etc.; while active character traits such as aggressiveness, stubbornness, obstinacy, impudence, insubordination and the desire for power and freedom are accepted as masculine. The goal is to rule, to be superior. Where it seems impossible to reach this goal by direct aggression, the nervous person chooses the variation of a "masculine protest with feminine means;" he tries to attain the dominating state of masculinity through a display of weakness, exaggerated malleability, or through the arrangement of sickness.

We can therefore conclude that this girl's wish, always to be the first, does not agree with the unhesitating acceptance of the feminine role. "Wouldn't it be easier if I were a boy?"

There was a big heap of sand in the courtyard. There we played grocers. The sand represented the food.

She describes their games. At this point I want to comment on the significance of children's games. Groos points out very clearly in his book, *The Play of Children*, how we must not interpret playing. I cannot comprehend how anyone can speak of a play instinct after reading this book.

The so-called play instinct is a child's attempt to prepare himself for the future by using the limited means at his disposal. He trains himself for the role of an adult with games that seem nothing more than playful to us. The imitation of adults is very significant and obvious, especially the imitation of those adults (or their conduct) who appear worthwhile to the child. The games are never senseless, but a step toward the future goal of the developing human being. It is all the same whether the child plays with a toy railroad or builds houses, or plays "husband and wife" or "Indian and princess." The child takes his play as seriously as an adult takes his work. Adults should therefore regard such games seriously and not interfere in a dominant, superior fashion. A child learns through play. Dostoevsky once remarked that the games of children have an artistic quality. We Individual Psychologists understand this train of thought very well. Children do not have the strength adults have with which to tackle a piece of work. Their greatest yearning, however, is to do as adults do. So they use tricks in order to make believe they are grown up.

There was a dog in our house named Bello which belonged to a box manufacturer.

Children and dogs generally have a close relationship because dogs comply with the children's striving for recognition; they obey, they let themselves be mastered. Children who have an excessive striving for recognition are strongly attracted to dogs. On the other hand, if all a child wants is to be watched continually by his mother, then he may be afraid of dogs. He will use the fear of dogs to compel his mother to always be present. Such children are more discouraged than those who make friends with dogs. Nevertheless, as the example clearly shows, the two methods grow out of the same root, the feeling of inferiority. Only the varying intensity of the feeling elicits different reactions.

This dog pulled a little carriage. It got lots of horsemeat sausages which lay by its hut. Poldi always wanted to steal one of the sausages, but the dog didn't like Poldi. One day Poldi crept carefully to the hut, grabbed a sausage and devoured it in an instant. That delighted him tremendously, I said to him, "The sausage lay next to the dog's feces and now you are eating it."

Again we see the tendency to degrade; the sausage lay next to the dog's feces. The wish to elevate herself over others never leaves her.

He did not care. The box manufacturer had a large, covered wagon. He sometimes took it with him. We were happy when we sat in the wagon.

She seems to like the company of boys.

Two old women lived on the second floor, and each of them kept several prostitutes. These prostitutes did not get up before noon or afternoon.

Children are often attracted to people wearing beautiful clothes. When their own circumstances are quite meager, when they have shabby clothes and are forced to suffer the bitterness and numerous discomforts of poverty, the contrast strikes them sharply. Limited by their childish judgment, they conclude that better clothes mean a better life, which they would also like to have. The purely social inferiority stings them, so they seek a simple, quick and sure compensation. We can understand how some children are thus drawn to the road of misery, and we shall not be surprised to see these girls playfully prepare for the profession of a prostitute when they believe they can reach the goal of superiority in this direction.

The prostitutes often threw money from their windows down to the street for us to buy them cigarettes and beer. Although I never saw more than the foyer of their apartment, I liked to be there. The furniture appeared very fashionable to me.

Prostitutes are not held in as much contempt by simple people as by the well-educated middle class. So we can see how the ranks of prostitutes are continually replenished.

I could watch them dress themselves from the hall window. I felt sorry for one of them who looked as if she were tubercular. But when she was dressed and had painted her face, she looked quite different than from the window. Some of the women were very vulgar and yelled through the house; it was bedlam.

That shows a ~~distinct aversion.~~ We do not suppose she will ever go the way of prostitution.

I remember a few things about Lina. We subscribed to "The Book for Everybody." Lina read the serial in it and was eager to get the installment each week. She always asked for the periodical. Father did not like to have her read the novel and we agreed to conceal the magazine when it came. I, too, promised not to say anything. However, when Lina came into the room, I cried, "The magazine is here."

She could not obey; she rebelled.

One evening Lina copied a love letter from a book. Father and Mother were in the kitchen; Lina was called out. I jumped out of bed, made a blot on the letter, went back to bed and pulled the blanket over my head.

Malice. She triumphs because she knows something the others do not know. Also, she feels powerful since she can obstruct her sister's plans, spoil her mood, and perhaps prevent her from making an important decision. Children resort to tricks and bad habits as a lever by which to raise themselves above the more powerful members of their environment. They usually damage, spoil, or destroy the property of others. Their hatred directs attention to their feeling of insignificance. We see their tricks as distinct acts of revenge produced by a feeling of inadequacy.

When Lina saw the ink spot, she cried. After a while she went out of the room again and I repeated my nasty trick. She scolded me. I imitated her in every way. She was nine years older and like a second mother to me.

She can imagine a kind woman only in the form of her mother. That is characteristic of spoiled children.

I tried hard to imitate Lina's handwriting. I liked her triangular flourishes. Father wanted me to write naturally.

There is no such thing as an imitative instinct. We imitate something because it pleases us, because it seems effective in our attempt to achieve superiority. Therefore, imitation is part of the striving for recognition and must be so understood. The imitation of her older sister indicates that she imitates only what fits into her style of life.

As a small child I would run up and down the steps in front of the church like one possessed. My mother had to drag me home with her by force.

Perhaps this shows pleasure in motion, or she runs away so her mother has to run after her.

Father was very religious; he taught me at an early age to make a cross when I passed a church and he gave me religious pictures. I began to collect religious pictures.

We believe that children collect things because it makes them feel strong. Some collections are absolutely senseless. This child collects in order to satisfy her striving for recognition.

I had a lot of pictures. In the evening I spread them in two rows under my pillow and on top I put a guardian angel. Otherwise, I could not have fallen asleep. I prayed until I was short of breath. I prayed for everyone I liked, for my grandmother, uncles and aunts.

It is not difficult to train a child for such behavior. What does, "I prayed for everyone," mean? The fate of this person is in my hand. Such a child feels superior. This form of praying, so incompatible with reality, is often a symptom of a compulsion neurosis.

(A rich man had to support his three poor sisters and this annoyed him a great deal. He prayed to God that He might protect them and prevent them from being burned to death. If he did not pray, he could not fall asleep for fear they might eventually be burned. Every day he rejoiced that they had not perished by fire. "I have their lives in my hand; I am responsible for their welfare.")

Christmas was a great event. Father sent me to the café "so that in the meantime Santa Claus could bring the presents."

Chapter IV

The Style of Life

Wherever a psychologist begins the study of a life story, he will find the particular life he is investigating directed toward a specific goal. In order to understand a person's life, we must discover the thread running through all his symptoms which can be traced directly to his goal. We call this thread the individual's style of life. The style of life is the special manner in which a person faces life and answers the challenge of existence; how he feels, thinks, wants, acts; how he perceives and uses his perceptions. The style of life is formed by early childhood influences, developed in early childhood, and guided by the goal of the person who follows it unquestionably.

A gloomy mood prevailed at home. My parents had quarreled again. I do not remember about what.

Children who are constantly the center of attraction, like this one, cannot bear having their parents quarrel. Not because they want peace, but because they feel excluded when the others are busy with each other. For that reason, they frequently try to prevent quarrels in the family. She does not remember what her parents quarreled about, only that they did quarrel.

Father asked me to stay in my room and turn my face to the wall because Santa Claus was just passing the window. So I turned around. Lina took my hand. Then a bell rang and we went into the Christmas room.

It is interesting for the Individual Psychologist to consider whether or not children should be told such fairy tales. We must not be too cautious. Those who insist on explaining everything in the light of sexual or other problems miss the point. Children do not care very much whether these tales are true or not; they take them as conventional nonsense, as a way of speaking. I have never seen a child as excited at the discovery that Santa Claus does not exist as those who were eager to explain the matter. We know that we tell our children too many fables; the question remains open as to how far we can go. However, in raising children, this issue is not a major problem, certainly not as serious as the tendency to impose excessive restrictions.

All restrictions not based on common sense have the effect of diminishing a child's courage and making him believe that the reality of life is much more dangerous than it is. What results is an attempt to evade the realities of life by resorting to neurotic alibis. Questions such as what fairy tales we should tell a child and up to what age answer themselves according to the law of common sense. We must not forget that children are initially not as stupid as many adults have unfortunately become.

A large Christmas tree stood on the table with candles burning. In front of it, I saw a big slate on a stand and beside it, a doll. I think I also got a picture book. I rushed to my presents, admired them, and immediately started to scribble on the slate with chalk. I could not write at that time.

Let us recall what we have said about her increasing interest in all visible things. Perhaps we shall find a verification. This scene, remembered for so many years, shows that she paid a great deal of attention to visible objects, even if it turns out later that the details remembered are not true. The extremes of beauty and ugliness attracted her notice.

Lina received a picture album and a red hat. I prepared a bed on the couch for my doll. Before falling asleep, I got up and looked to see whether it lay comfortably.

"I looked" confirms our assumption about her attraction to visual detail.

Next Christmas, Milli, a friend of mine, advised me to surprise my parents and Lina with written greetings. I bought stationary used for this purpose, trimmed with gold and angels.

We perceive this girl's qualifications for the decorative arts. Asked for what profession she should be trained, we would answer that she has trained in the direction of drawing. A vocational guidance advisor would have to keep this fact in mind. (Dressmaker or fashion designer.)

"Which profession would you advise?" is a question often put to psychologists. Many young people know very well what they would like to do; they have consciously or unconsciously prepared themselves for some occupation. The relatives like to assume that this is an instinctive choice. That is not correct. The choice of a vocation arises out of childhood influences, sometimes influences felt in infancy, and the so-called instinct is a manifest training for the future calling.

We have to deal with more difficulties in cases where the individual has no predominant inclination and obviously no talent. First, such people are probably much further away from and considerably more hostile to the question of work than those who have in some way prepared themselves. They have avoided coming to any decision on the problem of work, (one of the great social problems, as we know). They have shoved it aside for the time being as if it could be disposed of once and for all by such a maneuver. These tactics remind us somewhat of the ostrich which sticks its head in the sand when in danger, believing that no one sees it because it can see no one.

In order to decide for what profession a young person is best suited, we must draw the necessary conclusions from his life story, his remembrances, the statements of various family members, and his own behavior. From these factors, we can determine the type of environment from which he comes, and his sensory type (visual, auditory, motor) and so on. When a clear picture of the youth's character traits and compensatory striving has been formed, it is usually easy, with the help of our Individual Psychological experience, to find the occupation which best suits the pattern of his personality.

Milli had had a little book of Christmas wishes. She picked out three of the shortest for me and prepared to help me copy them.

This girl is capable of social contact.

Though she spelled every single word out for me, I spoiled a great many sheets. Again and again, I had to run downstairs to fetch fresh paper. I exerted myself to the utmost and was glad when I finished my letter at last. It was crammed with mistakes, but my parents and Lina enjoyed it immensely.

You see how others are induced to help this child, how well she is liked. She is accustomed to being favored. We can predict that when she is finally faced with a difficult situation, she will react acutely; she will bear misfortune less bravely than her step-sister, Lina. She is like a hot-house plant. When she is in a less sheltered position and faces a situation where she has to give and cannot take, she will break down.

As soon as I could write correctly, I composed long letters to Santa Claus, a whole list of things I wanted, written in a very affectionate manner.

Our assumption of the expectant attitude is confirmed. Her attitude in life is to expect things from others and give as little in return as possible.

I imagined that Santa Claus descended from heaven on a long ladder placed at the end of the world, in order to buy presents in the Christmas shops. I pictured him in detail.

Visual type.

Corpus Christi Day was almost as important a festival as Christmas Day. Father once gave a donation so that I could walk under a little canopy dressed up like an angel.

A sense for festivities.

The night before that day I could hardly sleep.

The anxiety which precedes decisions or unusual events is increasing.

I was awake at about five o'clock and peeked through the window to see if the weather was good. When I heard the hammering which accompanied the fastening of the little trees and saw flowers spread over the walks, I was overjoyed. At half-past eight, Father brought me to the gathering place of the procession. I wore an angel costume with a crown and wings. Then I was placed under my little canopy and permitted to carry an image of the Holy Virgin.

These recollections show the girl's interest in external beauty.

We had to wait quite a while. It was pretty cool, so Father brought me hot tea from a neighboring coffee house. My wings, made from goose feathers, became so heavy that Father had to take them off. Thus I trotted along, with a crown on my head, under the red canopy which was carried by four girls in white dresses. When we came near our house, I was too proud to look up to our windows. I imagined that I was almost an angel.

The child identifies herself with an angel to such an extent that she feels humiliated having to live in such a poor house.

Father followed along on the sidewalk, carrying the wings in his hand.

The girl's relation to her father signifies that she dominates him.

I liked to go to church and never omitted making the sign of the cross when I passed one. But when I passed a church in a trolley car or just happened to be with other girls who I knew would not make the cross, I was afraid to display my piety and fought with myself as to whether I should make the cross or not.

Children are naturally dependent upon the opinions of other and older people. They learn from their parents the latter's interpretation of the world and must believe it until they can or want to think sufficiently for themselves to correct it. Mass suggestion also operates somewhat along this line. An individual in a mass no longer acts as he would act if he were quite alone; he falls back into a childlike state where he credulously accepts and follows the declarations of supposedly more experienced, more learned people. In a mass, each individual tries to make himself a part of a unified whole.

The concept of a "mass" implies that everyone does not do what he wants, that he removes what separates and looks for at what unites. He who produces a slogan to which others are susceptible creates unity. We have to consider mass suggestion. An individual in a mass does not act according to his own opinion; all the individuals form a stream attempting to flow in one channel. It becomes the supreme task of a mass to act homogenously and without detailed investigation.

If I neglected to make the cross, I was conscience-stricken. I was afraid I would be punished by accidents.

She fights for what is instilled in her by tradition, namely, the preservation of her individual personality. The conscience pangs are an attempt to fight off mass suggestion.

I was painfully exact with my confessions. I searched through Father's old prayer books and wrote down a great many sins which I had never committed, and then explored my memory for more sins.

We find that frequently. She wants to boast of many sins.

Then I asked Father whether he knew a few more sins and if it was a sin to be troubled with flatulence. I had much trouble with the list of sins to be handed to the priest, which grew tremendously long. Since I was ashamed of having so many sins in front of the other children, I began to write such small, compressed letters that when I was in the confession chair, I could hardly decipher my own writing.

In reality such boasts tend to correct themselves. She boasts a great deal, but cannot make use of it.

At Easter, when I was in the fourth grade, I took Communion for the first time. I felt so peculiar that day, quite different from other days, so holy, I might say. I almost did not dare move around because I had eaten of Christ. I thought my friend, Olga, unworthy because she had not taken it as seriously as I.

She wants to be in the ranks of the highest.

I enjoyed the tales from the Arabian Nights immensely. Father and Lina read them to me before I could read. When I heard the story of the merchant and the ghost, in which the merchant slays the ghost with a date pit, I asked Father for some money and bought dates. Then I seated myself in a corner, threw pits into the air, and imagined that I had killed a lot of ghosts.

Such things happen when a child is about eight years old. A boy once thought that someone wanted to kill and devour him. Some people had made stupid remarks. The boy believed it still more when he was sent to a house to be "fed;" he thought he would be put to death there.

I never liked to eat. . .

Pampered, struggling child. The people around her overemphasize eating. When cleanliness is emphasized, a child becomes dirty; when the digestive function is emphasized, difficulties in the choice of food or defecation arise. We recommend that no overemphasis of natural functions ever becomes apparent to children.

I stimulated my appetite by the thought of fairy tales where sumptuous feasts were served. Or when I had to eat rice, for instance, I imagined a wicked witch who, in the shape of a beautiful woman, would eat only a few grains, but who secretly devoured corpses in the graves at night. In this way I consumed the rice grain by grain.

Notice how this girl identifies herself with every figure in the fairy tales. She could eventually have become an actress.

When we had cutlet, I imagined that was my own invention -- that the fork was a woman and the morsel on it her hat; then I let the hat-morsel on the fork-woman walk around the plate several times and ate it afterward.

This is the common foolishness of children. They constantly have to listen to, "Eat now; otherwise, you won't grow up!" They see clearly how important it is to the adults that they (the children) eat well. Only a child who feels inferior or oppressed gets the idea of protesting. He cannot find a better way to manifest an apparent superiority than by not yielding to the demands of the adults, or as here, by laughing at them. Especially when the protest appears so skillfully veiled, as in the play of this child with her food, the parents are quite powerless when they do not see through the trick. The child triumphs and proceeds to new strategies.

When I drank I often fancied that I was in a desert. All the others were dying of thirst and were sucking one another's blood.

She speaks on several occasions of things which might be called cruel. Children are often cruel without thinking anything of it. Who, as a child, has never tormented an animal? Not for the sake of tormenting, but out of pure curiosity. What will a fly do when I tear its wings off? How do the wings really look? It does not usually occur to children that they inflict pain on the fly; they themselves don't feel any pain.

Where the cruelty is conscious and deliberated, it serves, as in the case of the masculine protest, as a means of achieving one's objective by force or of giving oneself the impression of peculiar power. A child may train himself for cruelty or barbarity in order to harden himself and thereby feel manly, or he may use this hard-heartedness as a threat or instrument for oppression, always, however, with the same goal of self-elevation at another's expense. Daydreams of savagery are either a mental preparation, training, as it were, for the deed, or a weak substitute for cowardice. This is not to be understood as praise of cruelty. Courageous people need no cruel fantasies.

Sometimes fantasies of cruel acts are connected with sexual excitement, but we believe it a blunder to generalize by concluding that cruelty has a sexual origin. Children in whom fear is connected with sexual emotion belong to a special type, but not every child is capable of producing a sexual impulse with fear.

I imagined I was the only one who had some water left. Then I thoroughly relished drinking a whole bottle, sip by sip.

She fulfills the customary requirements of social life only under certain conditions.

In order to make my food taste better, I also liked to think that a famine had arisen and I was the only one who still had provisions.

We would not be astonished to hear that the Great Flood had come and she was the only human being saved. The legend of the Great Flood probably had its origin in a similar conceit.

I loved figs because they are mentioned in "The Arabian Nights."

This is a false causality. She deliberately makes something the cause and lets those consequences follow which serve her purpose, that is, to eat the figs.

I never liked potatoes.

We would not be surprised if she were to write, "because they are not spoken of in *The Arabian Nights*."

When we learned at school how potatoes had been discovered and how they had been wrongly prepared at first--it was not known then that only the roots were edible--I asked mother to boil a few for me and imagined that I had discovered them and nobody else knew how to prepare them.

Striving to be unique.

Mother made some sandwiches for me to take to school; sometimes I had chocolate, too. But I rarely touched my breakfast. I either gave my sandwiches away or took them home with me again. I felt a dislike for other children, for their hair and for their smell.

We expect such behavior from this type of spoiled child. In the parks we often see children who make gestures warding off others. That means the exclusion of others. Such a gesture indicates a pampered child who rejects strangers and wants to be only with the familiar, yielding members of her family.

And I often wondered how they could eat anything in that smelly atmosphere.

Her superciliousness increases.

Following Father's example, I acquired the habit of reading while I ate.

She dislikes her feminine role. She imitates her father's manners, expressing that she would prefer to be a man like him.

I enjoyed most reading some fairy tale, such as "Strong Hans," who has to eat through a mountain of delicious food for seven years. Even now my food tastes much better to me when I read with my meals.

In consideration of her ability to identify with someone else, we may say that she identifies with "Strong Hans." Again a boy.

Father told me one day that his former fiancé, Genevieve, had drunk her coffee without sugar. So I did the same. Mother took a lump of sugar in her mouth when she drank her coffee. I also imitated that.

She has not yet decided. She still hesitates. This will be a significant point in her development. She knows that she is a girl and cannot become a boy. Though her remembrances reveal her longing to be like a man, they also show a struggle to repress this longing, to reconcile herself to the feminine role and adjust to it.

My coffee had to be quite dark; milk horrified me.

This loathing of milk comes from the time when children begin to protest against the monotonous nourishment. All children are overfed with milk; they want to free themselves from a hated restriction. The food given to children should be varied; they should not be fed only with milk.

If we were served with sweet, milky coffee at a children's party, I felt as if I wanted to vomit.

We hear a good deal about eating which permits the assumption of an organ inferiority of the digestive apparatus. Experience has taught us that those memories retained over a period of many years and remaining particularly clear frequently point to bodily deficiencies either acquired or congenital. In a former chapter, we mentioned that those remembrances are significantly clear which fit in the individual's style of life and, because of that, they permit the therapist to make certain deductions from them about the style of life. But when we are told remembrances which, directly or indirectly, recurringly call attention to a particular organ of the body, we can conclude that this organ either is not now or did not, at some former time, function normally. When recollections concern themselves principally with eating or food, they indicate a weakness of the digestive apparatus. Sometimes that can be factually proven; sometimes compensation started at a time when the young child could not yet form words and sentences by which to remember pictures or impressions; or the defect in the functioning was very slight and the compensation begun by the body progressed so quickly and efficiently that only indirect associations remained in the memory. But they have been impressed on the memory and can be traced back in the purposive remembrances of our patients.

My digestion gave me much trouble. I was constantly bothered with constipation. Most of all I hated enemas and suppositories.

Spoiled children frequently experience difficulties with the simplest functions.

Sometimes I sat on the toilet for an hour and could not defecate. And when there finally was some result, Father used to be very glad. One day I was going to have an enema. Some friends of my parents were visiting us just then, among them a friend of Father's, a retired captain. I simply refused to have the rubber tube inserted. Mother didn't know what to do. The captain, who knew everything better, came in and said

187

to my mother, "You aren't managing that well; you have to do it this way," . . . and suddenly the rubber tube slipped and the water went right into his face. Once in a while, I found red spots in mother's bed or on her nightshirt.

Interest in what is visible.

Then I asked her, "Mama, why do you bleed from your back?" She replied that she had hemorrhoids from which she suffered at times. Then I crept to the seat where mother had sat and sniffed around it. Very soon I knew this smell so well that I could detect it on every woman.

A good sense of smell may signify an organ inferiority, but we would be wrong to assume that only the underfunctioning of an organ indicates a defect. Overfunctioning is just as much an inferiority and can lead to exactly the same difficulties as when the organ operates badly. Normal functioning means neither too much nor too little. A hyper-functioning of the sense of smell would, in our present culture, certainly lead to the same disastrous results as four hands instead of two hands and two feet.

I also tried to smell my own body so hard that I often got a headache from it. My main pleasure was to rub patches of silk against each other until they were hot and gave forth a peculiar odor. I sometimes called my friend, Olga, over to help me with this. We would sit down somewhere in a corner, rubbing and sniffing.

Pronounced faculty for smelling. The same tendency she has in regard to investigating spiritual matters.

I went to the theatre for the first time when I was four to see "Puss in Boots." The other children roared with laughter. I sat there and looked and listened with a serious expression. My parents asked me whether I liked it or not. Apparently they would rather have seen me laugh just as loudly as the others. They seemed disappointed because I did not move a muscle of my face and gave no sign of pleasure or displeasure.

The future grande dame! Setting herself apart.

Their inquisitiveness annoyed me. On the way home they insisted on my telling them why I had looked on as morosely as if I were seeing a tragedy. I did not answer. The next day, however, I recited the contents of the entire play. They were all startled. Only then did they realize what a deep impression the play had made on me.

We have said that this girl may be on her way to becoming an actress. The play made an indelible impression on her.

A poor, Swedish baron came to our house. He had been compelled to leave his country because of a duel in which he had killed his adversary. He had become the operator of a moving picture projector in a theatre. Once a week he invited us to the movies. We waited for him after the performances and then had supper together. Father ordered veal cutlet with fried potatoes and red wine. In a restaurant I could eat with great appetite.

The fussiest people consume everything in a restaurant. Our supposition is correct. Trouble while eating springs from the wish to make trouble.

Every week I looked forward with pleasure to that evening.

We could have foreseen that this child would be interested in the cinema.

When the baron received money from his people, he would treat all of us. Everybody drank a great deal of wine and the whole party was drunk. Only I remained sober which made me feel so lonely that I cried.

Everyone was occupied with his own happiness, not with her.

Later we used to frequently visit a restaurant in a building where there was also vaudeville. We always sat in the dining room. I could not stand it there very long so I stole away by myself to the vaudeville show, stood beside the band and listened. When the waiters drove me away, I went out through one door and came in again through another. And if there was no chance of getting in, I peeked through a crack in the door. During the intermissions, I would sneak in and take one of the empty seats.

I would like to comment on children visiting such performances. When I was two years old, my parents took me to hear some singers of popular songs. I heard good and bad things. I saw some operettas at the age of five or six. These things are not as harmful as they seem; the anxiety of parents is exaggerated. We should not take children to horrifying performances. But it is not justifiable to prohibit their seeing a funny piece. One of my oldest remembrances is this: My parents had to go away and leave me and my older brother in the care of our governess. When my father returned, he was greeted by a strange sight. I was standing on the table, roaring out a popular song dealing with a woman who was anguished by the sight of a slaughtered chicken; she even emphasized the fact that her heart was bleeding. The chorus of this song, however, told how this woman, in spite of her pity for slaughtered animals, threw pots at her poor husband. I find in this childhood remembrance an early interest in discovering how even contradictions can be united in one pattern.

I found great pleasure in the performances. My cheeks burned. I listened attentively to every word. But I could not stand comedians.

We would not be surprised if she became a movie actress.

I always loved animals.

That is a common trait among children who want to rule. Hardly anything in the world is more obedient than a dog or a rabbit. Even such children who avoid social contact because they feel their superiority endangered can be gentle to animals. We should not deny children an acquaintance with animals. The real motive of this preference, however, is the feeling of superiority.

I never tormented them. Only once, I cut a bedbug in half. Then I ran to my father to ask him whether it was a sin.

She wants to be the most pious of all.

I had a little rabbit. I trained him so that he hopped over to me when I called him. Once he bit me. I spanked him a little and decided not to look at him for the whole day.

Cruel punishment.

But no sooner had I taken him off my lap then I called him back, pardoned and kissed him, crying to think that he had forgotten himself so far as to bite me.

Feeling of grandeur.

I liked to play with his little tail, or I sat down with him on the couch, played the piano with his paws and sang a song.

What rabbits are good for!

No one else was allowed to come near him. I loved to scratch his nose softly with two fingers. He kept quite still. It seemed to do him good. After a while, I had scratched off all the hair around his nose.

If in complicated cases a question arises as to how someone gets the idea to rule by fear, the answer is that the person does not have the idea consciously, but he acts accordingly. At some time, he has observed and retained a strong, unconscious impression that it is possible to rule by fear. In much the same fashion, this girl finds out accidentally that we must scratch rabbits on the nose in order to please them and make them obedient. The origin of nervous symptoms is no more ridiculous than her discovery.

I was presented with a mouse by our boarder.

Fond of animals.

Later on the boarder gave me a hedgehog which spread its quills when I came near it. I thought: that animal is nasty; it only stings me. I don't like it.

All animals are not obedient.

One day a little bird flew in through our window. It was a canary and it had a sore foot. We bought a cage for her and took care of her. Then she laid an egg and sat on it, a phenomenon quite puzzling to me. I was greatly delighted with the tiny, bare little bird. But the old bird let the young one die of hunger. I put the little corpse in a box and the box under the couch. When it started to smell, I buried it in the courtyard.

She makes a pompous ceremony of everything.

I was immensely fond of ladybugs. When I found one, I took a box, pierced some holes through it, covered the bottom with cotton, put a fresh leaf over it and carefully put the lady bug on top of the leaf. I could play with it for hours and hours. And when it flew away, I began to cry and nobody could console me.

This girl searches for a way in which she can feel her superiority to the full.

Chapter V

The Jealousy Mania

Our boarder used to accompany us when we went on an outing. One day he stayed at home. Mother was quite angry; Father noticed it immediately. On our way to the trolley station, they began to quarrel.

At an early age, this girl is made aware of jealousy in the family. She feels that her father does not like it when her mother shows interest in other men. Jealousy shows a lack of self-confidence, representing an attempt to win power over a significant person. The victim of jealousy never realizes that by resorting to such means, he establishes at best only a semblance of power and more frequently, exercises an intolerable tyranny which backfires on the tyrant as surely as two and two make four. We commonly consider jealousy an instinctive feeling, but we are mistaken to believe that a feeling as complicated as jealousy is inborn. To accept such traits as inborn, inherited, or instinctive characteristics relieves us of personal responsibility for consequences resulting from their manifestation. In other words, such a stupid act can be more readily justified when we can blame this character trait on inheritance. Otherwise, we would have to assume full responsibility for what we have done. Severely neurotic cases of jealousy have clearly shown us that jealousy is nothing more than a combative mechanism to preserve prestige. It is combat assisted by feeling, and we reiterate: Feelings are not arguments.

In consideration of the prevalence of this disturbing trait, I will devote a few more words to the subject. A jealous person constantly searches for proofs of his influence, experimenting with every possible situation to prove this influence. The impossible demands with which a jealous person tests another person points clearly to his own lack of self-confidence, his minimal self-esteem, and his insecurity. We can easily see how his striving serves to thrust himself in the foreground, to attract attention to himself, and to increase his value in his own eyes.

A jealous individual is always ready to believe that he has been thwarted or shoved to one side. Such an unfortunate person reverts at once to his childish state of wanting everything. He makes the mistake of attempting to recover his superior position in relation to his partner.

Some individuals cannot bear having a fraction of attention withdrawn from them, and cannot suffer their partner's reading a book or newspaper in their presence. A glance, a conversation in company, a word of thanks for a courtesy, an expression of interest in another's picture, in a writer, or even in a relative, can lead, in serious cases, to violent outbursts of jealousy. It seems ridiculous for a wife to become indignant when her husband walks ahead with another woman, or talks to someone else at a party instead of devoting himself exclusively to her. Such cases are frequent. Other people cannot tolerate their partner's praising another person. The customary remark is, "How can you bother with such an idiot?"

In many cases it seems as if the unfortunate victim of jealousy can find no peace because he is not sufficiently secure personally to trust a peaceful happiness. He seizes every possible chance for new outbursts of jealousy designed to bind his partner more closely to him, to arouse pity, to punish the other, or to lay down rules. In such cases, what we consider ordinary jealousy is aggravated to the point where it becomes a severe neurosis, and finally becomes what we might call a jealous mania. The principle is always the same; the sole difference in various cases is quantitative.

Jealous rages are occasionally accompanied by hysterical weeping, nervous anxiety, or depression, which all become transparent as soon as we observe the effect. Or the jealousy is expressed in swearing, or condemnation of the other sex in its entirety, indicating the further progress of the effect of jealousy; namely, a preparation for the complete degradation of the opposite sex. Frequently, pride prevents the conscious realization of jealousy, but the behavior remains the same.

In many cases, jealousy is aggravated because the partner reacts to the helplessness of the jealous one with an unconscious aloofness, or indifference. The indifferent person in turn bases her feeling of superiority on the evident weakness of her jealous partner and, as a result, does not employ the right tone of voice or assume an attitude tactful enough to inhibit the growing feeling of jealousy in the other. Such a common character trait and its developments dramatically show how we poison our lives and relationships with others on the most trivial grounds, and how all this would be unnecessary if we were willing to assume responsibility for our actions more than we are currently taught to do. To resume our story.

"You are annoyed because the boarder is not with us."

Here a marital fight seems to be commencing.

"Be quiet!"

It sounds like a modest request and most people who ask for nothing but quietness believe that they demand little. But they fail to realize that, in fact, they demand a great deal. Life means activity and noise. When I demand quietness, it means that I make laws for the behavior of others. It may sound modest, but it is a battle cry.

"Go and get him! Or stay home if you want to. You can live with him; I'm not going to stop you! If the child weren't alive, I'd have left you long ago."

We see the child standing in the midst of a matrimonial scene. She knows what it is all about. She receives impressions of married life. As you will remember, we found some traits in this girl which made us anxious about her future. Such scenes certainly influence a child by giving her as graphic a picture of marriage as possible. Unfortunately, we become acquainted with the problem of marriage through our parents. Consequently, children frequently want to avoid marriage because it appears to them as a difficult problem, or they resolve to have a model marriage. Both resolutions lead to countless difficulties.

"What can you offer me? Not even a pair of stockings! You skinflint! What a life! You should have remained with your Genevieve!"

Genevieve had been an important person in the man's past life.

And they started yelling at each other.

A pampered child is made an involuntary witness of a quarrel between her parents. She is used to occupying the center of the stage. What does she do when she feels excluded? She interferes.

I cried and tried to reconcile Father and Mother. The quarrel was horrible for me.

That sounds well-meant. But it was horrible for her because she did not play a role in the argument, because she was a pure nobody.

Trembling all over (one cannot do enough in such a situation) I entered the streetcar with them. Father made a sullen face; Mother was furious.

We can deduce from this scene alone that her father must have been a timid man. A tyrant does not act like that. Her mother was a woman who did not seem weak in any way. She knew how to dominate her husband.

Mother wore a large straw hat which, according to the fashion in those days, sat pretty high on her head. We were sitting in an open car and while the trolley was going fast, a wind came along suddenly and tore her hat off, carrying it out of the car. Still boiling with rage, Father jumped from the car in the wrong direction and fell down full length. Mother and I were terrified; the passengers sprang from their seats; the conductor signaled; the car stopped. Some people on the street helped Father up and asked him whether he had hurt himself. He was deathly pale and could hardly answer. The conductor swore. Mother kept on saying, "My God, what do I care for that silly hat? How can you do such a thing?"

When someone is boiling with rage, he should not jump from a moving street car. He can easily have an accident if he is preoccupied with something else. We are not trained to do more than one thing at a time; two are too many.

I knew very well that Father would have not fallen headlong if he had not quarreled. But I was glad that he escaped with only a few bruises.

Now comes a remark which can be understood solely by applying the Individual Psychological method.

The sensation we created was very painful to me. All the people looked at us.

In light of our knowledge of the girl's personality, we understand that she dislikes that kind of situation. That seems to contradict our statement that she continually tries to be the center of attention. She wants to be the focus of all eyes, of course, only when she is sure of making a favorable impression. As intensely as neurotics want to make a good impression, they also fear any situation in which they may appear to unfavorable advantage. One of the important problems of most neurotics is: How do I look? What do they think of me?

We come to this conclusion because after so many years, she still remembers her feelings in the humiliating situation into which she believed she had fallen. How painful the emotion aroused by the general attention focused on her must have been. But still, it was attention.

A policeman came along and wrote down Father's name and address. When we were seated again in the trolley, I hooked my arm on his and did not leave his side again.

She is in the pleasant center again.

I was raving-mad at the boarder. "Because of this damn fool," I exclaimed, "there are always quarrels. The devil take him!"

We have learned from former incidents in her history that, even in a state which can be regarded as normal, she does not flinch from strong incentives. Therefore, we will not be surprised if she uses abusive language when she is in a severely neurotic state.

I never cared to go on outings with my parents from that time on. I was always afraid Father would contrive to do something which could not be rectified.

We see that the disagreeable sensation and the fact that she was in the background had a prejudicial effect on her.

As far as I can think back in my life, my parents always quarreled.

That is not quite correct, but since it is so strongly emphasized in her memory, we suspect she will have difficulties in her own future love relationships. She will hesitate, retreat, or try to escape. I want to expand on the idea of escaping. We believe a neurosis is a mistaken way of living, not a disease. Therefore, we cannot take refuge in what does not exist. I have no objection to using the terms illness or disease as figurative expressions, but the dynamics are different. We must remember that while a human being is not responsible for an infectious disease of which he is the innocent victim (such as pneumonia, diphtheria, typhoid, etc.), he is responsible for a neurosis. Disease causes damage to parts or the whole of the organism; neurosis in itself does not. When certain organs become ill or are kept in a weak condition because of a neurosis, they were either defective or ill before. Such defects have nothing to do with the neurosis as such. Definite relationships exist between bodily illnesses and neuroses, but that does not make a neurosis an illness in itself.

This girl does not know anything of disease; she is constructing, arranging, building up her life, and when something interferes with her normal progress, such an interference is called a disease. This conception, however, is far from her thoughts, even when they are compulsive. She knows quite well the difference between physical illness and these thoughts. The error consists in stating definitively that health lies on one side and disease on the other.

A constant source of trouble was that Father, in order to have Mother free for his work, always wanted my sister to take me for a walk. However, she preferred to read novels. She was a real bookworm and sometimes even read by the light of the moon. When Mother cooked Lina's favorite dish, Father became angry and said, "You are quite crazy about your Lina."

Discord is introduced between the two children. We are not surprised that both girls feel neglected. This girl's (the writer's) attachment to her father justifies the assumption that her mother has not played her role very well. For some reason her mother did not succeed in retaining this girl's affection, so she is in the second phase of preferring her father. A critical attitude toward her mother has set in. It is sometimes difficult to find out just when such an attitude begins. I, myself, liked my father more than my mother because he pampered me more. At the time, I did not understand why. I certainly esteemed my mother very highly as a human being, and yet I withdrew from her. When I thought about it, I came to the following conclusion: When I was three years old, a younger brother of mine died. On the day of the funeral, I was brought to my grandfather. My mother came to call for me there; she was crying bitterly. My grandfather consoled her and I noticed that she smiled. I could not forgive her for this smile for many years; how can a mother smile on the day she buries her child? Later on I understood it better; my grandfather probably held out hope of future children to her. On the other hand, I might have thought: How glad I am that she can smile on such a sad day. I was very critical of her. Another remembrance: An uncle of mine asked me, "Why are you so harsh to your mother?" This shows how critical my attitude was toward her. Reconstructing the past, I can understand it now. My mother pampered me during the first two years of my life because I was a sick child. I became accustomed to this pampering. But when a new child was born, I was dethroned. My mother could no longer give me so much attention since she had to take care of the newborn infant. I could not forgive her for that. Then in the second phase, my father took my mother's place, providing the pampering that I wanted.

The girl's father is also angry because the mother cares so much for his stepdaughter.

One day, in a rage, Father flung a dish of noodles on the floor. Mother often had secrets with my sister. Father could not stand it. When anger made him lose control of himself, he would begin to grind his teeth, throw dishes on the floor, tear his underwear, trample his hat underfoot and threaten to commit suicide. Once in a while we heard him say. "If only I had a revolver!"

We already know this man is inclined to be jealous. That seems plausible when the memory of his wife's first husband comes up, caused by observing her prefer her older daughter. We know how to cure this man; we would have to show him that he cannot bear being replaced. We understand that he feels helpless; only the helpless resort to such drastic means. This clamor for a revolver is typical; it is a threat frequently made.

Then he would run away, even leaving his meals untouched. I was crazy about Father, was beside myself when this happened, and was in terrible anxiety about him. When they quarreled, I always cried, begged him to be quiet and held his hand. That soothed him a little, but he would run away in spite of it. I waited apprehensively for his return, and when it took too long, I put on my hat and went to the café to look for him. I usually found him there and we embraced each other as heartily as if we had not seen each other for years.

We recognize clearly from the above description that this child witnessed domestic troubles and the problems of her parents' marriage disturbed her childish beliefs resulting in her complete confusion.

Chapter VI

Sexual Development

Let us survey the story of this girl through the magnifying glass of Individual Psychology, in order to uncover all the connecting links which make her life a single chain. Let us review the story as historians, or artists who study the development of a work of art. We want to examine how each fact, experience, and reaction fits in with the other parts in order to find the general thread, or as we call it, the style of life.

Here is a spoiled girl, excessively attached to her father, who gets what she wants whenever she expresses a wish, and in whose future, for that reason, we anticipate great difficulties. When a pampered child leaves the home where she has occupied a favorable position, she has not been trained to withstand hardship. Since she has some presentiment of what awaits her, she will try to preserve the old relationships as long as possible, fear decisions, and approach problems as slowly as she can. Her entire style of life then appears to have had a brake applied to it. The hesitating attitude, as I have termed this general characteristic, is typical for every neurosis. The neurotic is always busy preparing to do something, sometimes very busy indeed. But before he puts one foot forward, he objects. He makes what looks like a start, but stops in time to prevent anything happening. He says, "Yes," which is supposed to express his readiness and willingness, but right on the heels of "Yes" comes "But." And he remains in the same spot. "Yes-but" concretizes the typical attitude of all those who are nervous. It is possibly the most succinct expression we can find to define a neurosis.

We often compare the character traits revealed by the life story of the girl with the distinguishing characteristics of neurotics, so that we seem to imply that her character appears neurotic to us. The objection may be raised that the girl has developed no neurotic symptoms and as long as that is the case, a speculation as to her neurosis would be premature. As you will remember, however, at the beginning of the story, we emphasized strongly the necessity of using our collective store of psychological experience and knowledge, and this experience includes not only the picture of the fully developed neurosis, but also an individual's preparation for a neurosis. Determining indications point to such a preparation and turn up regularly again and again in the early life of almost every neurotic. When we look back in a life story and see the appearance and reappearance of these preparatory traits, we can draw the empirical conclusion, without knowing the rest of the story in advance, that the life of the person concerned will degenerate into a neurosis at the first suitable opportunity. Also, we must prepare ourselves for the eventual outbreak of this girl's neurosis, in order not to overlook anything essential, or to lose the thread of her story. Consequently, the examination of even minute details may be important.

In this biography, many apparently irrelevant details are mentioned, such as social relationships and people who have minimal effect on her life. In learning to understand her, we are not so much concerned with what is exciting in her experiences, but with what has attracted her. All the little incidents must be taken into consideration to gain a complete picture.

Father was often sad. The reason for that was my unusual bodily weakness.

We see how much she is influenced by the fact that her father is anxious about her and that his life is devoted to her.

And when he was in good humor for several days, a reaction would immediately follow.

We recall that she was this man's only child.

He used to sit in his accustomed place without saying a word and with a sad face, one leg outstretched, the other bent and drawn under. Or he would sit on the table with his legs doubled under him, sewing and sewing, and if you spoke to him, he answered absent-mindedly. That always annoyed Mother and so there was another quarrel.

We must remember that this girl was deeply impressed by her father's position in relation to her.

During an exasperating quarrel, Father hit the glass door with his fist, hurting his hand very badly.

The attitude of her father to her mother, so different from his attitude to his child, became apparent to the girl and she felt superior to her mother.

He couldn't work for several weeks and had to visit the doctor every day. At that time he went out with me a good deal. I felt ashamed of being alone with him; I wanted Mother to be there, too.

That is an interesting remark. The child clearly had a feeling of guilt toward her mother. Successful in supplanting her mother, she felt guilty. We have seen how this girl wishes to be superior under any circumstances, superior even to her mother. Certainly, a feeling of guilt can spring from such an attitude; the girl fights for her mother's position only because of a lust for power. Other writers may say that such a feeling of guilt can come only from an Oedipus Complex because this girl has a libidinous inclination toward her father. To such writers, we must respond that other authorities state that some girls have no Oedipus Complex. At this point, he who does not fully comprehend the significance of the struggle for power may think that the girl wanted something she was too frightened to take. In reality, however, she wants nothing but the dominating position in the family, and she has it.

When Mother gossiped with a neighbor, Father was beside himself. He was jealous of everyone, but most jealous of the boarder who really did have an eye on Mother.

We do not know how old the child was when she received these impressions. She is confused about time. When she was a small child, she kept a sharp eye on everything that happened around her. The position assumed by each member of the family grew clear to her. Living in the midst of active social relationships is how we learn to understand human nature. No one who has been carefully sheltered, before whom nothing was allowed to be said, can ever acquire such precise psychological perception. The more children are allowed to observe all that goes on in their home, the better their psychological understanding will be. The pedagogues say, however, that certain disagreements and tense situations should not be allowed to develop in the presence of children. While we do not claim infallibility for our recipe, Individual Psychology is in a good position. It does not matter what happens in the environment. What does matter is that the child connects to his family, that he develops social feeling, and then difficulties cannot produce negative results.

Acquiring information about sex is considered one of the great dangers for children. This view exposes the thoughtless inconsistency of the sexual experts. They say that the child is led astray by his school friends. This misleading is usually harmless and straightens itself out later, or the child simply does not believe what he has been told. When serious consequences follow such an explanation, we should blame the unintelligent parenting which prepared the ground for unpleasant results. There are many ugly things besides sex.

We should not assume that children believe everything they hear. When we were children, did we believe everything? When I was small, a boy told me that a butcher slaughtered human beings and sold the flesh. I didn't believe him. Similarly, a child may have serious doubts about a suggested explanation of sex. Children must be carefully taught the truth, so that they can have a firm hold on the useful side of life.

We once went walking and Father started to quarrel with Mother about the boarder, then raised his cane and threatened her, thereby accidentally striking me on the forehead. A swelling the size of a nut resulted. Father then controlled himself, but was most perplexed. I was so angry at the boarder that I said to Father, "Come Father, let us go and leave Mother behind."

The child's hostility is obvious. She uses everything to gain a victory over her mother.

Mother's position was not a favorable one. She was a pretty, cheerful woman and Father killed her cheerfulness. He wanted to keep her in the house to take care of the home and sew for him.

We are certain this fact had a harmful effect on the child. She will begin to dread the fate of her mother.

She fears that such a fate can change the course of one's entire existence, and that the same thing may happen to her that happened to her mother. In this way she nourishes her suspicions about the dangers of love and marriage. She will never be trustful; she will watch to avoid any indications that she also will be imprisoned in this fashion. She will be on her guard and learn to evade such problems.

One evening Father brought home a pearl-handled revolver from the neighboring café. Mother and I recalled his frequent threats of suicide and had no peace until he returned the revolver to the owner of the café. I always shivered when a quarrel began and they were almost always quarreling.

The child's trepidation during her parents' disagreements is not as simple as she implies. There is always the possibility that she will become of no importance. Two persons occupy themselves without giving her any consideration. A child's interjection into her parents' quarrels is often because she cannot endure being overlooked.

In spite of everything, however, I idolized my parents and watched over them jealously. Once when I noticed that my father started to follow a girl, I clung to his arm and cried, "You aren't going to follow that monkey-face!"

We are not surprised. Her goal is not to preserve harmony between her parents, but to be apprehensive about her own loss of power. That is often the root of jealousy, particularly where love does not exist and dividing relative power is the issue.

Most neurotics cling to their families to an extraordinary degree. This girl's form of expression is typical, "I idolized my parents and watched over them jealously." We are certainly not criticizing close family ties. The final judgment of every human attitude and action may be based, on the plus side, on this attitude's degree of social feeling or altruism, and on the minus side, the degree of superiority striving or egotism. The same action can therefore be useful or useless, depending on whether it works with, without, or against social feeling. The degree of social feeling may be used as a criterion for the evaluation of human deeds and for the human being as well.

Now that we have seen how all neurotic characteristics are distinctly opposed to social feeling, how the neurotic strives in a supremely egotistical manner for personal power at any price, we can assume that his devotion to his family is not based on sincere affection, but is used as a means to achieve an objective that feeds his lust for power. A neurotic needs the family which pities him, believes in him, and thinks he is ill, as he needs his daily bread. He knows that he would be an absolute nonentity without his family, abandoned without hope of reducing his feeling of insecurity and insufficiency. It is consequently to his advantage to make the ties between himself and his family as strong and lasting as possible, in which the usually uncritical attitude of his family helps him considerably. He often arranges an exaggerated affection for one or all members of his family, which naturally has nothing at all to do with wishes tainted by incest. Because this arrangement gives him domination over the family, family ties have been declared holy. In general, we find a nervous person more closely attached to his family than those who do not suffer from or complain of nervousness. The larger circle of the community frightens him back into the small circle of the family. Here he obtains what he does not believe himself capable of obtaining in a larger group. Wherever we meet a nervous person in the company of strangers, that is, outside the family, his gestures usually betray a backward tendency toward his family.

From this point, we will watch and see whether our general observations so far will be corroborated further in the remainder of her story.

And he had to return home with me. And whenever he thought a girl was pretty, I used to say, "All the women with monkey-faces seem to please you."

That is the expression of jealousy.

I came home one evening from the movies and found Mother in great excitement. Father had gone to deliver some material. Mother told me that Father's old assistant had been impudent and had wanted to attack her. I didn't quite understand what it was he wanted of her, but I was incensed and swore, crying, "That damn fellow. If I see him, I'll break his head!"

My best friend was my schoolmate, Olga. She did everything I wanted her to do.

We might have guessed it.

We used to play theatre together.

Again she emphasizes something visible. We have noticed before that this girl has an extraordinarily good visual sense, a penchant for everything visible. Those who have more experience with Individual Psychology know that such an interest must be trained. We have previously mentioned that training like this is usually started by some sight difficulty in early childhood or even in infancy. We presume that something similar has been the matter with this child. Her visual training is unusually strong. We must keep such points of special interest in mind.

Many dramatists have had bad eye defects; their training has sprung from such deficiencies. We must be able to see before we can visualize a stage scene. This visualization is easier for those who have placed seeing in the foreground. Such training is a disadvantage when the difficulties are overemphasized; on the other hand, an advantage can be seen in our appreciation of art.

We used to dress up in long robes and bind our heads with veils. Her brother was then a gypsy or a robber chief who stole me. Gradually he became annoying to me. He never wanted to let us alone.

We see here the strong preference for girls and the rejection of boys. He bothers her. We often find a choice like this, showing a preference for members of the same sex. If the boy was not much older, we can understand how the girls felt superior to him. That might also be a reason for rejecting him.

Once I locked myself with her in her room. We undressed ourselves, jumped around naked, and examined ourselves all around in the mirror.

Again the desire to see.

And because we had heard somewhere that two together could do something impure, we laid ourselves, first one, then the other, on top of each other. We were very disappointed because we didn't feel anything. Outside the door, her brother cried.

Now we hear another reason. At this point, we must address an important problem. Some might speak of a homosexual component. Psychological schools that believe in the inheritance of fully developed sexual tendencies will conclude from the girl's last remembrance that the primordial urge, fully developed, and dormant in her up to this moment has finally broken through. This conclusion appears to us somewhat superficial and mechanistic. Our interpretation is different. We know that in childhood, as soon as sexual desire manifests itself, nothing is received with so much shock as knowledge of normal sexual relations. This child's up-bringing and the impressions she receives from her environment have conspired at an early age to shock her with the first information about sexual relations between men and women. And what shocks a child will usually frighten her.

Premature exposure to even normal sexuality can lead to problems. Such youngsters either begin to masturbate or they seek homosexual relations; but whatever form their sexuality may take, it is only the sordid remains of normal sexuality. Homosexuality and masturbation certainly are not the normal forms of sexual development. In such cases, the normal has been frightened out of existence by shock and anxiety. An example will prove our statement. Consider those places where children are watched too carefully, the poorhouses, for instance, where boys and girls are not separated. There we find that no development of the sexual drive takes place other than the normal relationships. Should we assume that well-to-do children experience sexual development differently from poor children? Or consider those institutes exclusively for boys or girls, where cases of homosexuality often occur. Is it then just a coincidence that perverse sexual practices are more common among institutional children than among those who grow up in family homes? Or is the Individual Psychological conception more correct that the direction of an individual's sexual development is not inborn, but determined by his environment and upbringing?

Thus we can see the timid sexual expression of this girl in another light. The boy annoys her. Without knowing that, however, we may be sure that she will not increase her sexual experience by approaching boys; she is much too fearful for that. Consequently, she uses her friend, Olga, who, as she admits, did everything she wanted her to do and whom she likes for that very reason.

I don't remember who told me that love dies when one gives someone a needle. Anyway, I believed it. I talked it over with Olga and we decided to use this magic on her brother. I took a needle, broke it in two, gave him one half and told him that that made our friendship stronger and that it meant being true to each other forever after. He took his half of the needle happily and stuck it in his jacket. Then I laughed and said: "Now I can tell you that it's all over with love because the needle really means that love has been punctured!"

What did the boy do?

He began to cry bitterly.

He was obviously advanced in his development.

I was almost sorry for him. After a while it occurred to me to tell him that a gypsy had once prophesied that I would die when I was eighteen.

This theme of having an appointed time when she claims she must die occurs frequently. What happens when she makes this claim? We then begin to see through the veil: (1) if she really believes it, she feels herself superior to and excused from the prosaic duties of everyday existence. That is the end result. No matter what happens, there are no more tasks for her, a situation which suits a spoiled child; (2) when a girl makes such a statement, she immediately becomes the center of interest. Everyone is so upset that the girl is treated with more indulgence than ever--the consequence of her desire for indulgence.

The boy was inconsolable. Tears rolled down his cheeks. I was also very much distressed. I had said it so convincingly that I almost believed it myself.

I do not know whether I have emphasized yet this peculiarity of hers. Lying is quite common among neurotics. A pathological liar believes it when he says, "Our family is going to ruin." He feels it so much that he is shattered by it. A human being has the ability to make himself believe what he says. But just because all lies are not conscious lies (as for example, in neurotic and psychotic cases), they should not be treated with severity and punishment, but like all neurotic symptoms, with understanding and explanation. Neurotic lying is always an attempt to appear greater than one really is. Therefore, it indicates discouragement and an effort toward seeming greatness. The more a man believes he must lie, the more deeply he must be able to believe his own lies in order to appear so credible to himself and others that his story is absolutely convincing.

Similarly, we cannot fully appreciate the qualities of someone or something without some identification with him or it. Funny as it may sound, I have the feeling that I can identify with a bird. Or, for instance, bowling and watching the ball rolling, we begin to sway as if we were the ball ourselves. A feeling of this nature which we assume or into which we talk ourselves, as it were, is of much greater significance than previously recognized. Identification will, of course, come strongly to the fore when suitable for the goal in view. This girl likes to see the boy cry, so she tells her story all the more convincingly.

The boy was crazily in love with me. I am still surprised that a child of nine years can love so much.

We see here a love experience in a child of eight years. Those who have their eyes open will not wonder. We recognize such tendencies in early youth. Many are honestly in love with the other sex at the age of four or six.

I made Minna's acquaintance in the park. Her father was a cashier in a café. She invited me to her house. She had her own playroom, loads of toys, a child's dinner service, a little sideboard, even a set of doll's dishes, and always money for sweets.

We can imagine the consequences. She with her two poverty-stricken rooms; the other girl with the luxurious apartment. There will be difficulties. She will feel unable to invite the other girl. She will have to lie.

And now the following bothered me. Minna waited quite a while for an invitation from me. I was ashamed to have her at my house because we had only one room and a kitchen, lived so poorly, and had no pretty furnishings. Once when we were standing in front of my house, I said to her, "Look up there, at the first story, there is our apartment. The whole floor belongs to us, but mother keeps the key. We also have a room on the parlor floor, but there isn't much space there." And she looked up curiously. I always had an excuse. One day I couldn't keep my appointment with her. I had to do an errand and couldn't let her know in time. She waited and waited in front of the house and I didn't appear. Finally she screwed up enough courage to enter the house and to knock on our door. I was very embarrassed to see her in the house upon my return. But I saw at once that she felt quite at home, and that reassured me. In the course of our conversation, she asked me if we could go upstairs. I replied quickly, "Not today, it hasn't been cleaned." Soon after, however, she learned the truth, and we both laughed at my pretensions. We met almost every day and I neglected Olga. We liked most to play at cooking. We used to mix chocolate and slices of apples with milk and eat the mess. We used to buy "charlotte russes" and pickles. And for a small sum we could go to the movies. When children were not allowed to enter, we would become furious and swear at the theatre owner. Then we used to read fairy tales together and also books not suitable for our age. I remember a book I found in a chest, "Julia's Marriage," by Prevost. It tells the story of wedding night and I almost had a headache over it. And once I got hold of a book, "Children of the Divorced,"--the love and life story of a twelve or thirteen-year-old boy. He committed suicide at the end, and that made me very sad. I couldn't understand the reason for it. And I even read Ibsen in the fourth school year, naturally without understanding him. For example, I couldn't understand why Hedda Gabler shot herself.

Adults frequently do not understand why either.

I wanted to learn from the books, to learn to understand human nature.

This reveals the secret of many of those children who constantly read books. They want to fill the gaps in their knowledge of their fellow human beings. Children do not accept everything sight unseen; they test and compare; they imitate what they see in the moving pictures and in the theatre. They continually prepare for the role of the adult; they train in every direction. One aspect of this training lies in experiencing other people's fate from books. The strongest interest in beautiful literature arises because we can see how someone else attempts to solve his problems.

In the meantime, Father had established himself as an independent tailor. Our apartment served the double purpose of workroom and living quarters, which cramped us very much. Otherwise things did not go so very badly with us. Father could even assume the responsibility of new furniture on the installment plan: two chests, a table, chairs and beds. Before Christmas there was so much to do that, Mother, who continually had to help Father, found no time to cook. That annoyed me very much.

This child is upset because everyone is busy working instead of paying attention to her.

Minna's mother made the most elaborate preparations. They had been baking at her house for days; at our house we were sewing. On Christmas Eve, Mother went with Father to deliver the finished suits. Lina, who had moved away because of the limited apartment space, took me with her to her house. There she had a tiny Christmas tree. Everything was very nice, but the evening meal consisted only of herring, which didn't particularly appeal to me. When my parents called for me, I complained, "On Christmas Eve, I have to eat herring." Father answered that he had enough money, and we were going to eat in a restaurant. But I had lost all desire. There was a Christmas tree at home and I also got what I wanted, a child's set of dishes like Minna's and a rattle, but the mood had been destroyed.

She is severe; when everything does not go smoothly, her mood is destroyed.

I visited Minna the following day. She had a large Christmas tree with electric candles, and innumerable presents lay on her table. I did not envy her because of that. . .

This lack of envy might be pride.

. . . but when her mother asked me what I had received, I suddenly assumed the role of one to be pitied and said, "Nothing at all."

There lies the suppressed resentment, and at the same time the gesture of a beggar. We must watch this trait. To belittle oneself in order to produce a greater effect is the beggar's attitude.

I was greatly pitied and everyone hurried to make me a present -- a book of fairy tales and all sorts of pretty cakes. Among my father's customers was a young man who was friendly with a divorcee. This woman had a daughter my age, who resembled me very much. Her mother took a great fancy to me and often used to take me out. She rented a villa for the summer in a suburb and invited me to visit her. Father reluctantly let me go. Minna was away in the country for the summer and this suburb was my first country vacation, and for a long time the only one. In spite of the fact that I was extremely well treated there, I became so homesick after two days that I wept ceaselessly and demanded to be allowed to return home.

We must say something here about the psychology of homesickness. Anyone who is homesick feels that he is in a more favorable position at home. Spoiled children are usually homesick. Her position in the country seems to be a favorable one, but it is really less so; at home she is the center, in the country only a little girl; therefore the homesickness. She must yield to such homesickness; she was not prepared for the change in her situation.

There was nothing else to do but bring me home again as soon as possible. Lina studied for a whole year to be a nurse and how to assist at operations, and smelled dreadfully of carbolic acid. She fell in love with a Czech. Now and then she sent me to him with a note. Once the housekeeper opened the door and said, "You are Miss Rosa's sister, aren't you?" and told me some gossip.

How soon this child is initiated into love relationships!

I told my sister about Rosa, but she, of course, already knew about it. She often cried, and then Father and I would have to console her. When the Czech returned to his country, she took a position in a hospital in Prague to be near him. We tried in vain to dissuade her. Her departure irritated me exceedingly.

Why? She loses a person from her court. To exaggerate the situation somewhat, such a person needs to have a court around her. She does not consciously realize that by this strategy she assumes an extremely powerful position.

Chapter VII

The Problem of Love

I have forgotten to mention Tilda, my first friend. I met her on the street.

In spite of the pampering she received, she was able to make the acquaintance of children on the street. Probably the best way for a child to learn about human nature and people is on the street. If we could at the same time prevent the dissemination of so much evil knowledge, it would be a good way to raise children. If we could arrange for more supervision, and be reasonably sure that evil elements would not lead children astray, this may be the best way to obtain a many-sided experience. The common rivalry, the struggle to discover and influence relationships among human beings is the origin of social life. Large cities today cannot give children any sort of street life because of traffic dangers.

We have frequently remarked that this girl is an excellent observer and she has possibly developed this ability by associating with children on the street. Even if she has developed in a neurotic direction, she also has developed to an unusual degree the power to combine her perceptions.

Such abilities are trained to be used later as means for the easier attainment of the fictive goal. Again and again we perceive how valuable strength and talents, abilities and possibilities are spoiled and made worthless by a neurotic goal. Were a neurotic to turn into useful channels the collective strength and intelligence he employs pursuing a neurotic goal, the diverted energy would probably be enough to make a genius of him.

She had just climbed onto a delivery wagon; I climbed on after her; we began to speak to each other, played together, and promised to meet each other at the same place the following day. Her mother had a candy store in our neighborhood. I met her again in the fourth year at school and saw her often. She told me of her suitor, a ten-year old boy, Henry by name, who had already promised to marry her.

We see how far-reaching the preparation for future life is, even in a child's tenth year.

Then I made his acquaintance. I immediately tried . . .

To do what?

. . . to take him away from her.

Accustomed to being first, she had to choose this course when she found herself in such a situation.

I was half successful. We three went to the movies together, used to sneak into the garden of the insane asylum together and play at being married.

That is the beginning of sexual relations. These games, playing doctor, mother, and father, can be found among children the world over. The children make them up. I wonder why no one has yet discovered a repetition of forgotten, archaic rites in these games. It is superfluous to speculate on the theory that each individual must repeat the entire story of mankind, as some psychologists believe. Every individual uses the same sort of games as a preparation and training for adulthood, and he does not have to repeat the whole story of mankind in order to do this.

We often spoke of a friend of Henry's who was very good-looking, but who was also quite arrogant and didn't think much of girls.

We see how the variations in adult personalities are formed in early childhood. Children recognize these variations and also know how to react to them. Henry's friend made an impression on our heroine.

That sounded interesting to me, so I asked Tilda to arrange to have us meet. When she spoke to him about it, he said he would look me over.

I do not know if all my readers can comprehend how the girl is made to play a subordinate part. Obviously, the boy looked down on girls. His form of expression is degrading, which she understood. Anyone who is unable to hear this undertone, who is not musical enough to apprehend it, will not be able to grasp our way of thinking.

We all met. We walked around a bit and our talk was soon of kisses. I asserted that I would never in my life let myself be kissed by

214

anyone. The boy answered that he would prove the contrary to me, by force if necessary. I did not take him seriously. It was already twilight when we crossed the square, and he threw his arms around me. I struggled, called to Tilda for help, and freed myself after some effort.

The picture recurs. Man is the aggressor, the girl the hunted animal. How hard things are; how careful one must be to avoid such attacks.

I upbraided him for his impudence and pointed out that a stolen kiss was not the same as one given voluntarily.

Notice how the ten-year old girl can argue; she has learned it in her family.

And that, if I were a boy, I would never bother about stealing a kiss.

With that she degrades him.

I walked alongside him cautiously. What angered me most was that he had rumpled my hat and hair. Soon after, he asked for another appointment through Tilda, but I didn't care about seeing him again since I knew I could have him.

For the first time, this girl faces the problem of love. She must formulate a response. Unquestioningly, the form of response or reaction will be influenced to some extent by the behavior of the other person. Nevertheless, I believe we may definitely conclude from all that has gone before, and from the little test we have just read, that our girl will not regard love as a means of development, and certainly not as an expression of social feeling, but as a means to win power and significance. Provided, naturally, that she does not run away from the problem completely. We have to watch carefully in her story how she reacts further to the question of love as one of the three great life problems--whether she approaches or withdraws from it. We can measure the degree to which an individual is normal or neurotic by the degree to which he attempts to solve or evade his problems.

During my fifth year at school, I became friendly with a girl named Sophie. She could play the piano and I envied her on that account.

We see how her striving for recognition proceeds in all directions.

I had long wanted a piano.

I know that I shall now hear the objection: Is it a sin to want to play the piano? We find it quite worthwhile, but is that all? No matter what comes along, she will say, "I want to have that, too; I want to have that, too." This constant wanting is characteristic. Anything forced into the foreground to the exclusion or detriment of other factors, disturbs the smooth course of our existence. Cleanliness is worthwhile, but when I make it the salient feature in my life and think only of how to make everything clean, I then not only neglect all other important tasks, but I also discover that everything is so dirty that it is not even worth the trouble to continue living. Thus constant washing becomes the symptom of a compulsion neurosis.[1] A person may say that everything is dirty. Is he right? We shall not even discuss it. If we make cleanliness the most important thing in life, we can no longer live.

It is the same with sexuality. When I make sexuality the pivot of my existence, the world is then so topsy-turvey that I don't know the difference between left and right. One person makes this problem of major importance; another individual chooses another problem to overemphasize. To understand this mistake, we must also understand that everything starts in early childhood and therefore must be false, because children cannot approach the absolute truth and cannot judge the world correctly. Stressing one problem to the exclusion of others disturbs the harmony of life.

And yet, the overemphasis of one principle does not have to disturb life, and that is the principle of social feeling. When I maintain the belief that, under any circumstances, I will go only in the direction of general usefulness, I can make no important mistakes. No one has been able to disprove this principle.

To this point we hear the objection: But the personality is lost. This view misconstrues social feeling as conformity to an existing culture rather than attempting to improve it. In the case at hand, however, we find a greatly exaggerated striving for recognition. The goal of superiority is also expressed in the desire for a piano.

---

[1] A compulsion neurosis produces symptoms which the patient believes force him to do certain things against his conscious will.

Sophie's foster parents--her parents were dead--had a grocery store where Mother often used to make her purchases. In this way our two families became acquainted with each other. Her mother suggested to my father that he send me to the same music school her daughter attended which boasted an excellent teacher. I could then practice at their house. Father took her suggestion and I entered the music school.

This intense struggle to attain greater heights will not be hindered or censored. We would all agree that she should learn to play and that everything was still in the direction of general usefulness.

Girls and boys were together at the school. Many of the boys fell in love with me. I thought they were all fools and ran away from them. One in particular never left me in peace. He always greeted me with, "I kiss your hand, Fraulein." That pleased me somewhat, but otherwise I didn't like him because his father was a shoemaker.

Her father was a tailor. We see how significant social rank is to her. If her father had been a shoemaker, and his a tailor, she would have argued in the same way; that is to say, the shoemaker would then have been better. From this one sentence we can deduce that this girl wants to surpass everyone, not only in the family, but in the outside community as well. Consequently, she has little to give the community. Her problem is: How can I be first? She stumbles on obstacles and opposition. She must be careful not to fall in love because her hat and hair may be rumpled.

I liked to make believe . . . that I was of better family and if I could avoid it, I never said that my father was a tailor. When I was younger and someone asked me what his occupation was, I used to answer that he was a fire engine inspector. Our boarder, who had been a fireman, often told us about fires and how dangerous a fireman's job was. That made a deep impression on me.

If he had told some heroic story, she would also have made use of it.

I treated the shoemaker's son badly. When I was in good humor, I permitted him to accompany me part way, but when I was in bad humor, he was not allowed to come near me. I used to say "sir" to him and order him about, "Just see that you go your own way, sir, or I'll call a policeman." That made him angry, so he got two other boys to watch for me and throw stones at me. Then I would run away. I saw them waiting for me in the schoolhouse and that frightened me very much. I was afraid our teacher might see them and think that I had something to do with them.

She dreads a bad reputation, a trait which appears in intensified form in a neurosis as, "What will the others say?" It is the anxious, consequent slogan of those who want to be first. Most people live in fear of the opinion of others, permitting their actions to be influenced by it. When we become aware of how much superfluous anxiety and worry govern our conduct, and of how little true courage there is in the world, we cannot wonder that our epoch is called the "neurotic age." It was probably not much different in other times; perhaps the only distinction is in the changing fashions of living.

There was a high school student at the music school who used to lend me detective stories. Henry also used to lend me some. I devoured them with Olga or Sophie. Detective stories gradually became my passion. At night I was so terror-stricken that I couldn't sleep.

Many children prefer detective stories because they like the tense excitement produced by reading them and, further, because they like to discover tricks in such stories which they can utilize to achieve some superiority over others.

The type of book or the life style of the reader determines the reasons for the fascination with detective stories. In most case, the reader likes to identify with the detective whose superior ability to uncover trails and detect clues, whose strength and dominating position are all so impressive. Here is a man who obviously knows nothing of impeding weakness in mind or body which makes so much trouble for the reader in his daily life. In his imagination, the reader elevates himself to the role of a fictive personality (the detective) and obtains the laurels of success without exertion. The value of such identification lies often in the carrying over and retention in daily life of some of the courage inherent in the imagined role of the detective.

The appeal of detective stories lies as well in the excitement and anxiety evoked. The reader frequently finds himself in a tense state by identifying with the pursued, and this tension enables him to come up with ideas for saving himself. This is especially true of those books in which the author gives the role of hero or adventurer to the fugitive who must overcome innumerable obstacles in his path. The reader usually identifies with the character assigned the role of the hero, no matter whether detective, adventurer, or thief. Only those individuals who always choose the opposite select a disagreeable character with which to identify themselves.

All readers extract some form of pseudo-superiority from detective, mystery, or adventure stories. They like to play with dangers which are really no dangers for them and which, as they know in advance, they are going to conquer. They abstract, as it were, from reality without having any responsibility. And therein lies the danger of fantastic tales. They estrange from reality and open the way to irresponsible, neurotic dreaming. Courageous individuals do not need such fictions and will not resort to them.

I was also passionately fond of films dealing with criminals. One of the theatres once played "The Man in the Cellar." Children were denied admission. I schemed the whole day how to get in. Finally I got one of the older girls to buy a ticket for me, pulled my hat down over my face, and got in.

You see the effect of the detective stories and crime films.

The picture had a terrible effect on me. I couldn't fall asleep for a whole week. I was afraid to breathe in the dark, I would wake Mother up, and when she fell asleep, I would then awaken Father.

We have known for some time about her tendency to disturb her parents in the night. When her mood became one of anxiety through identifying with the characters in the motion picture, the result was what her style of life compelled. The result would have been the same without the feeling of anxiety, but with it, she feels more justified.

Terrible fear also caused the following:

This girl begins to describe how she gathers anxieties as a miser gathers treasure, collecting situations which can produce anxiety.

Father had the habit of letting the shutters down, but not closing them. Every passerby could look in. Once I was lying awake in bed between my parents. Father was still reading. He used to read an hour before going to sleep. Suddenly I saw two eyes glaring into the room like those of one crazed.

The erotic reason for the peeping can be recognized distinctly from the way she describes the incident. When she speaks of horrible shocks, we must not forget her tendency to harp on and exaggerate situations producing anxiety.

I was very ambitious and learned quickly during my first three years at school. I liked chorus practice best. I didn't have a good voice, but had a good ear. Some children always sang off key.

Here also we see how sharply she notes the difference between herself and others. For someone else, this difference would not have been significant enough to remember.

They trembled when called on to sing and didn't even dare open their mouths.

She has recognized very early the unfortunate inferiority feeling of those children who lack some accomplishment, and who lose control of themselves when they must reveal this lack. I have seen children almost desperate because they could not whistle. I once met a boy who told me that he could not whistle for a long time. One day he succeeded in whistling and felt as if God were going to whistle through him. We can see from this description what immense importance is ascribed to these abilities.

They made me laugh so much that I had to stick my head under my seat.

We have known for some time that laughter is also a language and has significance. Dostoevsky says that we can tell a man's character from the way he laughs. She laughs so heartily that she must hide her head under the chair. That looks as if it would pain her to show others how superior she is. Anyone who can recall the picture of a classroom knows that nothing is more noticeable than hiding one's head beneath one's seat. It is an exaggeration which looks more harmless than it really is.

And sometimes I laughed so much that a little accident would happen . . . When I was ten years old, in the fourth year at school, I began to neglect my schoolwork. I became lazy, inattentive, and very dreamy.

We do not know why this girl grew less studious in her fourth school year. She may have had another teacher whom she liked less; maybe she was scolded. Suddenly she applied the brakes and stopped. Spoiled children often progress as long as the way is smooth, and neglect their work as soon as a difficulty presents itself.

The teacher said I could have been one of the best students, but that I was too lazy.

She is fully satisfied with that. That is the pronouncement which often attracts children to laziness; they satisfy themselves with the possibility. They do not speculate badly. "One bird in the hand is worth two in the bush" is taken to be the greatest of wisdom. The feeling, "I could be the best," is sufficient; they do not go further so as not to destroy this illusion. When they really accomplish something, they have the advantage of being praised by others; consistently studious children are not noticed much. Lazy children stumble on a paying road; like all unmanageable children, they work under less trying conditions.

Father was indifferent to my progress at school. He only concerned himself with my health. He was always careful to see that I had enough fresh air. In the evening, when he was through working, he often went walking with me. We would pace quickly along the streets to the railroad viaduct. Then I waited, shuddering, until the train shot out of the tunnel. It could be heard thundering a long way off. It appeared to me like a monster, a dragon, a devil. The moment it rushed passed me, I swore at it out of the smoke which threatened to obscure me.

Even this little incident is exaggerated, comparisons made to increase the effect of the sight of the train. Even out of that she extracts the advantage of the possibility for anxiety. She will construct groundless fears until she cannot rid herself of her anxiety. That is the development of training toward an anxiety neurosis.

I was not a good student in high school either. When Christmas came during my first year in high school, I wanted a piano badly. Father wanted to buy me a used one, but could not find any good enough. Christmas morning had already come. I cried, yelled, scolded, threatened neither to eat nor drink, if there were no piano in the house by evening.

Undoubtedly, her relationship even with her father is poisoned by her desire to rule.

At that time Father's earnings were quite good and he had intended to buy me a piano anyway. When I became so wildly furious, he dressed himself and promised that he would try to buy one on the installment plan. After some delay, he succeeded in getting one and it arrived just in time. I was never so happy in my life. I immediately opened it and began to play. Then I ran over to Sophie's and invited her to return with me and see it. Then I played again and played and played until Father made me stop. I was really happy that day. The next day I arose very early and practiced diligently. Before that, I had always said that I had a piano. Now I didn't have to lie anymore.

I used to play pieces for four hands with Sophie. At the end of the year, a concert was arranged at the music school. I wanted to be nicely dressed for it and asked for white shoes. Father didn't want to buy me any and painted an old pair white for me. The general examination took place at the school on a Sunday morning. We played our pieces. We even had to learn to bow correctly. Everything went off smoothly. I had no stage fright and played my pieces without any mistakes. I played one piece with Sophie.

We would like to use this opportunity to say a few words about stage fright, a frequent symptom. Stage fright usually appears when people confronted with a task are less concerned with the accomplishment of the task than with worry about what people are going to say about them. We have already seen that many neurotics are greatly dependent on the opinions of others. When their striving to accomplish something extraordinary is excessively intensified, the success of this striving becomes increasingly uncertain and the possibility of failure looms that much nearer. In stage fright, we clearly see the general, neurotic anxiety before a decision, the hesitating attitude, and the distance between the person frightened and his fellow human beings. If that pinnacle of success which inordinate ambition has set is not achieved, stage fright offers an excellent alibi. If the task (a speech, an examination, or whatever it may be) is crowned with success, the value of such a success is doubled, for it has been achieved in spite of the handicap of stage fright.

Various reasons explain the absence of stage fright before a public appearance. Such absence may indicate perfect objectivity and adjustment to life, routine training, or the naivete of one who has never suffered a defeat. Stage fright is naturally no inborn characteristic, but results from early experiences. The reason for the absence of stage fright in this girl is unquestionably the last named, that is, the naivete of one who has never suffered a defeat. We can imagine how it will be when she faces a failure or a dangerous situation. As long as she continues to progress, she has no stage fright.

My friend distinguished herself and recited a poem at the end of the performance. A year later we found, in addition, that something practical and lucrative could be done with my piano playing. Tilda's father, Mr. Stockinger, who was a waiter in a wine restaurant, suggested that we play together in the restaurant. One evening Tilda and I collected our music, small pieces, quadrilles, waltzes, and so on and went over to the restaurant. We lost our courage at the entrance. We quarreled as to who should enter first and squeezed through together. Mr. Stockinger immediately brought us to a table and gave us some wine. Then we were asked to go to the piano. At first we were too shy. After some coaxing, however, we went to the piano, and looking neither left nor right, began to pound the keys. There was much applause and that flattered us. After a short pause, we played a second piece in our best style. When we had gone through our repertoire, we took a plate and went around collecting money which we later divided. We bought a lot of chocolate cake on the way home. I gave Father a silver coin.

There was a restaurant next door to us, in which an athletic society met every Wednesday and Saturday. They always engaged a musician to play for them. I often saw the men exercising. They made the funniest faces when they marched to the music and when they exercised with the heavy iron dumbbells which they couldn't quite manage to raise aloft completely. Their arms trembled and their bellies shook. I could hardly restrain my laughter.

How she tried to revenge herself on those who were strong. She laughs at them because of their facial expressions and for any reason she can find.

The musician was ill once and the restaurant owner didn't know what to do about getting a substitute on such short notice. He thought of me. I was quite willing since I could earn a little money.

We should say something here about the desire of children to earn money. Children have an intense longing to earn money and we must try to channel this longing in the proper direction. We see the same longing in adults who have always been financially dependent on others and who have never earned any money themselves. It is wrong to speak here of miserliness, thrift, or the desire for money per se. We see it better in the light of Individual Psychology. It represents the struggle for equality. In our civilization, since money has become the measure of a man's worth, even though a most inadequate one, everybody exerts himself to realize his worth in money. In this way, we understand the child's desire to possess money as the attempt to be equal.

The athletes were pleased with me and offered me tarts and beer. One of the men was very fat. Later I received another tip. At home I assumed all sorts of airs, snubbed my family, answered their questions nervously, and then told them they ought to have some consideration for me after the strain of such hard work.

We see how this girl begins to assume airs. She has done it before in order to appear greater.

I substituted for the pianist as long as he was ill, and later played once in a while when he was away. There was hardly room to move in our tiny flat. An apartment was vacant in Sophie's house which had an additional room; the living room and kitchen were also larger there. We moved over, but my proximity to Sophie lasted only a short time. For some reason or other, the landlord gave Sophie's parents notice. Her parents sold their store and moved to Ottakring, quite some distance away from us. I visited her often. She told me about a boy with whom she had fallen in love and pointed him out to me. I surveyed him, and then gave her my opinion. "I wouldn't have anything to do with a boy like that. Get him out of your head."

We are already familiar with this attitude. What another has is worthless.

That didn't stop me from flirting with him . . . I always dressed myself carefully when I went over to see her and would parade in front of her. She admired me very much.

There we have the ideal friend for this girl. Her friend must admire her, must put up with criticism and let herself be ordered about.

She adored me. She took literally whatever I said. She met a girl in her new neighborhood whom we both mocked. Sophie explained to me that she only went around with her because she was bored, but that she always thought of me. To make her jealous, I told her that I had fallen in love with a boy, described him in detail, and told her how we kissed and how we talked to each other in the movies. I said he was surely going to marry me. And I promised her that I would hide her under my bed on my bridal night and she promised to do the same, in case she married before I did.

Again her penetrating curiosity.

Then we kissed each other and swore to always be true to one another. She often complained of her foster father. He used to tell nasty jokes which thoroughly disgusted her. He even wanted to "touch" her. She was very afraid of him. I shuddered when I heard this. Her foster father was also very strict; he boxed her ears when she brought home a bad report card from school. My father would laugh and say, "Five is more than one." (Five was a bad mark, one a good mark.) I once got a mark of five in the class on religion. It happened this way. I had not gone to mass on Sunday and had to give a suitable excuse. Instead of doing that, when I was asked why I had not attended, I replied, "Because I didn't want to."

We know that in school nothing is more dangerous than to tell the truth about such things. As long as we lie, we are respectable, but when we tell the truth, then we get into trouble. I do not know how children emerge from this training in school. Woe to the child who says, "I was bored," or who answers the question, "Why didn't you greet me?" with "Because I didn't want to." When he lies, he is a valued member of human society; when he tells the truth, he is lost.

Here we see a further reason why children lie. Often it is the way of least resistance. Children learn to save themselves many disagreeable moments by lying. They sometimes have the example of an adult whom they detect in a lie and whom they then imitate. The latter event has the added attraction of being able to imitate an adult, in other words, to appear greater than they really are.

The class was as still as a mouse. It sounded like blasphemy. It was at least honest. Only the teacher didn't know enough to appreciate honesty.

We understand how this girl came to do it. She must also feel superior to her teacher.

I believe that was in the first class at public school. At that time Father had a book with pictures illustrating the whole story of the persecution of the Christians in Rome. I couldn't read very well at that time, so he explained the pictures and told me the whole story. I would arrange stage scenes with my doll. Most of the time, she would take the part of a king's daughter. Presumably under the influence of those pictures which presented the crucifixion, I composed the following play: a strange knight steals my doll and kisses her in front of her husband who has just come in. Her husband starts to scream. The knight, with the consent of the stolen princess (the doll) has the husband knifed by a couple of hangman's assistants, tortured with heated tongs, and then orders his skin torn off. And while I was imagining all that to myself, I suddenly had the most peculiar feeling.

There we have the emerging of a sadistic-sexual fantasy. She is merely an onlooker, but she is inclined to observe closely the difficulties of others. We have often remarked how she attempts to degrade others. We must consider two points in attempting to explain how she comes to create such images: (1) her father, with the story of the persecution of Christians, has really opened the door for sexual stimulation under cover of sadistic, painful scenes and pictures; (2) she discovers at the same time that she belongs to that type which, at the sight of such scenes is not affected by accelerated heartbeat, gooseflesh, or loss of control of the sphincter muscles (muscles controlling discharge of bodily waste), but is stimulated sexually. We gather that her anxiety dreams, her liking for criminal films, do not remain merely as anxiety images in her, but go further and excite her erotically.

When the feeling subsided, I got up and thought to myself, "Now you have made a marvelous discovery. No one suspects what a wonderful feeling such images can produce."

We have heard how she was in the process of training herself to produce anxiety images and now that her type takes clearer form, she begins to train more strongly in this direction.

The first time I really heard anything about sexual intercourse was in the first high school class. There was a clique of girls in that class who had matured at an early age and had well-developed bodies.

226

They were supposed to understand jokes with a double meaning and to go around with boys. During rest periods, they could always be seen whispering to each other. I wanted to learn what they knew, so I approached them, behaved like them in order to win their confidence and walked home from school with them.

Children frequently pretend to know more than they really do in order to learn something. Here we see quite clearly how information about sex spreads in school. I am convinced that we cannot prevent it. Whatever he who attempts to explain sex to children does in an effort to combat such dissemination is useless against the elementary force which pervades the school. At that age children are critical and do not believe everything.

When I was finally alone with one girl who was supposed to know a great deal, I asked her if she knew where children come from. She said, "Yes." I begged her to tell me. I had heard different things, but didn't believe them. She didn't want to tell me at first. I teased her so long, however, that she finally consented. I had to swear that I would never tell anyone.

Notice how the girl who is supposed to be the most experienced is ashamed and embarrassed, demanding that it be kept a secret.

Then she put her head close to mine, walked up and down with me, and said that one must have sexual intercourse in order to have a child. The expression "sexual intercourse" was not clear to me, so she described the procedure. Horrified, I cried, "That can't be true!"

Chapter VIII

The Shock of Sexual Knowledge

Individual Psychology has always believed that man is an indivisible whole, a concentrated bundle of life, striving toward a goal. To attain this goal, he constructs a system embracing everything that may help him and rejecting all that may hinder his progress. When a man has an experience that registers in his memory, it becomes a part of and belongs to his system. This system continues throughout his life, including all forms of expression. The life of an ordinary healthy person conceals this system; serious mental disorders reveal it distinctly. Psychiatrists have long recognized the rigid schematicism of mental illnesses, especially noticeable in paranoia. Individual Psychological investigations have gone a step further and have pointed out that a similar life scheme is present in every human being, with the modification that in relatively normal individuals it is not so prominently noticeable.

When we apply this idea to our story, we come much closer to an understanding of this girl's system. Until now, we have been able to harmonize every trait and expression with her system. We are dealing here with a spoiled child who wants to occupy the leading position and avoid every situation which does not fit into her style of life. Let us see whether our hypothesis is confirmed.

My lack of confidence seemed to offend her somewhat, so she described the whole thing to me again. Then I wanted to know if only certain people had intercourse, or really everybody.

This is one of the common questions children ask as soon as they learn something about sex.

She answered, "Everybody, otherwise there would be no children," and then promised to tell me more about it the next time.

Here we now have the point of which I have often spoken. We should not believe that explanations by children are more pernicious than those by educated adults. When we compare the explanations given by children and by scientists, we often prefer the children's explanation. Their description is more human, more delicate. This child does not have to believe the other who is supposed to know more; she can doubt and in this way prepare herself for the truth. When an adult with his officious authority, comes and gives a brusque and dogmatic explanation, the child has no time for preparation, no time to doubt, to adjust, or to protect herself. We merely have to examine a pamphlet on sexual enlightenment to see that children are more delicate.

In spite of the exact description, I still doubted her words. It seemed too piggish to me. I came home quite excited. The more I thought about it, the more the alleged intercourse seemed grotesque. I grew nauseous when I thought of all other people. I exempted my parents, for I really didn't believe they would do anything so filthy. It even occurred to me that it was probably a dirty joke which some man had concocted and spread about.

You see the attempt to soften the blow.

I did think, however, that it was quite beyond good people, and in particular, my parents, to do anything of the sort. And a girl who would permit herself to do that was, in my eyes, contaminated and degraded. It was inconceivable to me how one could live after it.

Here appears the snag which seems unavoidable when enlightening a child about sex, since the child already has a fixed form of life. When such a child strives to be foremost, to shine in every respect, she receives the impression from such an explanation that sex is concerned with something debasing so she will, sooner or later, protect herself from the approach of the opposite sex. Even the most careful explanation cannot avoid this danger. The degree to which she will repel advances will depend on how much she has fed her ambition. She will have difficulties and begin to resent her sex. The superiority of the feminine role appears to be threatened because our culture grants men privileges whereby they appear superior in sexual intercourse. It is a cultural lie. If we could stamp it out, permit men no privileges and achieve equality, there would be no place for the thought of debasement or inferiority. If I believed this pitfall could be avoided by explanation, I would be manifesting an excessive naïveté.

It was incomprehensible that people could go on living afterward.

We can imagine that such a fiercely ambitious girl will try her utmost to ward off all thought of love and marriage. She will struggle desperately to avoid any solution when these thoughts become a serious problem. She will appear like someone who has set herself the task of building a life from which love and marriage are excluded.

How I myself came to be I did not think of at all.

That is one of the forms in which the rejection of the feminine role, the elimination of sexual activity, makes itself manifest. She did not think. What she does is active and difficult work. It is mental strain not to see, think, or face the question: How did I come to be?

I confided in Sophie what I had learned and added that I couldn't believe it. Then she told me that some time ago, she had heard her parents' bed creaking loudly. She couldn't see anything because it was too dark, but the creaking was very suspicious--her parents surely had an intercourse. I made her describe the creaking in detail. Then I said to her, "It may well be fine for your parents, but mine surely don't do it. I lie between them in bed and I would have noticed something long before this. My father is entirely too proper anyway. He originally wanted to be a priest.

You see how her first reaction comes primarily from her longing for superiority. Just as she didn't say before that her father was a tailor, now she surrounds him with the glory of having wanted to be a priest.

Soon after, I again walked home with my knowing schoolmate. She told me a whole lot more, all of which was disgusting to me; that all married women had intercourse; that it hurt very much the first time and that one bled the first time; that prostitutes did it for money and then had operations so as not to have any children; and that men wore a rubber protector.

We are now in the realm of sexual clarification.

Another girl said later that she had a thick medical book at home which she used to read secretly. Sexual intercourse was explained in that book in detail as well as the sexual organs, and there were also pictures. I asked her to lend me the book. She answered that she was afraid her parents might discover the book was missing or that my parents might discover the book in my possession. I persuaded her that everything would be kept secret and she promised to let me have the book for two hours.

A frequent procedure during the time of sexual clarification is to look in books. The dictionary plays an important role.

She invited me to her house. We wrapped the book in newspapers and with a beating heart carried it to my house and hid it beneath a chest. After supper, I got it out and sat down in a corner. My parents were very busy just then and didn't watch me. I read with boundless excitement. Now I had it in black and white and could do nothing but accept the sexual act as a fact. But I still thought my parents incapable of doing any such thing. And I decided then never to marry.

We have here the confirmation of what we expected, so we can anticipate precisely what she is going to do or not do, according to the style of life developed up to now. She collects reasons to avoid love in which she fears a defeat.

On the rare occasions that Father and Mother were affectionate to each other, I would throw myself energetically between them and make them understand that I alone was the one to receive caresses.

Again, she expresses a vigorous reaction against sexuality. When we assume that she does this because she is jealous of her mother and wants her mother's place in relation to her father, we disturb the clear unity of her behavior pattern. Freud called childish jealousy of one of the parents the Oedipus Complex. Oedipus was a Greek who unknowingly married his mother after he had killed his father. We believe that only in a few cases is childish jealousy based on sexual reasons. In general, the jealousy of children does not express desire for sexual possession of the father or mother, but merely a wish to occupy a higher and more powerful position. It is an expression of the struggle for superiority.

During the night I lay like a Cerberus between them. I often remained awake for hours--not purposely to watch. I simply fell asleep with difficulty. And when Father snored, I tickled him with my braid and when Mother snored, I shook her. I couldn't stand snoring.

A partial diversion from the theme. Even here there is nothing but "I" and "I." Everything must happen as I want it. We often find in the later lives of adults that they cannot bear certain habits, for example, snoring. Our girl objects to disturbances like snoring or turning on the light. We see how these trivialities mirror the lust for power. She seizes the slightest opportunity to lay down a law for someone else. We can see her powerful compulsion most clearly in the demand for quiet, a common method for asserting power. It is a means which appears modest, but is, in reality, tyrannical. As if such a thing as quiet were possible. The other must pattern his life rules on mine; he must live so that my demands become his general guideline.

When it grew dark, the prostitutes used to walk the streets. I watched them now with entirely different eyes. I wished I could hide myself in the room of one of them to see what happened. And once when it was evening, a man stood outside a house on the street and his trousers were open.

Such people are called exhibitionists. They are cowards in life who avoid normal sexual relationships and achieve their sordid satisfaction by exhibiting their sexual organs to desirable women, usually young girls. They are excited by the fright and nervousness aroused in the girl; they extract a cheap triumph from their seeming power to force another person into a wretched situation.

Most girls and women have probably encountered an exhibitionist. It is a frequent occurrence of which men are less aware. I have learned from personal experience that it is a widespread abuse. It makes a strong impression on such a girl, diverting her still further from the normal road.

In telling her story, she knows that she is stepping on the road of desertion. While she plans and follows her behavior pattern, she lays one brick after another, cemented by her striving for superiority and her fight to exclude everything which does not fit into her system.

I screamed and ran away madly. I never ran so quickly in my life.

You see how forcefully she emphasizes the flight which will be manifest in everything and everywhere.

When I was in the second year at high school, I suddenly imagined that the calves of my legs were too thin . . .

232

That is doubt of one's own beauty. The girl doubts easily. If she imagined that she were pretty, it would be an impulse in the direction of love. If she made her longed-for superiority a reality, she might be forced to face and accept a problem.

An objection could be made here that she is taking pains to make herself prettier, that she really wants to attract men, eventually to have a normal relationship. She does want to attract, but merely to secure her superiority. Deep down, she doubts whether she is really attractive enough for someone to love her. And this doubt is more important than all the useless puttering about which seems to flatter her vanity. This doubt is arranged. We must not forget that doubt does not come from heaven; it fits exactly into a person's system. We can look at doubt in two ways. Either we doubt because we have some unsolved problem or we doubt in order to have an excuse for evading a decision.

Our girl needs doubt in her system; therefore, she makes these discoveries of which we will undoubtedly hear more.

. . . and put on three pairs of stockings. Father was angry about it because it was summer and he said my feet would perspire. So I cut off the feet of the stockings and wore only the top parts. Then I stuffed them with cotton and even put on a pair of Father's knitted trunks.

In addition to springing from a doubt of her power to attract, this procedure is a symptom of a nervous condition already known to us. It is an activity on the useless side of life, overemphasizing useless things. It destroys the harmony of life.

My arms too . . .

You see how this progresses.

. . . seemed to me too thin.

We expect her to find many ugly points about herself with the consequence, "I cannot marry; I must exclude love completely from my life." She gathers reasons like a honeybee in order to avoid a love relationship.

I wouldn't have gone out with a short-sleeved dress for anything. Then I imagined I had shaky hands. So I tried to hide my hands as much as possible. At school there were girls with curved bodies. There was nothing to see on me. Olga and I measured our chests with tape measures. The result was very discouraging. Then we stuffed our bosoms with handkerchiefs and paraded on the street.

That looks like an attempt to attract others. In connection with other facts, however, we perceive that this girl considers herself of little worth. She makes attempts, as she says, to improve her appearance. These attempts hide a deep feeling of inferiority. In all that she has done until now, she shows no indication of moving in the direction of love and marriage. The attempts she makes are sufficient for parading on the street, but not for marriage.

Once when I passed my hand over my head, it seemed pointed and angular to me.

Now she is at the end of her art. She can stuff her stockings to make her calves appear larger, she can stuff her dress front to swell her bosom, but what about her head? You see how this training goes on. Up to her head everything has been patchwork; she must come to the point where she proves to herself that she is not suited for love.

I used to keep my hat on as long as I could. Sometimes the perspiration would run down underneath and I would not take it off. I remember now that when I was eight years old, I forgot to take off my hat in the classroom. The teacher had to remind me of it.

At this point, we should say something more about remembered and forgotten facts. We have already seen that conclusions for an individual's style of life can be drawn from remembrances and incidents. They have a definite psychological worth. These factual incidents usually have no significance to the individual himself.

What happens here? The girl tells us more than once that she has hidden her head. She does not say so directly, but intimates that she has wanted to hide her head when she was a child. In itself that is an inconsequential remark. Why does she report it? She jumps from one fact to another, and we often receive the impression that one fact is supposed to justify the other. This is very common among neurotic people. They establish a private logic, seeking the most irrational justifications and proofs for the correctness of their conduct. They relate experiences which are quite ordinary, but to which they ascribe such importance that we wonder why they carry so much weight, until we discover that these experiences or facts are supposed to be justifications.

The psychic machinery of the neurotic is so delicate that its functioning is jarred by the slightest disturbance from the outside, and so it is protected with a defensive shield of handy justifications. Nothing is permitted entry into the system until it is clubbed into form so that it fits.

We wonder at the dexterity of such a person who manipulates experiences and events until they fit into her style of life. If we did not know that the soul is a unity on which we work in order to arrange it more artistically, we would wonder why so insignificant a matter is emphasized. That emphasis is the compulsion of our psychic life to unity, a part of the general creative power of the life of the soul.

I was accustomed to making my hats myself, usually from the remnants of the things Father made. For the most part they were impossible, but sometimes one was wearable. The making of hats gradually became a mania. It went so far that Father had to lock up all the extra pieces of material in the house.

Again, she shows a good visual sense. We can imagine that the joy of designing something pleasing to the eye stimulated her. To that we add that she has never been scolded, that everything she does or says is praised, and we can thus understand that hatmaking also represented a training. She clearly shows a deeper desire to create something pleasing so that she can shine.

Father had an old coat which he had promised to remodel for me. He never took the time off to do it. I became angry and scolded him. I believe, I said, "bum" to him.

You know what friendly relations exist between her and her father, but you see how easily they can be broken when the question of power comes to the fore and he does not want to follow her wish. We could say she is impulsive.

Impulsiveness is a question of temperament. What is temperament? Doctors, psychologists and philosophers all differ on the meaning of temperament. Since the days of the Greeks, temperament has been divided into four distinct classifications: sanguine, choleric, melancholy and phlegmatic. Such divisions are purely descriptive and merely satisfy the desire for order in human thought. Pure forms of temperament seldom occur; what we usually see are mixtures. A human being, during the course of his life, can also change from one temperament to another. The representatives of the natural sciences believe that temperaments are produced by the various activities of the inner glands, such as the thyroid gland, the sexual glands, the suprarenal glands and so on. This assumption is quite mechanical and has not been proven. On the contrary, we regard the temperament as an expedient safety device, the development of which is determined by the degree of the feeling of inferiority and discouragement. Temperament is a means by which to attain one's fictive goal.

For centuries, we thought that temperament was inborn and inherited, a belief which serves to relieve us of responsibility. When we ascribe a deed to temperament, we absolve the doer of responsibility. And even when bodily conditions (so-called dispositions) do have some influence in the development of a temperamental quality, the objection may be raised that no bodily condition compels an individual to assume a particular attitude toward life. Of course, specific physical conditions suggest an abnormal attitude and make a normal one more difficult.

Like most mental qualities, temperament is trained to serve as means to the attainment of the goal. He who believes he will achieve his objective by being quiet and indolent will become phlegmatic, but will remain phlegmatic only as long as it appears advantageous to him. He who believes he must storm ahead will become impulsive. Naturally, the environment and the experiences as well as the physical constitution play an important but never compelling role in the formation and development of temperament. Every child is impulsive if she grows up pampered and then has her wishes refused. Mention might be made of psychopathy, but she handles the matter quite correctly; with the same goal, we would not act differently.

Father got up, gritted his teeth and struck me lightly. He didn't hurt me, but a little accident happened again because of my fear.

We may assume that this girl belongs to the physical type which loses control of the bladder in a condition of fear.

When the war came, we had to knit all sorts of things for the soldiers, mittens, socks and so on. I had to knit a pair of mittens. I knit an index finger in the place of the thumb and vice versa and then I tried to stretch the fingers. When we had to deliver the knitted stuff, I was afraid to hand mine in, but luckily the teacher didn't notice anything.

Many worse things than that were handed out to the soldiers during the war.

I pitied the soldier who would get those mittens. After an absence of two years, Lina returned from Prague. She was quite elegant and had a lot of trunks with her. While she was unpacking, I took a pair of her shoes and tried them on. They fit perfectly. They were the first ones with high heels I ever had on; Father allowed me shoes with only low heels. Later when I was sent out to get some beer, I went quickly to the neighboring café. There were usually two men there, one of whom had once asked me to play cards with him. I was a little in love with him.

The mention of love may seem surprising. We are not certain whether it is love or power; it is possibly a relationship consisting almost entirely of a striving for superiority. If this girl proceeds further, something will surely happen to prevent the complete development of the affair.

He was there when I entered, but no matter how hard I tried to draw his attention to the high heels, he didn't notice them.

Something begins here to which we usually do not pay much attention, an attempt to make an impression. Another striving lies underneath the one usually considered, namely, the power motive.

Lina brought me some Bohemian slippers, a writing book and many other things which I do not remember. But when the perfume and mouthwash appeared, I seized them, ran to rinse my mouth out, and sprayed my clothes with the perfume. Now we were all together again-- that made me happy.

We know what makes her happy; the fulfillment of her desire for superiority. The more she approaches her ideal of being the center, the closer she is to happiness. The bigger her court, the better.

We had a mouse in the house. When mother baked something, the mouse used to come through a crack in the door. The smell attracted it. Mother and I were terribly afraid of mice.

Girls usually dread and are disgusted by mice. Their behavior reveals their reluctance to being taken by surprise, and a fear of being harmed by the mouse. It is not always a sexual symbol, but when we remember how girls act as soon as they hear a mouse, how they protect themselves as if they were going to be assaulted, we can understand how it could be such a symbol in some cases.

I was sitting in my room and brooding. It was a habit of mine then.

The tendency of busying herself with useless things grows more marked.

Father carried the petroleum lamp to the kitchen and sat down at the sewing machine. And as I sat there in the shadow, something scurried across the floor from one side of the room to the other. I ran to Father and cried, "A mouse!" Father was of the opinion that I was seeing mice everywhere and that it was only a moving shadow. . . . I had a good nose for the smell of a mouse.

We have already heard of her nose.

I could smell it distinctly on my music; I was always an extremely good smeller. One night, as so often happened, I was lying between my parents who were already asleep. It was dark and very quiet. I heard something breathing and scratching at the door. I was terror-stricken and thought at first it was a burglar. I drew the cover over my head, listening intently. Then I realized that it was a mouse and woke Mother, who was as frightened as I. Then I awakened Father. He laughed at us. Jokingly, I promised him a piece of silver if he would get out of bed and chase the mouse away. When he lit the lamp, the scratching ceased. Obviously the mouse was afraid of the light. . . . We bought a mousetrap, but it did not catch the mouse. The rodent became more and more impudent. We often heard it scratching in broad daylight. The mouse nauseated me so much that I tried to force my parents to move out. In order to quiet me, they used to tell the funniest mouse stories. They said that a mouse had once sprung into the pocket of our assistant, Krassny. Mother's brother liked to play with mice and once he even put one inside his shirt.

You see how the idea turns up that a mouse can hide itself in one's clothing in some way.

My dread could not be overcome. I couldn't eat another thing whenever I happened to hear the mouse scratching during mealtime. Finally, Mother borrowed another mousetrap from a neighbor, and we caught the mouse with it. Father wanted to drown it, but when I saw it in the cage, it filled me with pity because of its pleading eyes and troubled movements and I begged for its life.

How can we reconcile that with the girl's style of life? No matter how small this object is, she can now be the merciful one; she controls life and death. It gives her a feeling of strength. She will probably have her own way.

We went out into the street and let the mouse run free. . . . Soon after we caught a second mouse. But by that time, I was so bitter that I agreed when they decided to drown it. Mother poured water into the pail; Father took hold of the trap; I got up on the table to be safe. Unfortunately, the mouse was too quick for them and sprang like a flash out of the trap and hid itself. Mother and I were furious. We knew that it would take care not to go into the trap again. A week later, when I came home one evening (our apartment was at the end of the house corridor), a mouse was sitting in front of our door.

She talks so much about mice that we are now attentive. There must be some connection with a former preparation for the sexual question; something is reflected here which has already been started.

I screamed, ran to the house door, and shouted to my parents through the window for help.

She behaves as she did when she saw the exhibitionist.

Mother immediately came out with a broom. The mouse had disappeared. It was doubtless the same one which we had already caught, so it did not dare, therefore, to enter our apartment. I believe it also warned the other mice about our house since, from that time on, we were spared any mice. Also, like most people, I was very afraid of rats. There were many in our courtyard. They used to creep out of the sewer pipe. Father often used to say that one could hear them whistling down the toilet pipe. When I heard that, I did not want to use the toilet any more. I was afraid that a rat could bite me when I sat down. We let the dog, Bello, hunt the rats. There was a wild scramble in the yard. The housekeeper with a broom, Bello running after her, and all us children who were scared, but who ran around here and there. A mad mix-up. I also couldn't stand spiders.

She continues to list all things she hated; she does not seem to emerge from this train of thought.

One morning when I was polishing my shoes, I felt something sticky in one of them. I thrust my hand inside and there was a partially crushed spider. I hurled the shoe in the corner and did not wear that pair for a long time. Once there was one on the wall just above my bed. I sprang out of bed and called my parents. Father wanted to kill it. I was of the opinion, however, that that might mean bad luck and seized his arm. The spider finally landed in the pail.

One day Olga found in the trunk of her father, who had been in Siberia . . .

A spider? A mouse? No. ... *the memoirs of Casanova.*

The close thought connection leads one to infer that a mouse was a sexual symbol in the life of this girl.

At that time I was in the third year of high school. We devoured the book. Then she discovered a lot of erotic books, bound in black, with the title, "The Secret Library," stamped in white. Trembling with excitement, we got the books out on the floor and read them aloud to each other. The books were called, "The Black Don Juan," "The Lady with the Dark Spot," "The Swimming Instructor in the Women's Bath," and so on. The most awful things happened in those stories.

Naturally, superficial observers will take this as an expression of eroticism. It is more correctly understood as a deviation from eroticism, as an effort to give very little place in her real life to it. The reading of erotic descriptions indicated the exclusion of eroticism in reality.

I saw a postcard which fascinated me in the window of a stationary store. It depicted a centaur embracing a nymph in a suggestive fashion, while whispering something in her ear. I wanted very much to buy the card, but was ashamed. The picture troubled me constantly. Day after day, it drew me to the store. Finally, I made up my mind, entered the store and asked to be shown postcards. The one I wanted was among them. Full of joy, I returned home and hid it among my underwear. When I was alone, I would take it out and concentrate on it, imagining myself sometimes the centaur and sometimes the nymph.

While we formerly found that she sought sexual excitement in her reading, she goes further here and begins to interest herself in pictures. She goes over into the visual.

The postcard made no impression on Olga.

We may conclude that they go different ways in their erotic development. Olga is another type; possibly she is not so frightened.

Funny that boys could not attract me when I thought they were superior.

Here we find a corroboration of the reason given for examining pictures and reading erotic books. She shuns love by occupying her fantasy with useless things. Boys are only there to be made fools of.

When we depreciate the value of something which we originally wanted, we rid ourselves of a disagreeable duty or responsibility, and retain our good humor. That is also the meaning of the fable of the fox and sour grapes. When the fox saw he could not reach the grapes, he consoled himself by saying they were sour, thereby retaining his good humor.

I never kissed one. The love life of my youth existed in fantasies. I used to imagine the story of King Saul in which he sent the husband of the woman he loved to war. And again that a woman was stolen by a knight, raped and her husband pursued by servants. There always had to be a broken marriage.

We remember that she has already had sexual fantasies.

Gradually erotic images no longer satisfied me, and I went about making them visible. On a piece of paper I drew a woman with a voluptuous figure, and a strong man, cut out the figures and laid them together so that they embraced. But I was a bad artist and my silhouettes looked awful. Therefore, I decided to write a story.

A new training begins at this point, or it is the continuation of one already begun which is preparation for her life story. She writes skillfully and fluently.

I first composed an introduction which told of a blond, immaculate girl and her betrothed. I described the person of the girl in detail; the man interested me less. Then the novel began. I let a friend of the fiancé appear, an untrustworthy fellow who immediately desired the girl. And she who treated her lover badly fell in love with the brutal friend. In a scene where the friend, from a hiding place, watches the girl bathing, I described her again in minute detail and was fascinated by my own description.

Here also those who have some understanding of human nature can recognize this deviation and how she searches for a new road in order to escape the normal in eroticism. Here we see how this aberration is nothing but the shoddy rest which remains when the normal is excluded.

At the end I describe an embrace between them. . . . I loved to watch myself in the mirror.

We see the predisposition to the visual. Such girls who remind us of the voyeur type are strongly attracted by mirrors.

Other girls disgusted me.

This is an attempt not to proceed further in the direction of homosexuality.

My own person pleased me most. . . . At that time I was in low spirits and went around with bowed head, not daring to look people in the face, imagined everyone could see through me and was afraid I wouldn't grow anymore. I was horribly unhappy. Finally I went to Father and whispered to him, "I have a confession to make." He asked me what was the matter now.

This sort of question is heard only in connection with spoiled children. They keep us busy with them the whole day long.

And I confessed with shame that I had done a certain thing. He said it didn't matter once, but I had better not do it again or I would harm myself.

She has found a more advanced road in eroticism; she has arrived at auto-eroticism. We can predict, in accordance with the girl's style of life, that she will cling to it for a long time. This satisfaction offers her several advantages. First, she derives physical pleasure. This pleasure is not only harmless, producible at will, but carries with it no binding consequences. It releases tense emotions which might force her to solve her love problem in more realistic fashion. The problem of love is circumvented. The question of power is solved to her satisfaction since she threatens her father with the possibility of a sordid habit and is unstopable. Retention of the habit over a long period indicates an asocial attitude. It is the eroticism of the lonely.

Now I felt better. But on the next day, I began again. And every time I did it, I would go and confess to Father.

We can explain why she did not hide it. She has her father in her power; she will force him to watch her more closely. She has secured a further protection for herself and given her father something else to do. He must watch so that she does not repeat it.

They used to watch me in bed, but in bed nothing happened.

Chapter IX

The Masculine Protest

When I was fourteen, I resumed my swearing at my parents and at God.

We must assume that difficulties have entered the life of this girl, as they obstruct the path of every spoiled child. Pampering cannot continue forever and this swearing represents anger at the deprivation expressed in degrading remarks.

The pampered child struggles for the continuation of the pampering. We can give the word "pampering" various meanings and say, "I understand pampering means this or that." But that is a waste of time. The moment she believes she is not being sufficiently pampered, she attempts in her rage to degrade others. For herself at least, she is in the foreground and overrides everyone else. Scolding is an attempt to degrade others. With a few exceptions, every child goes through some phase of being spoiled. This phase is present in the style of life. The interest in favorable situations is sharpened. The chief concern lies in the endeavor to regain the pampering. The trait to dominate and tyrannize is developed. Scolding stronger individuals and God cannot be separated from the feeling of one's own superiority.

(Case: A girl who had an illicit love relationship suffered from the fixed idea that everyone was a murderer. She was the oldest child, spoiled, ambitious, and brought up by her grandmother. When we hear the word grandmother, we can predict the pampering. When she was sixteen, she began an affair with an older man, which signifies weakness and a desire to be pampered. The saying goes, "An old man's darling." The affair lasted a long time and can be explained thus: I am stubborn and want to have my own way, and this man is also stubborn, so we have decided to marry. That is the logic of the neurotic. The man was good and gave in to her in almost everything, withholding his approval of only one thing, her cooking. The girl took particular exception to this. One day, she witnessed a murder in the neighborhood, a terrifying incident that made a deep impression on her. She used the word as a condemnation of civilization in order to degrade everyone and everything so that, as a consequence, she seemed to herself to be the only pure and innocent one left. We shall see how and why she does it.

Her lover had avoided introducing her to his family, and she could not endure it. We could have predicted that she would not be able to endure a free love relationship. She would feel herself confined and protest vigorously. During the war, her lover was sick and she went to great trouble to provide milk for him. When she finally had procured some milk, his mother took it from her, but then shut the door in her face. This girl was in a situation where she valued the man because she needed him. The love relationship had much more significance for her than for a balanced person. She wanted to be ahead of everyone and exert her own will through force. She preferred to continue the relationship, but there was something offensive about it. She achieved a measure of freedom for herself when she cursed people she did not know. We can compare this conflict somewhat with the feminine gesture directed against the disadvantaged falling to the lot of the female sex (the masculine protest). She did not get far--she reached only resentment and anger. She revenged herself in that she looked on every respectable person as a murderer, thus condemning our culture. In the beginning she condemned herself with the rest, later she excluded herself. Consequently, she was a saint and everyone else a devil.)

Without moving my lips, the most abominable words used to enter my mind. I felt terribly depressed.

Depression is often found with a compulsion neurosis. A depression usually starts when an individual believes he is forced by some power to pursue a particular course of action. Since these courses of action usually obstruct the activities of others or, at least, prevent a focus on useful things, the resulting depression resembles a self-accusation and is viewed that way. Frequently, the depressed person expresses guilt about his depression, but we should not be fooled by it. We want to study how depression fits into the system of this girl and we will also make some comments on depression in general.

Depression is a weapon used to elevate one's own position. The necessity for help from strangers is demonstrated through weakness, tears, sad moods and complaining, forcing others into service. Depression is related to melancholy, a miniature of it, so to speak.

An individual who fears a failure in life, or whom failure has overtaken, can point to depression or melancholy as the reason for the failure, thereby freeing himself of responsibility by demonstrating his own weakness and need for help. The neurotic logic thus finds a justification for dominating others. Insufficient social activity in youth sometimes results in the peculiarly aggressive attitude of depressed or melancholy people, which can be compared to partial suicide in that one damages oneself and threatens revenge on the environment. When a depressed person reproaches himself, he reveals an exaggerated notion of his own importance. In addition, we can always detect a complaint that it is partly, if not altogether, the fault of others. Supported by this grumbling, the subordination and assistance of the others is demanded and one's own irresponsibility and superiority realized. Depressions grow out of a suspicious and harshly critical attitude toward society and are usually developed in early youth.

We can see in a general description of the depressed mood the same characteristics which the writer of this life story reveals, the manifest striving over and control of her environment to strengthen her own security. Her system does not prefer to rule primarily through weakness. She will use this means only when she cannot succeed with direct aggression, or when she has gone too far and is forced to apply the brakes. Here she needs the depression in order to have a justifiable burden. The feeling of being heavily burdened she exaggerates thus: "I fight against it, but cannot rid myself of it. To be forced to do or say things is a terrible burden."

And often I was at the point of confessing to my father.

She has the tendency to make her father her confidant; she wants to indicate to him: "I am unhappy, one must give in to me, everyone must let himself be dominated by me."

I couldn't bring myself to do it. It was the only thing I kept secret from him. I felt miserable.

Even if she doesn't tell her father anything, he will notice the change soon enough. She will attract his attention through her ill appearance, her sickly and absent-minded manner.

And when I saw him before me with his weak arms, it hurt me dreadfully. I thought, "If he only knew."

She feels herself superior through her degradation of him. His weak arms!

I tried in vain to convince myself that I meant someone else when I thought of a bad name.

246

She wants to feel noble.

Then came the thought in between, "Father is a . . ." In order to prove to myself that father was not a . . . I thought, "Father is not a . . . ; his assistant is a . . . ," and cried, "He can go to the devil." Then I kept still and heard within me again, "Father is a . . ." Then it seemed to me as if all my cursing were aimed at Father, and I felt as if someone had hit me a hard blow on the head.

When we ask ourselves whether someone can demand anything from this girl, we have to answer in the negative. She busies herself with useless things, letting them consume all her energy. She has no confidence in herself. Her attitude expresses her doubts whether she will have a position in life similar to the one she has now in her family, and whether she will be able to solve her problems in a way that enables her to remain in the center of the stage.

Her neurosis begins here. When we look back, we become aware of the prolonged preparation consistently leading to this point. Her entire behavior tends toward evading the duties of a normal life in the society of her fellow human beings. She fills her time instead by occupying herself constantly with the matter of superiority in her own circle. When her superiority is endangered, and the problems of life approach more and more closely, the first compulsion symptoms appear. She curses her family and God, a habit she has practiced since childhood. We can now definitely determine that she is on the road to a neurosis. Her exaggerated desire for superiority and what we have termed her hesitating attitude have indicated this development for some time. Undoubtedly, she will sink more and more deeply into the mire of neurotic thought and behavior. In the vicious circle of a neurosis, a neurotic act provokes a strong reaction that triggers a still stronger act in the same false direction, arousing a still stronger reaction, and so on. In general, a neurotic cannot possibly find his way alone out of the labyrinth of his neurosis. Because of the patient's lack of penetrating understanding and his obsession with power, he has little chance of improvement without some outside, objectively comprehensive assistance.

Following the advancement of this compulsion neurosis can teach us a great deal. I would like to explain in more detail the character of a compulsion neurosis to prepare a better understanding of this girl's story. Compulsion neuroses are those forms of neurosis in which certain compulsive symptoms, such as compulsive-washing, praying, brooding, etc. govern an individual's life. These compulsions work like commands, and according to the patient's arguments, disobedience leads to direst consequences. Such compulsive symptoms torment the person who has them, arousing in him an anxious, painful mood.

When we observe what really happens (as we always do in Individual Psychology) and what the patient achieves with his symptoms, the meaning of a compulsion becomes clear. The compulsion neurotic has approached life's demands pretty closely. His retreat is all the more complete and demonstrative. Like all neurotics, he is ambitious, but discouraged. When he faces an imagined difficulty that he does not have sufficient courage to tackle, he shoves between himself and this difficulty a barrier constructed by his teetering ambition; this barrier assumes the character of a compulsion. He piles up a mountain of obstacles in front of him like a mountain of refuse, and when life demands something of him, he excuses himself by pointing to the refuse heap. He seems to use up all his energy overcoming this mountain that he himself has built, but what he really does is avoid the problem or demand. The diligence and haste with which he works, the severity and ostensible inevitableness of his compulsion are supposed to legitimatize his good intention.

In his attempt to combat the symptom, the patient assumes the right to produce it and, arguing according to his own private logic, becomes at the same time judge, complainant and defendant. As in all neuroses, the goal of a compulsion neurosis is superiority. We claim that the neurosis (including the compulsion neurosis) is an illness of position and not of disposition. The compulsion neurotic substitutes his own compulsion for the compulsion of the world upon him. His own self-elevation and lust for power is mirrored in the substitute compulsion. The main reason for and probably the main purpose of the arrangement of a compulsion neurosis is the frittering away of time which protects him from the necessity of solving, or even making an attempt to solve his problems. Only when we look ahead to the goal and result of a neurosis can we understand the sense of it. Like a revolt, the outbreak of a compulsion neurosis prevents a yielding to the demands of communal life. That is its purpose.

The objection may be raised that the patient may well be satisfied and happy with the superiority which he wins, and with the certainty with which he protects himself from the imagined danger of facing his problems. This would indeed be so, were it not a seeming superiority, a seeming certainty. A patient does not construct a neurosis by purely intellectual means; he brings to his aid his entire being, all his abilities and feelings in the arrangement of this "yes-but" mode of life. The neurosis is a weapon, a club; that is to say, the neurotic believes himself surrounded by enemies against whom he must fight until he has secured that which he considers the prize of victory. These circumstances leave no room for joyous feelings which would hinder him in fulfilling his intentions. He must pay dearly for the waste heap he piles up.

If we apply this general explanation to the life story of our young girl, we see her energetically occupied in establishing between herself and the community a barrier, a waste heap. She feels herself compelled to curse God and her relatives, reproaches herself when she is depressed, rules her environment, and wastes her time with useless things. Like every neurotic, she uses her neurosis in order to be able to say: I have not been able to solve my life problems because I have been so overburdened with these things. This "because" is typical. It is the neurotic justification in a private logic arranged to evade the true logic of life and to fit the patient's needs. Every person with some common sense can see how weak this justification is. And yet the neurotic must believe in it as he believes in something holy, whereby he indicates to us that in him is some glimmering of the distance between his conduct and the real demands of communal life. Otherwise, why would he have to justify himself?

I was never safe from the compulsion of swearing in the street or in company.

We see how she answers the first question of life (social contact). She creates a great distance between herself and others. Her swearing prevents contact with other people.

I was even afraid of myself. I was always worried that some accident would happen to punish me.

Here we can see what the feeling of guilt really intends. Its only purpose is to increase the waste heap on which it is thrown. Nietzche is right when he says, "Conscience pricks are indecent."

I endeavored to distract myself by every means possible.

We know in advance that she will not be successful.

Once when Minna and I were returning from the gymnasium, I talked continually in order to drown my thoughts. Suddenly I choked, had to stop and listen . . . Once I saw a criminal film, "The Man with Nine Fingers." It was horrible. An old woman was murdered in the film. My parents waited for me after the performance. My father said it was poison for me, but he did not divine the principal cause of my excitement. I seemed to myself like the murderer of my parents. In my thoughts I also had to swear at God. And then I heard a shriek as if it were from a devil, "You, you have said all that." Inwardly I answered at once: "God is the most beautiful man, and the best one there is." While I was saying, "Our Father," I heard, "Holy Mary, I pray to thee. No, I don't pray to thee."

There you have a pretty picture. When we move to the left and then to the right nothing happens; it looks as if we have done something, and while we waste our time in this way, we avoid solving problems.

Then there was an inward whisper again: "I pray to thee, Maria." I was perspiring with fear.

Such fixed ideas must shatter their thinker. In this shattering lies the principal purpose of the neurosis. Now we understand the significance of feelings a little better. Feelings are never arguments; they run in the direction demanded by the individual style of life. We can go a step further; the arrangement works toward the goal of producing the appropriate feelings to help the neurotic obey (follow) his style of life. This girl helps herself by producing feelings which build themselves into an impassable barrier for her. We hear that she does not want to go out into society, that she does not train for a vocation, and that she will fail in the third test imposed by life, the task of love.

Then the swearing proceeded with full force. I would have to start praying again. I tried with all my strength, but the nasty thoughts would come in between; it often took an hour before I could finish a prayer.

She has no connection with religion.

At that time I began to interest myself in men.

God helps the righteous.

I wanted to please all. I received compliments about my eyes and paid special attention to them.

Other psychologists would be happy. She is beginning to flirt a bit. We know that she will remain where she is.

I took some trouble to protect my eyes so that they would not lose their luster.

A new occupation. Another compulsion.

Sometimes I used to take a neighbor's little girl in her carriage to the park.

She would prefer to be in the child's carriage herself with someone else pushing her. We know that this activity will have a bad end.

It was very sunny there. I became apprehensive that the sun might dazzle my vision.

Refer to Freud's monograph on paranoia. She invents a new obstacle.

From that moment I avoided the sun.

She protects her eyes. Many psychologists would say it indicates that she wants to find a man, and would not notice that we can change something into its opposite. We can exaggerate self-protection to a point where we will be totally isolated.

When we want to understand such vague symptoms, we must approach them with the Individual Psychological question: What happens when a girl like this attempts to avoid the sun? All attachments are prevented by it, especially love, from which she draws further and further away.

I used to watch, anxiously fearing that a ray of sunlight might fall on me. I avoided all sunny spots. When I was forced to leave the shadow . . .

We see how much she has to occupy herself with it.

. . . and accidentally raised my head in the sun, I would talk it into myself that I had been dazzled by the sun.

When we glance back at the superstitions of people, at the mythological details that mention similar things, we can discern the marvelous phantoms of the ancients. Even in *Hamlet* there is a warning to women not to go into the sun or a pregnancy may follow. That comes from an old superstition. However, we do not have to assume that archaic thoughts were behind the girl's phantoms; it is sufficient that she has found something to cut her off from the problem she seeks to avoid.

I thought it out thus, that the sun had taken away some of my power of sight, and that I would have to go blind. Day by day, this thought came to me. Consciousness of the fact that I saw as well as ever was lacking.

She would have been able to do nothing with such insight; it would not have helped her system. Only when she imagines that she has been harmed can she withdraw from, that is to say, escape, the solution of life's problems.

When Lina went out with me, I begged her to avoid the sun. I wanted to find out if she trusted herself in the sun. She laughed and declined to follow this procedure. Then Mother came along. That didn't satisfy me at all.

We see how she hardens herself and that common sense no longer helps. He who asks the naïve question, "Why is common sense of no more use?" overlooks that she does not behave sensibly, but wants to run away. We can describe the wonder of the thundering guns at the front to a deserter a hundred times, but he will permit himself only those thoughts which help him to flee.

I used to get hold of Olga or some other friend and make her look at the sun.

That is her unsocial trait. She is possessed by the idea that the sun weakens the power of sight and permits all others to look at it.

So that they would not think I had become a fool, I arranged it so they noticed nothing. For example, I said: "I don't know what is in my eye; I can't look at the sun, can you?" And as soon as she raised her eyes to the sun, I had to laugh uproariously.

That looks as if she were purposely trying to do harm, as if she thought it desirable for the others to have their sight weakened. It is the laugh of the victor, probably an attempt to be physically superior to the others, supported by the idea that she knows a secret. She is superior because the others do not know it.

I believed their eyes were dazzled by it and that made me glad.

We see again how that is confirmed.

I always had my eyes cast down on the street. When I raised my eyes, I protected them with my hand. In spite of my precautions, however, the idea pursued me. Then I would run home like one possessed and say to my father, weeping: "I have been dazzled by the sun. I'm disgusted with everything, I'm going to kill myself."

She pushes her desertion to the extreme and plays with thoughts of suicide. She has lost hope. Arms, legs, eyes have lost their appeal.

Then I complained bitterly to my parents because they wanted to let me go away. At first they laughed and asked whether I had gone crazy. Father assured me that the sun had great healing power. He often went to the window, opened it, and cried to me, "Look here, how I open my eyes in the sun. I would be glad if I could go walking in the sun every day." When I saw how Father let the sun shine one him, I became confused. Then I began to lament all over again . . . I had a feeling of anxiety continuously, as if I were always sensing a terrible danger.

This danger is, of course, a defeat in love as we have found up to now. She is too proud. A girl who wants to be ahead of everyone cannot reconcile herself to the possibility of defeat, so her anxiety is concretized.

Finally, I hardly dared to go out on the street. I was also afraid that a stroke of lightening could hit and dazzle me. If the sun barely shone through a window on me, or if someone played with a mirror and the reflected light passed over me, I was terror-stricken.

Don't go in the sun. Let no one see you; you cannot compete.

Nowhere did I feel safe. I said to myself that the accident fated to happen to someone was inescapable, even if one locked oneself in a room. I was already sick of life and wondered, if things did not improve with me, whether it would he better to kill myself instead of going on to meet such a fate.

Now we see the consequences of this idea. She pushes the problem of seeing into the foreground. In order to justify this attitude, she has to find other measures. So we hear:

In order not to strain my eyes, I read as little as possible.

We are reminded here that she has spoken with emphasis of reading salacious books. This can be a withdrawal from them and a confirmation that she must protect her eyes.

When I read, I was always annoyed by being able to see the tip of my nose.

We can understand that very well because she was always looking at the tip of her nose. That would hold for others too, but others have no interest in the matter. It is a good excuse for eliminating reading.

I talked it into myself ...

We are approaching a beauty defect.

... that I was cross-eyed. I turned myself here and there, held the book in different positions; the tip of my nose followed me like a bad conscience.

We see how she preoccupies herself more and more with things that make it possible for her to think her eyes are weakening. I can imagine what would happen if she were to lose her sight completely.

I once read in the Bible that when some dirt was blown into the eyes of a saint, he became blind. This I now recalled. Dirt meant bird dung to me. And I watched carefully when I passed a tree. I also tried to avoid drain pipes where the sparrows and pigeons gathered. I used to look often at green lawns and bushes because I had heard that green was good for the eyes.

The more tricks she conjures up to strengthen her eyes, the more her conviction grows that the condition of her eyes is bad.

If the lampshade was not put on the oil lamp, I would become absolutely mad with rage.

We see how this tendency reflects her lust for power so that the others must follow her wishes.

I never looked at light or fire. Here and there people talked of diseases of the eye, for example, of cataracts. When they talked, they pointed to their eyes. I strictly avoided doing that. When I noticed that I had done it unknowingly, I was immediately afraid I would get the disease of which they were then speaking.

That behavior is one of the usual marks of hypochondriacs or compulsion neurotics. They include everything they can possibly fit into the neurotic mess in order to fritter away the time, protect themselves, and gain security against being dragged into the life stream. They feel danger in the stream of life and hang on to their neurotic life preservers.

I imagined that my eyes could jump out of the sockets as a result of straining them. I pressed them back carefully with my fingers.

We are astonished at the ostensible nonsense. This girl is possessed by the thought: How can I protect myself from having to accept love, marriage, and the role of a woman? She is indifferent to everything else and feels safe. Behind this confusion a star shines dimly, released from the role of a woman. She pays the price, she suffers, but merely to get her reward in the future.

I refused to let a blind piano tuner come to the house. It seemed to me that blindness might be contagious. After that, I even imagined that I had bumped my eyes against something and they had been knocked out. This delusion lasted for three months and was followed by a disturbance again started by a compliment.

Compliments were paid to her eyes, so she attempted to destroy them.

This time it was my teeth with which my disordered imagination began to busy itself.

Someone has complimented her on her teeth; however, that means she is fit for the role of a woman.

I was drinking from a glass and struck the glass against the edge of one of my upper front teeth. I suddenly imagined that I had broken off a piece of the tooth. I ran anxiously to Father and cried; "For God's sake! Have I broken off a piece of my tooth?"

Again exit beauty!

Then I opened my mouth and let Father look inside. "Where?" he asked astonished. In order to see whether he could find the damaged tooth himself, I didn't tell him which one I thought I had hurt. But when he could find nothing, I cried, "A front tooth," and pointed to the one. Mother and Father examined the tooth carefully from all sides, and could not discover a scratch. I became angrier, ran to the mirror, and looked at it myself.

Picture this girl: In her eyes a compliment works like a call to the front of life. Now that a compliment has been paid to her teeth, she must attack them.

And it seemed to me that it was a shade shorter than the adjoining tooth. So now I was quite convinced that I had broken off a piece and began to cry wretchedly. When Lina came home . . .

We remember that she is a professional, a dentist's assistant.

. . . she had to look into my mouth. She could find nothing. I asked her if she would dare to strike a glass against her teeth. She laughed, took a glass and tapped her teeth with it. I stood there and watched her earnestly. I had always been very particular about my teeth. I remember the following:

This is the tooth complex. She will now prove that everything was not always as it should have been with her teeth.

The front milk teeth were very shaky. It would have been necessary to tug only slightly to have pulled them out. Father wanted to try it with a string. I preferred to try it myself, tied a piece of thread around a tooth, made the other end fast to the door knob and began to pull carefully. I became afraid and let the thing go. Then a dentist who was a friend of the family looked at my teeth. I opened my mouth unwillingly. And before I knew what was happening, the shakiest tooth was already out. But he let the tooth fall into my mouth and in my excitement, I swallowed it. My parents were very upset. For a few days I had to eat cabbage. When I was six, one of my teeth hurt. On the way to the dentist, I cried and complained and didn't want to go. Father promised me a pocketbook if I permitted the dentist to pull out the tooth. I wanted the pocketbook first and Father really bought me a very pretty bag. Then he advised me to think of the brave "Tin Soldier" and everything he had had to go through. When we got to the dentist's house, I halted for a moment in front of his door, and then said to Father, "Let's go to another--I'll surely cry with this one, and with another I'll have more courage." We turned around and went to another. He looked at the aching tooth and advised pulling it. I whispered to my father: "I have to consider it--he has such an angry face--let's go to another." And with some excuse or other we left him and finally returned home. I got such an awful toothache that night, however, that mother had to go with me the first thing the next morning to the dentist. I concentrated on the "Tin Soldier" and finally let the tooth be pulled.

But that was long ago. Now I had my anxiety about my teeth without any visible reason, without any pain. The idea alone that I might, in some way, strike my mouth against some object, was enough to make me think I had knocked a tooth out. When the idea occurred to me, I always used to consider the position in which I found myself at the moment and measure the distance between me and the nearest object, such as a box or the piano. I wanted to prove to myself that it was impossible for me to have hit myself against it. I had retained that much sense. But the only result of this proof was that I became still more excited. For then I believed I had not taken enough care and had really damaged a tooth. And then I would measure distances again. Then I would again imagine that I had broken a tooth or at least scratched one. I experimented so long until I was exhausted by my efforts and excitement. Finally, quite discouraged, I would upbraid myself: "How can a person be so stupid as to knock out a tooth on purpose?"

Now she imagines that she has already knocked one out. A tooth plays an extraordinarily important part. We can clearly see how someone arrives at a tooth fetish. Her tooth-complex is not fully developed, but we cannot deny that she greatly overvalues a tooth.

My parents had to look into my mouth constantly.

We see how the wasting of time grows to undue proportions and how she becomes the center of the family.

Naturally they never found anything. No one could find the slightest thing the matter, not even I. I didn't believe the others or myself.

She helps herself quite simply in order to be able to go further. She cares about her teeth, not her duties as a woman.

And so when I discovered tiny irregularities in my teeth which I had not noticed before, I imagined they were the damages I had inflicted on myself and began again to fume. Sometimes when I was eating cherries, I bit on a cherry stone. That depressed me to such an extent and drove me into such a condition that I needed a whole day to recover. Finally, I used to squeeze the pits out of the cherries before I ate the fruit. I even had a peculiar way of eating apples. I cut them in thin slices, laid a slice at a time on the knife, and inserted the knife carefully into my mouth. Once the knife struck against my teeth and I immediately thought I had bitten on the knife. I was beside myself and shrieked: "No one has ever done that before, to bite on a knife and break one's teeth off." My parents demanded to know what the matter was now. Lina happened to be there. Everyone was amused, as if glad about what had happened. Father was of the opinion that I deserved it, because of my exaggerated carefulness. I became still more excited, thought Father really meant that I had broken off my teeth by my own fault. Chokingly I cried: "Now you do admit that I have knocked out my teeth?" Father rejoined, "I don't admit anything. But when you are so stupid as to imagine anything like that, it's about time you ate apples like everyone else." I did not stop crying. Lina picked up a knife and tapped her teeth with it. Then she asked me smilingly if the performance was sufficient. Little by little, I became quieter. About two months later, I noticed that there was some tartar on my teeth. I had scratched it off before with a needle. When I remembered that, I became terribly unhappy. "My God!" I said to myself, "certainly no one does that--scratch the enamel of one's teeth." I wanted to commit suicide. When I drank coffee, I used to think that the heat of the coffee might crack the enamel. I refused to drink anything too hot or too cold, and drank coffee, tea, soup, beer, even water, lukewarm. I ate nothing hard. I was afraid to break a tooth if I did. I ate no more bread crusts, no meat in which there was a bone. No chocolate and no sugar. Then I didn't chew anything any more. I let the foods melt in my mouth and then swallowed them like a toothless hag. That looked so funny that my parents used to laugh until they cried. Then I avoided even bringing an eating utensil in contact with my teeth. I opened my mouth as wide as possible and inserted the food as carefully as I could or sucked the food up from the spoon or plate. Finally I ate only with my fingers. In the tram, when a window rattled, I became anxious and thought it might fall and knock out a tooth.

She arranges her life so that she is freed from every occupation.

This delusion also lasted several months. But a still worse one followed. I had an excruciating youth.

I was just returning from school. I had accompanied a friend and wanted to cross the street. A man approached us from the other side. He had a cloth around his face. I thought at first he had a toothache. When he came nearer, I noticed that his whole face was eaten away. There was no nose, no lips, only a number of red holes. I felt as if someone had struck me. I was seized with such dread of this man that in order not to retrace his footsteps, I turned around and made a detour home.

Now comes the lupus phobia[1] and with it the fear of infection. We now see more clearly and can prophesy that this fear of infection will lead her to strengthen her feeling of security and support her still more in her attempt to exclude love and marriage from her life.

---

[1] Fear of lupus, which is a tuberculosis of the skin.

Chapter X

A Lupus Phobia

The last thing she collected in her effort to rid herself of reality was a man with a rash.

I was seized with such dread of this man, that in order not to retrace his footsteps, I turned around and made a detour home.

The impact of these impressions, driving her further and further away from life, is intensified. Again and again, she finds an excuse for continuing her flight.

Still extremely frightened, I told Father what had happened.

Significantly, she tells it to her father and we may well ask why. The obvious answer would be that she is on good terms with him and has confidence in him. But we can find another reason for her behavior; she wants to make him understand what will follow--that she must attach herself still more closely to her family, lessen her contact with the outside world, appear laden with burdens and incapable of doing anything or of solving any problems.

He thought it was probably lupus. What was that? A devouring disease whose name in Latin means wolf.

The father, who had a morbid fear of tuberculosis, had two or three medical books which he often read--hence his knowledge. We might say that he also has a phobia, and therefore she has inherited his fear. But it is not so. The girl trains herself. She takes the means which she can use and which appear serviceable to her in the specific situation-- whether from her father or elsewhere. Supported by her fear of an infectious disease, she now believes she has the right to separate herself from the outside world. Why should that be an inherited trait? She wants to be at the top and observes that she cannot possibly attain in the outside world the favorable, central place she occupies in the bosom of her family. We would like to ask anyone who doubts this: Who would leave a favorable situation for an unfavorable one? Common sense speaks here; we do not need profound hypotheses. If someone wishes to object, he first has to show us whether he would willingly leave an agreeable situation to enter a disagreeable one.

I wanted to know if this disease was infectious.

I have already indicated that this girl may already know something of infectious diseases of the sex organs.

He assured me that it was not the case. But I did not believe him. Not even when Lina confirmed his words. From the beginning, I was firmly convinced that lupus was infectious.

I would like to comment about the peculiar methods of the nervous when they establish their conceptions. They must be right, and everything is turned about until they have proven what they set out to prove. This disease must be infectious. Even if all authorities were to say it was not; she would still assert it was. We find with almost every neurosis this false logic whose force lies in the fact that it permits the patient to do what she otherwise would do without proof. For example, I knew a patient who had always played the leading role in her family and whose situation suddenly became unfavorable through an unsuccessful marriage. She arranged a hunger strike, explained that she could eat nothing because she had a weak lung and got an attack of coughing when she had to swallow the food, consequently doing real damage to her lung. Her behavior was an attempt at suicide. When such a patient gets to the point where she asserts that the most important thing at that moment is to get up and go for a walk to stimulate her appetite, she arranges matters so the conditions cannot possibly be fulfilled and her insight will not interfere with her neurotic striving. A "no" in answer to life is clear.

Even though two people who know about it insist that lupus is not infectious, she will not be convinced.

I would have preferred never to set foot again on that street. But we lived just around the corner, and the way to school was through it, so I could not avoid it. Gradually, this fear vanished.

How are we to explain this? We hear that such a disorder can disappear only when it is treated by means of psychological interpretation. Symptoms of illness as the outer, visible signs of a neurosis are labile and vanish for a time, or sometimes change into other symptoms without psychological treatment. The patient constantly tries to adjust himself to the varying pressure exerted on him by his environment. The girl says: Gradually this fear disappeared itself. If we believed her symptom was of sexual origin (repressed libidinous wishes, for instance), then we would have to assume her libido has undergone a transformation. Such an interpretation is too far-fetched and, in addition, false. We know that she has temporarily lost her courage. As soon as she regains it in some measure, she feels her schemes are superfluous and tries once more to find a way to life. Obviously, when her courage increases a little, she loses her anxiety. We see her hesitating attitude toward the question of love. We observe how she seeks to escape it. We want further confirmation as to whether we are on the right road. All these phases represent attempts to escape an answer to the question of love.

One afternoon a boy called for me, an acquaintance of Olga's who was attentive to both of us. We went for a walk together and happened to pass a street where there was a home for people suffering from lupus. The windows of the home were covered with green netting similar to the netting used to make nets to catch butterflies. I heard the whirring sound of some apparatus. All at once, I noticed where we were. I was horribly depressed, spoke not another word and turned to go home completely broken. I was as if lamed. My thoughts stood still and only one thing filled me, dread of lupus.

Just when she is with the boy attentive to two girls, something fills her with dread. Two reasons may explain: (1) the boy also likes another girl; (2) she can use her lupus phobia to escape the solution of any problem.

At first I could not answer at all the worried questions of my parents as to why I was so upset. Horrible thoughts whirled in my head. I thought that the people who accidentally trod in the footsteps of a lupus sufferer would spread the germs over the whole city.

Now the whole town is full of lupus. Now she cannot go anywhere any more. The distance between her and the question of love grows step by step.

I asked myself, "Where on earth is there a place with no lupus? Where is there a spot where no lupus sufferer has left bacteria behind him?" The whole world appeared infected to me.

We see here the gesture of exclusion of the spoiled child.

I felt as if I were surrounded by bars through which there was no way out. At the same time I felt I hated and loathed the lupus sufferers.

At this point, we shall also pause a moment. Most people would say that was a natural and understandable gesture of rejection. But in other situations in the life of a neurotic person, the same gesture appears without being natural and understandable. For example, what does an exaggerated fear of mice or spiders signify? Why does a nervous individual emphasize his hate and loathing so forcibly? There is no logical rationale for it. The gesture demonstrates a feeling and aims at something other than an imaginary fear. In our case, it serves to preserve the distance which the fear of lupus has created between her and life. Nothing agreeable to her can be used as a means to attain her end. She must make use of something disgusting in order to create a justifiable distance between herself and life.

She acts correctly according to her system. If she did not have the accompanying feeling of hatred and loathing, then her behavior could rightly be called idiotic. There lies the difference between feeblemindedness and neurosis. A neurosis is always consistent, constructed on a scheme of private logic. Feeble-mindedness is inconsistent; it has no logical coherence or sequence whatsoever.

Father's objection that all other people existed without such fear was of no avail. It seemed as if lupus was there for me alone.

Here we see how well she says it and still does not understand. The disease really exists for her.

A punishment for me alone.

This punishment must not be taken seriously. Nervous people say, "This is the punishment for my sins." This girl does not care about constructing a guilt complex if she can merely exclude love.

Like a horrible, gigantic spider, the dread of the devouring disease crawled through me. If I had known of some way by which I could have killed myself quickly, I would have done it. But I knew none.

She has not gotten far enough to cut off her life completely. She still has one resource, her family. Such a girl could be driven to suicide by separating her completely from her family, for instance, in a sanatorium where she was not well treated, or if her parents were to withdraw from her and declare her hopelessly insane. "Better dead than to live like this." She might then commit suicide as an act of revenge.

Miserable to the point of being almost feelingless, I commenced washing my hands and face with potassium permanganate. I rinsed my mouth thoroughly with Lina's antiseptic. I would not wear my coat again. I imagined that I had infected it by wearing it when I passed the lupus hospital. I wore gloves when I took my shoes off and was careful never to let the shoelaces touch the soles of the shoes, which I regarded as particularly badly infected. My parents watched my activities with great apprehension. Then I asked Father whether it was possible to be infected by the air which came out of the lupus hospital. He laughed at me and answered that it was quite impossible, for otherwise, all the people who lived there or passed by would become ill.

That gave me little hope. But I clung to the belief that the soles of my shoes were infected by having stepped on the same pavement on which the man with lupus had walked, and consequently, that the floor of our apartment was also infected. . . .

People who feel forced to wash themselves constantly (washing compulsion) usually use the argument that everything around them is dirty or infected. Such an argument serves to shut out some part of life in which they anticipate a defeat and in which they consequently do not feel secure. We have heard that the delusion was strengthened when she went out with the boy who praised another girl.

. . . and that perhaps one of the inmates had spit out the window and I might have trodden on the slime. My parents tried desperately to pry me loose from this idea, but in vain.

Her position in the house has now been firmly established. She has become the central figure, much more than before in that she has succeeded in cutting off all connection with the outside world.

From that time on, I touched any shoes and coat only with gloves. One day a piece of lace slipped out of my hand to the floor. Mother had to give it away. I did not even want to touch Mother any more since she had to come in contact with the floor when she washed and cleaned. My terrible excitement found vent in frequent crying spells. To quiet me, my parents and Lina would touch the floor and my shoes with their fingers before my eyes. But later when Mother cut the bread without first having washed her hands, I shrieked and refused to eat. She had to get a new loaf. Even the doorknobs I touched only with gloves and, in addition, would cover the gloves with a piece of paper.

This is the usual trick of patients with a washing compulsion. Consequently, what follows is such filth in the room as we can expect only from people who ceaselessly wash themselves and, at the same time, continuously fight dirt.

They had been infected by the infected hands of my family! Then I got the idea that one could never know whether money had been touched by a lupus sufferer or not. So I did not touch it any more unless I first covered my hand with a piece of paper. When I had to buy something, I wrapped the money in the inevitable paper and carried it to Minna. She had to accompany me and pay the bills.

Now she has a court attendant. Somebody has to accompany her on the street. That is agoraphobia.

She also had to open doors for me because doorknobs were suspicious. A beggar suffering from lupus might have touched them! Dirt, misery, poverty seemed to me grounds for lupus.

In this respect she is not quite wrong.

Finally I did not touch anything any more without paper. When I wanted to move a chair from one spot to another, or when I had to pass an object, for instance, a brush, to someone, I first protected myself with paper. I threw away a pair of gloves I had used to pick up some money because I had forgotten the paper. I wrapped pencils in paper before writing with them. My frightened thoughts were running in so many different directions that at last there was nothing left that I did not believe to be infected.

I remember a wild discussion between a patient with a washing compulsion neurosis and a chemist in which the patient wanted to prove that no place in the world was absolutely free from particles of dirt.

The chemist denied it. I was on the patient's side; it seemed to me that she was right. But whether she was right or not was of no consequence. What matters is to make progress in life, to make ourselves useful. We do not make ourselves useful by declaring that everything is dirty and then resting on our oars.

One day I took a walk with a school friend and her mother. Suddenly I saw a terrible looking man with a red, swollen face full of holes. He was standing near the curb. I asked my friend to look at him. She did and burst out laughing. I myself was not able to look again in his direction. I was glad we were walking on the other side of the pavement. I thought this girl would surely become infected with lupus as punishment for ridiculing him.

Again, I must insert a few remarks. People suffering from phobias and other forms of neurosis frequently imagine they are pursued by diabolic, relentless misfortune. I do not believe that many among you have met a lupus sufferer more than once. This girl has met such a diseased person at least twice. We often hear that neurotics constantly have an experience repeated. I remember a case of washing compulsion--a woman who examined everything in the world for dirt in order to eliminate dirt. I have never seen anyone who was so much in contact with dirt as she was. I shall try to explain this in a few words.

A neurotic seeks justifications to protect and strengthen his asocial attitude. His feelings have led him into a neurosis; his understanding which is not distorted has not followed his feelings, cannot follow, and is forced continually to produce means to lessen the tension between intellect and feeling. Reason is taken in tow by feeling and therefore completes its task by demonstrating that such a restricted field of activity is inevitable. And so we see the patient pursuing vindicating arguments or facts, especially those facts that appear to him fatefully inevitable, like acts of God for which he is not responsible.

We must remember the extraordinary ability of the psyche to arrange, correct, choose, exclude and purposively apperceive. When we remember this, we can then understand that where the psychical apparatus has become the instrument of a neurotic goal, the intellect, governed by feelings, arranges, chooses, and purposely apperceives those facts that will not disturb the neurotic development or goal, and the neurotic finally appears to us as a poor, pitiable victim of circumstance. He plays a trick and is fooled by it himself.

For example, a man says he wants to get married and have a child. He falls in love with one girl after another and each one rejects him. Consequently, after twenty years, he is in exactly the same spot as he was when he started, namely, unmarried. The world pities him since he obviously makes every effort to win a wife. The world does not bother to examine the sincerity of his efforts very closely. If it did, it would see that he probably approaches a type which he knows in advance will refuse him; or that he makes his courtship so clumsy an affair that he is sure to be unsuccessful; or that his behavior toward the woman makes him impossible as a prospective husband; in short, that he does everything to prevent the actual steps leading to marriage in order to remain within the fortress he has built because of his fear of women.

This pattern is an example of the art and cunning of neurotic thought and argument, somewhat simplified and schematized, naturally, in order to make it more understandable. But the example achieves its purpose when it clarifies that the experiences we have are not important, but the lessons we learn from these experiences, and that correct interpretation of experience is necessary to understand another human being. With this peculiarity of the human intellect in mind, we no longer question whether frequently repeated disturbances and misfortunes in neurotic life are merely accidents, or whether neurotics tend to seek their troubles.

I brought Minna two pieces of sugar which I had first rubbed on the soles of my shoes.

You see how far the tendency to degrade goes. She attacks all other people as if she had to exterminate them because she feels unable to cope with them. She alone is worthwhile, and she alone is to be respected.

I was frantic with joy when she ate them.

This excessive form of egotism is converted into criminal trends. Clearly, her egotism expresses itself in the tendency to degrade. She approaches her fellow human beings in an aggressive manner; that is egotism. We may call it by another name, but everyone will have to agree that she is interested exclusively in herself. The Freudian school calls this manifestation narcissism. The word "narcissism" is taken from the story of the Greek youth who fell in love with his mirrored reflection. Narcissism plays an important role in Freudian psychology. It is the libidinous love of a person for himself. Every person is supposed to have a greater or smaller narcissistic love for himself. To those acquainted with psychological literature, I suggest that the Freudian view of narcissism does not include the tendency to degrade.

I really thought she would get a little lupus from eating the sugar. I then fed all my friends with that sort of sugar, but gave none to my family. When I had to go through the street where the lupus man passed, I held my clothes close to my body for fear that the lupus man might have touched the walls of the houses and the lampposts. But I often imagined that a part of the dress had somehow grazed one of those spots. Then I ran straight home and hurriedly took off all my clothes. When I passed this street with a friend, I would push her, seemingly by accident, against the walls and lampposts so that she should get some bacilli on her dress, too.

At this point, we must remember that the outbreak of lupus phobia occurred when she took a walk with a boy who liked another girl as well. Her gesture expresses clearly that she wants to exclude this other girl--every girl.

And when I thought that a piece of clothing had become infected, I threw it away. But since my wardrobe was in a sad condition, I wondered how I could help myself. I conceived the idea of letting Father destroy the bacteria with his hot iron and moist cloth.

She has discovered a working method which was later proven correct by scientific research.

My family frequently had to go through the dangerous street. I asked them repeatedly to be careful not to touch anything there. Although they promised it over and over again, the suspicion would not leave me that they did not pay any attention to my caution. Now none of them was allowed to come near me any more.

We see how she aggravates her condition. Her radius of activity becomes smaller and smaller. She is the only one in the world who is pure, free from bacilli, the only one who realizes how all others plunge into misery. All other people are profane, depraved, infected; she alone is not. She is a saint. She achieves her goal of superiority on the useless side of life by cheap means.

And when someone touched me by accident, I raved and stormed, had crying spells, and threatened to kill myself. I did not know any more where to sit down so as to be far enough from the others. I used only one chair and no one else was allowed to sit on it.

This reminds me of the customs of monarchs or religions where a particular seat may be touched only by a sacred person. If someone were to assert now that the girl derives these ideas from archaic, inherited traditions, we have just one response: everybody gets the same silly ideas under similar, restrictive conditions.

I also selected my own knives, forks and spoons which were put in a certain place to be protected from infection by the rest of the furniture. I took strict care of my things. Woe if mother happened to put a wrong fork on my special plate!

We see what we can observe in every neurotic; she is sick. That means a law for the others. The others receive regulations for their lives from the disease of the neurotic. That gives her a feeling of superiority even if she does not notice it. I do not believe this fact can be overlooked by anybody whose attention has ever been called to it.

One day, during house cleaning, my water glass with my toothbrush in it was accidentally put on the table. When I saw that I grew furious, swore at my mother in vile language, menaced her, threatened to kill her--I don't know what else I did in my rage.

It almost looks like the divine wrath of a god when someone has violated his sacred commands.

Such scenes occurred practically every day. Then my parents would wrangle about me. Father would accuse Mother of not having been careful enough and thus having excited me. Mother would reply angrily that she could not keep all my caprices in mind, that she had other things to think of. Our employees also trembled in my presence.

I do not know whether that is quite true, but it is sufficient that she has the impression.

When I was on the street, I was always anticipating meeting perforated faces. The whole city was soon inhabited by lupus sufferers. I saw them everywhere. I did not dare go out any more at night for fear I might bump into one of them in the dark.

The restriction goes farther.

In the daytime I stared at all faces, and when someone passed by too quickly for me to see whether he had a nose or not, I ran after him and stared at him again. Every time I imagined, "This one has lupus." Then I would rush home crying and complain to Father, "I have seen a lupus sufferer again." Father always tried to talk me out of my delusion. His clear and sensible explanations quieted me every time to a certain degree. He was the only one able to console me a little from time to time.

This "from time to time" needs some further consideration. It means almost nothing. She may permit herself to be consoled by her father--in order to be able to start again. Physicians often hear their patients say, "When I leave your office I feel fine. But as soon as I am out, it starts all over again." Many doctors believe it is a magic power emanating from them. However, a patient merely compliments the physician in order to lead him astray. We usually answer, "Then you should stay here all day." The fascination then vanishes quickly.

I washed myself constantly with potassium permanganate. The skin of my hands became terribly rough, as hard as leather and full of cracks.

That is correct. People who feel compelled to wash themselves all day have the dirtiest hands in the world.

My teeth become brown from continual rinsing. When the soap or a brush fell on the floor, I did not use it again. Not for a kingdom would I have picked up something from the floor. Mother also had to wash her hands ceaselessly. I watched her carefully, especially before she started to cook. If she forgot to wash her hands, I did not eat one morsel, however hungry I may have been. The restrictions I imposed on her irritated her and she complained to Father. He begged her to indulge me.

Her power extends farther and farther. He who does not comprehend this does not comprehend the most important facts. Unlimited power is most important to her, and although she has only a small circle at her disposal, she does as much as possible to dominate it.

I had the most inconvenient difficulties with my shoelaces. If one of them touched the soles of my shoes or the floor, Mother had to pull it out immediately and buy a new one. I had assembled a whole collection of infected shoelaces in a drawer. I also had a full line of hair pins, soaps, toothbrushes and dental creams. Father was already considering consulting a physician. My delusion was kept secret from outsiders.

As a rule, parents keep the ailment secret in a kind of false shame without helping the child by doing so. On the other hand, if they speak too much about it, that does not help, either. A method needs to be found which helps everybody.

When I found an illustration of the so-called lupus spoon in Lina's instrument book, I shuddered. I wondered why there was only one instrument for such an abominable disease.

She regards it as an insult, a degradation of her phantom, that there is but one instrument for it.

Lina told me that one could get lupus not only on the face, but all over the body as well. I did not dread that so much as the image of a face full of holes.

He who observes a little more closely knows why. "She is the fairest in the land." Therefore the stress laid on the facial lupus.

I brooded ceaselessly on the lupus disease. Horrible things came to my mind. I imagined, for instance, that a lupus sufferer touches someone with his fingers after having touched his wounds or scratched them. Or that a drop of pus comes in contact with a coin which one unsuspectingly takes in one's hand--then one may scratch one's own eye which would, no doubt, infect a person with lupus.

She understands something about inoculation; that is, infecting an eye by bringing a germ in direct contact with it.

The thought especially that a lupus sufferer might kiss me made me shiver with fright.

This "especially" is charming.

Finally I fancied that the mere thought of contact with lupus might produce the disease, that the thought might be as much as the act.

Here again she anticipates some of the modern theories and hypotheses. Right now the conception of "mind over matter" is widely spread.

When such thoughts came to my mind, I became extremely excited, washed my face in a hurry, and ran to Father to get some consolation. However, I had to overcome some reluctance to speak of these ideas, tried first to indicate, to circumscribe them, never said directly: "I have imagined this or that," but: "If a girl were to imagine this, and so on."

Her conscience is not clear. She does not want to assume any responsibility for her neurosis. She has some glimmering that her attitude is unjustifiable and will not admit it. As long as she does not understand and interpret correctly her intentions and striving, she finds no way out and proceeds further, like a Don Quixote, to fight windmills.

I also often thought--we lived on the ground floor--how easily someone could climb in the window--and, what is more, it might be a lupus sufferer!

Two evils at once.

"Such sufferers," I said to myself, "must always be in great need because they are avoided by other people."

Here again let us find out what lies behind those words. We could say, for instance: as a result they have to be helped. He who speaks thus is on the useful side. She continues differently. We have to beware of such cunning rascals. When two people have the same impression, the same experience, they draw different conclusions according to their different goals and different styles of life.

The idea of a burglar with lupus scared me to death. Then I remembered a story which I had read or heard somewhere in which God tests a saint with a leper--I thought that was the same as lupus. The leper very soon turned out to be the Lord Himself. And I said to myself: "Even were the Lord Himself to come as a lupus sufferer to me, I would not admit Him; indeed, I would not touch Him--or should I make an exception in that case?

One day we went on an excursion. I was in the third grade in school, I believe. Coming back we passed a new lupus hospital; in fact, I don't know whether there were or are two lupus hospitals in this city. I'll find out. Suddenly I read in big letters, "Hospital for Lupus Sufferers." That gave me a sad feeling. I must have known at that time what lupus is. There was a milkstand in the station where we had to transfer to another car. Our boarder was with us. Father bought hot milk for us. I also drank a glass. But with the lupus hospital before my eyes, I detested the milk. I had a dim feeling that a lupus sufferer had drunk out of my glass.

That is an old remembrance. What conclusion can we draw from it? No more and no less than that she now tries to support her lupus phobia. She searches until she finds new justifications for the continuation of her neurosis. We frequently find neurotics search for support for the present scheme in their past life.

In the meantime, our circumstances had changed for the worse. Many of Father's customers had been drafted for military service, some of them without having paid their bills. We could hardly pay the relatively high rent of our apartment. At the first opportunity, we moved into a house some blocks further on. It was an old house and our new home was cheaper and roomier than the old one and was on the first floor. Up to that time, I had slept between my parents. Now I got a little room to share with Lina and, for the first time, a bed of my own. Lina slept on the couch.

We already understand enough of this girl's character to be able to predict what will follow. She will probably not want to lie there alone. She will not let herself be driven out of an agreeable situation. She has mentioned this fact before. It is supposed to express: "I am the center." That means a description in space for her psychic construction.

I did not want to be driven so abruptly out of the bed of my parents in which I had slept so long. For some time I remained--as a temporary arrangement--in Mother's bed. Gradually, I decided to reconcile myself to the new custom. Little by little the lupus delusion, which had harassed me for over a year, disappeared.

What that has to do with sleeping alone is not quite intelligible. However, the two facts might be related. We have assumed that the lupus phobia is directed against every possible relationship with men, that she fears the love problem. She sleeps alone; she emphasizes that the lupus phobia is disappearing. Perhaps she is relieved by the thought:

"One can remain single." I do not know whether we find my assumption confirmed. I will follow this idea carefully, awaiting further corroboration.

I could not put up with lying alone at night very long. Besides, my bed was unsteady and I was afraid that the upper part might fall down on me and smash my teeth or crush my nose.

Again a beauty defect.

I was quite particular about my nose. When Lina gave me a kiss, I often imagined she had distorted it. Then the tapping of a termite made me nervous. Every other day my sister had night duty, and I felt all the more lonely.

The sister suits her purpose very well. We see how the tendency to withdraw from men leads her to her sister. Before she slept alone, she chose to lie beside her mother. We will have to see whether she struggles to save herself from the confused state of her erotic problems, whether or not her refusal of men and attachment to women grows stronger.

I asked Mother to sleep in my bed, while I slept in hers.

This would disprove our combination if we, like other psychological schools, recognized the man in her father. According to their interpretation, the desire to sleep in her mother's bed indicates a wish to approach her father sexually and eliminate her mother of whom she is jealous. However, her father is unquestionably asexual for her; we do not know yet why she goes through this performance.

At that time I had the custom of hanging my stockings and garters over Father's bedstead before going to sleep; on top I put my hairpins; I spread my shirt, petticoat and bloomers on his comforter, and put my shoes under his bed. I laid my dress, sweater, coat and hat carefully on the table. No one was permitted to touch these things lest I become wild with fury. One night, lying awake, I noticed that Father continually slapped his face in his sleep. The action frightened me; I thought he was going crazy. Suddenly he opened his eyes and exclaimed: "What is tickling my nose?" And then I saw that my garters were doing it. The fear that the headpiece of the bed might fall on me did not let me sleep peacefully in Mother's bed, so I had to take it down every evening before getting into bed. Soon a new cause for alarm appeared. Over the little night table, standing between Father's and Mother's beds . . .

The beds are separated. She plays the role of the mother since she is using her mother's bed, but sleeping separated from her father.

. . . hung an image of the Holy Virgin. The image was a little closer to my side. I became anxious about that. I imagined it might fall down on me. On the other hand, I was too superstitious to have it removed. So I went back to my own bedroom and bed.

When we consider the situation of this girl, we realize that pampered children are very reluctant to leave places to which they have been long accustomed.

In the middle of one night I fell through my bed with a crash. That made the bed all the more unattractive to me and I slept thereafter in Mother's bed with her. In order to be safe from the holy image, I moved over to the very edge of the bed. I cannot say that this position was very comfortable. Besides, I still did not feel safe enough. I often got up when all the others were asleep, stood for a while somewhere in the room in my nightgown and pondered how I could get rid of the bed troubles. One night, while I was standing in my former bedroom and brooding, I accidentally made some noise. Lina awoke, jumped up terror-stricken and began to cry pitifully. She believed she was face to face with a ghost. I crept quickly back to bed. The menacing image on the wall drove my sleep away. I then tried to lie in bed the other way round, my head near Mother's feet. But that was more uncomfortable than before. Our feet hit each other's face during the night. Finally Father took my vacant bed and let me sleep in his bed. Even there I did not feel quite at ease. I do not know why I believed this bed would bring me bad luck.

That seems to agree with the idea that it is dangerous to get too near a man.

Then it was arranged in the following way: Father returned to his bed, Lina took my bed and I slept on Lina's couch. But the couch was too short for me. I was considerably taller than my sister and had long legs. My feet hung over the end of the couch. I had to wrap them in a special blanket. Then Mother had the idea of preparing my bed in the kitchen on the sewing table. But the table was too hard and a draft from a nearby window disturbed me.

This child certainly has many difficulties in bed.

Now we resolved that I should try to sleep with Father in his bed. But since, in fear of the holy image, I lay down in the direction reverse to the one in which he lay, the arrangement was as awkward as it had been in Mother's bed. At last, Father ordered a carpenter to repair my bed while I watched him do it. Then I lay down, head at the wrong end, and so it remained.

The position a person assumes in sleep is not accidental and seems to have some significance in terms of his style of life. Individual Psychological investigation has shown us that even the phenomenon of sleep is patterned on the person's style of life. Those who understand Individual Psychology can often guess the position someone assumes in sleep.

Experience has taught us, for instance, that people who sleep on their stomachs are usually stubborn. We can hardly expect a person to exhibit much courage in life who goes to sleep by rolling himself up like a porcupine and pulling the blankets over his head. A young man sleeps with his arms crossed on his chest. His style of life reveals a desire to imitate Napoleon. Later, when life becomes hard, he conceives the insane idea that he has been chosen general to lead troops to Russia. Our girl lies in bed the wrong way around. Her position expresses opposition--nothing else, although, of course, such people may also assume an oppositional attitude in regard to their love relationships.

Father wanted me to take up dressmaking after I finished high school.

We doubt she will take up dressmaking because that is a subordinate profession.

But I did not care for it. I would rather have entered business school like Olga who set the example for me in every way. Father did not consent. He suggested that it would cost too much. He preferred to have me become a pianist and spoke of a scholarship in a conservatory. I replied; "And then? Then I shall be a stupid piano teacher!" Finally we came to no decision whatsoever and I remained at home.

That is the right place.

Next fall I registered for a one-year course at business school. I was the only one in the class who paid her tuition fee monthly. All but two or three of my classmates came from wealthy families. I felt happy in their company. I made friends with the prettiest and most distinguished ones and was invited to their homes. But since I could never invite them to our house--I had told them a lot of lies about our circumstances--our friendship did not become as intimate as any friendship with Olga. I could speak of things with her which would have shocked the wealthier girls. Although I hated moral conversations, I always made myself listen patiently. My greatest wish was to prolong these acquaintanceships. . . . I remember a very disagreeable episode. We could buy liberty bonds at school. This was done in the following way: The professor called out our names in alphabetical order and asked every one of us, naming in addition our father's profession, how many bonds we wanted to buy. Almost all the girls had permission from their parents to buy bonds and named smaller or larger amounts. Meanwhile I was on pins and needles. Not only that Father could not spare one cent more for war contributions--we were glad when we could get an extra loaf of bread from time to time--but it was going to be revealed in public that Father was a tailor. Slowly, my doom approached. When my name was called out, I arose, blushing all over. The professor had cast a glance at the list and said "Your father is a tailor. Tailors make much money nowadays." I do not remember what I stammered in answer. . . I was a pretty good scholar in general, but arithmetic and bookkeeping were my weak points. The morning before an examination in arithmetic, I would say to my father: "I feel so ill, I can hardly stand up straight."

That is a common reaction. If a child trains for it properly it becomes automatic, so that she feels sick merely hearing the word arithmetic. "It makes me sick to hear of it." We also notice this behavior in other situations where it is harder to explain. Headaches, tiredness, even vomiting, often originate this way. A teacher, for instance, had a fright spell when he approached the city hall in his town. Without knowing anything about him, we cannot possibly understand what the city hall has to do with the spell. The reason in this case was that he had to report to the higher school officials. Another time, at a party, he was asked when he had to go to school. Five minutes later he had another fear spell. This becomes intelligible only when we consider the facts that have led to this condition.

". . . *and went back to bed. The following day I went to school again. Eventually the professor of arithmetic discovered my trick and gave me the lowest mark every time I did not attend school. One day I was impertinent to a professor and got a low mark in conduct. On such occasions, we had to take a report card home and return it with one parent's signature. Although I had no reason to be afraid of Father, I decided to get his signature on that piece of paper without letting him know what he was signing. To that end I proceeded as follows: I took a sheet of white paper, covered it with a small strip of red blotting paper, leaving only a small margin, went to Father and begged him to write his name in the white margin. First, of course, he wanted to see what was under the blotting paper. I took it away and there was nothing but a blank sheet of white paper. Astonished, he asked what I wanted it for. I only smiled. He probably thought this was another one of my whims, wrote his name, and shook his head.*

The fight with her teacher is almost a pleasure to her; she tries to get the upper hand over him and succeeds. She won a lasting victory over her father long ago.

After a while I did the same thing again, and once more Father wanted to see the covered paper first. The third time, however, he signed without looking. This time he had signed the conduct report. . . . Our classes were between two and six o'clock. In the morning I studied, as a matter of fact only before an examination. Mother then heated the little stove in the bedroom. Father worked in the kitchen with his assistants late into the night. The customers came and went during the day. We were never by ourselves, never undisturbed. The assistants had to work on Sunday morning and in the afternoon customers tried on their suits. Mother, Lina and I hated this state of affairs. We tried to persuade Father to work at certain hours, like other tailors, and then rest. But we could not convince him. He always answered: "You hate the tailoring business. But without my work you wouldn't have anything to eat." We had just enough to eat, but otherwise, in spite of all the work, we were in need of almost everything. Father had gradually acquired the fixed idea of working for an unusually low price, for almost cost price. Sewing was his passion, to produce good suits his pleasure, to satisfy his customers his ambition and pride. Even when he had so many orders that the assistants had to work overtime, there was often hardly enough money left at the end of the week to pay them their wages. Lina always had to help, although all she had was her meager salary. A relative wanted to keep the books for Father or even help him to open a store where he would have had nothing to do but cut and fit. But Father's initiative had been killed; we could not get him away from sewing.

That illustrates well the inflexible habit of older age. A life's training cannot be easily broken and should be broken only when it is necessary for the individual and his environment. I must confess I would not try either to detach such a habitual worker from his work. I would not say to an elderly man that he ought to stop working, or entirely rearrange his pattern of work, because he would feel life pressing on him heavily as soon as the routine ceased.

Father's craze to make a present of his labor to his customers brought about terrible family quarrels. Mother, with Lina's backing, showered Father with reproaches, scolded him, yelled that this life was no life and that he was ruining all of us, asked him what he thought would become of the child. At first he would answer, but as soon as Mother mentioned my name he became silent, went into the bedroom, and tore his hair.

One day, brushing crumbs off the table, I carelessly dropped my pocket mirror on the floor. While picking it up, I saw that it had a few cracks. "How silly," I thought, "now I won't have good luck for seven years."

Here is another opportunity for compulsive thoughts and acts. This is the third time, proof that the disappearance of one symptom (the lupus phobia, for example) does not indicate a cure, but rather that a new symptom will be produced, and that the appearance of symptoms will not stop as long as she does not change her goal and style of life. Besides, I want to emphasize that neurotics are always superstitious. Everyone who does not believe in himself has to believe in something else, whatever it may be. Of course, it does not follow that because we believe in something else, we do not believe in ourselves.

On that day I was somewhat depressed. I went to Olga to ask her whether she had ever broken a mirror. She could not remember ever having done so. I thereupon decided to have her break a mirror at an opportune moment so that she would have no good luck for seven years either.

She constantly strives for equality so that others are no better off than she.

A little later Lina was angry for some reason or other and broke her mirror in a fit of wrath. I approached the fragments gingerly, looked at them, and wondered how my sister could break a mirror, knowing that she would not have good luck for seven years. . . . In the coatroom of the business school, one of the girls accidentally dropped her pocket mirror while taking off her coat. I was standing behind her at the moment and she cried jokingly: Oh, goodness now you have broken my mirror!" I was startled. She quieted me, assuring me that she herself had broken it, not I. I was badly frightened and asked her if she were quite sure of it. She swore that it was so. I believed her since I had hardly touched the mirror, and when I looked at her, I thought: "Whether or not she has broken a mirror makes no difference. She is not pretty and will have no good luck anyway."

Here we have further evidence for the correctness of our assumption that her main object is to be pretty enough to be the first one in life.

I remember, by the way . . .

She is collecting memories again to support her neurotic behavior.

. . . that as a small child I was once afraid of a mirror. I was passing a glassware store and looked into one of the mirrors on display. From it a horribly swollen face stared back at me.

Again the swollen face!

I recoiled, but could not resist looking back a second time. Alongside this mirror hung another that distorted my face lengthwise in a weird fashion. Father explained to me afterward that these were mirrors which distorted all they reflected. Our petroleum lamp had a reflector to make the light shine more brightly. This mirror, or reflector, had already bothered me, as I remember now, at the time of my eye phobia. It now began to disturb me very much. I would not touch the lamp. I was often asked to carry it from the kitchen to the living room when Father had a customer, but even if fifty customers had waited outside, I could no longer be made to touch that lamp. I was afraid the mirror might break because of the intense heat of the petroleum flame and the resulting bad luck would attach itself to me if I just happened to be present. I let the others sit by the lamp and took my seat further away. Realizing, however, that it was all the same whether my parents or Lina or I were near the mirror when it broke, since the mischief would then pursue us all, I begged Father to take the reflector off the lamp. This done, I worried about what they would do with it. Mother wanted to throw it in the garbage can. I objected because it might break in there. Then she proposed giving it away. I did not like that either. I thought that might also mean bad luck. Finally, we stored it in a wooden box in the cellar.

We see to what lengths she goes to avoid all possible bad luck. We also see with what super-caution, wrongly placed of course, she nourishes the idea that we can somehow force our fate. This wretched phobia contains the idea of godliness. What must I do in order to control fate?

Chapter XI

Yes! But—

Father had a little work basket of plaited straw in which he kept, among other things, several pocket mirrors. I was afraid to break them, and was always very careful not to touch the basket. Finally Father decided to sell the mirrors to the same man who bought our remnants.

Her attention is concentrated on all the mirrors around her. Significant for the structure of every neurosis, this type of preoccupation becomes most conspicuous in a compulsion neurosis. The Individual Psychologist can easily understand what really happens. By placing all the social tasks of life in the background, the patient has abandoned her duties. She stands a greater distance away from the important problems of her life. In order not to suffer a defeat in trying to solve her problems on the useful side of life, she spends all her time on useless activities.

We know this extremely spoiled child is striving for a goal of superiority, that she wants to be more than all the others. We have seen how she succeeded in attaining her goal within her family. As she grows older, she now has to approach the community outside her family where her success is thoroughly uncertain. Like all pampered children, she avoids new situations, especially when she is less certain of her success. Her striving to remain within the old situation and attempt to achieve the goal of superiority there becomes more apparent. This striving is easily accomplished by means of a neurosis whose intensity can be increased in accordance with the purpose. The father especially, and the other members of the family as well, are drawn into the whirl of her fixed ideas which gives her the impression of her superiority in the house.

The symptomatic choice of the mirror now becomes obvious. As in former years, she makes her principal aim being first or foremost although she now moves in a broader circle and nearer the front of life. Problems of love and marriage come closer. Will I be able to surpass other girls in my relationships with men; will I gain power over men? Her interest concentrates itself distinctly around the mirror, probably stimulated by her visual training. Occasionally, she complains of her weak eyes. Children with minor eye defects understandably increase their interest in all visible objects in order to conquer their difficulties. In this way they become more closely acquainted with colors, lines, shades, perspective and usually retain this visual interest for the rest of their lives.

However, this girl has become uncertain, vacillating, as almost all pampered children do when they have to face a new situation. She tends to solve the problems of love and sex in the same fashion as she has tried to solve all problems up to now; that is to say, she wants to be the first. Love and marriage, however, are social problems. Their solution requires interest in others. Her prototype lacks such interest in others almost entirely, which is typical for pampered children. She wants to master the others, force them to obey her command. Will she be able to do the same in love? The marriage of her parents, her whole environment perhaps, does not give her the impression of the unimpeded victoriousness of a woman. Love becomes a dangerous obstacle to her desire to rule; she is not at all certain of conquering it in her favor. The thus intensified feeling of uncertainty causes her to shake off responsibility from her and shift it onto mirrors. Her fate depends on mirrors now. But suppose the mirror breaks?

A widely spread superstition makes a happy marriage depend on whether we have broken a mirror. A strange, spiteful magic has to decide, not the magic effect of our own personality. If she is not the first in the contest of love, then the mirror bears the blame, and her superiority remains untouched. The superstition states that she who breaks a mirror cannot marry for seven years. That would exempt her from having to decide whether she is the "first in the country." But she could continue to believe so. Like all pampered children, she hunts for easier means of gaining the final victory.

Two general remarks may be inserted here. A few of my critics, unfortunately blinded by rage, believe that I have eradicated sexuality and love from my psychological conception. However, I wish to point out that in all cases of neuroses and psychoses, as well as in perversions, the patient does not approach love in the light of common sense, that is, as an attitude of social feeling, but merely as sexual desire in the service of a striving for power on the useless side of life. Both sexual desire and striving for power have switched over from the tracks of general usefulness onto the tracks of neurosis, and both no longer share in the progress of humanity, but are part of personal egotism.

Second, I want to emphasize that this unwise use of our love potential encounters difficulties everywhere. Because love and marriage are tasks for two people, they have no room for egocentric presumptions on the part of one of them. Moreover, the partner's response to the unsatisfactory advances of the neurotic is naturally unfavorable. And above all, the neurotic always feels hurt when his timid social feeling is challenged as it is by all problems of life, since all problems (birth of children, school, friendship, interest in mankind, political standpoint, profession, love, marriage) are social problems. Regarding the love problems of the neurotic, we will perceive a diminishing speed in his activities to the point of a hesitating attitude or complete standstill. The violent aggression in the beginning comes to a sudden end. From a physical point of view, this description is sufficiently clear. Physical expression of the disturbance is found in impotence, vaginism, frigidity, perversions, ejaculation precox, etc. This superstitious occupation with mirrors exhibits the hesitating attitude of the girl. If a mirror breaks, this accident is blamed in case she does not win, and her superiority is saved. Every now and then, the thought of committing suicide appears. Death seems salvation, the last consolation of the desperate.

The objection might be raised: Why is she anxious about breaking a mirror if the resulting bad luck would help her avoid the problem of love, and protected by her superstition, she would not even have to attempt to occupy herself with the dangerous question? The neurotic does not think so simply. She wants to appear to make every effort to respond to the demands of communal life. That is her "yes." But then she throws a stone in her way which impedes her progress. That is her "but." The result is that she has a good alibi for the evasion of the danger of love; she has reneged. I want to very much, BUT I cannot. That is the meaning of her fear of mirrors. As long as someone wants to, but excuses herself with a "but," she does not want to.

Several mirrors were displayed in the shop window of the candy store that Tilda's mother owned. Until then I had not noticed them. One day I suddenly imagined I had smashed one of the mirrors by closing the store door, and I was seized with a terrible fright. Tilda carefully examined all the mirrors in the window and swore that she could not detect a crack in any one of them. But I did not believe her and was so unhappy all day long that I wanted to die. I said to myself: "I'll have misfortune for seven years anyway, and now seven more years in addition; then I'll have no more happiness at all in life and it would be better to die now."

The next day I was quiet again; but from then on when I went to see Tilda, I took Minna with me to open and close the door.

Every time I accidentally touched a woman with a pocketbook, on the street or in the street car, the fearful thought struck me like lightning that I had demolished her pocket-mirror and thus caused myself seven more years of misfortune. Frequently, I followed such a woman and wanted to ask her whether she really carried a mirror in her pocketbook and, if so, whether it was still intact. But I never dared do so.

As long as the question is not answered, the possibility remains that a mirror has been broken. Therefore, she does not dare to ask.

I had to use a mirror when I wanted to comb my hair. I possessed a square hand mirror which I touched only with the greatest precaution. Sometimes I fancied that I had put it too roughly on the table, and, at the same time, thought I had heard it crack. Then I ran to my parents or Lina full of fear; they had to inspect it thoroughly. And even if they swore by all they held holy that they could not see any crack, not even a scratch, I did not believe them and I trusted my own eyes still less. I was bent madly on the thought that there was a crack in it, perhaps not perceptible to the naked eye.

In order to see whether it would break, I now put the mirror on the table as carefully as possible. And immediately I fancied again that I had broken it. The longer I manipulated it in this manner, the more strongly I labored under this delusion and the more excited I became. After a while, I was raving.

One day on the street, we passed the fragments of a mirror. The idea that I had touched them with my foot grew in an instant to the conviction that I had stepped on them. I ran home weeping and complained to Father: "Something terrible has happened to me."

In an alarmed tone, he asked what it was. At first I did not want to tell. Merely to speak about it seemed calamitous to me. I felt as miserable as if I had just been sentenced to death. At his insistent request, I told him what had happened.

The mirror story cannot be exaggerated enough. A frequent occurrence in a neurosis to achieve the purpose at any cost.

Father laughed and said that according to my own description, someone else and not I had broken the mirror. I had only come in contact with the fragments which certainly did not mean anything. But this time, he could not console me. Then I called Minna and led her to the spot where the fragments were lying, without letting her know my aim. I took her arm and ingeniously arranged to have her step unsuspectingly on the glass. Now I felt easier. I thought, "If I have no more luck, you shall not have any more luck either!"

Struggling against the superiority of others. As if it were proof that this actually has to do with her love problem, the son of the proprietor of the café appears on the scene at the right moment.

I was very friendly with the son of the proprietor of our favorite café. We had already played together when we were children. His name was Hans and he was just as old as I. He had a speech defect. His vocal cords had been hurt in a tonsil operation.

We often took walks together. But since I disliked being alone with a boy and wanted to make some new acquaintances, I asked him one day whether he knew of a friend for me.

Two are less than one. This frequent neurotic phenomenon occurs in the event of a possibility of affection for a person, in order to prevent a love affair. Someone cannot be in love with two people at the same time without lying to herself. When an individual cannot decide in favor of one or the other, this indecision is the decision. Neither one is wanted. The phenomenon of indecision appears frequently in life and always indicates a tendency to refuse.

The attempts of the girl to approach love relationships although they are very careful, do not surprise us. They are attempts to say "yes" in situations of little danger, in much the same way as someone who seems about to decide to withdraw, yet makes a few hesitating steps forward only to express her "but." This "yes!-but . . ." as we said before, is perhaps the best definition of neurosis. In the following paragraphs, our opinion will be confirmed and we will see how she handles a love affair.

In return for it, I was to introduce him to my friend Olga. Then the four of us could go out together. He replied that he knew many boys and that he would find a suitable one. I made it a condition that my boyfriend had to be handsome.

Fritz, the friend, was a tall, blond fellow who, in spite of his youth, liked to show off as a man of the world. He was immediately attracted to me and told me a lot of nonsense. I also told him a pack of lies....

When I asked Hans how he liked Olga, he said, "Quite well, only her manners are not so good yet!"; and then, for his taste she was too dull . . . he likes a lively girl better. He was only fifteen years old and stole money from his father when he wanted to go to the movies with a girl. I replied: "What do you think? You must know how to take her. My dear, she has had a lot of experience—why don't you try it?"

And I summed up all her nice qualities. I myself did not want to be alone with Fritz. I always wanted the other two to be with us. Hans, who was easily influenced by me, promised to go with us the next time. In return, I gave him my word to find another girl for him if he did not want Olga any more.

Fritz was very much in love with me. In the movies he made bashful advances. But I rejected him with the words: "I prefer to talk at a certain distance." He had to follow suit.

One evening Hans rushed into the room in great excitement, saying that Fritz had taken a box at the People's Opera House for "Rigoletto" and that I should get dressed in a hurry. I did not quite like the idea. I was a little ashamed to appear with the two boys in a box. But since my parents did not object, I got ready quickly. Fritz was already awaiting us in the box. He handed me a bunch of flowers and kissed my hand. Blushing with embarrassment, I took my seat.

I liked the music very well, but I should have preferred to listen to it without company. Fritz held my hand all the time and kissed it constantly. That was very bothersome. During the intermissions, we spoke about the opera. I pretended that I had heard this opera several times and knew every singer. I answered a certain question with: "The singer doesn't seem to be well disposed today."

After the performance, Fritz made a proud declaration of love and asked how I thought our relationship would be in the future. I answered: "My nature is pretty cool. You'll see that."

I decided to shake him off as soon as possible. Hans and Olga did not get along very well together. I therefore tried to talk him into another girl friend of mine, Elsa. I called his attention to the fact, however, that she was more or less engaged to another fellow. But if he, Hans, did not proceed too stupidly, it would be quite easy to estrange her from her boyfriend who, by the way, was a disagreeable chap.

Elsa was just giving a party for several of her friends, when I came in with my two boys. During a game of forfeits, Hans wanted to give me a kiss. However, I was already disgusted with him to such a degree that I refused to let him kiss me. All the others made a fuss about that because the other girls kissed their boys without ado. The most I granted him was permission to kiss my hand—and even that with reluctance. They called me pretentious, which I really was at that time. I spoke affectedly, turned continuously from one side to the other and said on every occasion: "That is much too low for me!"

On the way home, I informed Hans that Elsa had invited us to her birthday party. If he wanted to wheedle himself into her good graces, he probably would have to give her a present. At my suggestion, he bought her a manicure set.

Elsa was really surprised at the generosity of my boyfriend—in general he was considered as such. Between him and me, however, there existed merely a friendship, except that Hans did everything I wanted him to do.

I did not allow him to bring the obtrusive Fritz along this time.

After a while, Hans complained to me that Elsa did not seem to be interested in him. He could not get any further with her.

Then I went to her to sound her out about him. She answered very reservedly. While we were talking, she combed her hair. Suddenly the thought occurred to me to take a wisp of her hair that had come out in combing and bring it to Hans. I do not know myself why I was so eager to procure a girl for him.

The tendency to play matchmaker is distinctly based on the malicious intention to harm, which we can also notice on other occasions. Her intrigues are always intended to injure girls, her rivals.

When he came to me the next time, I gave him the hair in an envelope and said: "Elsa sends you this as a souvenir." At the same time, I gave him the strict injunction not to speak about it to her because she did not wish it.

Thereupon Hans conceived new hope and began to court Elsa again.

But when I noticed that she was in love with her fool, the whole business started to annoy me. I decided not to see her any more and instructed Hans: "Leave that silly girl alone! You come along with me now to another one!"

And I brought him to Walli, a girl whom I knew through Elsa. I talked to him so long until he told her he loved her and begged her for a kiss.

A long time afterward, Hans came to us one day and said to me, smiling peculiarly, that he did not feel quite well. I went out with him for a while and, on my insistent questioning, he finally confessed to me that he had contracted gonorrhea. He added, "A real man of the world must have such a thing." Although I thought his disease very interesting, I avoided giving him my hand for fear of infection.

Obvious fear of infection, probably used for the purpose of eliminating the problem of love.

Furthermore, I found out that he had stolen some of his mother's jewelry and had taken it to a pawnbroker. He had also stolen money from his father's safe. The result was that, from now on, his parents were very strict with him; he was allowed to go out only on Sunday afternoon. Then he called for me, and we merely took a walk.

My father liked Hans very much and was amused when I told him that it was the boy's greatest ambition to be a man of the world. In the black suit which Father had made for him, the little fellow really looked quite good. . .

One Sunday afternoon I went with Olga to the city park. Young as I was, my parents gave me every freedom. We strolled up and down in front of the music pavilion. Two naval officers came along, looked and smiled at us. Olga and I blinked at each other, turned our heads slowly around and saw that the two men were following us. And suddenly they addressed us. We were so embarrassed that we could hardly answer. We had met with many an adventure with young fellows before; but young men like these, that was something entirely new. My companion introduced himself to me and started to relate stories about life at sea. In order to make ourselves more interesting, we pretended to be foreigners—Olga was a Hungarian and I a Romanian—and spoke broken German. We could not, however, maintain the deception. Our embarrassment threw us into still greater confusion—we were timid anyway. We grew more and more silent; the two men almost had to pull every word from our lips. But my naval officer seemed to be very pleased with my timidity. He never took his eyes off me, showed me every courtesy, and inquired interestedly about my home conditions. Olga also blushed continuously and did not quite know what to reply. Then we went to a café. Gradually, we became more lively. Time passed by in cheerful conversation. We were startled when the clock struck seven. The officers brought us to the trolley station. They would have liked to bring us home, but we declined this offer for reasons of decency. My officer, who had not ceased his attentions to me, emphasized how he regretted that this was the last day of his leave of absence and that he had to return to port the following day. He begged me to come to the railroad station. Since I did not know whether Olga or another girl would have time to go with me and I was afraid to go alone, I made up some excuse. Then he wanted to have my address in order to write to me. I replied that he must not write to me at home, but I gave him the address of Olga's brother who was serving his apprenticeship in another shop. *When he said goodbye to me, my new admirer was quite moved; he admonished me to be good and promised me to be back soon. "Little girl," he called me. Again, he declared it a pity that he had not met me sooner. He would never forget me, he said. Would I permit him to address me by my first name? Once in a while I was to think of him. He had tears in his eyes when he pressed my hands. I remained completely unmoved. It merely seemed strange to me that a man who sees a girl for the first time can fall so deeply in love.*

Two weeks passed. I had gradually forgotten our meeting. One day Olga came to our house and whispered to me that I should come with her immediately because she had several letters and postcards which had accumulated at her brother's place. At first I was very much surprised. Then I was happy, if only for the fact that the other officer, in spite of his promise, had not written to Olga.

The letters were extremely tender. For that reason they caused unpleasant sensation in me. While I read them, a trembling came over me. I felt urged to something that was against my nature. I presumed that he wanted to chain me to himself, which roused my indignation to such an extent that I was restless all day long. I was still almost a child. I had not even had my period yet. The mere thought of having to be alone with a man horrified me. I sat down in my bedroom and imagined what would happen to me if I were his wife. This made me angry with him and disgusted with myself.

Distinct expression of evasion of love.

Olga advised me to answer, but in a cool manner. And then we talked about that certain thing which he surely would demand. We started to ridicule him, and I sneered: "If he thinks I am going to kiss him, he'll have to wait a long time." I had never kissed before. A kiss alone seemed to be the worst. Then I received a letter or a postcard from him almost daily. He also sent me his photograph. At last he inquired whether, on his next sojourn in Vienna, he might propose to me. That disquieted me still more. The thought of being torn from my accustomed surroundings was unbearable. I made an evasive and short answer. My parents, who did not object to such an advantageous marriage, teased me when they noticed my embarrassment. I said to my father, "I will marry only you."

Psychoanalysts of the Freudian school would regard this remark as proof that the sexual desires of this girl are directed toward her father. It would be an example of this girl's Oedipus complex, on which Freud later laid less stress. However, we have long seen from the context that a sexual relationship between her and her father is not possible; for her, her father is asexual. Not every desire of a girl is a sexual desire or concerns itself with sexuality (libido). But every wish is a wish to rise, to win more power and security, to improve one's situation and position in the community. When sexuality appears a suitable means for this purpose, it is adapted to the striving for power and serves as a weapon to achieve success. We do not believe sexuality is the primal urge, neither for the beginning nor the end, but believe it is a means which we use as necessity arises, and which we abandon as easily as we resort to it, when other ways lead to the goal.

The father of this girl is a comparatively weak man. She knows that she can rule him. "I will marry only Father" means in the language of her system: "I want to rule Father, I alone and as completely as possible."

Her first acquaintance with marriage led her to believe it was a battleground on which one loses or wins. Reasonably sure of her victory, she wants to proceed on that battlefield where she has no defeat to dread, and refuses to make one step on another field which she does not know, and where she may experience defeat.

I was still pretty childish.

The naval officer did not abandon his suit. In one of his next letters, he informed me that one of his comrades would come to see me in his name. That terrified me again. Moreover, we were not in a position to receive an officer in our apartment. We did not even have one room where one could talk alone to a person. Every corner was crowded with Father's tailoring business.

In the meantime, we had often talked about putting me into an office.

She will now be brought face to face with the great, human problem of work or vocational occupation. She has solved most incompletely, the two other major social problems: friendship and love. Our expectations are not very high, but we are most interested to see what she will do with the question of work. As a pampered child, she will also be badly prepared for this problem of life and will hesitate, stop, or run away.

After finishing business school, I did not do any work at all. I got up at ten in the morning, demanded food at once, and ate an awful lot. All day long, I visited friends and came home only for meals. Father was of the opinion that it could not go on like that any longer; I could either help a little at home or else get a job in an office. Household work did not interest me in the least. In an office, I could make some money.

So, one morning, Father looked through the newspaper and found an advertisement inserted by a chemical factory for an office girl.

Mother and I went out to the plant. They engaged me right away.

Then we rode to Lina who was at the hospital. My sister was on night duty, so we could speak to her during the day; otherwise, I would not have seen her any more before starting my new job. In the trolley car, I could see from my mother's face that she had something on her mind. She sat silently beside me. Soon she confessed that she would rather see me refuse the position; the factory was too far from home; it would be too much of a rush for me.

When Lina heard the news, she embraced and kissed me and gave me plenty of advice on my conduct. Then we went home.

Father also seemed to regret his idea. He probably did not think that I should get a job so easily. He, too, was of the opinion that the location of the office was too far from home. And what is more, I had continuous working hours with only one-half hour for lunch. I would not be able to stand it, he said. He was quite excited. But I insisted on trying at least. "First you chase me out of the house," I reproached him, "and then you want to stop me."

The next morning I woke up very early. Mother helped me dress. Then she gave me a thermos-bottle with hot tea, cold pork, bread and a few lumps of sugar. Father blessed me as if I were going on a long journey and told me to come home if there was anything I did not like. My parents were both quite upset. In a rather depressed mood, I started.

She probably expects great honor from her job. According to the usual nature of such office positions, we may assume that she will soon find her way back to her parents. The excitement she speaks of indicates the intense tension such people feel who do not think of the work or of other people, but solely of their triumph or possible defeat. In this increased tension, the aforementioned stage fright originated as a sign of poorly developed social feeling and an exaggerated interest in one's own person. At the same time, we find courage, self-confidence, and an optimistic attitude only among individuals who feel they are in contact with other human beings and at home with them. Courage is the result of a perfect social feeling.

A few old maids were working in the office. My first task was to rule lines in a large notebook. I was so excited that I made a few ink spots in it. Then I had to file copes alphabetically. That hurt my eyes.

Her intense interest in her eyes, probably fostered by her parents—she was near-sighted and was frequently admonished to take care of her eyes—breaks through as a signal for retreat.

The manager of the office was a young man in uniform. He took me into his office, showed me around, encouraged me, and said that, of course, everything was new the first day, but that I would soon be acclimated. However, I had had enough already from what I had seen so far.

During my lunch time, I ate the bread and cold pork and drank the tea. But that was as good as nothing. I was used to devouring tremendous portions, several plates of soup and so on, reading all the time I ate. The old maids made me nervous, too. Suddenly, I got severe abdominal cramps. I went to the ladies' room and had to keep going there all afternoon.

It is merely an assumption and would have to be confirmed by other facts that this girl belongs to the type which reacts to increased psychical tension with gastrointestinal disturbances.

Later on I broke the thermos bottle. And then it was five o'clock at last. I staggered exhausted to the trolley car.

At home each member of my family surpassed the other in pitying me. Lina took me in her arms and sighed: "Poor child, you have had to work so hard!" Mother also embraced and kissed me. Father descended from his sewing table, stroked me, looked lovingly into my eyes and kissed my forehead. Then mother cooked a delicious meal, all my favorite dishes. But I was so exhausted that I could not eat. That made Father excited. "Don't you see," he exclaimed, "she'll break down? If she goes to this office for only a few days, I'll have her lying here sick in bed! How she looks! Pale, drawn cheeks! She can't stand that! She needs an office where there are many young girls, where she isn't watched so closely, where she doesn't have to work so hard and has a little time to amuse herself, an office that isn't so far from here! She isn't going to go there again!"

Her attitude incites the pampering group to help her in her intention to give up her position. The retreat is complete.

Just as we finished our dinner, the bell rang. Mother and Lina went to open the door. From the kitchen, I heard the voice of a man whom I did not know. Lina came back to the kitchen. It was the friend of the naval officer. I was startled. I did not feel like saying two words to him and therefore asked my sister to pretend that I had gone out. In a way, I was sorry. However, because I was still weak from the abdominal pain of the afternoon, I was afraid of making a bad impression. And, besides, the whole affair annoyed me.

Evasion from love and possible marriage. We must not be surprised or become dubious when we notice that she tries to attain her goal with sound reasons. Such reasons are often used merely as an alibi; or something occurs that is considered a strong counter-reason. If we are certain of our interpretation, the counter-reasons are not so important. We do not see any positive act leading to the solution of the love problem.

Mother and Lina talked to the officer for a while. I did not move. When he had gone, I slipped into my bed completely exhausted. I could hear Father say to Mother that she should let me sleep as long as I wanted, so that I could recuperate from the hardships of the day. Then I fell asleep.

The next morning Father went to the office to give notice on the pretext that I was sick. When he asked for my papers, the manager did not give them to him, but said I should come back to the office as soon as I felt better. However, Father forbade me to go there. After two weeks, I received my papers back. I received only one more letter from the naval officer written in a sad mood. Thereafter, I did not hear from him any more. . . .

One day I went shopping downtown with a girlfriend of mine. Two young officers addressed us on the street. We refused to talk to them, but that did not discourage them and they inveigled us in a conversation. I went on ahead with one of them and lost sight of the other two. The young lieutenant led me through narrow, quiet streets. It was evening. Suddenly, he seized me and wanted to kiss me. I resisted with all my might. He tore my veil, which I had borrowed from Lina. I was furious and cried: "Now you leave me alone right away!" He grew pale and apologized. I replied that I did not want to have anything to do with him and that I did not care to see him any longer. He said he had torn my veil and would compensate. I refused any compensation and walked away. He came after me, apologized again, and threatened to give the money for the veil to a beggar unless I gave him my address. I told him to do as he pleased and again left him. But he followed right on my heels and talked and talked to me, until I relented and even agreed to meet him again socially. In order to show off with an officer, I decided to meet him in our neighborhood. But when I saw him waiting on the square with a bunch of roses in his hand, I felt embarrassed. I carried the roses bashfully with their heads down.

The justified repulse of a too aggressive officer (who certainly had a right to expect more of girls who permitted themselves to be accosted on the street) is followed by her agreeing to see him again in order to show him off to her acquaintances. That illustrates again how she evades the challenge of love, how she misuses it to feed her vanity, which is nothing more than her longing to appear more than she really is.

He proposed going to a café. At first I did not want to. But since it was quite chilly, I went in with him. While we were talking, he asked me if I would not rather be alone with him. I answered that no one was disturbing us anyway. Then he said he did not mean it that way, it was so uncomfortable here, he would like to be all alone with me. Now I understood. "What do you mean? You can't have me for that! I want to go home!" He seemed indignant. We left the café.

On the street, he tried to persuade me again, and asked if I were afraid of him. He gave me his word of honor as an officer that he would not do me any harm. And while we were walking along, he suddenly tried to push me into a house—I believe it was hotel. I ran away. He came after me. When he caught up with me, I screamed at him furiously that he could not force me to do anything he wanted, that I had never been alone with a man and had no desire to be either. "Is that so? You don't believe what I say!" he shouted back. "That is an insult! I have given you my word of honor! I am not a scamp! Think it over, please!"

"I have nothing to think over. Don't fool yourself!"

Finally, after much coaxing, I made another engagement with him. This time, he brought his photograph. That, I thought, was silly. We rode to a park. There he asked me at once to kiss him. I said to him: "Now, look here. I have never kissed a man, and if I ever do, it will be only for love. But I am not in love with you."

"For that you don't have to be in love. You'll learn how to fall in love with me, just wait. Probably you don't even know what a real kiss is."

That made me curious. I thought it might be a shame not to know what a real kiss was like, and decided not to oppose him, in case he should try to steal one from me. I did not have to wait long until he gave me a kiss. But I only felt disgusted. Then I said to him that I was cold and wanted to go home. He was obviously offended that his kiss had not made me warm instead of cold, and shouted at me in an angry voice: "Either-or! Either I shall never see you again or we shall love each other, which you certainly will not have to repent. Didn't I give you my word of honor as an officer? What on earth do you think I am?"

"With that sort of voice you won't get anywhere with me. I will not—that settles it."

"Think it over! I'll give you a week's time! And if you don't agree, return my picture."

"Your picture—there it is. Take it! Goodbye!"

I handed it to him, turned around and went off.

Early the next day I ran over to Tilda, told her that I had been kissed and that I knew at last what a real kiss was. I described in detail all sorts of delight which I had not felt at all. And then I advised her to obtain the same pleasure for herself as soon as possible.

We see her approaching the limit of her relationships with the other sex, an arena in which she fears defeat. She no longer has any fear about being the first one. She wants only to play with fire. Immediately after, she boasts to Tilda and tries to make her go over the dangerous road which she herself detests.

The evening after the kiss, I washed my mouth out thoroughly with potassium permanganate and spit out ten times. . . .

Tilda had a friend with whom she was quite deeply in love. That vexed me. I tried to incite her against him; I endeavored to persuade her that he was not suited to her. I did not succeed with this method, so I called on Minna for assistance and suggested that she make some disparaging remarks about him to Tilda. So she said to Tilda: "My, that boy is a homely fellow!" Tilda replied scornfully: "I don't care if you like him or not—as long as I like him."

This endeavor to disturb others in their love happiness expresses her general aversion to love and, at the same time, her inclination to be a saboteur when she is not the center of attention. Similarly, in school spoiled children who do not lead in classwork or games disturb the others because they feel incapable of obtaining the leading role.

What follows is an attempt to make a joke out of the love play, which is too dangerous to her ambition; by fooling men, she preserves her feeling of superiority over them.

In order to change Tilda's ideas, I took her out with me every afternoon. We put on large hats and pressed them down on our faces. A fur which Father had made for me covered my face up to the eyes. Tilda did the same with a fox fur. One could see nothing of our faces but the eyes which we rolled crazily when we met a man. We were frequently addressed by men who took us to cafes; there we devoured a lot of pastry and afterward made our escape. One day an elderly gentleman between forty and fifty addressed us and invited us to a barroom. That was something new. At first we hesitated, but as we were two against one, we thought that nothing could happen to us. An elaborately dressed woman with bleached hair received us, whispered a few words in the gentleman's ear, and showed us to a little booth with a curtain in front of it. The gentleman ordered wine. We began to feel alarmed. The curtain, however, was not drawn. Except for a piano-player, who was just starting to play a dance, no other person was in the restaurant. The wine had scarcely been poured into the glasses, when Tilda whispered to me that I should be careful because the man might perhaps have put some narcotic or exciting drug into the wine. That sufficed to terrify me.

Although we were constantly urged to drink, we took only small sips of the wine. We made up instead on the cookies. The man then took a seat between us. We receded anxiously. I had already repented having accepted the invitation and was wondering how we could manage to get away as soon as possible. The man did not look as if he could be easily fooled. He was angry because we withdrew from him and asked in an irritated tone what we were supposed to be here for. We became more and more dejected. When he left the room for a moment, we wanted to use the opportunity to get out. We deliberated on what to do in case he attempted to rape us. There were no weapons, of course, with which we could have defended ourselves. Tilda had the idea of attacking him if necessary with the two empty chairs beside us. In order to be prepared in time, we laid our hands on the armrest. After coming back, he started to sidle up to us. We repulsed him again. He became furious, called us silly kids, impertinent dumbbells, and accused us of having cheated him. That was very disagreeable to us. He renewed his advances. But we succeeded in pushing him away without the assistance of the chairs. Finally nothing remained for him to do but pay. The lady with the yellow hair looked dumbfounded when she saw him leave the place without having achieved his purpose. On the street, the man swore at us again. But now we felt safe; we told him to go to hell and marched off. We were glad to have gotten away with a mere fright and decided to be a little more careful the next time.

Lina induced me to take dancing lessons twice a week. I let a different boy take me home each time. But I never kissed one of them. One day Tilda came to me with another girl and told me that there was going to be a masquerade in our neighborhood. The three of us could go in old-fashioned Viennese costumes.

I was delighted at this idea, all the more so since I had never attended a ball. I agreed at once, although I did not know how to arrange about getting out. Father had always opposed my going to dances and balls because of my poor health. Also, I had no suitable dress and by no means the money to buy a new costume. Tilda and Gretel had prepared their white dresses and black masks; whereas, I had not yet had the courage to tell Father about it. At the last moment, I resolved to ask a rich girl whom I knew to lend me a dress and whatever else I needed for the ball. She agreed, and I picked from her numerous dresses one that seemed to be best suited for the ball. She also let me have a mask and a little fan; patent leather shoes I had myself. I told Father that I was going to see Tilda; I had let Mother into the secret. She also gave me the money to buy a ticket.

Tilda had already left for the ball when I came to her house with my parcel, containing, among other things, some powder and a lipstick from Lina. Tilda's mother helped me dress. But since the rich girl whose dress I was going to wear was about three times as stout as I, her dress was far too wide for me. We had to pin it together hastily with safety-pins. Then I tried on the mask. It pressed against my face and screwed up my eyelids. However, there was no more time to adjust it. When I mounted the stairs to the ballroom, I noticed that all the other girls came in accompanied by men. Only I was alone, which troubled me a little. For that reason, I put on the mask. But I had to lift it several times in order not to stumble.

The dance floor was packed. There was an intermission just when I entered. I searched for my friends and soon found them. They were sitting on a bench whispering to one another. I took a seat beside them, but they did not recognize me. After a while I went over to Tilda and said: "How do you do, Miss Tilda." Both girls were quite perplexed and then very glad I had been able to come. The music began to play; we were asked to dance and danced incessantly. We had paid for our tickets, but unfortunately possessed not one more penny to buy something to eat or drink. And we were both hungry and thirsty.

A gentleman with quite a bourgeois appearance asked me for a dance. He looked much too old for me, had a funny pronunciation and did not dance very well. However, I hoped that he would help me quench my thirst and so I talked to him after the dance for a while. Then I introduced him to my friends. Before that, I had whispered to Tilda; "Listen, I have caught a fish who can't even dance decently. But I hope he takes us to the restaurant. You two must flirt with him."

The gentleman did not seem exceedingly delighted to suddenly have three girls with him instead of one. But I made him understand, either all three—or none! Thus the four of us went to the restaurant and drank wine.

After a quarter of an hour, I asked him to excuse me and left the dancing gentleman to my girlfriends. He soon followed me and wanted to dance with me continuously. I escaped whenever I could.

A large cap was suspended from the ceiling at one end of the hall. The couple that happened to pass under the cap during a dance had to get "married"; that is, they had to kiss each other in a separate room. Most unfortunately, I danced under the cap with the old man. But I refused to let him kiss me. I said, "I'll send you my girlfriend, Tilda. I don't want to." Tilda in turn referred him to Gretel, who did not want to do it either. Thus the poor man was done out of a kiss and had incurred expenses for nothing.

Afterwards I danced eagerly and received many flowers in little bunches. I fled from one man to another. Only the mask disturbed me. I was glad when midnight came and I could take it off. Now I danced all the more; I made several engagements with men but I did not keep one of them. And then the ball was over. Several young chaps asked if they might take us home. We refused politely.

I dressed in Tilda's house. Her mother laughed at our experience with the poor fish, as we called him. Then I went home. Father was still awake. He made an angry face when he saw me. I did not let him get a word in edgewise, and told him so many funny stories about the ball that he could not help laughing. At last he only said, "You are never to go alone to a ball. The next time I'll go with you if I have time. Dancing all night and then expecting others to pay for you."

I always had to wear the same dress for my dancing lessons. For a long time I had wanted to get a new one. But we never had enough money to buy one. I thought my head off trying to find a way to manage to make a little money. Of course, I did not want to be chained to an office. I simply hated office work.

Every now and then I looked through the advertisements in our newspaper. One day I happened to see the following advertisement;

"Help wanted. Easy work. Good pay, etc." I showed this advertisement to my parents. They did not like the idea of my taking such a job. They asked what good it had done to send me to business school. I replied that I cared only to make some money; how I earned it made no difference to me.

The next day I was already sitting at a long table, stripping feathers apart.

The other women looked at me with curious eyes. But I did not take any notice of them and stripped my feathers mechanically. Much dust was caused by this work which continually irritated my throat. I had to cough a lot. I tried to combat the cough by thinking of the money that I would earn and the dress that I would buy for it. Then I remembered a moving picture in which an assistant worker like me married the boss. Unfortunately, my boss was a small old man with a paunch. When I told Father about my debut as a feather-stripper, he said the job was no good because it would endanger my lungs. I went there once again. Then Father forbade it. I got my few cents and decided to look for another position.

I thought I had found the right one when, after some time, I read the following advertisement: "School for moving picture actresses. Professor N. N." This time Lina had to accompany me. We were received by the alleged professor, who still looked quite young, in a room decorated with red wallpaper and a good grand piano. He asked us to attend a rehearsal first. After that he would examine me.

Two young men and a very gay young woman came in and rehearsed a love scene. Then it was my turn. One of the men was to be my partner and was to represent my father, who objected to my being married. The young man immediately commenced making grimaces. I played the sad one. And then I imagined how I acted when Father denied me a wish. I stamped my feet on the floor and bawled: "Don't be so nasty!" Everyone began to laugh; they all applauded and cried: "Excellent." The professor thought I had much talent and wanted to arrange to give me lessons at once. But Lina told him that she had to talk to our parents first. When Father heard about the new plan, he was dubious about its value. Moreover, it was impossible for him to procure the fee for lessons. Thus, this career also found its premature end.

A little later on the idea came to my mind to become assistant to a dentist such as Lina had been. I thought this sort of work pretty easy. Besides, I was curious to see how people behaved when they had a tooth pulled. Soon I found an advertisement in the paper and applied as a nurse in a dentist's office. The dentist, an elderly man with whiskers, did not please me. He asked me if I had had any previous experience and I had to answer in the negative. Then he murmured something, put down my name and address in his notebook and dismissed me.

Two days later I got a postcard from him asking me to come see him. Before he decided to employ me, he asked me at length about my family and other personal details. He seemed to be a pedantic man. Then his wife came in and looked me over. She wore a dressing gown. It was most repugnant to me to have to shake hands with her. In addition to the tiny salary, he promised me plentiful tips. He also told me that my predecessor had gotten married. The last thing he did was to caution me to always have my hair neatly combed.

The following morning I had to be at his office at half past seven. The dentist showed me the most important of his instruments, explained how to fix the drill, etc. My head ached from seeing so many instruments. The first patient came in. I took a place at her left, covered her neck with a small towel, and put water in a glass. The dentist lit the little spirit flame and pumped hot air on the tooth. I had to heat a tiny mirror over the flame so that it would not become misty from the patient's breath. I was so excited I held the mirror over the flame too long, and suddenly my chief cried: "Enough! Otherwise the mirror will crack." My old fear of mirrors came over me like lightning. I could see the little mirror cracked and myself burdened with seven years of misfortune. And at the same time, I reflected on how to get away. Besides, I disliked very much the rubber plate which served to isolate the tooth under treatment and dripped with saliva.

At first sight the frequent change of occupation seems to be justified, but this girl will have difficulty finding a suitable position as long as she does not change her style of life. In the dentist's office, her whole attention is directed toward finding a way of escape. The old, apparently, forgotten fear of mirrors comes in at the right time. "Besides, I also felt a strong dislike." The famous "besides" in a neurosis.

Finally, I had to carry out the brass pot into which the patient spit, and sterilize the instruments. All this and the obnoxious odor of my hands sickened me to such a degree that I could hardly eat anything for lunch.

At two o'clock I had to be back. Then the dentist showed me how to wind absorbent cotton around a nerve needle and advised me to practice that thoroughly. His wife appeared again, saying I was to help her mend the linen when I had some time. I thought to myself: "You can wait a long time. What else? All day long on my feet and in addition, mend her laundry."

Now the parade of patients began. However, I was cheated of the spectacle that I wanted to see most of all; no one had a tooth pulled.

Those who feel inferior and weak want to be present at the misfortune of others. Some children train and practice to be cruel because they are ashamed of their weakness. They stand around shivering when a pig is slaughtered, but the spectacle nevertheless attracts them over and over again. They intend to harden themselves, they read continually or listen to ghost stories, and so on. The accomplished tyrant is always a coward and a weakling as well.

I finished my work with difficulty. In the evening I went home and never returned to the office.

Chapter XII

The Goal of Superiority

One day, while we were taking a walk, Tilda's friend pulled her onto a gutter drain and held her on it. Both shook with laughter. Surprised, I asked them what that meant. Tilda answered: "Don't you know that a girl doesn't get a husband if she stands on a gutter drain?" I cocked my ears at once and thought: "Peculiar. I always disliked stepping on one of these gutter drains, sort of a dull presentiment that it would mean mischief!" Now I believed I had found out at last what was behind that feeling. Afraid of being pushed or pulled onto a gutter drain like Tilda with the result of never being able to acquire a husband, I went out with them quite reluctantly from that time on.

Again a new compulsion idea. The symptoms change like the colors of a chameleon, adjusting themselves along neurotic lines to changing environment and conditions. The chameleon, the neurosis, remains the same. Even if the symptoms disappeared temporarily (and on closer inspection there would be enough neurotic signs to discover) that would not guarantee the disappearance of the neurosis. It signifies that the neurosis, for the time being, needs fewer alarming symptoms or does not consider them necessary. Patients often overlook that fact when they believe themselves to be quite cured because they have been temporarily freed of their troublesome symptoms. Symptoms are small parts, but we are interested in the whole human being. The criterion for a cure lies solely in how the entire individual reacts in the future to life and its demands.

This girl goes further, step by step, in her compulsion neurosis. One restriction follows another, each more comprehensive. The entire construction of her neurosis is intelligent and consistent, demonstrating that even intelligence is merely an instrument used either to overcome life's obstacles or evade them, depending on the goal.

She felt reluctant probably because she was not the center of the situation. The gutter drain idea could free her from the fatal thought of being superfluous, or one among many, showing why the logical arguments and explanations of her friends cannot help her. The gutter drain idea has another purpose than to be logically discussed, and the idea is perfectly correct and intelligent for this other purpose. Private intelligence fights common sense. We find this private intelligence throughout the reflections of all kinds of people with conduct disorders, such as problem children ("because I don't want to . . ."), neurotics as in the present case, insane people ("because I am influenced by electric currents"), criminals (because he has better clothes than I"), suicides ("because life has no meaning"), perverts ("because perversions are a higher form of sexual expression"), drunkards, drug addicts (because I cannot live without these remedies"), superstitious people ("because something brings good luck or bad luck") and so on. All these forms of private logic serve to justify the attainment of personal goals, but not one considers the general, human purpose of the community. That is why they belong in a neurotic system.

Soon I could do nothing but believe in the mysterious connection between a gutter drain and its various consequences. Even if I could have been furnished with clear proof that this remark of Tilda's was merely a silly saying--Finni, a friend of Lina's, whom I had repeatedly seen stepping on gutter drains, got married in spite of it--even then no one could have changed my mind anymore. My friends wondered why I made a big detour around the gutter drains or became frightened when I saw one. When they asked me why I avoided them so carefully, I answered: "Why, they stink so badly. I can't stand the smell."

One day, when we passed a gutter drain and I had shown my usual signs of fright, I explained to a young man how my fear originated. He placed himself on a gutter drain before my eyes and stood there for a while. That seemed so funny to me that I had a fit of laughter. At the same time I felt sorry for him. I said to myself: "Now he can wait a long time until he gets a wife." There was no doubt in my mind as to the truth of this superstition.

I noticed that there was a gutter drain near the trolley station where I had to get off. I immediately re-entered the car and got off at the next station. Another day I arrived at the same station with a girl who knew that we had to get off there. I did not see any other way out of my dilemma but to jump over the drain. In spite of this precaution, I imagined I had touched the drain with my foot. I became very despondent, said good-bye to the girl and went straight home. I told my parents that something terrible had happened to me. They were terrified. But when they heard what had happened, they became almost hysterical with laughter. Father put on his overcoat and promised to show me that he could step on a gutter drain a hundred times. Sobbing, I answered that this was not the same in his case since he already had a wife and therefore did not have to be afraid anymore. It would be different if Lina were to do it. So my sister really placed herself on a gutter drain right in front of me. But that did not quiet me. On the contrary, I cried all the more, reproaching myself with the thought that if Lina did not get a husband, I would be guilty.

It was often merely necessary for me to be near a gutter drain to start the fixed idea that I had somehow touched it. Only when I had succeeded in inducing all my friends, one after the other, to step on the drain, without letting them know what I was aiming at, did I feel somewhat relieved. But when winter came and the streets were covered with snow, I dared to venture out only with the most elaborate precautions. I was continually on the watch for gutter drains covered by snow. One evening, I felt as if I had stepped on one. I ran home in a frenzy of despair, crying and raving. Then I returned to the spot where the accident had happened to find out whether there really was a gutter drain. There was none at all, just a puddle.

The fear of gutter drains made going out almost impossible for me. I had examined my own neighborhood very carefully to see where all the drains were located, but further out there were innumerable, unknown, spiteful gutter drains. In spite of my apprehensiveness about going around with men, the prospect of having to remain an old maid for the rest of my life seemed to me the most despicable fate. "Old maid" -- the mere name terrified me. In sheer desperation, the idea came to me to retreat from this world and enter a cloister.

This fear of gutter drains places all responsibility for possible failure to find a husband on the drain, and leaves her personal attractiveness intact. Her vanity and pride are saved. If no one wants her, it is the fault of the gutter drain, just as before it was the fault of the broken mirror. Children who make certain acts responsible for failure in schoolwork frequently have similar superstitions, such as: stepping on the dividing lines between sidewalk squares, leaping over a number of stairs, and so on.

Almost every person can remember periods in his life when he had certain compulsive thoughts or felt forced to do things which led him into such difficulties. To illustrate: one man feels compelled to doubt everything he hears; another feels compelled, under certain circumstances or at certain hours of the day, to pray in order to maintain a mental balance; a third believes that he exists only by means of supernatural assistance and behaves as if everything were a present from this supernatural power. We see lighter forms of compulsive action in ordinary superstitions compelling the person concerned to do or not do specific things, such as: never to start a journey on Friday, never to light three cigarettes from the same match, never to put the left shoe or stocking on before the right, never to let a lamppost or similar street object come between him and his companion, and the like. Later on, compulsion neuroses and phobias occasionally branch off from such traits.

These forms of childish superstition evidently reveal an aggravated inferiority feeling and the lack of confidence in our own strength. Now and again, however, a successful attempt to busy ourselves on the generally useful side of life can run parallel with the attempt to win laurels in the realm of superstition. Success in such cases is usually attributed to a fortunate omen. For instance, the patient who suffered from the fixed idea that his sisters might burn to death if he did not pray for their safety from fire every night, saved his sisters not only from burning to death, but he also constantly thought and took care of them, which was probably the deeper purpose of his fixed idea.

He was unconsciously forced to carry out his charitable intention and he would surely have been able to accomplish it consciously, if the meaning of this unconscious compulsion had been made clear to him. The conscious and unconscious are not opposite poles, as Freud thinks; thoughts passing over into the unconscious is a means, a deception of the psyche utilized when the personal feeling of integrity or the unity of the personality is threatened by some conscious misinterpretation.

In the course of analysis, we have frequently seen that this girl's psyche resorts to all sorts of artifices to overcome real and imaginary difficulties of life, as well as to aid in her tendency to exaggerate or falsify reality, her choice and purposive use of experience, and similar mechanisms. The nervous psyche must use such tricks to be able to even approach the fictive, tension-producing goal. One of these artifices is the location of the goal in the unconscious, or the substitution of one neurotic goal for another in the unconscious. When there seems to be a stark contrast between the conscious and the unconscious (a fiction which the Freudian school takes as truth), the difference is merely in the means and has no significance in the final object of elevating the personality and achieving the fictive goal of godliness.

We find this concept confirmed in the example of the man who prays for his sister's life. The conscious and unconscious pursue the same road, both guided by the goal of superiority on the useful side of life, that is, to take care of his sisters despite all obstacles.

Another trait in the gutter drain episode should be familiar to us. She feels relieved when her friends deprive themselves of their chance of marrying by stepping on the drain.

My fear of gutter drains was supplemented by the following. One day I began to imagine that the trolley lines J and J2 would bring me misfortune. Eventually, I added to them the numbers 13, 3, 63, 43, and the letters A, Ak, B, Bk., D, and C, from the outskirts of the city to the center. It became absolutely impossible for me to use these lines. I often walked many blocks, even when the weather was bad. J and J2 were the most strictly forbidden cars--I do not use them up to the present. I had to face the worst difficulties because of these prohibitions which I positively had to follow. I could tell many stories about my sufferings. One evening I got out of Car F at a crossing where I had to change to Car II. A car came along which I thought was Car H; I am somewhat nearsighted. I got in, and sat down. Suddenly, I was surprised to notice that the supposed Car H ran straight down the "Loop" instead of turning into Alser Street. I jumped up and looked at the sign. What did I read? Car D. I rushed out and jumped off the car like one bereft of her senses. This mistake depressed me horribly. I believed I was going to have one misfortune after another from then on. Again I resolved to enter a cloister.

We see how she restricts her radius of action by the car phobia and, faced with the problem of love, seeks a way to avoid possible defeat by means of a cloister.

For the time being, however, I ironed the dress I had worn in that detested car in order to break the wicked spell. If I had been rich, I would have thrown away or burned all the things I had worn, including my hairpins. But I, poor devil, had to be satisfied with ironing out that ill-fated dress, washing myself from head to foot and performing a counter-magic. I repeated a number three times.

Then it became quite impossible for me to go through certain streets. When I had to pass through one of them, I held my breath so that the air from it could not enter me and go down my throat. And if I had already breathed, I spat out three times and wiped my mouth with saliva. Which streets were they? I am still afraid to name them.

Lina used to be terribly angry when I dragged her along a street in a zigzag, and constantly forced her to make detours.

The members of my family were also forbidden to ride in the cars with the unfortunate numbers, or walk through streets taboo for me. If I found out that they had done it anyway, I did not let them come near me. I remembered with great care the clothes they had worn in those cars and streets and did not touch them again. And if I accidentally came in contact with them, I swore and fretted, tore off my dress and underwear, placed myself in front of the open window without a bit of clothing on in order to catch pneumonia and die, and finally threw myself in complete desperation on the bed.

The longing for death, closely related to suicidal tendencies, appears as a trial solution to escape defeat in the love problem. As always, this attempt results from a tendency to exclude life when all other ways to a satisfactory solution of life's problems seem blocked. Instead of overcoming her difficulties by means of creative power and choice of a generally useful occupation, which would also help her overcome her feeling of inferiority, she chooses to detach herself from and condemn the community and its offering, revenge herself on those who stand in her way, and acquire a fleeting feeling of superiority in experiencing mastery over her life and death. These choices represent the confession of the weakling, of the hopeless.

The streetcar phobia, and the way this girl builds it up, again gives her power over her family, the weakest part in her environment.

I was once walking along a certain street and grazed a woman carrying a handbag. The idea suddenly struck me that she might live on one of those forbidden streets. I followed her to see whether I was right or not, but eventually lost track of her.

I did not visit the moving picture theatres on that street any more. There might be people from forbidden streets in them. Not even a fine program could induce me. Then a number of coffee restaurants in different sections of the city became so repugnant to me that I closed my mouth and nose when I had to pass them. One day I forgot to protect myself in this manner in front of the Café Central. I remembered afterward that I had passed this place and that a disastrous wind had blown on me from the revolving door of the Café. I felt as if I had been poisoned and turned about, raced home, flung my hat in a corner, tore off my clothing, cleaned my face with soap and water, and washed out my mouth.

The streets abhorrent to me bred as rapidly as rabbits. I already detested a whole district. When people from this forbidden district came to see us, I felt as if I were in a room with people infected with the plague, whose mere breath brought ruin and who infected everything they touched. I would never use a chair on which one of them had sat. At last, nothing remained for me to use but my own tattered and torn easychair which I guarded like a dragon. If someone showed the slightest intention of sitting on it, I made a great fuss and prevented him. I dragged the chair with my own hands from the kitchen to the living room to use when I played the piano. My clothes were not allowed to be put on another chair.

One day Mother was making hash. I was delighted in spite of the fact that it was horsemeat. While she was serving some of the hash to me, she accidentally brushed her arm against the armrest of a chair on which a forbidden person had been seated a short while before. I was furious and did not eat one bite of hash. That made Mother so angry that she almost threw the whole pot on the floor.

Remarkably, even her love for the good midday meals her mother cooks cannot lessen her fear of uncleanliness. We might think that a strong desire, like one for physical pleasure, would have enough power to suppress at least temporarily her lust for power. That would be a superficial thought. Man is a unity. He does not consist of two or three wishes, fighting each other, with one or another conquering from time to time; he has only one goal and everything he does aims toward this goal. In the patient's opinion, if physical pleasure can be used as a means toward this goal, such pleasure will be utilized or any other means which seems practical. But here the physical desire is unimportant in her struggle toward her objective, superiority, so her desire is disregarded and secondarily used to illuminate her difficulties which makes her struggle for superiority such an exhausting one. Our girl eats hash with great relish, and when she refuses to eat it, she regards her sacrifice as a heroic act, extracting an additional bit of superiority.

Plates, cups, forks and knives used by forbidden people I never touched again. Mother had to stow away such utensils in another place apart from the rest of the pots and pans, so that I could always easily recognize them as untouchable for me. I grew accustomed to eating with knives, forks and spoons used only by me and had plates only for my use, just as during the time of my lupus phobia. If someone I did not like or anyone of my family happened to touch one of my things after being contaminated by touching or using one of the obnoxious objects, I did not touch my things any more. Mother had to buy new implements.

One Saturday night something happened which "soiled" my specific knife and fork. I immediately began to rave and scold Mother because she had not been careful enough. The stores were already closed. It was impossible to buy me another set of eating utensils. Mother borrowed a fork from a neighbor.

To evade direct contact with all forbidden people who came to the house, I would withdraw to the bedroom. There I felt as if the evil eye which I ascribed to them penetrated the wall and brought misfortune upon me. So I went to bed and crept under the blankets.

When misfortune happens because of the evil eye, of course, she is not responsible. The evil eye is to blame. What patients call bad luck is usually their own mistakes and stupidities, the cause of which they seek somewhere outside instead of inside. The evil eye is one of those goblins which would become a real danger for a neurotic only if it were absent or could not be resorted to.

Certain stores were also prohibited and Mother was not allowed to shop in them. When I suspected that she had bought supplies in such a store, I cross-examined her, asked her the most cunning questions, and set traps for her like a detective. When I found out that she had lied to me, I swore at her in abusive language and behaved as if I had lost my head.

We remember that her use of abusive language began in her childhood (her first neurosis commenced with swearing). At that time, she did it secretly and her conscience pricked her afterward. Now she feels her swearing justified and does not bother to conceal it. Obviously, the neurosis is progressing.

After the slightest contact with forbidden people or things, I washed myself.

We could have predicted that the last stage of this phobia would be a washing compulsion. Quite in contradistinction to the mentally defective, she proves her intelligence by choosing an intelligent plan for attaining her goal.

This girl appears superior again in the washing compulsion. She is the only clean human being in the world. Everyone else is dirty. Again, we see the parallel between the conscious and the unconscious. Unconsciously, the striving for power is a cheap, hidden road to superiority, customary among pampered children. The conscious aversion to the dirt of others expresses the unconscious road to superiority. The result is that the patient, without quite comprehending the full meaning of her actions, is the only one clean and superior. She would not deny it if we told her so, but she would constantly reiterate and point to her torments. The more she is tormented by the dirt of others, the cleaner she remains.

I frequently washed my whole body. I never again used a piece of soap which fell on the floor. My parents and Lina were not permitted to wash themselves with this cake of soap either. So the soap which had fallen on the floor accumulated and soon there was a pile of unusable soap.

I had a number of garments which I could no longer wear. I gave some of them to Mother. But she was not allowed to come near me when she wore any of them.

At home I wore an old, torn dress consisting of a green, worn-out skirt and a red blouse much too tight for one. I wore a pair of Bohemian slippers; if I could have managed it, I would never have taken them off. Thus I sat like Cinderella in a corner of the kitchen on my broken chair with the rusty nails, in front of me all the things whose mere presence seemed pernicious to me, all the objects bewitched by the touch of residents of those execrated districts and streets, outside the gutter drains, streets, houses, gas lampposts, coffee restaurants, trolley cars, stores threatening with their wicked magi; danger, mischief, and misfortune dogged my steps.

She describes her suffering with much skill and penetration. An antisocial, selfish life never leads to pleasure in the power which has been won over a few people at the expense of so much exertion. She sits like a tyrant on a throne which can be overturned at any moment; she rules by fear and is ruled by fear. She has to make her position in the "enemy country" secure by cunning and brute force. She has no real friends, no help, merely oppressed subordinates who, she instinctively feels, would desert her if they could. No confidence, no candor, no love comes to her, only obscure mistrust, unwillingness of those she has made into servants, and dangerous counter pressure. The protecting measures which have been arranged for her own security become weapons in the hands of her enemies. The more she thinks of her security and how to preserve it, the more insecure she becomes.

The suffering of the neurotic grows to an unbelievable torment and drives him into those great crises in which he either breaks down or hardens himself to the point where he becomes psychotic; or where he reaches the point of dim comprehension of the faulty construction of his happy struggle for recognition and then seeks enlightenment.

So-called logical arguments are of no avail in attempting to free this girl of her compulsion ideas and compulsion acts. She must be shown, step by step, the real construction of her behavior as we see it. She would have to learn to recognize what the purpose of her symptoms is and what she achieves thereby; that she wants unconsciously to detach herself by compulsion from the compulsion of communal demands; that she has built a secondary battlefield in her intense desire to avoid the principal battlefield of life; that she wants to fritter away her time so as to have none left for the accomplishment of her daily tasks; that she intends to evade life's demands with excuses, curses, alibis or ostensibly good reasons. In addition, the erroneous views acquired in her childhood must be set aside; her exaggerated ambition and vanity, and the tendency to isolate herself must all be explained to her with great delicacy and tact. She can then be led to change her style of life by unmasking the technical apparatus of her compulsion neurosis and helping her understand the whole course and consistency of her conduct.

I started to menstruate unusually late. All my friends had started long ago. Olga, for example, had her period when she was fourteen. I remember that very well. One day she took my hand, and while her eyes twinkled, led me into the bathroom and suddenly lifted her skirts. I saw bloodstains on her bloomers. "What do you think of that?" she asked proudly. I was quite depressed and resolved to tell her in about two weeks that I was so far, too. Later on, I always made my friends believe I had already begun menstruating. However, year after year went by and the period did not set in.

Most likely, an innate inferiority of her sexual organs, for which there was apparently no compensation, was responsible for the retardation of her menstruation. This inferiority was probably indicated on other parts of her body.

My parents were quite worried and had me examined by a doctor. The doctor ordered hot sitz baths. When I was seventeen, the function finally set in. When I discovered the signs, I ran at once to Father and told him. He embraced me happily and said, "Now you are a grown-up girl. You are no longer a child. We must celebrate that." And my first menstruation was celebrated by a good supper.

I frequently had a depressing dream. I dreamt that Father or Mother were very sick. I woke up crying in the middle of the night, burdened with a bad conscience, and it took me a long time to fall asleep again. While I tossed in bed from one side to the other, I resolved to change myself, assist my parents with their work, go run errands for Father, and help Mother with her housework.

Most children occasionally dream about the death or serious illness of one of their parents. To interpret such a dream by the saying,

"The wish is father to the thought," is the privilege of a schematic, insinuating psychology. On rare occasions, this interpretation is correct. However, we will make such a decision only when the general mood of the dream speaks for it and, most of all, when the behavior of the dreamer otherwise justifies such an interpretation. A mitigation of the death-wish can be found at such times when, in spite of a strongly antagonistic attitude toward the parents, such a dream occurs as part of severe depression and sadness. This would be a sign that the child's struggle against the parents does not go so far as to wish for the parents' death. This dream usually attempts to foresee the future. What will happen when my parents die?

Permit me at this point to insert a few general remarks on the purpose and significance of dreams. The dream is an obvious fiction in which a person arranges advance attempts and tests for controlling a future situation or solving a future problem. It is a fiction because an individual never views a dream situation in accordance with reality, but always transposes it as if it were reality and always as he would like to have it; he never really approaches reality, but tests his abilities under the influence of the dream and attempts a trial solution in it. A person dreaming is not different from a person awake; the only difference is in the form of expression. In his waking life he occupies himself with the present, in dreams (daydreams or dreams in sleep) he busies himself with the future by means of the past, that is to say by his experiences. Dreaming, he thinks in advance. And the way in which he thinks in advance mirrors graphically the psychic attitude of the dreamer, his courage, his adjustment to his environment, his character traits and their neurotic evasions, his own peculiar way of facing problems. The dream creates a mood whose purpose is to encourage or discourage the dreamer in approaching his problem. Such moods appear in gradations from anxiety to indifference to outspoken courage. All the dreams of an individual agree with his style of life; they belong to a system and form part of the individual unity. Conscious thought has little to do in a dream. The criticism and opposition of the sleeping sense organs are silenced. Thought in the dream is more abstract, simplified and symbolized, inclined toward a more childish state, as it were. The dream must remain unintelligible to the dreamer to protect the unity of his personality, to preserve the mood aroused in him, and to veil the goal and direction of the dreamer in the unconscious.

I do not have sufficient space her to explain more in detail the means used in dreams to accomplish their objective, to explain the technique of dream interpretation. It will suffice to indicate that the dream, like every other soul manifestation, can be employed to gain insight into the psychic machinery of a human being.

In our case, the girl is apparently anxious about her future. She needs her parents to be able to maintain a feeling of superiority. Although she emphasizes in the following paragraphs that the frequently recurring dream left no impression on the following day, the mood produced in the dream and its frequent repetition, a distinctly emotional training, has surely alleviated her attitude toward her parents. Therefore, this dream signifies a degree of social feeling, interest in her parents.

In the morning, however, everything was forgotten again. The day, the light, the morning blotted out my feelings. At this time, I had another tormenting worry. I fancied I was extremely old. Sometimes I wondered seriously whether it would not be best to end my life. Then I said to myself: "The years are passing by so quickly and misfortune approaches at a rapid pace." I never told my true age. Such thoughts came to me especially before falling asleep. Sometimes I woke up frightened, my age flashed into my mind and I thought: "How wonderful it would be to be born now!"

So old, and nothing done yet for immortality!

The thoughts mentioned obviously touch the problem of love for which she does not feel prepared because of her exaggerated desire to rule. Then she looks back at those ideal times when, in early childhood, the pampered girl actually possessed unlimited power and did not have to face new problems.

Father had had a weak heart for many years. When he was fifty-eight, the malady suddenly grew worse. He would frequently jump out of bed at night, and rush to the window struggling for breath. During the day, he was also often short of breath. Then he would stop working and have Mother take him for a walk. Up to that time, he had never rested during the day. Now he always lay down for an hour after dinner. Gradually, he seemed to lose all interest in his family. Every now and then, we heard him complain of being concerned about me. I gave no thought to the morrow, like a child, and there was no money in the house. Father felt that he did not have much longer to live and spoke of it, too. But I could not comprehend the seriousness of his disease. I never thought that he might die. Soon he was hardly able to stand on his legs any more. Lina and the doctor had to give him injections which refreshed him for a while, but the improvement never lasted long.

Father was very restless in bed. He could not live without his tailoring business. My sister was on vacation and nursed him. She and Mother alternately sat up with him during the night. I always stayed awake until about eleven o'clock; then I grew so tired that I had to go to bed.

To protect himself from becoming cold, Father wrapped a broad gray shawl around his chest. This shawl unfortunately belonged to the objects which I could not touch. I asked Mother in vain to take something else for this purpose. She said that the shawl was just right. So I could not embrace and kiss Father any more, which I wanted so much to do. I was even afraid to come near him; later on I regretted it many times although it was absolutely impossible for me to act differently.

For a short while, it seemed he was going to recover in spite of everything. We put him in a comfortable chair and he told me a lot of funny stories about his boyhood. Everyone laughed and we all hoped again. But the next day, he was again in a somnolent state, sitting upright in his bed. I often saw him moving his hands in restless sleep, as if he were sewing. One evening he arose suddenly, staggered to the sewing table in the kitchen, and stretched out his trembling hands for a coat. We asked him to go back to bed. His feet were already swollen.

My parents were still not married. Mother was much troubled that I might remain an illegitimate child. Then the doctor left her in no further doubt as to Father's condition; I only learned about this afterward, and prepared her for the worst. Mother talked matters over with Olga's mother. This woman ran straight for a priest. She learned from him that a marriage ceremony that evening at eight o'clock could be performed upon producing a certificate from a physician. Our doctor wrote out such a certificate. But it was difficult for Mother to speak to Father about the impending marriage ceremony. I remember her saying, "Look here, dear; you know we are not married yet—what will become of our Clara?" Father murmured, "yes", once in a while and nodded his head to what she said. When I heard that the ceremony was going to take place that very day, I was glad despite my grief. At last—I was almost eighteen years old—I would be able to use Father's name. Until that time, I had always told others that that was my name anyway. But now it really would be mine.

We bought two candles, borrowed a crucifix from a neighbor, a pious old woman, got some holy water, and put these things on a table covered with a white tablecloth. Everybody was very excited. I trembled all over. At eight o'clock the priest came with the sacristan who had to serve as witness as well. During the ceremony, Lina and I remained in the kitchen. Before leaving, the priest spoke to Lina and me and asked us to come to confession to him.

The ceremony exhausted Father, especially because he had to confess and receive extreme unction at the same time. Mother wanted to make him believe he was not very sick. Completely spent, he whispered that everything was all right, but would she please spare him the sight of the priest in the future.

A few days later, I was visiting Minna in the evening when Mother came into the room and said in a sad voice that I should go home with her as Father was sinking. Mrs. K. accompanied us. Father was asleep, sitting up in bed. I sat down beside him quietly. His breath was heavy and slow. Then I stole away to the kitchen. From time to time Mother came into my room. I did not know that the doctor had told her Father would not live through the night. Suddenly, I heard mother cry, "Father! Father!" I rushed into the room and could just see Father falling back onto his pillows. Lina embraced him. He had taken his last breath. I threw myself over his bed, kissed him, called for him, begged him to forgive me. I did not want to let go of him. Lina had to carry me out. When I got to the kitchen, I felt nauseous and vomited.

Again we see that she belongs to the type of person who responds to excitement with nervous disturbances in the digestive apparatus. All our inner organs are supplied by a separate nervous system, the involuntary nervous system which is older in evolution than the central nervous system and was formerly supposed to be the seat of life. When we are joyous and our heart beats more quickly as a consequence, when we blush with shame, perspire with fear or have a stomachache because we dread something, it is because of the activity of the "emotional" nerves which have been correctly classified as the sympathetic nervous system (N. sympathicus). In some cases, this involuntary nervous system is abnormally sensitive (an organ inferiority) and consequently functions more strongly than usual. We might add, however, that the source of irritation lies in the psychic structure of such people, in their style of life. In such cases a minor irritation produces a major reaction in those organs attached to this nerve system: the heart, the bladder, perspiration glands or digestive apparatus, as in the case of this girl.

In order to treat such disturbances successfully, we must go back to the psychic source and from that point, change the patient. If we find, as in this case, that the super-strong desires of the patient increase the psychic tension, then we have to change her whole style of life. We can accomplish this change only by strengthening her social feeling. Her private intelligence will be transformed into common sense in direct proportion to the strength of her social feeling. She will feel at home with and agree to the problems of life with all their advantages and disadvantages and lose her anxiety. From now on she will no longer live in a hostile world and no longer depend for her self-esteem on the opinions of others. On the useful side of life, she will feel herself a respected human being, and her feeling of inferiority will be reduced to the point where it can be well utilized as an impetus to useful accomplishments.

The room windows were opened; a candle was lit. We crouched in a corner of the kitchen side by side, weeping and unable to sleep. When Mrs. K. left us, a neighbor came to take her place. We lay down only at dawn. We were stiff all over. The next day, when I woke up, I felt as if there were a great weight on my mind. I went to Father, stroked and kissed him and put his cover in order. He looked so peaceful, not at all like a dead man. At night the men came with a coffin, laid Father in it and carried him away. We were afraid to sleep at home, so we slept for a few nights at Mrs. K's. Mother told us that she had had a vision of a skeleton two nights before Father's death.

In the chapel at the cemetery, I saw Father for the last time. His body was not altered. I still could not believe that he was dead. I stood in front of the coffin and expected him to open his eyes.

I was always looking at Father's work table. I could not comprehend his being dead. I thought he might merely have seemed dead. Mother and I locked ourselves in the bedroom at night. Saturday night the key to this room broke; we could not open the door the following morning. Mother called for the janitor through the window and let down a cord on which to hang all sorts of keys. None of them fitted. Finally a plumber opened the door for us.

I longed terribly for Father; I cried without ceasing. Frequently, I woke up frightened in the middle of the night; I could not breathe and felt grieved to death.

We can feel with the girl how deeply the separation from her father disturbed her. As long as he lived, he was the pedestal on which she had built her triumph. From now on, her mother has to replace him inasmuch as she is fitted for the position.

Then I dreamed that a dog with a muzzle bored his snout into me and turned and twisted it around. It gave me an extremely painful sensation. I turned on the light looking, to see whether I was bleeding or hurt anywhere. But I did not find anything. This dream was repeated frequently.

I also dreamed many times of a tall, bearded man standing at the foot of my bed, and woke up frightened to death. I could see him as distinctly as if he were really there.

And then I saw in my dreams a flower rising slowly and bending toward me, one single flower with five leaves like fingers. Again I woke up full of anxiety.

We could interpret these dreams correctly only if she gave us some information about her thoughts and remembrances in association with the dream material. However, we have two important supporting points. We know her life style and the problems that oppress her, and we can understand the mood emanating from her dreams. Correctly interpreted, these dreams should give evidence of the road she is using as a bridge to her goal of superiority, away from the road of logic and common sense. The moods springing from these dreams should also aim in the same direction.

In the first dream, we find love as the present central problem in the life of this girl. Her aim is to escape union with a man. We can safely assume that the dog represents a man. We frequently find a similar tendency to degrade in dreams. Because she has clearly demonstrated this tendency in former parts of her life story and because as we have read before, she occasionally has called a man a dog, our assumption is certainly justified. The muzzle is a little confusing. But if we remember that she always endeavored to provide men with a muzzle, to play tricks on them, to eliminate dangers and evade possible consequences, our attention will be more strongly directed to the fact that her "yes-but" has not only had a reinforcement of the "yes," but also a reinforcement of the "but." The pain and the fear of being hurt, of bleeding, lead her to assume that no precautionary measure is sufficient.

The second dream, also frequently repeated, permits the conclusion that in the mood of the dream she is alone with a man. As a precaution, this man is not pictured as friendly, either. It is impossible to identify him at this place. However, the second dream confirms the conclusions drawn from the first dream.

The third dream is ambiguous. We will go only so far as to suppose that the situation represents a hand stretching out after her. Here again we find the threatening approach and purposive generation of anxiety which characterizes the life of this girl plainly enough as the life of a pampered child.

Here the story ends and with it our analysis. I emphasized at the beginning of the book that we were not concerned here with the complete biography of a human being, but merely with a portion of a life story. We were more interested in seeking what we could extract from the material given than in the completeness of the story. In private consultations as well, we learn nothing more than parts of life stories from which we must draw our conclusions. I have tried to give the reader a picture of the procedure followed in a psychological analysis. I want my reader to see how a psychologist armed with a store of experience listens to, apprehends, works over, and understands an ordinary and otherwise insignificant life story. The very ordinariness of this biography is significant in illustrating how much a psychologist can get out of it.

A patient whose life is so confused can be cured only by thorough understanding of how the condition developed. In addition, our task is to give a patient the insight which we have won ourselves by means of experience and common sense. Such a procedure encourages him. He merely needs to use common sense to understand. Because common sense is much rarer than the word implies, we must beware, in attempts at analysis, of premature inferences. Superficial, mistaken judgments serve to discredit those who make them.

As I have said, I was much more concerned with the events and results of this partial biography than with the completion of the story. I fear, however, that an incomplete story will not satisfy most of my readers. The human intellect strives toward fulfillment; an unfinished fragment stimulates the imagination to create for itself a suitable ending. As much as I would like to help the reader in this respect, I know no more than he does. As I said in my preface, I have never seen this girl. All that I know about her has been written by her and by me in the present book. She mentions her present condition only once in the story, when she tells us that to this very day she still cannot bring herself to use certain street cars. We may assume from that remark that her compulsion neurosis has probably improved a great deal, but has not entirely disappeared.

Experience also teaches us that when a person has done a right-about-face and set foot on the road to normal conduct, she progresses along this road in the right direction as quickly as she retrogressed before in the wrong direction. Just as every step into a neurosis inevitably destroys courage, every step out of a neurosis builds up courage and with it strength and social feeling. That idea agrees with what I have heard about the writer of this story; namely, that insofar as she has been able to help herself without the aid of a psychologist, she has freed herself of her compulsion neurosis, and is taking courageous steps to solve her difficult life problems. I shall leave to the imaginative power, psychological understanding, and intuition of my readers to divine how.

Index

A

abnormality..75

above 2, 4, 27, 35, 57, 119, 126, 132, 147, 149, 169, 172, 176, 199, 240, 283

abuse..36, 73, 108, 232

accusation 15, 16, 53, 58, 78, 90, 110, 120, 131

    accuse 15, 121, 269

achievement...4, 26, 87, 150

acquisition 35, 161

activity...3, 5, 8, 9, 10, 20, 22, 26, 31, 33, 48, 51, 53, 64, 68, 70, 73, 79, 80, 81, 86, 106, 150, 169, 195, 230, 233, 245, 251, 266, 268, 316

    active 104, 134, 173, 202, 230

adapt 13, 37, 46, 74, 90

    adaptation 6, 13, 22, 27, 31, 32, 34, 43, 98, 107

addiction 16, 146

adjustment 12, 36, 50, 51, 75, 80, 90, 98, 104, 114, 143, 145, 223, 313

adolescence..45, 81

affection...53, 76, 77, 129, 154, 162, 198, 204, 286

aggression...17, 102, 120, 121, 147, 173, 246, 284

agoraphobia 5, 20, 60, 62, 92, 94, 148, 265

alcohol

    alcoholism 16, 89

alibi...146, 170, 222, 284, 294

altruism...204

ambition............10, 15, 26, 39, 40, 55, 71, 93, 94, 99, 117, 146, 222, 229, 248, 278, 289, 297, 312

    ambitious............28, 35, 39, 55, 91, 106, 116, 117, 120, 122, 123, 125, 171, 220, 230, 244, 248

ambivalence..57, 132

anger... 15, 20, 24, 29, 34, 38, 39, 40, 59, 132, 199, 244, 245

antithesis...132

    antithetical...147

anxiety ...3, 5, 8, 20, 21, 24, 37, 55, 60, 62, 72, 74, 80, 92, 102, 117, 118, 129, 163, 165, 168, 181, 190, 194, 199, 206, 218, 219, 220, 221, 222, 226, 253, 257, 262, 313, 317, 318

    anxious 4, 35, 71, 100, 158, 166, 195, 201, 218, 248, 259, 275, 284, 314

arrangement.. 12, 89, 138, 139, 147, 173, 204, 248, 250, 273, 276

arrogance 21, 102

art 22, 26, 27, 51, 59, 60, 70, 96, 103, 123, 150, 200, 205, 234, 267

    artist..23, 241

    artists 23, 37, 67, 145, 200

as if 32, 42, 44, 45, 67, 85, 86, 88, 89, 104, 108, 109, 130, 138, 153, 161, 162, 164, 165, 166, 170, 171, 175, 180, 187, 188, 194, 199, 208, 220, 238, 247, 250, 253, 258, 259, 262, 263, 267, 285, 292, 297, 305, 308, 309, 310, 313, 315, 317, 318

assertion..161

association 33, 318

assumption..................... 4, 11, 48, 51, 148, 162, 167, 179, 181, 187, 198, 236, 274, 280, 293, 318

    assumptions..115

asthma 64, 88 attention.9, 15, 17, 23, 24, 25, 43, 46, 52, 53, 56, 59, 60, 62, 63, 64, 65, 67, 72, 77, 82, 84, 87, 88, 90, 93, 98, 100, 106, 115, 134, 139, 151, 152, 153, 154, 156, 157, 160, 163, 169, 170, 176, 179, 187, 193, 194, 196, 197, 199, 210, 237, 246, 250, 268, 269, 282, 287, 296, 301, 318

attitude.2, 3, 4, 5, 7, 9, 11, 13, 14, 15, 27, 28, 32, 33, 34, 36, 37, 38, 39, 41, 42, 44, 49, 51, 52, 57, 58, 59, 61, 64, 68, 69, 71, 73, 74, 75, 76, 77, 78, 80, 85, 86, 87, 90, 92, 94, 99, 100, 101, 102, 104, 107, 109, 114, 115, 120, 122, 123, 125, 127, 134, 139, 142, 145, 147, 149, 150, 151, 152, 161, 181, 194, 198, 200, 201, 202, 204, 211, 224, 236, 243, 245, 247, 254, 266, 272, 276, 283, 284, 292, 294, 313, 314

avoiding 68, 96, 119, 145, 171

   avoidance 85, 104, 119

awareness 96, 108

awkward 276

B

beauty 32, 155, 164, 179, 181, 233, 254, 256, 274

becoming 38, 55, 87, 99, 104, 161, 189, 315

being....2, 3, 6, 7, 8, 9, 14, 21, 22, 26, 30, 31, 32, 36, 39, 40, 43, 44, 45, 50, 56, 58, 62, 63, 65, 67, 70, 72, 73, 75, 77, 78, 80, 81, 84, 85, 86, 87, 88, 93, 96, 102, 104, 105, 106, 117, 121, 128, 132, 134, 139, 147, 148, 151, 157, 158, 160, 162, 165, 168, 172, 173, 177, 180, 185, 197, 198, 199, 202, 204, 207, 208, 214, 221, 225, 228, 235, 236, 237, 244, 246, 248, 254, 255, 263, 264, 267, 282, 286, 290, 296, 300, 303, 307, 309, 310, 314, 317, 318, 319

belief 30, 40, 41, 42, 71, 72, 77, 78, 86, 90, 109, 145, 173, 216, 236, 264

below 2, 18, 33, 43, 57, 147, 172

blind 101, 169, 252, 254, 255

   blindness 255

blushing 82, 83, 87, 277

body 27, 42, 43, 74, 119, 143, 144, 187, 188, 218, 268, 271, 311, 312, 317

C

case....2, 3, 4, 5, 6, 7, 8, 9, 11, 12, 13, 14, 15, 16, 17, 19, 25, 26, 27, 29, 30, 33, 34, 35, 36, 38, 39, 46, 49, 53, 55, 56, 58, 60, 61, 64, 65, 67, 70, 71, 72, 73, 75, 76, 77, 78, 80, 81, 82, 85, 86, 87, 88, 89, 90, 91, 92, 94, 96, 97, 102, 103, 104, 106, 108, 109, 113, 114, 115, 116, 119, 122, 124, 128, 130, 132, 133, 138, 140, 142, 147, 152, 153, 160, 164, 169, 184, 200, 216, 218, 225, 261, 263, 266, 272, 277, 284, 296, 297, 304, 314, 316

   cases ...3, 8, 10, 15, 17, 18, 19, 20, 28, 33, 34, 36, 39, 40, 44, 46, 47, 53, 59, 63, 67, 69, 70, 75, 77, 79, 81, 82, 84, 85, 86, 88, 90, 91, 93, 97, 99, 102, 103, 104, 108, 110, 115, 117, 118, 120, 123, 126, 128, 135, 143, 144, 148, 153, 154, 165, 168, 180, 191, 193, 194, 206, 208, 231, 238, 283, 306, 316

castration 44

catatonic

   catatonia 11

causality 132, 185

caution 268, 281, 301

central nervous system 316

change9, 14, 17, 21, 35, 36, 39, 44, 59, 63, 64, 65, 78, 81, 108, 134, 149, 151, 169, 172, 203, 211, 235, 246, 251, 261, 279, 297, 301, 303, 307, 312, 316

character 20, 21, 25, 27, 55, 61, 63, 64, 70, 77, 97, 99, 100, 103, 104, 105, 134, 144, 146, 147, 171, 173, 180, 193, 194, 200, 219, 220, 247, 248, 273, 313

   character traits 146, 173, 180, 200, 313

   characteristics 47, 57, 60, 64, 76, 114, 122, 127, 128, 154, 173, 193, 200, 204, 246

child.4, 13, 14, 15, 17, 20, 21, 23, 24, 27, 31, 34, 35, 37, 38, 40, 42, 43, 45, 49, 50, 52, 53, 57, 59, 60, 61, 62, 63, 64, 65, 67, 69, 70, 72, 73, 74, 75, 76, 77, 78, 79, 80, 82, 88, 92, 93, 96, 98, 99,

100, 110, 116, 118, 122, 123, 124, 125, 126, 127, 128, 129, 136, 138, 139, 142, 144, 145, 151, 152, 153, 154, 155, 156, 157, 158, 160, 161, 162, 163, 164, 165, 166, 170, 171, 172, 173, 174, 176, 177, 178, 179, 180, 182, 183, 184, 185, 186, 187, 189, 195, 198, 199, 200, 201, 202, 203, 205, 206, 208, 209, 210, 211, 213, 224, 225, 227, 228, 229, 234, 236, 244, 251, 263, 266, 271, 276, 277, 279, 280, 282, 290, 291, 293, 312, 313, 314, 315, 318

children 4, 5, 6, 14, 15, 22, 23, 24, 25, 28, 29, 34, 37, 38, 39, 40, 42, 43, 46, 53, 56, 57, 58, 61, 63, 67, 69, 70, 72, 74, 76, 77, 79, 81, 82, 86, 94, 96, 98, 99, 100, 101, 102, 104, 107, 109, 110, 116, 117, 118, 120, 121, 122, 123, 124, 125, 126, 127, 128, 129, 132, 134, 138, 139, 153, 156, 158, 160, 161, 162, 163, 164, 170, 172, 173, 174, 175, 176, 177, 178, 179, 183, 184, 186, 187, 188, 189, 190, 195, 198, 202, 203, 207, 209, 210, 211, 213, 214, 216, 218, 220, 221, 223, 225, 227, 228, 230, 231, 239, 242, 275, 282, 283, 284, 286, 296, 302, 310, 312

choice 16, 23, 24, 59, 68, 73, 79, 97, 98, 99, 106, 180, 184, 206, 282, 306, 308
clean 68, 118, 130, 148, 216, 310
    cleaning 9, 118, 269
    cleanliness 118, 119, 120, 148, 183, 216
collective 162, 200, 213
common sense11, 19, 24, 32, 48, 52, 82, 84, 89, 108, 144, 145, 150, 179, 249, 252, 283, 303, 316, 318, 319
community..142, 143, 144, 204, 217, 249, 282, 291, 304, 308
    communal..22, 23, 52, 108, 168, 248, 249, 284, 312
    communal life 108, 168, 248, 249, 284
comparison 110, 160, 172
compensation.....6, 21, 23, 24, 28, 55, 68, 81, 90, 96, 143, 144, 145, 146, 161, 165, 175, 187, 295, 312
    compensatory 2, 23, 143, 144, 165, 180
competition.. 10, 33, 38, 65, 67, 75, 82
completion..319
complex 17, 36, 40, 44, 55, 94, 114, 154, 256, 258
compulsion 8, 10, 25, 26, 68, 81, 103, 117, 118, 119, 127, 132, 135, 138, 146, 166, 168, 177, 216, 232, 235, 245, 247, 248, 249, 251, 255, 282, 303, 306, 311, 319, 320
    compulsive 117, 148, 167, 198, 247, 279, 305
concentrate 43, 80, 240
    concentration... 8, 24, 37, 60
concept 182, 306
    conception 2, 11, 13, 21, 22, 27, 59, 99, 108, 114, 143, 173, 198, 207, 272, 283
conflict... 34, 62, 120, 245
conscience 26, 168, 169, 182, 254, 272, 310, 312
conscious 20, 23, 43, 50, 79, 91, 93, 104, 106, 108, 136, 144, 162, 184, 194, 208, 216, 306, 310
    consciousness..3, 4, 14, 34, 37, 44, 56, 96, 108
constitution 158, 236
contact13, 14, 21, 25, 32, 52, 96, 101, 106, 107, 145, 152, 180, 190, 249, 259, 260, 264, 266, 271, 285, 292, 307, 309, 310
contempt..175
contribution 11
cooperate 117, 118, 120, 121, 124
    cooperation..2, 13, 21, 73, 114, 118, 120, 123, 124, 126, 130, 149
cosmos...24
courage 4, 7, 12, 14, 16, 18, 21, 22, 23, 33, 37, 43, 44, 46, 48, 52, 66, 67, 68, 79, 80, 87, 88, 90, 99, 100, 107, 114, 142, 144, 145, 161, 179, 209, 218, 223, 248, 257, 262, 276, 292, 298, 313, 319
    courageous 22, 39, 44, 84, 89, 100, 109, 145, 149, 320
coward.. 21, 52, 84, 302
    cowardice...18, 38, 45, 70, 84, 89, 94, 147, 161, 173, 185
creative 32, 123, 235, 308
    creative power 32, 235, 308
crime... 54, 67, 84, 85, 219

criminal 9, 76, 85, 226, 249, 267

critical 9, 11, 18, 35, 37, 59, 64, 68, 99, 115, 139, 152, 198, 227, 246

cruel 127, 164, 184, 185, 302

cruelty 46, 127, 147, 184, 185

cry 25, 101, 127, 157, 192, 195, 207, 208, 256, 257, 275, 316

crying 16, 25, 26, 40, 53, 58, 106, 190, 198, 205, 258, 264, 268, 270, 305, 312

culture 16, 21, 23, 42, 96, 172, 188, 216, 229, 245

cure 6, 27, 36, 42, 45, 48, 58, 104, 107, 149, 199, 279, 303

curse 127, 249

cursing 120, 247

cyclothymia 18

D

daydream 94

deaf

deafness 23

death 22, 36, 55, 65, 76, 92, 93, 96, 97, 110, 117, 118, 119, 131, 139, 148, 177, 183, 239, 272, 285, 306, 308, 312, 317, 318

defeat ... 8, 9, 11, 12, 28, 29, 30, 35, 46, 49, 50, 52, 64, 67, 68, 85, 94, 98, 105, 147, 148, 149, 168, 172, 223, 231, 253, 264, 282, 291, 292, 296, 307, 308

defense 48, 64, 69, 103

deficiency 38, 77, 80, 114, 165, 173

delinquency 146

delinquent 78, 99, 168

delusion 255, 259, 264, 270, 271, 273, 285

delusions 149

Demosthenes 23

dependence 14, 21, 24, 172

dependency 172

depreciation 73

depression 10, 15, 16, 17, 18, 25, 42, 53, 55, 56, 58, 106, 128, 194, 245, 246, 313

depressed 16, 53, 56, 60, 64, 106, 245, 246, 249, 258, 262, 279, 292, 307, 312

deprivation 244

desire to dominate 134

despair 105, 305

destruction 15, 67, 166

dethronement 64, 67, 89

detour 100, 110, 155, 259, 260, 304

detours 147, 307

development 4, 5, 6, 9, 13, 14, 15, 28, 37, 38, 43, 49, 65, 69, 70, 71, 73, 74, 75, 76, 84, 85, 97, 98, 99, 101, 102, 105, 114, 142, 143, 144, 145, 147, 151, 162, 186, 200, 206, 207, 215, 221, 236, 237, 241, 247, 266

dexterity 23, 42, 235

diagnosis 6, 19, 22, 40, 48, 91, 114, 115, 120, 121

difficulty 10, 29, 30, 32, 42, 43, 46, 47, 60, 62, 64, 69, 75, 92, 98, 104, 110, 114, 117, 129, 130, 171, 205, 221, 231, 248, 301, 302

difficulties 3, 4, 7, 9, 13, 22, 26, 27, 32, 36, 38, 42, 43, 44, 45, 58, 67, 72, 77, 79, 81, 84, 92, 106, 114, 121, 125, 129, 150, 160, 161, 165, 171, 180, 183, 187, 188, 195, 197, 200, 202, 205, 209, 226, 229, 244, 270, 276, 282, 283, 305, 306, 307, 308, 309

discontent 24, 93, 117

discouraged 11, 30, 67, 75, 161, 174, 248, 257

discouragement 66, 98, 146, 208, 236

disease 56, 107, 146, 162, 197, 198, 255, 260, 261, 263, 269, 271, 288, 314

disorderly

disorderliness 24
displace
   displacement..38
disposition 35, 37, 47, 50, 73, 107, 248
distance.........4, 8, 13, 24, 30, 72, 80, 87, 92, 94, 100, 169, 222, 224, 249, 257, 262, 263, 282, 287
division of labor..98
dog..166, 167, 169, 174, 190, 239, 317, 318
   dogs...174
dominance 11, 38, 48, 87, 90
   dominant 21, 47, 59, 97, 134, 174
Don Juan...85, 240
doubt...24, 73, 229, 233, 271, 276, 304, 305, 315
   doubtful 93, 99
dream............5, 11, 40, 46, 58, 70, 72, 75, 88, 91, 93, 105, 107, 108, 109, 139, 312, 313, 314, 318
   dreams 5, 11, 20, 46, 70, 75, 107, 108, 110, 137, 149, 226, 313, 318
dreams 5, 11, 20, 46, 70, 75, 107, 108, 110, 137, 149, 226, 313, 318
drive.. 50, 145, 207
   drives.. 89, 146, 147, 311
drug
   drugs...146
Drug... 35, 36, 297, 304

E

early memories
   earliest memory... 28, 50, 59, 80, 89
   earliest recollections...82, 123
   early recollections 79, 83
eating... 37, 64, 89, 91, 131, 170, 174, 183, 187, 189, 258, 268, 309
economy
   economic 70
education 3, 4, 14, 21, 29, 45, 74, 76, 77, 142
   educators 142
ego..5
   egotism.. 64, 147, 204, 267, 283
eldest child...63, 64, 65, 66
emotion..25, 38, 39, 70, 77, 107, 108, 121, 165, 185, 197
   emotional.......................................24, 38, 77, 81, 105, 111, 121, 130, 166, 314, 316
empathy 73
encourage 313
   encouragement 27, 36, 43, 46, 149
enemy 49, 67, 122, 311
   enemies 170, 249, 311
energy..145, 213, 247, 248
enuresis..24
environment.....13, 14, 18, 21, 22, 23, 24, 32, 34, 37, 38, 43, 45, 50, 51, 63, 64, 72, 74, 76, 77, 79, 106, 121, 136, 143, 147, 148, 164, 170, 171, 176, 180, 202, 206, 207, 236, 246, 249, 262, 279, 283, 303, 308, 313
envy..59, 60, 64, 67, 211
epileptic 34
epoch 218
equal 4, 16, 26, 32, 44, 72, 102, 103, 224
   equality.. 67, 69, 73, 224, 229, 279
error 46, 50, 56, 168, 198
Esau 69, 128

escape 3, 8, 10, 11, 12, 13, 14, 24, 26, 35, 36, 39, 44, 47, 48, 50, 51, 58, 67, 72, 85, 87, 92, 94, 98, 99, 101, 103, 147, 148, 149, 169, 197, 242, 252, 262, 297, 301, 308, 318

Eve..57, 163, 210

evil...84, 213, 309, 310

evolution..316

examination 19, 26, 48, 50, 52, 82, 88, 109, 115, 124, 201, 222, 277, 278

   examinations 26, 71, 80, 124

exclusion...26, 33, 36, 41, 47, 96, 139, 186, 216, 240, 263

excuse..4, 30, 36, 103, 110, 138, 146, 148, 169, 171, 209, 225, 233, 248, 254, 257, 260, 284, 289, 299, 312

   excuses 148, 248, 284, 312

exhibitionism

   exhibitionist..94, 232, 239

expectation 33

   expecting 51, 58, 299

experience....7, 10, 14, 20, 21, 23, 24, 25, 27, 29, 31, 48, 49, 57, 61, 63, 65, 67, 74, 75, 81, 83, 85, 88, 93, 94, 97, 104, 115, 117, 118, 119, 121, 124, 144, 147, 151, 171, 180, 187, 200, 205, 207, 208, 213, 228, 232, 266, 267, 272, 287, 291, 299, 300, 306, 319

F

failure 14, 35, 48, 49, 57, 59, 65, 104, 171, 222, 223, 245, 305

   failures...107, 132

fainting 34

fairy tale..70, 178, 179, 184, 186, 209, 211

family ..3, 4, 8, 10, 16, 24, 25, 26, 29, 34, 37, 38, 52, 53, 55, 57, 58, 60, 63, 66, 69, 70, 71, 72, 73, 76, 77, 81, 97, 98, 99, 102, 104, 115, 117, 119, 124, 125, 128, 129, 131, 134, 139, 145, 148, 149, 155, 178, 180, 186, 193, 202, 204, 207, 208, 215, 217, 224, 245, 247, 257, 258, 260, 261, 263, 265, 268, 279, 282, 293, 301, 307, 308, 309, 314

family constellation 37

fantasy 44, 46, 58, 59, 65, 74, 79, 86, 87, 89, 93, 94, 99, 156, 226, 241

fate..32, 55, 57, 70, 119, 171, 177, 203, 210, 254, 281, 283, 305

father .3, 4, 16, 25, 27, 28, 29, 30, 34, 35, 36, 38, 50, 53, 55, 60, 61, 64, 65, 66, 73, 74, 75, 76, 77, 81, 89, 93, 94, 98, 99, 104, 105, 125, 126, 127, 128, 129, 131, 132, 133, 135, 136, 144, 151, 152, 153, 155, 156, 157, 158, 162, 163, 164, 166, 167, 169, 170, 171, 182, 186, 190, 193, 196, 198, 199, 200, 201, 202, 204, 208, 211, 214, 217, 222, 223, 225, 226, 230, 231, 235, 240, 243, 246, 247, 250, 253, 257, 260, 270, 274, 275, 277, 278, 282, 286, 289, 290, 291, 300, 313, 317

fatigue...8, 105

favoritism 38

fear.......3, 5, 8, 9, 10, 12, 24, 26, 39, 40, 48, 49, 52, 62, 64, 71, 81, 82, 84, 87, 89, 93, 96, 97, 106, 109, 117, 118, 119, 122, 123, 131, 133, 147, 148, 163, 164, 170, 174, 177, 185, 191, 196, 200, 218, 219, 236, 237, 250, 259, 260, 261, 262, 263, 267, 268, 269, 274, 276, 277, 284, 285, 288, 289, 296, 301, 304, 305, 306, 309, 311, 316, 318, 319

feeling 2, 3, 4, 7, 8, 13, 14, 15, 17, 20, 21, 22, 24, 25, 26, 28, 29, 32, 33, 36, 37, 40, 43, 44, 48, 49, 52, 54, 55, 56, 59, 68, 70, 71, 74, 75, 78, 79, 80, 83, 84, 85, 86, 87, 88, 89, 91, 94, 98, 99, 100, 102, 103, 104, 106, 107, 109, 114, 120, 121, 127, 128, 142, 144, 145, 146, 147, 160, 161, 168, 169, 171, 172, 173, 174, 176, 190, 193, 194, 202, 204, 208, 215, 216, 219, 221, 226, 234, 236, 239, 244, 246, 249, 253, 259, 263, 266, 269, 273, 283, 292, 297, 303, 306, 308, 314, 316, 319

   feeling of inferiority 2, 3, 7, 8, 22, 25, 28, 74, 86, 88, 99, 144, 145, 146, 147, 160, 161, 169, 172, 173, 174, 234, 236, 308, 317

   feeling of superiority 25, 55, 86, 144, 190, 194, 269, 297, 308, 314

   feeling of worth 52

fellow man...81

female...28, 44, 75, 76, 94, 104, 105, 130, 136, 147, 245

   feminine 27, 28, 29, 30, 33, 74, 76, 147, 172, 173, 186, 229, 230, 245

fetish 258
fiction 32, 110, 306, 313
    fictitious 8, 62, 80, 85, 89, 145, 148
    fictitious goal 148
    fictitious superiority 145
    fictive goal 11, 144, 146, 148, 168, 213, 236, 306
firstborn 63
forget 92, 130, 179, 220, 233, 290
form 5, 8, 9, 10, 18, 22, 28, 31, 32, 40, 41, 65, 71, 78, 79, 80, 85, 86, 93, 94, 97, 99, 103, 109, 114,
    120, 127, 129, 132, 142, 143, 146, 147, 150, 154, 165, 168, 176, 177, 182, 187, 204, 206, 214,
    215, 218, 219, 226, 229, 235, 267, 304, 313
freedom 21, 22, 24, 45, 115, 156, 172, 173, 245, 289
Freud 107, 162, 231, 251, 290, 306
Freytag, Gustav 43
friendship 3, 7, 13, 14, 50, 65, 124, 207, 277, 284, 288, 291
frigidity 33, 104, 109, 120, 284
future . 5, 38, 41, 51, 59, 82, 96, 97, 98, 99, 107, 173, 180, 188, 195, 197, 198, 200, 213, 255, 287,
    303, 313, 314, 316

G

game 17, 66, 139, 287
    games 28, 73, 74, 155, 173, 214, 296
genius 23, 76, 213
glance 6, 49, 194, 252, 277
glands 27, 49, 74, 81, 236, 316
goal 2, 4, 6, 7, 8, 9, 10, 11, 12, 15, 20, 21, 23, 24, 25, 27, 28, 31, 32, 33, 36, 37, 39, 41, 46, 48, 52,
    55, 59, 61, 63, 64, 65, 68, 73, 74, 75, 76, 79, 84, 85, 86, 90, 92, 93, 94, 98, 100, 102, 103, 108,
    114, 123, 126, 127, 128, 143, 144, 145, 146, 147, 148, 149, 169, 171, 173, 175, 178, 185, 204,
    208, 213, 216, 228, 236, 248, 250, 266, 268, 279, 282, 291, 294, 303, 306, 309, 310, 313, 318
God 26, 46, 105, 166, 177, 196, 220, 244, 247, 249, 250, 256, 258, 266, 272
Goethe 43
greed 147
grief 148, 315
Groos, Karl 173
group 52, 142, 205, 294
guessing 115
guidance 152, 179
guilt 16, 17, 25, 55, 109, 127, 128, 166, 168, 202, 245, 249, 263
    guilt complex 16, 55, 263

H

habit 35, 36, 50, 60, 62, 88, 102, 186, 219, 238, 243, 247, 279
hallucination 57, 90, 101
    hallucinations 101
handshake 100
handwriting 18, 43, 150, 176
happy 6, 7, 10, 20, 53, 56, 78, 91, 102, 105, 117, 128, 138, 155, 160, 174, 222, 237, 248, 251, 277,
    283, 290, 311
    happiness 12, 20, 71, 189, 194, 237, 284, 296
hate 147, 148, 166, 263, 278
    hated child 24
hate 118, 119, 176, 263

headache 64, 188, 209

    headaches 8, 38, 39, 101, 105, 109, 110

heart 5, 8, 40, 60, 88, 91, 99, 100, 103, 107, 115, 190, 231, 314, 316

Herder, Johann Gottfried 44

heredity 3, 69, 77, 124

hero 84, 219

hesitiation

    hesitating attitude 7, 65, 114, 200, 222, 247, 262, 284

homosexuality 29, 31, 62, 73, 74, 75, 76, 85, 207, 242

    homosexual 61, 74, 75, 93, 206

hostility 23, 136, 203

    hostile 37, 65, 73, 89, 93, 98, 121, 122, 125, 139, 149, 180, 317

human .. 9, 14, 15, 21, 23, 27, 31, 32, 40, 41, 88, 114, 142, 144, 145, 147, 148, 150, 151, 158, 160, 162, 173, 185, 197, 198, 202, 203, 204, 208, 210, 213, 222, 225, 228, 235, 242, 247, 267, 291, 292, 303, 304, 310, 314, 317, 319

human nature 88, 202, 210, 213, 242

humiliation 62, 86, 94, 104, 105, 116

hunger 191, 261

hurting 201

hypnosis 107

hypnotic 107

hypothesis 117, 228

hysteria 146

I

Ibsen, Henrik 209

idea .. 7, 9, 10, 22, 30, 35, 40, 46, 57, 69, 77, 83, 84, 86, 92, 94, 96, 97, 98, 99, 104, 105, 106, 111, 114, 118, 119, 123, 126, 127, 130, 131, 135, 139, 158, 172, 184, 191, 197, 228, 238, 244, 252, 253, 254, 257, 264, 265, 268, 272, 274, 275, 276, 278, 281, 285, 287, 292, 297, 298, 300, 303, 305, 306, 308, 319

ideal 33, 85, 99, 114, 118, 133, 172, 224, 237, 314

    ideal final form 99, 114

identification 69, 208, 218

illness ... 9, 12, 16, 18, 22, 39, 47, 53, 55, 56, 68, 82, 96, 97, 99, 100, 106, 131, 139, 148, 160, 168, 170, 171, 197, 198, 248, 261, 312

image 30, 86, 154, 181, 271, 275, 276

    images 5, 86, 148, 154, 226, 241

imagination 43, 94, 114, 119, 218, 256, 319

    imaginary 9, 10, 25, 28, 86, 93, 263, 306

imitation 8, 69, 74, 156, 173, 176

immortality 97, 314

impatience 38, 60

imperfection 23, 129

    imperfect 11, 38, 42, 43, 118, 124

impotence 22, 23, 33, 47, 48, 56, 57, 58, 90, 103, 138, 284

inborn 21, 62, 74, 193, 207, 223, 236

incest 89, 204

incomplete 10, 319

indecision 3, 33, 286

independence 22, 29, 45

    independent 24, 53, 93, 98, 151, 210

Individual Psychology .. 3, 4, 11, 17, 20, 21, 22, 23, 24, 27, 32, 34, 38, 41, 43, 47, 48, 79, 84, 104, 107, 113, 114, 115, 116, 121, 142, 143, 146, 150, 168, 200, 202, 205, 224, 228, 248, 276

infantile .... 34, 40, 107, 147 inferiority.....2, 3, 4, 6, 7, 23, 27, 37, 42, 44, 47, 49, 52, 57, 59, 60, 65, 75, 86, 114, 136, 143, 144, 145, 149, 158, 160, 161, 165, 168, 173, 175, 188, 220, 229, 306, 312

    inferiority complex 114

    inferiority feeling 3, 145, 149, 158, 160, 161, 168, 220, 306

insane 214, 264, 276, 304

insatiable 8

insecurity 7, 24, 38, 71, 144, 193, 204

insight 20, 31, 108, 150, 252, 261, 314, 319

insomnia 170

instinct 21, 69, 96, 173, 176, 180

intelligence 52, 75, 213, 303, 310

    intelligent 3, 15, 49, 63, 78, 92, 104, 157, 166, 303, 310

intention 33, 40, 103, 123, 143, 150, 168, 248, 288, 294, 306, 308

    intentions 50, 249, 272

interest . 15, 22, 25, 26, 32, 33, 35, 36, 37, 39, 42, 47, 49, 52, 55, 60, 66, 73, 75, 80, 81, 84, 92, 94, 96, 97, 98, 99, 108, 113, 119, 127, 133, 142, 143, 152, 154, 179, 181, 190, 193, 194, 205, 208, 210, 241, 244, 250, 254, 282, 283, 284, 292, 293, 314

intolerance 95

intuition 23, 320

irritability 37

    irritable 18, 38, 60

isolation 24, 35, 49, 51, 80, 84

J

Jacob 69, 128

jealousy 33, 34, 64, 67, 90, 91, 92, 134, 136, 157, 158, 193, 194, 204, 205, 231

    jealous 67, 85, 89, 91, 109, 137, 157, 193, 194, 199, 202, 225, 231, 274

joke 7, 125, 132, 229, 297

    jokes 225, 227

joy 235, 240, 267

Jung, Carl Gustav 162

K

Kant. Emanuel 44

L

language 45, 75, 103, 147, 150, 197, 220, 269, 291, 310

laughter 188, 220, 223, 303, 304

law 15, 33, 37, 41, 66, 85, 119, 121, 138, 139, 143, 179, 232, 269

    laws 69, 77, 168, 195

laziness 16, 67, 93, 221

    lazy 221

leadership 69

    leader 152

learning 43, 52, 59, 92, 201

left-handedness 42

libido 40, 262, 291

Lichtenberg, George 107

life problems 103, 215, 249, 320

life style (see also style of life) 113, 140, 170, 218, 318
life tasks 65
liveliness 57
logic 5, 10, 11, 15, 72, 82, 108, 146, 244, 245, 249, 261, 318
love 3, 7, 8, 10, 13, 14, 15, 22, 25, 28, 29, 30, 31, 32, 33, 34, 35, 38, 40, 41, 44, 49, 50, 55, 56, 57,
      58, 62, 63, 65, 68, 71, 80, 85, 86, 87, 88, 89, 94, 96, 102, 104, 106, 109, 118, 119, 133, 134,
      142, 145, 148, 149, 154, 157, 171, 175, 197, 203, 204, 207, 208, 209, 211, 215, 217, 224, 225,
      230, 231, 233, 234, 237, 241, 242, 243, 244, 245, 250, 251, 253, 255, 259, 262, 263, 266, 267,
      273, 276, 282, 283, 284, 286, 287, 288, 289, 290, 291, 294, 295, 296, 297, 300, 307, 308, 309,
      311, 314, 318
loyalty 31
lying 58, 67, 80, 109, 119, 208, 219, 225, 238, 274, 285, 286, 293

M

male 28, 44, 57, 136
manic-depressive 18, 84
mania 9, 10, 18, 19, 166, 194, 235
mankind 51, 69, 84, 96, 162, 214, 284
marriage 5, 7, 8, 10, 12, 15, 22, 30, 31, 32, 33, 34, 35, 36, 38, 39, 41, 44, 48, 49, 53, 56, 57, 58,
      61, 68, 74, 80, 85, 86, 88, 89, 91, 94, 98, 102, 103, 104, 105, 106, 109, 116, 123, 124, 133,
      135, 142, 195, 199, 203, 230, 234, 241, 255, 259, 261, 267, 282, 283, 290, 291, 294, 315
marry 5, 8, 29, 39, 48, 57, 58, 68, 71, 88, 89, 105, 106, 135, 148, 154, 157, 213, 225, 231, 233,
      244, 283, 290, 291
masculine protest 28, 30, 45, 89, 132, 147, 172, 173, 184, 245
masculinity 27, 173
masculine 27, 28, 30, 33, 44, 45, 77, 89, 93, 132, 147, 172, 173, 184, 245
masochism 86, 94
mastery 36, 308
masturbation 3, 26, 49, 58, 62, 71, 80, 86, 87, 206
mathematics 92
maturity 21, 151
May, Karl 65
melancholy 55, 56, 235, 245
memory 6, 56, 57, 59, 61, 79, 83, 92, 93, 105, 108, 144, 158, 183, 187, 197, 199, 228
menstruation 29, 312
mental disorder 18, 27, 228
metaphor 108
migraine 38, 64
mind ...7, 14, 27, 28, 32, 52, 58, 72, 74, 91, 104, 114, 116, 117, 119, 126, 143, 144, 150, 154, 172,
      179, 205, 218, 240, 245, 267, 269, 271, 272, 292, 300, 304, 314, 317
misbehavior 81
misinterpretation 306
mistrust 80, 311
mood 8, 11, 21, 70, 105, 165, 169, 176, 178, 210, 219, 246, 248, 292, 294, 313, 314, 318
morphine 16, 35, 36, 48, 53
mother .3, 6, 7, 10, 13, 14, 15, 20, 21, 28, 34, 35, 36, 38, 46, 50, 51, 53, 58, 59, 60, 61, 64, 65, 71,
      72, 73, 74, 75, 77, 78, 79, 80, 82, 83, 87, 88, 89, 92, 93, 94, 97, 101, 109, 121, 125, 126, 128,
      132, 136, 138, 139, 151, 152, 153, 154, 155, 156, 157, 163, 166, 170, 174, 176, 185, 188, 193,
      196, 198, 199, 201, 202, 203, 209, 210, 211, 213, 214, 217, 231, 237, 245, 257, 266, 269, 274,
      275, 284, 289, 292, 293, 298, 299, 309, 315, 316, 317
motives 6, 36, 99
movement 43, 60, 81, 99, 110, 142, 165
murder 17, 55, 244
murderer 84, 244, 245, 250

muscles..37, 93, 226
music 60, 164, 217, 218, 222, 223, 238, 287, 289, 298
musical...214
musician...223
myths..86

N

narcissism...267
nation..45
national..52
need ..6, 7, 17, 18, 45, 47, 57, 74, 92, 93, 94, 97, 121, 153, 160, 170, 185, 219, 245, 260, 272, 278
neglect 9, 15, 106, 109, 119, 163, 216, 221
    neglected child 118
neuralgia...38, 39
neurasthenia..146
neurosis..2, 4, 5, 8, 9, 10, 13, 14, 26, 38, 43, 46, 52, 60, 67, 68, 71, 88, 91, 92, 102, 103, 108, 117,
    118, 119, 124, 132, 138, 142, 147, 149, 166, 168, 169, 172, 177, 194, 197, 200, 216, 218, 221,
    245, 247, 248, 249, 250, 261, 263, 265, 266, 272, 273, 282, 283, 285, 286, 301, 303, 310, 312,
    319
    neuroses......................................5, 18, 27, 41, 52, 118, 146, 168, 170, 198, 247, 248, 283, 306
    neurotic 8, 9, 10, 12, 13, 14, 15, 16, 17, 20, 21, 23, 25, 28, 33, 36, 38, 39, 41, 48, 51, 53, 57,
        59, 65, 72, 78, 86, 88, 89, 92, 101, 103, 107, 108, 113, 118, 120, 124, 127, 129, 131, 132,
        136, 137, 138, 145, 146, 147, 148, 149, 161, 166, 168, 169, 171, 173, 179, 193, 197, 200,
        204, 208, 213, 215, 218, 219, 222, 234, 244, 245, 247, 248, 249, 250, 255, 261, 263, 266,
        267, 269, 280, 283, 284, 286, 303, 304, 306, 310, 311, 313
Nietzsche, Friedrich...17
normal4, 9, 13, 14, 23, 26, 27, 28, 29, 32, 33, 37, 39, 41, 43, 44, 62, 66, 75, 89, 94, 100, 101, 103,
    118, 123, 132, 144, 145, 148, 160, 197, 198, 206, 215, 228, 232, 233, 236, 242, 247, 319

O

obedience..65, 66, 68, 90, 107, 147, 163
objective 2, 15, 16, 33, 69, 71, 82, 94, 184, 204, 236, 309, 313
obstacle...62, 251, 283
obstinacy...173
occupation .3, 5, 10, 13, 14, 15, 26, 34, 35, 49, 50, 57, 65, 71, 80, 97, 98, 124, 142, 155, 156, 180,
    217, 251, 259, 284, 291, 301, 308
Oedipus complex...290
only child...63, 72, 73, 75, 91, 125, 152, 201
opinion.......................... 12, 33, 38, 82, 93, 129, 130, 182, 218, 224, 238, 240, 258, 286, 292, 309
opponent..53
optimistic 22, 32, 33, 46, 52, 292
organ...8, 103, 143, 145, 187, 188, 316
    organ dialect..103
    organ inferiority 187, 188, 316
    organ jargon...103
orientation...41
overcoming...32, 68, 85, 121, 128, 143, 248, 308
oversensitivity
    overcompensation 143

P

pain 29, 47, 66, 71, 72, 84, 145, 184, 220, 257, 294, 318
painter 23
palpitation
    palpitations 8, 38, 40, 60, 62, 115
pampering 149, 152, 166, 199, 213, 244, 294
    pampered 28, 34, 35, 49, 51, 53, 61, 62, 72, 75, 79, 82, 88, 92, 93, 106, 115, 118, 128, 152,
        158, 161, 165, 186, 195, 198, 200, 236, 244, 275, 282, 283, 291, 310, 314, 318
pantomime 121
paralysis 18, 56, 84
paranoia 10, 84, 89, 138, 228, 251
    paranoid 87, 138
parent 60, 65, 73, 278
    parents 4, 7, 32, 38, 46, 49, 50, 51, 55, 56, 61, 64, 68, 69, 70, 71, 72, 73, 75, 76, 77, 78, 82, 86,
        115, 125, 129, 132, 135, 139, 153, 163, 164, 166, 168, 169, 178, 179, 180, 182, 184, 187,
        188, 189, 195, 197, 199, 203, 204, 210, 217, 219, 224, 229, 230, 231, 238, 239, 240, 244,
        250, 253, 257, 258, 262, 264, 269, 271, 273, 277, 281, 283, 285, 287, 289, 290, 292, 293,
        300, 304, 311, 312, 314, 315
passivity 104
    passive 104, 147, 173
patient 2, 3, 4, 6, 7, 8, 9, 10, 11, 12, 13, 14, 16, 17, 18, 19, 26, 27, 28, 29, 33, 34, 35, 36, 38, 39,
        40, 46, 47, 48, 50, 51, 53, 55, 56, 59, 60, 61, 62, 64, 65, 71, 72, 74, 75, 76, 79, 80, 83, 84, 86,
        88, 89, 90, 91, 93, 94, 102, 103, 104, 105, 106, 107, 108, 110, 114, 115, 116, 120, 125, 133,
        146, 147, 148, 149, 150, 166, 170, 171, 216, 247, 248, 249, 261, 265, 266, 270, 282, 283, 301,
        306, 309, 310, 316, 319
pattern 12, 18, 24, 26, 34, 69, 70, 76, 77, 80, 146, 148, 164, 165, 166, 168, 180, 190, 231, 232,
        267, 279
peace 178, 194, 203, 217
perception 2, 9, 51, 66, 80, 144, 152, 165, 202
perfection 144
personal superiority 85, 90, 94
personality 15, 31, 36, 151, 180, 182, 196, 216, 218, 283, 306, 313
perspective 14, 24, 115, 283
perverse 207
perversion 34, 58, 85
philosophy 82, 132
phobia 8, 119, 120, 260, 262, 268, 273, 279, 280, 281, 307, 308, 309, 310
    phobias 266, 306
physician 2, 14, 18, 26, 27, 48, 51, 53, 70, 110, 113, 149, 153, 270, 271, 315
pity 25, 109, 158, 169, 190, 194, 239, 290
play ..7, 13, 17, 28, 45, 64, 66, 69, 73, 75, 88, 89, 97, 100, 154, 155, 156, 173, 184, 189, 191, 192,
        195, 205, 209, 214, 215, 216, 217, 219, 222, 223, 226, 236, 237, 238, 288, 296, 297, 298, 318
pleasure 17, 18, 66, 176, 188, 189, 190, 242, 278, 296, 309, 311
poetry 70
polarity 132
possession 5, 155, 231
poverty 16, 123, 175, 209, 265
power 15, 18, 23, 27, 31, 35, 36, 59, 66, 69, 85, 86, 87, 90, 93, 96, 98, 101, 106, 128, 134, 142,
        143, 145, 157, 161, 162, 163, 173, 184, 193, 202, 204, 213, 215, 232, 233, 235, 237, 243, 245,
        247, 248, 252, 253, 255, 270, 282, 283, 291, 305, 308, 309, 310, 311, 314, 320
practical 10, 11, 20, 22, 60, 81, 150, 223, 309
praise 69, 123, 185
pregnancy 44, 88, 105, 135, 252
pregnant 40, 68, 135, 139

preparation.....11, 13, 28, 29, 32, 45, 52, 76, 80, 84, 92, 93, 97, 115, 156, 185, 194, 200, 213, 214, 229, 239, 241, 247

prestige 13, 16, 22, 148, 157, 193

pride.. 15, 133, 194, 211, 278, 305

primitive 147

private intelligence 303, 316

private logic.. 19, 52, 147, 148, 234, 248, 249, 263, 304

probability 125

problem....2, 4, 7, 8, 9, 14, 15, 18, 22, 30, 32, 36, 41, 47, 49, 50, 53, 55, 57, 58, 59, 65, 67, 72, 73, 77, 80, 87, 94, 103, 105, 108, 109, 110, 114, 115, 116, 120, 127, 130, 142, 169, 170, 179, 180, 195, 206, 215, 216, 217, 230, 233, 243, 248, 252, 254, 262, 273, 284, 286, 289, 291, 294, 304, 307, 308, 313, 314, 318

    problem child 4, 9, 67, 77, 127, 304

profession 71, 98, 99, 142, 156, 175, 179, 180, 276, 277, 284

proof......................5, 12, 62, 86, 107, 109, 110, 121, 130, 134, 167, 257, 261, 279, 286, 290, 304

prophesy 259

prostitute... 86, 175

prostitution 175

protection.. 4, 21, 101, 160, 243, 251

prototype... 21, 31, 35, 36, 37, 41, 45, 51, 64, 79, 93, 97, 98, 283

provocation 127

psyche... 14, 22, 23, 32, 41, 143, 266, 306

psychic...2, 14, 20, 21, 31, 35, 45, 47, 63, 69, 80, 85, 88, 96, 97, 98, 107, 143, 144, 146, 150, 171, 235, 273, 313, 314, 316

psychology 3, 11, 84, 86, 143, 150, 167, 211, 267, 313

    psychological20, 25, 31, 39, 70, 73, 74, 114, 130, 150, 165, 172, 200, 202, 234, 261, 267, 274, 283, 319, 320

psychosis 9, 15, 18, 119

    psychotic 15, 113, 146, 208, 311

psychotherapist... 48

punishment 28, 126, 137, 190, 208, 263, 266

purpose 8, 9, 11, 21, 33, 50, 70, 85, 96, 101, 108, 144, 148, 150, 153, 163, 166, 179, 185, 210, 248, 249, 250, 257, 267, 274, 282, 285, 289, 291, 297, 303, 306, 311, 313, 315

purposeful... 163

Q

quantitative 194

R

race 7, 67, 68, 69, 81, 96, 128, 129, 144

radius.. 142, 268, 307

rage.. 15, 34, 39, 86, 109, 132, 196, 199, 244, 255, 269, 283

rational.. 148

readiness 98, 200

reality.2, 10, 11, 13, 20, 28, 37, 52, 59, 69, 71, 84, 86, 87, 89, 90, 98, 99, 106, 107, 108, 122, 138, 144, 148, 149, 150, 161, 177, 179, 183, 202, 219, 232, 233, 240, 260, 306, 313

reason 4, 8, 31, 37, 42, 45, 48, 55, 57, 58, 61, 82, 84, 86, 89, 99, 100, 101, 109, 128, 132, 133, 138, 160, 171, 178, 198, 200, 201, 206, 207, 209, 220, 223, 224, 225, 241, 245, 248, 257, 260, 277, 278, 280, 290, 294, 298

recollection... 6, 51, 61, 79, 80, 92, 93, 94, 97

rejection... 42, 48, 94, 104, 154, 206, 230, 263

religion .... 51, 225, 250 religious...81, 97, 107, 176

remorse 50, 168, 169

repression 76, 165

    repressed..87, 94, 165, 262

resentment 34, 132, 138, 211, 245

resistance 16, 27, 48, 58, 61, 68, 94, 225

responsibility 3, 6, 31, 50, 53, 125, 146, 160, 168, 171, 193, 194, 210, 219, 236, 241, 245, 272, 283, 305

    responsible 3, 11, 14, 23, 27, 59, 122, 170, 177, 197, 266, 305, 310, 312

retreat...146, 161, 197, 248, 293, 294, 305

retreating...82

revenge 53, 61, 78, 104, 105, 107, 120, 166, 176, 223, 246, 264, 308

revolutionary 69

ridicule..125, 162, 290

rigid 148, 163, 228

role.8, 15, 17, 27, 28, 33, 44, 45, 46, 57, 59, 70, 74, 75, 77, 93, 104, 105, 134, 143, 149, 156, 167, 172, 173, 186, 195, 198, 210, 211, 218, 219, 229, 230, 231, 236, 255, 256, 261, 267, 275, 296

roughness...126

rule.....16, 17, 31, 37, 41, 48, 51, 67, 74, 88, 95, 117, 120, 123, 125, 126, 129, 130, 132, 133, 134, 136, 161, 171, 173, 190, 191, 222, 246, 271, 283, 291, 293, 314

    rules...31, 53, 72, 89, 122, 128, 147, 170, 194, 232, 249, 311

S

sadism...66, 85, 138, 166

    sadistic...66, 85, 87, 125, 137, 138, 226

safety 92, 127, 147, 168, 236, 298, 306

salvation 121, 284

Saul...70, 241

scheme...146, 147, 148, 152, 163, 173, 228, 263, 273

Schiller, Friedrich 43

schizophrenia...10, 13, 45, 84

school ..3, 6, 7, 13, 22, 24, 25, 27, 35, 42, 45, 50, 52, 65, 67, 68, 73, 75, 77, 80, 87, 88, 93, 98, 99, 109, 130, 142, 156, 158, 165, 168, 169, 185, 186, 202, 206, 209, 213, 215, 217, 218, 220, 221, 222, 225, 226, 227, 232, 233, 240, 259, 261, 266, 267, 272, 274, 276, 277, 278, 280, 284, 290, 291, 296, 300, 306

science 24, 26, 51, 96, 123

second child....................................3, 7, 25, 38, 56, 63, 65, 67, 68, 69, 70, 74, 122, 124, 128, 138

security 24, 65, 98, 108, 144, 161, 172, 246, 255, 259, 291, 311

self.....7, 9, 12, 15, 17, 22, 26, 34, 48, 51, 56, 59, 67, 69, 79, 89, 91, 92, 96, 97, 98, 104, 107, 108, 110, 111, 114, 135, 144, 145, 171, 185, 193, 245, 248, 251, 292, 317

    self-accusation...17, 56, 245

    self-confidence 7, 12, 48, 67, 89, 104, 114, 193, 292

    self-esteem 145, 171, 193, 317

    self-evaluation 59, 91

    self-preservation...96

    self-reproach..26

    self-training 79, 97, 98

semblance 147, 160, 193

senile 68

sensation...46, 136, 196, 197, 290, 317

sense organ 313

sensitive..103, 104, 121, 316

sensitiveness 48

sensory type..180

sex 27, 28, 31, 53, 68, 74, 75, 85, 87, 89, 94, 124, 136, 142, 147, 194, 202, 203, 206, 208, 227, 228, 229, 245, 261, 283, 296

sexual 3, 11, 14, 18, 22, 23, 27, 28, 29, 30, 31, 32, 33, 45, 48, 49, 56, 58, 62, 65, 66, 68, 73, 74, 75, 76, 81, 85, 86, 87, 89, 92, 94, 99, 103, 104, 106, 107, 120, 125, 135, 138, 148, 157, 162, 163, 165, 178, 185, 202, 206, 207, 214, 226, 227, 229, 230, 231, 232, 236, 237, 239, 240, 241, 262, 283, 290, 304, 312

sexuality 20, 27, 31, 61, 71, 75, 80, 94, 120, 157, 206, 216, 231, 283, 291

Shakespeare 156

shame.. 242, 271, 296, 316

shock 93, 94, 164, 206

shyness 44

sickness.. 88, 160, 161, 173

significance...........4, 21, 79, 131, 151, 171, 173, 202, 208, 215, 220, 234, 245, 250, 276, 306, 313

significant..2, 92, 100, 173, 186, 193, 217, 220, 319

sin 183, 190, 216

skin 11, 226, 259, 270

sleep...11, 16, 17, 62, 80, 88, 91, 100, 101, 105, 106, 107, 163, 170, 171, 181, 218, 220, 274, 275, 276, 294, 313, 315, 317

sleep...100, 106, 107, 170, 171, 273, 275, 313

sleepsleeplessness... 8, 39, 170, 171

smell 119, 186, 188, 191, 237, 238, 304

social 9, 13, 14, 15, 16, 21, 22, 25, 26, 27, 29, 30, 32, 33, 35, 36, 37, 40, 41, 42, 44, 45, 46, 48, 49, 50, 51, 52, 53, 59, 64, 67, 68, 75, 78, 79, 80, 81, 84, 85, 86, 88, 89, 90, 92, 98, 99, 100, 104, 105, 109, 114, 118, 119, 120, 122, 123, 124, 133, 142, 144, 145, 149, 168, 175, 180, 185, 190, 201, 202, 204, 213, 215, 216, 217, 245, 249, 282, 283, 291, 292, 314, 316, 319

social interest...25, 35, 40, 48, 80, 86, 88, 98, 99, 114, 119, 123

social usefulness 81

socially useful.. 44, 114, 123

society ...14, 15, 21, 31, 46, 49, 50, 52, 53, 58, 65, 71, 75, 82, 87, 96, 97, 102, 127, 142, 223, 225, 246, 247, 250

sorrow.. 56, 162

soul 10, 18, 20, 24, 85, 97, 150, 235, 314

spasms 38, 64

speech 45, 150, 222, 286

stage fright... 71, 222, 292

stammer 42

status.. 56, 66, 133

stealing 67, 215

stomach..3, 37, 38, 62, 64, 88, 100, 103

stress 68, 129, 271, 291

striving.....2, 9, 10, 11, 15, 20, 21, 25, 27, 29, 33, 35, 39, 44, 55, 57, 59, 63, 64, 68, 70, 74, 79, 80, 81, 82, 83, 85, 90, 96, 97, 98, 100, 114, 118, 128, 130, 143, 144, 145, 147, 157, 158, 163, 169, 174, 176, 177, 180, 193, 216, 222, 228, 232, 237, 246, 261, 272, 282, 283, 291, 310

striving to overcome... 114

stupid..75, 179, 183, 193, 257, 258, 276

stuttering.. 23, 42

style of life.....5, 9, 11, 12, 14, 18, 20, 21, 22, 25, 26, 27, 28, 31, 32, 33, 36, 47, 53, 57, 58, 63, 70, 72, 76, 79, 81, 83, 93, 96, 100, 103, 105, 107, 108, 117, 118, 121, 123, 125, 128, 134, 144, 147, 149, 176, 178, 187, 200, 219, 228, 231, 234, 235, 239, 242, 244, 250, 276, 279, 301, 312, 313, 316

submission 90, 94

success...5, 22, 26, 36, 44, 48, 50, 59, 61, 64, 68, 82, 85, 88, 93, 97, 102, 108, 125, 149, 171, 218, 222, 282, 291

sucking 184

suffering 6, 12, 20, 47, 68, 88, 91, 100, 110, 118, 119, 142, 149, 158, 262, 265, 266, 311

suggestion.. 17, 40, 107, 182, 217, 288 suicide .7, 9, 18, 34, 35, 36, 53, 54, 92, 93, 120, 139, 162, 199, 203, 209, 246, 253, 258, 261, 263, 284

    suicides...22, 304

superiority....2, 3, 4, 6, 7, 8, 9, 10, 11, 12, 15, 16, 20, 22, 24, 25, 26, 27, 28, 31, 32, 33, 34, 35, 36, 37, 39, 41, 44, 45, 46, 50, 55, 56, 57, 59, 68, 73, 74, 75, 76, 79, 84, 85, 86, 89, 93, 98, 102, 108, 114, 121, 126, 127, 144, 145, 146, 147, 148, 157, 158, 160, 163, 169, 170, 173, 175, 176, 184, 190, 192, 204, 216, 218, 219, 229, 230, 231, 232, 233, 237, 244, 246, 247, 248, 268, 282, 283, 284, 286, 306, 309, 310, 318

    superior ..3, 5, 10, 18, 33, 39, 49, 56, 60, 86, 114, 117, 127, 138, 148, 149, 169, 170, 172, 173, 174, 177, 193, 201, 202, 206, 207, 218, 220, 226, 229, 241, 246, 253, 310

    superiority complex..57

    superiority striving 204

superstition 4, 77, 84, 252, 283, 284, 304, 306

suspicion...7, 33, 80, 268

syle ..2, 5, 6, 9, 11, 12, 14, 18, 20, 21, 22, 25, 26, 27, 28, 31, 32, 33, 36, 47, 48, 49, 53, 57, 58, 59, 63, 64, 70, 72, 76, 79, 81, 83, 93, 96, 100, 103, 105, 107, 108, 117, 118, 121, 123, 125, 128, 134, 144, 147, 149, 176, 178, 187, 200, 219, 223, 228, 231, 234, 235, 239, 242, 244, 250, 276, 279, 301, 312, 313, 316

symbol 99, 105, 237, 240

    symbols 108, 150

sympathy 87, 117, 136, 164

    sympathetic 17, 20, 61, 316

symptom ..28, 30, 40, 64, 71, 82, 114, 127, 129, 131, 133, 138, 147, 161, 163, 171, 177, 216, 222, 233, 248, 262, 279

symptoms 5, 8, 9, 12, 19, 24, 27, 33, 36, 38, 42, 45, 60, 64, 65, 71, 72, 80, 82, 85, 87, 91, 104, 107, 115, 124, 127, 131, 137, 138, 139, 147, 160, 168, 170, 171, 178, 191, 200, 208, 216, 247, 248, 251, 261, 279, 303, 311

T

teacher 25, 77, 78, 98, 154, 156, 217, 218, 221, 225, 226, 234, 236, 276, 277, 278

    teachers 4, 42, 50, 77, 86

teeth 71, 86, 137, 199, 236, 256, 257, 258, 270, 274

temper...34, 38, 39, 162

    temper tantrums..162

temperament 235, 236

tenderness 154, 160, 171, 172

tension ...6, 8, 9, 18, 24, 37, 38, 46, 62, 63, 64, 71, 72, 77, 82, 87, 88, 92, 105, 218, 266, 292, 293, 306, 316

the question 5, 9, 14, 24, 26, 29, 67, 90, 98, 101, 123, 178, 180, 215, 225, 230, 235, 262, 285, 291

theoretical 143

thinking......................................2, 11, 19, 29, 91, 92, 106, 107, 115, 117, 118, 127, 184, 214, 300

thirst..184, 299

thought.6, 22, 29, 40, 48, 75, 97, 109, 110, 134, 139, 143, 148, 152, 157, 158, 168, 174, 183, 184, 191, 198, 205, 217, 223, 225, 226, 229, 230, 231, 235, 236, 238, 240, 241, 246, 247, 252, 253, 255, 256, 258, 259, 260, 262, 266, 267, 268, 271, 272, 273, 274, 278, 279, 280, 281, 284, 285, 287, 288, 290, 295, 296, 297, 299, 300, 301, 303, 305, 306, 307, 309, 313, 314, 317

thyroid 129, 236

time..5, 10, 13, 16, 17, 22, 26, 29, 31, 38, 40, 44, 45, 46, 47, 50, 53, 55, 56, 57, 58, 65, 67, 68, 70, 71, 72, 73, 76, 79, 81, 87, 89, 90, 91, 92, 93, 94, 98, 99, 103, 104, 106, 113, 116, 117, 124, 125, 126, 129, 130, 131, 132, 133, 134, 135, 137, 138, 139, 145, 150, 151, 153, 155, 163, 168, 171, 179, 180, 183, 187, 188, 191, 196, 197, 198, 200, 202, 207, 209, 210, 211, 213, 215, 219, 220, 222, 224, 226, 228, 229, 230, 231, 235, 239, 240, 242, 243, 244, 247, 248, 249, 250, 255, 256, 258, 261, 263, 264, 265, 270, 273, 274, 277, 278, 279, 280, 282, 284, 285, 286, 287, 288,

289, 290, 292, 293, 295, 296, 297, 298, 299, 300, 301, 303, 304, 307, 309, 310, 312, 314, 315, 316, 317

timidity 289

Tolstoy, Nikolayevich 96

tooth...256, 257, 259, 300, 301, 302

training 4, 13, 18, 26, 28, 29, 42, 74, 75, 77, 78, 94, 98, 104, 123, 130, 160, 165, 180, 185, 205, 210, 214, 221, 223, 225, 226, 234, 235, 241, 279, 282, 314

trait 134, 153, 155, 172, 190, 193, 194, 211, 218, 228, 244, 252, 260, 306

    traits...27, 124, 147, 193, 195, 201, 306

transference 48

trap...83, 239

treatment....4, 16, 17, 18, 24, 35, 40, 47, 48, 51, 59, 78, 79, 81, 102, 103, 107, 109, 114, 116, 117, 129, 130, 131, 133, 137, 140, 146, 149, 153, 170, 261, 301

truth 5, 16, 17, 25, 28, 41, 48, 59, 78, 84, 94, 106, 203, 209, 216, 225, 229, 304, 306

twin

    twins...63

tyrant 34, 53, 193, 196, 302, 311

U

ugliness...65, 179

uncertainty 45, 71, 283

unconscious 20, 108, 144, 147, 148, 162, 191, 194, 306, 310, 313

understanding 2, 5, 9, 11, 22, 25, 36, 41, 48, 52, 84, 85, 113, 115, 123, 124, 128, 142, 143, 146, 202, 208, 209, 228, 242, 247, 266, 319, 320

unfaithful 35, 92

    unfaithfulness 53, 90

unhappy 7, 29, 32, 53, 61, 68, 69, 135, 142, 242, 246, 258, 284

    unhappiness 15, 30, 139

unique 45, 46, 185

unity............................... 2, 47, 48, 57, 79, 107, 123, 150, 182, 231, 235, 306, 309, 313

unmasking 312

upward striving...22

V

vaginism 284

vain..33, 212, 246, 264, 315

value 2, 5, 9, 16, 20, 23, 47, 51, 52, 77, 120, 171, 193, 218, 222, 241, 300

    values 83, 132, 142

vanity...76, 138, 155, 233, 295, 305, 312

virtue 26, 56, 65, 105

vomiting 62, 88, 91, 277

W

war..109, 116, 133, 236, 241, 245, 277

washing compulsion 147, 264, 265, 266, 310

weakness..2, 3, 8, 15, 23, 47, 51, 53, 58, 64, 92, 143, 147, 160, 172, 173, 187, 194, 201, 218, 244, 245, 246, 302

weapon 17, 52, 59, 102, 109, 171, 245, 248, 291

Weber, Frederick 113

weeping 69, 194, 253, 285, 317

Wild.. 28, 65, 239, 265, 274

wisdom 130, 221

wish .6, 7, 40, 42, 45, 53, 55, 74, 77, 82, 86, 88, 100, 108, 110, 120, 121, 134, 135, 138, 144, 157, 167, 172, 173, 174, 189, 200, 231, 235, 274, 277, 283, 288, 291, 300, 313

withdrawal...51, 254

woman6, 7, 10, 15, 16, 28, 30, 31, 35, 40, 44, 53, 56, 58, 65, 66, 71, 72, 74, 75, 76, 77, 80, 81, 82, 87, 89, 90, 91, 93, 102, 104, 109, 116, 117, 118, 119, 120, 121, 122, 123, 124, 125, 127, 130, 131, 132, 134, 137, 138, 149, 172, 173, 176, 184, 188, 190, 194, 196, 203, 211, 241, 249, 255, 256, 258, 266, 267, 283, 284, 297, 300, 308, 315

work...2, 7, 8, 14, 23, 25, 26, 32, 36, 48, 50, 53, 73, 77, 81, 88, 92, 96, 97, 98, 103, 105, 107, 108, 109, 110, 115, 123, 124, 130, 131, 132, 134, 142, 145, 149, 155, 170, 174, 180, 198, 200, 202, 221, 224, 230, 235, 247, 278, 279, 282, 291, 292, 293, 299, 300, 302, 312, 317

world14, 21, 22, 33, 39, 41, 42, 44, 45, 51, 55, 57, 60, 69, 75, 83, 85, 92, 101, 126, 143, 144, 145, 146, 147, 151, 165, 172, 181, 182, 190, 214, 216, 218, 248, 260, 262, 264, 265, 266, 268, 270, 286, 288, 289, 305, 310, 317

worthlessness...27, 49

Y

yes-but.. 148, 248, 318

younger.7, 38, 39, 45, 60, 61, 64, 65, 67, 68, 70, 72, 76, 80, 81, 82, 89, 93, 95, 122, 128, 198, 217

youngest 6, 35, 36, 58, 60, 69, 70, 71, 93, 102, 103, 104, 106, 110, 152

   youngest child 35, 36, 69, 70, 93, 152

Appendix:

Basic Principles of Classical Adlerian Psychology

Henry T. Stein, Ph.D.[1]

Alfred Adler (1870-1937) developed a rare, holistic theory of psychology, pedagogy, and philosophy of living. His lectures and books for the general public are characterized by common sense. His clinical books and journal articles reveal an uncommon understanding of mental disorder, insight into the art of healing, and inspiration for encouraging optimal human development. Adler's essential principles are as follows.

Unity of the Individual

Thinking, feeling, emotion, and behavior can only be understood as subordinated to the individual's style of life, or consistent pattern of dealing with life tasks. The individual is not internally divided or the battleground of conflicting forces. Each aspect of the personality points in the same direction, toward an unconscious, fictional final goal.

Goal Orientation

One central personality dynamic originates from the growth and forward movement of life itself. It is a future-oriented striving toward a goal of significance, superiority, or success. In mental health, it is a realistic goal of socially useful significance or superiority over general difficulties; in mental disorder, it is an unrealistic goal of exaggerated significance or superiority over others. The natural childhood feeling of inferiority (being "small in a too-big world"), for which we aim to compensate, leads to the creation of a fictional final goal that subjectively seems to promise future security and success. The depth of the inferiority feeling usually determines the height of the goal, which

---

[1] This brief overview was first published in 1997 on the Classical Adlerian Psychology web site at http://www.Adlerian.us/principl.htm. A more comprehensive exposition of principles, "Classical Adlerian Theory and Practice," may be found in Volume 1 of *The Collected Clinical Works of Alfred Adler*, or on the web at http://www.Adlerian.us/theoprac.htm.

then becomes the "final cause" and organizing principle for all behavior patterns and expressive movements.

Self-Determination and Uniqueness

The unconscious, fictional goal may be influenced by hereditary and cultural factors, but it ultimately springs from the creative power of the individual, and is consequently unique. Individuals are not consciously aware of their goal. By analyzing birth order, repeated coping patterns, and earliest memories, the psychotherapist infers the goal as a working hypothesis. The therapeutic process consists of ultimately making the client's unconscious goal conscious, and encouraging him to move in a more socially useful, and thereby more satisfying, direction.

Social Context

As an indivisible whole, a system, the human being is also a part of larger wholes or systems: the family, the community, all of humanity, our planet, the cosmos. In these contexts, we meet the three important life tasks: occupation, love and sex, and our relationship with other people – all social challenges. Our way of responding to our first social system, the family constellation, may become the prototype of our world view and attitude toward life, solidified as a psychological "style of life."

The Feeling of Community

Each human being has the capacity for learning to live in harmony with society. This innate potential for social connectedness has to be deliberately nurtured (a crucial, early parental task). Social interest and feeling imply "social improvement," quite different from conformity, allowing for innovation even through cultural resistance or rebellion. The feeling of genuine security is rooted in a deep sense of belonging and embeddedness within the stream of social evolution.

Mental Health

A feeling of human connectedness, and a willingness to develop ourselves fully so that we contribute to the welfare of others, are the main criteria of mental health. When these qualities are underdeveloped, feelings of inferiority may haunt an individual, or an attitude of superiority may antagonize others. Consequently, the unconscious fictional goal will be self-centered and emotionally or materially exploitative of other people. When the feeling of connectedness and the willingness to contribute are stronger, a feeling of equality emerges, and the individual's goal will be self-transcending and beneficial to others.

Treatment

Classical Adlerian Depth Psychotherapy, brief therapy, couple therapy, and family therapy follow parallel paths. Clients are encouraged to overcome their feelings of insecurity, develop deeper feelings of connectedness, and to redirect their striving for significance into more socially beneficial directions. Through a respectful Socratic dialogue, they are challenged to correct mistaken assumptions, attitudes, behaviors, and feelings about themselves and the world. Constant encouragement stimulates clients to attempt what was previously felt as impossible. The growth of confidence, pride, and gratification leads to a greater desire and ability to cooperate. The objective of therapy is to replace exaggerated self-protection, self-enhancement, and self-indulgence with courageous social contribution. Ideally, we help the client live more creatively by dissolving the self-limiting style of life and the fictional final goal.

For Additional Information About Distance Training in Classical Adlerian Depth Psychotherapy:

Visit www.Adlerian.us.

Made in the USA
Lexington, KY
26 June 2013